The late **Dianne Haworth** w
journalist and author who established a name for herself
as a leading contemporary biographer and sports writer.
She died in 2008.

Sir Patrick Hogan KNZM, CBE, established the
Cambridge Stud in 1976 and went on to become one of
the most successful breeders of thoroughbred racehorses
in New Zealand (and Australasian) history. Throughout
his glittering career, Sir Patrick has brought an enduring
passion to the industry he has served so well, and is the
only person to have been inducted into both the New
Zealand and Australian Racing Halls of Fame.

'Sir Patrick has earned and deserves all the accolades and honours that have come his way, from his success with breed-shaping stallions like Sir Tristram and Zabeel, to his knighthood for services to the New Zealand, Australian and global breeding industries.'

— John Magnier, Coolmore Stud, Ireland

'He's just been a wonderful contributor to the thoroughbred industry, and Sir Tristram and Zabeel have been quite incomprehensible in terms of the contribution that they have made. A lot of people attribute it to great good fortune — but you make your own luck, and I don't think there's anyone who could have developed those stallions more than Patrick did.'

— Peter Vela, founder/owner, New Zealand Bloodstock

'Sir Patrick Hogan is significantly responsible for putting New Zealand on the world map as a breeding country. I think New Zealand has a lot to thank him for.'

— John Messara, Arrowfield Stud, Australia

'People like Patrick Hogan are fantastic to work with. Internationally they are top of their class, and there are not many industries in New Zealand you can say that of. Promotion, marketing, he images an aspiration to perfection and that's what makes him a wonderful example in all respects in terms of presentation of this industry.'

— Hon Winston Peters, Minister for Racing, New Zealand

'It's a very tough world and Patrick has sharpened his teeth against the best. I don't care if he was in New Zealand, Siberia or running a stud in England or Kentucky — Patrick would be supreme. He'd be the leading studmaster wherever he was.'

— Gai Waterhouse, Australian trainer

'We need him to keep going for the next 30-odd years. I'd like to see if we could clone him for New Zealand — that would be a great thing!'

— Graeme Rogerson, New Zealand trainer

'In all the studs around the world, he wins it by the length of the home straight.'

— Tony Arrold, editor, thoroughbred section, *The Australian*

'In racing terms, he's our royalty. He relates so well to everyone and is held in such high respect.'

— Aidan Rodley, *Waikato Times*

'He's flamboyant — he's a born showman. His horses are him. That's Patrick. Always said he wanted to be a millionaire by the time he was 40, and he was.'

— Shane Keating, former Cambridge Stud manager

'The breeding industry is awash with potentially great stallions that never quite make it, but not so Cambridge Stud. This, I am sure, is a direct result of the exemplary knowledge, dedication and devotion of Sir Patrick Hogan, who history will judge as one of the great breeders of our time.'

— Lloyd J. Williams, owner

GIVE A MAN A HORSE

THE REMARKABLE STORY OF SIR PATRICK HOGAN

DIANNE HAWORTH

HarperCollins*Publishers*

Sir Patrick and Lady Hogan will kindly donate all royalties from this book to the True Colours Charitable Trust, a non-profit organisation in the Waikato-Midland area, which supports children and young people living with a chronic, serious or life-threatening illness.

HarperCollins_Publishers_

First published in 2007
This edition published in 2016
by HarperCollins_Publishers_ (New Zealand) Limited
Unit D1, 63 Apollo Drive, Rosedale, Auckland 0632, New Zealand
harpercollins.co.nz

HarperCollins_Publishers_
Unit D1, 63 Apollo Drive, Rosedale, Auckland 0632, New Zealand
Level 13, 201 Elizabeth Street, Sydney NSW 2000, Australia
A 53, Sector 57, Noida, UP, India
1 London Bridge Street, London, SE1 9GF, United Kingdom
2 Bloor Street East, 20th floor, Toronto, Ontario M4W 1A8, Canada
195 Broadway, New York NY 10007, USA

A catalogue record for this book is available from the National Library of New Zealand

ISBN 978 1 7755 4096 0 (pbk)
ISBN 978 1 7754 9134 7 (ebook)

Cover design by Shirley Tran Thai, HarperCollins Design Studio
Cover image of Sir Patrick Hogan with Sir Tristram © Jenny Scown Photography & Inspirit Gallery, www.inspirit.co.nz
Text updated and Chapters 18, 19 and 20 written by Aidan Rodley
Typeset in Imprint MT
Printed and bound in Australia by Griffin Press
The papers used by HarperCollins in the manufacture of this book are a natural, recyclable product made from wood grown in sustainable plantation forests. The fibre source and manufacturing processes meet recognised international environmental standards, and carry certification.

Dedication

This book is dedicated to my wife Justine and daughters Nicola and Erin, who gave me 'the wings to fly'; also to New Zealand thoroughbred breeders past, present and future, and my staff at Cambridge Stud.

CONTENTS

ACKNOWLEDGEMENTS

To HAVE BEEN given the privilege of writing the biography of Sir Patrick Hogan, an icon of thoroughbred breeding on the world scene, has been a fascinating and absorbing undertaking.

It was a journey that started with a small boy from comparatively humble circumstances in Cambridge who nursed high ambitions: to one day build himself a fine career working with the farm animals and horses that he so loved. That Sir Patrick has succeeded beyond all expectations is, of course, a matter of public record. Not only has he put Cambridge Stud on the world map for thoroughbred breeding, but he has also lifted the profile of New Zealand generally in this sphere.

Sir Tristram and his son Zabeel have been his flagship horses and are remarkable stories in themselves, but here I ran into a dilemma. How should I refer to Sir Tristram in the book? Sir Tristram was affectionately called Paddy — his stable name — by Patrick and his wife Justine, along with the staff of Cambridge Stud and everyone who knew him. Frequently, when speaking of him for this book, the stallion was referred to by both names within the space of a single sentence! After mulling it over, I decided to follow in the spirit of Cambridge Stud and refer to Sir Tristram by both his official and stable name throughout, as did his many friends in their reminiscences of this incomparable horse. I hope it is not confusing.

A second challenge on the word front cropped up when Sir Patrick was knighted. Should 'Patrick' become 'Sir Patrick' at every reference, or for ease of reading, should it remain as

Patrick, with 'Sir Patrick' being used only when applying direct media quotes? After discussing it with Sir Patrick, this was the path we decided to take.

This was an undertaking that stretched across two countries, reflecting Sir Patrick's close involvement with both the New Zealand and Australian racing industry, and it was one that I could not have adequately covered without the support and help of so many people — friends and colleagues of Sir Patrick's within the industry.

In particular I would like to thank the staff of Cambridge Stud, Barry Lee, John and Peter Hogan, Joe Walls, my brother Peter Buckland, Jenny Kain, John Costello, Sonia and David Bradford, Phillip Quay, Mike Dillon, Barry Street, Aidan Rodley, Peter Vela, Barry Lichter, Wally O'Hearn, the Merlin Press, Sister Charles (Constance Hurley), Joe McGrath of the VRC, Graeme Rogerson, Nick Columb, Adam Sangster, John Hogan (in Ireland), Sir Michael Fay, John Messara, Gerry Harvey, Bart Cummings, Gai Waterhouse, Trevor Lobb, Bill Charles and Carlo Rossi.

Dianne Haworth, 2007
Auckland, New Zealand

Foreword

THE FIRST PERSON I met from the Hogan family was Patrick's father Tom, whom I ran into at my first visit to the New Zealand National Yearling Sales, which were held at that time at Trentham in Upper Hutt.

Patrick's father would catch my attention as he stood near the entrance to the yearling boxes at the sales complex by catching my arm or leg with the end of his walking stick and, in good Irish humour, urge me to inspect his horses. 'You'll find your winners here!' he'd say.

I first had the pleasure of meeting Patrick in either 1958 or 1959, and from that time onwards our association has developed into a firm friendship that has lasted almost five decades. In those years Patrick was a young budding thoroughbred horse breeder with a penchant for developing the breeding industry in New Zealand.

It took him a number of years to acquire his now world-renowned Cambridge Stud, which is located in the Waikato, south of Auckland, in New Zealand's North Island. Since its foundation, Cambridge Stud under Sir Patrick's astute guidance has stood several phenomenal and successful stallions, led by Sir Tristram, whose progeny produced 45 individual Group 1 winners, a total of 127 Group and Listed Stakes winners and, in all, 220 black-type performers [horses that have won or been placed in Stakes races], which equate to almost 25 per cent of all his runners.

The success of Sir Tristram has flowed on through the winners which continue to be produced by his progeny, male and female lines alike. Following in Sir Tristram's footsteps is his son Zabeel who to date has sired 36 individual Group 1 winners, including Melbourne Cup winner Jezabeel, and the multiple Group 1 winners Octagonal and Might And Power.

The deeds of these wonderful stallions have brought the New Zealand breeding industry to the forefront of world breeding, with Sir Patrick at the helm steering the ship. Through the powerful sire lines that these two stallions have, Sir Patrick has ensured the continuing recognition, integrity and success of the New Zealand breeding industry.

I am honoured to be his friend, and accepted, without hesitation, the invitation to provide the foreword to this book, his biography. Sir Patrick is an eminent thoroughbred breeder who possesses a touch of genius, and I am sure everyone will find this publication most interesting and informative.

J. Bart Cummings, A.M.

GALLOPING HOGAN

SCENE 1: IRELAND, 17TH CENTURY

THE YEAR WAS 1649, and Oliver Cromwell was raising hell in Ireland. Drogheda lay in ashes, its defenders and townspeople butchered most brutally. Wexford shared a similar fate. The Puritan general was systematically quelling a rebellion set in train by the royalist adherents of Charles of England. Now his Ironsides, the cavalry, roamed the countryside in search of surviving rebels and those who'd succoured them.

John Hogan, blacksmith, must have been expecting trouble when a troop of Cromwell's cavalry clattered into the village of Kilfeacle, County Tipperary, and halted at his little forge. They had come for a purpose. Most blacksmiths had made weapons for the insurgents. The troopers dismounted: confident, hard faces beneath close-fitting skull helmets, all alike with their cropped heads and brown leather jerkins.

John Hogan was being assisted by his son Daniel. Man and boy stood sullenly as the roundheads ransacked the forge. They found nothing and this seemed to infuriate them. They rounded on the father and beat him unconscious.

Next they turned their attention to the boy. A trooper produced a length of rope, made a noose in it and flung the rope over a bough, swearing an oath to hang Daniel. Just as they were about to string up the young Hogan, the commanding officer noticed that his charger had lost a shoe and ordered Daniel to replace it.

The boy set to work, having learned the farrier's trade from his father, and soon the shoe was ready. Sweating and shaking with fright — for he knew that once the horse was shod he'd lose his life — Daniel grasped the horse's foot. But the animal must have sensed his fear because it lashed out, sending him sprawling.

The officer agreed to hold the horse's reins while Daniel nailed on the shoe, all the while berating the boy for his incompetence. But when the last nail was in place, Daniel suddenly straightened up, hammer in hand.

He struck the bully a fierce blow to the head, grabbed the charger's reins, leapt into the saddle and raced away, leaving the astonished troops dumbstruck. When they regained their composure, they set off in pursuit. They failed to catch the boy — the roundhead officer's charger was swift, and Daniel had an intimate knowledge of the countryside.

It's fitting that a horse was involved and that the lad made his escape at the gallop. The soldiers and their masters would, in time, have much cause to regret that Daniel's neck wasn't stretched when the opportunity arose. For Daniel Hogan went on to become Galloping Hogan, one of the most celebrated of Ireland's outlaw rapparees.

The Hogans were descended from the Dalcassions, whose territories extended over parts of Clare, Tipperary and Limerick. Daniel's forebears occupied lands around the stronghold of Ardcrony and his ancestry can be traced back to Ogan, an 11th century warrior prince. Along with many other old Irish families, the Hogans were driven off their lands to make way for the plantations and settlements of Henry VIII and forced to live in the heavily wooded hills and mountains of Munster and west Leinster.

The conqueror could not have known at that time that he was sowing the wind to reap a whirlwind. The dispossessed organised themselves into irregular bands of foot soldiers and horses, capable of swooping down and attacking the numerically superior English forces before melting back into the hills.

Such companies of determined 'kerns' gradually developed into larger and more lethal forces. Their commanders and instructors were experienced Irish soldiers, lately returned from the battlefields of Europe. These 'swordsmen' had an ancient model: the Chinese guerrilla fighters who'd operated with deadly efficiency for centuries, and whose methods were widely used by military strategists on the Continent.

Thus began in Ireland a system of warfare that would endure almost up to the present day. The armies of the interloper were relatively safe when ensconced behind the stout walls of their keeps, but once out in the open they were vulnerable to the hit-and-run strategy of the Irish. The guerrillas knew the terrain and were more mobile, thus could they wreak havoc on army convoys and supply lines. Some operated alone while others struck in bands, but all employed the same tactics of speed and agility. They also had the people on their side — an enviable advantage.

Over time, the daring guerrilla bands matured into formidable cavalry units and, to a lesser extent, infantry who assisted the Irish armies in their wars with England. Though they never became 'regular' soldiers, the generals nevertheless welcomed them with open arms, and prized their martial skills highly. One man stood out among the best of the rapparees. He was Daniel Hogan, one of the finest horsemen and swordsmen Ireland ever produced.

To be given the sobriquet 'Galloping Hogan' in that era — when most men handled horses as easily as we drive cars today — you had to be an exceptional rider. You had to 'be one' with your horse. The rapparees had a secret riding trick which they used only in emergencies: they were able to summon their horses by means of a whistle or some other signal. As the animal galloped towards him, the rapparee would grab hold of the left ear of the careering animal and, using the horse's momentum, would then swing neatly into the saddle and race to safety.

No doubt Hogan was capable of this feat. Legend has it that he acquired the nickname 'Galloping' because of the great skill with which he rode and handled his huge mare. It was in all likelihood a Cashel, one of the great old breeds of Irish horse originating in Tipperary — one of the biggest, strongest and noblest breeds in Europe, renowned also for its speed.

(From *The Irish Highwaymen*, Merlin Press)

CHAPTER 1

THE CALF CLUB CHAMPION

'Despite his enormous financial success, the game to Sir Patrick wasn't ever the money; it was the competition — the winning.'

— Shane Keating

SCENE 2: NEW ZEALAND, 1949

TEN-YEAR-OLD PATRICK HOGAN frowned with concentration as he put his jersey calf, Neatness, through his paces again. Tugging firmly on the calf's head collar and rope, the pair marched up and down the Waikato farm paddock on a grey, drizzly, September afternoon. 'Once more, Neatness, you're not walking alongside me properly,' the boy said sternly. Presentation, he knew, was all-important with the judges who came to Cambridge's Goodwood Primary School each November for the biggest event in a New Zealand country school's calendar — Calf Club Day.

He had to teach Neatness to walk sedately alongside him and in exact synchronisation with his own movements — stopping when he stopped, starting when he started, halting for dramatic effect to be shown off to his best advantage to the judges. 'Again!' the boy insisted stubbornly as the calf faltered.

17

He had chosen his calf carefully, selecting one on his parents' mixed dairy farm that bore the tabulated Neatness pedigree, knowing he would present well. Patrick planned to feed him up with oil in his diet, groom him each day and spend every spare minute for the next two months training him in readiness for the great event.

The prize Patrick so coveted was the winner's blue ribbon, and the one person standing between him and success was an equally determined contestant, Margaret Hunt, who had beaten him for first prize the year before. That wouldn't happen again, he vowed to himself. 'Once more, Neatness. Stop here . . . now turn around . . .'

Watching his youngest from an adjacent paddock where he was working his Clydesdale horses, Thomas Hogan allowed himself a small smile of pride. The boy shared his passion for the land and its livestock, particularly the horses. Like his ancestor Daniel 'Galloping Hogan' had done 300 years before, this boy would leave his mark, of that Tom Hogan was sure. The steely combination of competitiveness and determination didn't acknowledge a second place.

NEWSPAPER ITEM, GALWAY, IRELAND, 1909:

'A small farmer named Patrick Hogan dropped dead at his residence, Ballindooley, on Wednesday. Deceased had been several times threatened that if he didn't give up a farm which he held under the eleven months' system* he should mark the consequences, and finally he surrendered the place at considerable loss.

Another which he held under the same system he refused to give up, as it was his only means of support with notice of surrender on the 1st of May, and this it is believed so preyed on his mind that it resulted in his sudden demise. He leaves a wife and eight young children to mourn his loss. Deceased was only 45 years of age.'

(*Held at the landlord's whim and not subject to the fairer rent-fixing mechanisms of the land courts.)

Twelve-year-old Tom Hogan was one of those eight children left fatherless at Ballindooley in 1909. Within five years he was living in New Zealand, his decision to emigrate triggered by the financial struggles of life in Ireland and a letter he had received from his cousin, Mick Hogan, urging him to follow his lead and come to the new country — a land he claimed that was full of opportunity for hardworking young men. His family at Ballindooley were distraught, and his six-year-old brother Paddy was never to recover from the departure of his much-adored older brother. But yes, they said, they understood — with family to support him out there, this was an opportunity Tom could not turn down.

In New Zealand, Mick's brother, P.T. 'Put' Hogan, had made his name in racing circles in the early 1900s, and was famed as a hard-case Southland/Irish character. Put Hogan had first worked with Clydesdales before discovering thoroughbreds and in the 1918–19 season he trained 45 winners, a record total that was to go down in history. He was not above a little equine skulduggery either, teaching one of his champion mares to limp before a race to improve her odds.

Tom loved New Zealand's open lifestyle, but when two of his sisters, Mary and Bridget, and his brother Tim died in the worldwide influenza epidemic within the space of four years from 1917 to 1921, Tom was devastated. Here he was, on the other side of the world, unable to grieve alongside the remaining members of his family. Mary had been his favourite — the two had been inseparable in Ireland and were only 12 months apart in age. Tom would mourn her for the rest of his life.

He found employment shovelling metal for the New Zealand Railways at Wellington and later at Taranaki, working on the construction of a branch line from Te Roti to Opunake. He left the railways to work and live with his bachelor uncle, Jack Casserly, on his 2500-acre farm set on Maori lease land at Hawera. Jack was a highly successful farmer at a time when Taranaki was a major force in New Zealand due to its dairying wealth, and his nephew was a fast learner.

Casserly, who bred draught horses, owned a Clydesdale stallion by the name of Blue Peter, igniting Tom's dream to import his own Clydesdale stallion to New Zealand one day. It was Tom's job to take Blue Peter as a visiting stallion to local farmers who kept a mare or two in their paddocks to supply them with foals for their next generation of four-legged farm workers. In the era before tractors, Clydesdales were a vital part of New Zealand farming life, pulling the carts that took the cans of milk to local dairy factories early each morning, before returning to the farm to plough the fields or be used for general work.

In 1919, aged 22, Tom married Sarah Small, a local girl whose parents had also emigrated from Galway. Cannily, Tom established social contacts that would stand him in good stead in the community, including that of Clem Trotter, head of the Farmers' Cooperative in Taranaki (coincidentally, that acquaintanceship was to extend to the next generation and two future Knights of the Realm, in Clem's son Ron and Tom's son Patrick).

Tom and Sarah farmed a couple of hundred acres at Matapu, and Tom played for the local rugby team where he made several lifelong friends. It was the onset of the Depression in 1929 that forced the young Hogans' next initiative. Butterfat had slumped to sixpence a pound and, to make ends meet, Tom moved into the draught horse business, gaining early recognition as a successful trader, the owner of visiting stallions and an astute judge of Clydesdales. Each year he would make the journey north to Cambridge for its annual six-day horse fair — the largest in the Southern Hemisphere — to buy, sell and trade. He also travelled to fairs in the South Island, Hawke's Bay and the central North Island. As owner of the contract to supply the South Taranaki County Council with their horses, his income grew along with his success.

He bought a second farm in Matamata, Waikato, in 1934, had it managed for him by a rugby friend from Taranaki, and then decided the family should move north in 1938. 'The days of working horses are finished,' he told his eldest son John. 'I'm going to sell all of my stallions.' And off they went to Cambridge, where Tom had spent so many happy hours trading his horses. They bought a mixed dairy farm at Fencourt, on the outskirts of Cambridge, where they retained a satisfying link to their past — the Hogans' living room mantelpiece was awash with the many ribbons and cups that Tom had won from showing his Clydesdales.

He stocked Fencourt with dairy cows, pigs, cattle and a couple of Clydesdales to work in the fields. And, satisfying his marketing desires, he continued trading in draught horses. Tom liked to head off to a sale in Cambridge and buy a young

21

horse, get it on the truck as soon as he could and bring it home. He'd shampoo it, clean its mane, tail and forelocks, trim its feet, put it on the truck and drive back to the sale yards. By the afternoon session he'd have that horse in the line-up, looking entirely different, and sold for a reasonable profit.

This was a deeply satisfying way of making money, Hogan chuckled to himself. There was the adrenaline rush that came from the thrill of the chase when he'd turned a bargain into a good profit, and it was also great marketing.

If you were a Hogan, it was to town once a week, watching rugby on Saturday — especially when John and Peter, Tom and Sarah's two older sons, were playing for Hautapu or representing their province of Waikato — and to St Peter's Catholic Church on Sunday. The Friday night trips to town were the highlight of the week for the country children of the district. Pleading with their parents, they would make a beeline for Cummings and Cooper's toyshop in the main street, where the generous shopkeepers would allow them to play for as long as they liked with the shiny, new toys on sale.

Four-year-old Patrick had been given a smart red tractor from the shop as a Christmas present and seemed delighted with it. Where was his beautiful tractor which he had spent the whole day playing with? Sarah asked him late one afternoon. He pointed to the fireplace where the remains of the tractor lay splintered to smithereens. 'I was helping you,' he responded quick as a flash, 'so you didn't have to cut up the firewood tonight.'

From the outset and by inclination, Patrick's life was intertwined with animals. He was tender-hearted — bird nesting or rabbit shooting were never for him — and formed great attachments with the animals at Fencourt, particularly the working Clydesdales whom he loved and who fired his passion to work with horses throughout his adult life. Pigs were his favourites: in farrowing time there would be anything up to 16 piglets born in a litter at Fencourt, and that was something special. Pigs were the most intelligent animals of all, Patrick decided.

Hay and silage-making, working the rake and the grab, driving the team of Clydesdales to the local milk factory, backing the milk cart in, helping roll out the milk cans and tipping milk into the vat, then over to the whey tanks to fill up and take back home for the pigs' feed, then washing out the cans at the back of the cow shed . . . the life of a country kid who relished farm life was never short of excitement. Calving time was a high point of activity at Fencourt. It was Patrick's job to help bring up the calves that had been taken from their mothers 48 hours after their birth. He'd feed them by hand and teach them to drink from buckets — experience that would give him a head start in animal husbandry and management.

At Goodwood Primary School, life was one of pattern and order. Each Monday morning the national anthem was sung; every morning there was a bottle of pasteurised milk plus an apple in summer. In winter, the boys begged to be chosen to light up the potbelly stove and boil the water in a large urn to make cocoa drinks that were loaded up with sugar. Times tables were chanted by rote, and each child had a little orange-coloured Post Office bankbook with serrated steel teeth in which to place their pennies and sixpences. They could get their money in, but maddeningly it could not come out — saving was a habit to be encouraged.

Patrick's introduction to St Peter's Catholic School was daunting. A tough old nun had lined him up on his first day, scaring the hell out of him. 'I'll be knocking all the cheek out of you, young man. I know what you'll be like coming from a Protestant school!'

Then there was singing class. He couldn't sing to save his life and had no idea why he had been picked to join the group of 10 pupils. At the group's first practice, the nun stopped playing with an almighty bang on one of the final notes: 'Who cannot sing a note?' she demanded.

How could he own up and face the public shame attached to such an admission? Patrick resolved to try to tough it out and prayed the spotlight fell elsewhere, but an elimination process got underway. First one child sang alone, then a second, third, fourth and fifth, and then it was Patrick's turn and he knew he was a goner.

'Stop!' the nun thundered, glaring at the boy as he stumbled his way through a chorus. 'Why didn't you own up? Have you ever been in a singing group before?'

'No, sister,' Patrick admitted.

'They teach you nothing at those non-Catholic schools,' she snorted. 'Get back to your classroom.'

Was this going to continue for the rest of his days at the convent? Patrick wondered. After a solid whacking from the same nun one afternoon, first on the palms of his hand then around his legs with a large white strap, before being sent out into the porch to stand in the corner facing inwards for an hour, Patrick was in a black mood. He had probably deserved it, he admitted to himself, but there was no way he could go home and squeal about what had happened — that would only bring another whacking from his father.

Thank God for Sister Charles who arrived on the scene. Her surname was Hurley — another staunchly Irish name — so there had to be a good chance of her understanding the 11-year-old Hogan's personality. She was young and liberal, and thought nothing of coaching or playing rugby with the boys, climbing into the depths of the scrum or booting the rugby ball downfield, her floor-length nun's habit trailing in the mud. She made the boys form a netball team to play the girls, calmly ignoring the boys' howls of protest: 'We don't want to play that sissy's game!'

On the religious front Patrick made his first Holy Communion and became an altar boy, lighting candles to make smoke wriggles on the ceiling of the sacristy which never failed to infuriate St Peter's priest, Father Frank Quinn. Father Quinn was, some claimed, a despot who arrived in Cambridge after the war and struck up a friendship with Tom Hogan. Both were from Ireland and both had an uncanny eye for picking horses. They shared the ownership of a couple of steeplechasers — Ballinsloe, named after a great Irish horse fair of the same name, and Kinvara — and reckoned they had beaten the odds by making more than they lost.

Frank Quinn liked to visit the Hogans on Sundays and it was Patrick's job to open the farm gate and close it as the priest left. 'Here you are boy,' Father Quinn would say as he drove out. 'Sixpence for you — and don't spend it all at once.'

The satisfaction that came from showing his calves and pigs at school Calf Club Days was lodged deeply in Patrick's psyche. There was no Calf Club Day at St Peter's, so the 11-year-old decided he would continue showing calves by himself. A trip down the road to the Morelands' farm where there was a pedigree jersey herd was all that it took. He would ask them if he could borrow a bull calf and, as he had done from the age of seven, he would rear it and prepare it for the Waikato district shows.

Patrick was learning what it took to prepare young stock for the show ring while devising his own little tricks to attract the judges' attention. It would prove the best training ground on earth for the day when his father allowed him to lead Fencourt Stud's first thoroughbred yearlings through the ring at the Trentham National Yearling Sales. Later in his career, and largely due to that early Calf Club Day savvy, Patrick would have no peer at leading around and showing off his million-dollar yearlings at the Karaka sale ring.

Patrick refused point-blank to go to boarding school for his secondary schooling. 'I will run away or get expelled if you send me down there,' he threatened his parents. 'I want to stay at home.'

'Down there' was St Patrick's College, Silverstream, a school considered to be the finest Catholic boys' boarding school in the country. 'Your brothers John and Peter went there and it didn't hurt them,' Tom Hogan countered. 'They play fine rugby too at Silverstream — you could make the school's first XV like your brothers.'

No, no, no, Patrick was adamant — he would not go.

Tom and Sarah relented and agreed to let him attend Marist Brothers' College in Hamilton. Not that Patrick was interested in school anyway, they knew. He was at his happiest working on the farm, or in the school holidays staying with his eldest sister, Eileen Whiteman, who was 20 years his senior and married with four children. The kids would all troop off at night from the Whitemans' farm near Morrinsville and, armed with torches and four-gallon buckets, go eeling in nearby rivers, proudly returning with their wriggling catches. The eels were dumped in the washhouse tub that had been filled with water in preparation, and the next morning, before the family's washing went into the tub, the eels would come out to be processed by Eileen's husband Vern for the evening feast.

Patrick told Tom and Sarah that he hated going to Marist. Why? asked his bewildered parents. Patrick shrugged his shoulders: 'I just want to be working on the farm.' He would be out of the place as soon as he could — his 15th birthday, when he could legally quit school, couldn't come fast enough. Tom experienced the disappointment of a traditional Catholic father. He'd nursed a quiet desire to have his youngest look at a stint in the seminary with the idea of becoming a priest. Patrick was the seventh child and third son, and in a large Catholic family there was always an expectation that one of the children would go into a religious order.

Then the realist in Tom kicked in. The boy probably had too much spirit and rebelliousness for the cloisters. He and Sarah had been shocked to hear a whisper from a source close to the Catholic boys' college that Patrick was arguing against some of the basic tenets of the Catholic religion — the confession box, birth control, and priests not being able to marry — with the priest during divinity class! They knew that sitting through lessons of compulsory Latin, French, English, maths and religion was just too tough for Patrick.

Ahead of him lay his fifth form and School Certificate year, an exam he feared he would most probably fail. As the dreaded twice-yearly school examinations loomed, he came up with a bright idea. 'I'll pay you blokes two shillings each for some answers,' he promised classmates who sat on either side of him. With an ounce of luck he'd land the school's most elderly brother as supervisor for their examinations. He was prone to nod off in his chair during exams, leaving his pupils to their own devices. But Patrick's plans came unstuck. He tripped himself up by getting too many answers right and topping the class in a subject. Back in the classroom, the priest challenged the boys: 'Who in this class has done best in the examination?'

One name after another was called out. Wrong, wrong, he said. 'Top of the class is a certain person called Patrick Hogan — and I would pick that some tricks have taken place,' he added. Well, Patrick justified, he was an honest cheat — at least he had paid for the information!

But much as he disliked Marist, it would have been foreign to his nature to spend a couple of years in a place — any place — without turning it into some sort of profit. Patrick and a classmate began collecting scrap metal, specialising in squirreling out small quantities of the high-value lead that had been discarded at the dump near to their school. At lunch time the two boys would disappear, sneaking down through the gully and into the tip. Patrick's partner would then take the lead back home to Huntly to sell, with the two boys splitting the profits of sale 50/50.

On the upside, Patrick was meeting students from other parts of the Waikato, and others on the school bus. Then there were the girls from Cambridge High School, who just happened to be walking past or talking to each other at the local bus stop when the boys from Marist and Hamilton High School alighted in Cambridge. As the bus slowed down for the

Cambridge town stop, the boys, anxious to impress the girls, pulled up their socks in an attempt to look their best. The girls would offer some words of cheek while coolly appraising which of the boys appealed most to them.

Fourteen-year-old Patrick was in no doubt which of these girls most appealed to him. She was a dark-haired girl who lived in the town and had a warm attractive smile that sat well with her direct manner. Her name was Justine Heath.

Finally, the great day arrived. Patrick celebrated his 15th birthday in October like no other, secure in the knowledge that he could now leave school and not be forced to sit the dreaded School Certificate examination. He was already helping his brother Peter with his contracting and hay-making business at weekends and school holidays, and in particular he loved driving the Ferguson tractor. Now he could throw away the school books and work all day, every day, at Fencourt.

There was a piece of advice that he wanted to pass on to him, Tom said one day. 'Patrick, remember one thing. Don't ever get yourself into a position where you will lose your good name. Once you have lost your name, you will never regain it, no matter how hard you try or how much money you have.'

Tom Hogan was sitting at the kitchen table, poring through the fine print of an English stud publication. The farm was doing well, their family were self-sufficient, and perhaps now — after decades of sacrificing everything for their children's well-being and the welfare of the farm — it was the time to indulge in the secret dream he had nursed for so long. He loved his Clydesdales, but their working days were at an end as New Zealand farmers had switched lock, stock and barrel to tractors.

He no longer wanted an imported Clydesdale stallion like Blue Peter, which his uncle in Taranaki had once bred from. What Tom Hogan wanted in 1956 was to enter the heady world of thoroughbred breeding. He had always had a fine eye for a horse, and what had stood him in good stead when he bought and showed Clydesdales would work as well for thoroughbreds, he believed. This would be the greatest of challenges, and Tom knew that in the enterprise he would have a strong ally in horse-mad Patrick, who was now working full-time on the farm.

'Patrick, I have in mind to buy a hoss.' His father's Irish accent had never been diluted from the time he had first arrived as a penniless immigrant from Ireland at the age of 18.

What kind of a horse, Patrick wondered. Glancing down at the paper his father was staring at, his heart raced. 'Are you getting into thoroughbreds, Dad?' he asked.

'I am,' his father replied. 'There's a stallion standing in England called Blueskin, which fits the bill nicely. And would you believe it, his sire is also called Blue Peter? This has to be a very good omen, Patrick,' the deeply superstitious Irishman added, staring at the paper that showed Blueskin's pedigree. 'This horse had the same name as my uncle Jack Casserley's stallion, the Clydesdale I took around the farms of Taranaki when I first arrived in New Zealand all those years ago. That Blue Peter made me want to own a stallion one day — now I have the chance to buy the progeny of another Blue Peter. I'll talk to Tom Laird and see if he wants to come into the venture with me. If he does, we'll each have a 50 per cent shareholding in him.'

Tom Laird was a fellow Irishman who lived a couple of miles down the road on a small farm called Cambridge Stud. And, as Tom Hogan had anticipated, his friend responded enthusiastically to the idea. Yes, he would be happy to share the ownership of Blueskin with his old mate, Laird nodded in agreement, as Tom outlined the English horse's pedigree. But the stallion would not stand at the Hogans' Fencourt farm. It would be more practical for Blueskin to be lodged at Cambridge Stud, they decided.

Patrick was over the moon. Blueskin could be his pathway to future thoroughbred breeding of his own, he dreamed. For the present though, there was substantial maintenance work to be done by Patrick, along with Joe Burns and Jim Coventry who also worked on the Fencourt farm, at the Lairds' place, putting in fence rails and generally setting things in order in preparation for the stallion's arrival.

Blueskin (Blueskin II as he would be known, as there was a Blueskin already registered in the New Zealand Stud Book) was to be one of four stallions who were coming out to stud in New Zealand on a six-week-long ship voyage from England. The others were Chatsworth, that had been purchased by Sir James Fletcher of Alton Lodge Stud, Astreus for Sir Woolf Fisher at Ra Ora Stud, and Alpenhorn purchased by J.A. Mitchell of Santa Rosa Stud in Taranaki. All three studs were at the top of the ladder commercially in New Zealand, in contrast to Blueskin's owners, Tom Hogan and Tom Laird, who were virtually unknown.

Twenty-four hours before the ship was due to arrive, Tom and Patrick travelled north to stay in Auckland with their relatives, the Coynes. In a mood of high anticipation, they arrived at the wharves the following morning to meet their stallion, only to be told that the ship had to remain out in the stream in the Waitemata Harbour for a further 24 hours before it could berth. The infuriating thing was that they could see the ship across the water, with the four horses' heads sticking out of boxes that had been lined up in a row on the deck.

He couldn't identify Blueskin from that distance; Tom shook his head with annoyance. They would have to return to the Coynes, he told Patrick. Then a launch pulled up alongside and out of it climbed three grim-faced breeders — James Fletcher, Woolf Fisher and J.A. Mitchell. 'Are you Tom Hogan?' Woolf Fisher asked.

'I am,' Hogan replied.

'Well,' Fisher offered generously, 'take our launch and go and have a look at your horse. He's the best bloody stallion on that boat.'

Twenty minutes later, father and son were on board inspecting Blueskin. Both were drawn to the magnificent dark-brown horse with a perfect star in the middle of his forehead, who responded to their strokes with a friendly whinny.

'Yes,' Tom Hogan nodded with satisfaction as he stroked the horse's nose. 'I think Blueskin will do a grand job for us.'

SISTER CHARLES ON PATRICK HOGAN

In 2006, Sister Charles (Constance Hurley) says the character she sees in the man today is largely that of the little boy she once taught.

'Sir Patrick is a very focused individual, a man striving for perfection all the time, a man who likes to come first all the time. As a child at the convent, he was also very focused, striving for perfection and always wanting to come first! He could never tolerate anyone telling a lie, or putting the dirty across him, and he would be mortally offended if someone didn't believe what he told them. He was above average academically, but he became that way because he was so focused on whatever he was doing — maths, English, spelling . . .

'He was kind to other children, very respectful, first to stand up on his feet when someone entered the room, and so immaculately clean. Patrick had that serious side to him, but when he went out and played, a totally different side of his nature emerged. He was fun — he loved games and having a good time.

'You couldn't help but love the boy. He had those blue piercing eyes and a lovely smile with dimples. Sometimes you wanted to get mad with him, but you just couldn't. When he hadn't done so well, he could look very solemn, very withdrawn. He was surprisingly complex for a child. He longed to be affirmed when things were going well, but there was this "don't probe too deeply" standoffishness in him too.

'Patrick was always pleased when you were pleased with him, and he would be a little hurt when you weren't!'

CHAPTER 2

A FARMHAND FROM CAMBRIDGE

'But perhaps Blueskin II's greatest claim to fame was setting in concrete the desire of a young Cambridge farmhand to frame a career around breeding thoroughbreds.'
— David Bradford, *New Zealand Thoroughbred Racing Annual*

THREE FARMHANDS SAT on the top rail of the cow shed fence, heads bent over a small black transistor radio, too excited to shout and break through Peter Kelly's race commentary. Calling the Awatea Handicap at Trentham, Kelly's voice rose to fever pitch. 'They've swung into the home straight, and Bargoed has challenged the leaders . . . Bargoed! . . . Bargoed on the outside . . . Bargoed!!! . . . The winner of the Avondale Guineas has taken out the open sprint this afternoon!'

'Yeeeehah!' Patrick Hogan, Jim Coventry and Joe Burns punched the air with joy. Another race day, another first placing for one of the country's two top three-year-old colts and progeny of their stallion, Blueskin II — his first crop. Just the day before, on the first day of the meeting, Blueskin's other

34

top colt, Blue Lodge, had competed in Trentham's 1960 Spring Carnival, and had won the prestigious Wellington Guineas. That was the kind of one-two to make the world sit up and take notice of the Cambridge stallion!

Time to come down to earth and bring the cows into Fencourt's walk-through shed for milking. Later that evening they would celebrate with a few beers. Jim and Patrick were mates at the Hautapu Rugby Club, as well as working together on the farm. As for Joe Burns . . . he was employed to do general work and milk the cows at Fencourt, but he was the man who taught Patrick the meaning of hard work when he first left school to work on his father's farm.

Joe had a phrase he never tired of repeating to the 15-year-old as they fed the pigs, milked the cows, did the hay and silage-making, or worked the draught horses. 'Listen boy, you've got to do a fair day's work for a fair day's pay.' It sure was a fair day's work, Patrick reflected, that started at 4.30 a.m. each day — mornings of chill dank fogs, frosts that crunched thick on the grass, or miserable, driving Waikato rain. Nothing ever got in the way of milking the cows.

And, from the mid-1950s, there was another dawn tyrant on the scene, in Fencourt's unwieldy irrigation plant: a new technology Peter Hogan had persuaded Tom to introduce to improve their farm's efficiency. Peter was the one with the flash ideas, according to his younger brother. 'You should have this machinery, hay baler, harvesting gear . . . ' he would tell his father.

Peter's latest idea was the irrigation of the farm. The land was to be bulldozed to create dams and holes sufficiently large to form lakes that could tap into Fencourt's two natural springs lying about six metres underground, with pumps inserted to suck out the water and irrigate the paddocks. To achieve this, Patrick and Joe had to manually shift the bulky irrigation pipes and sprinklers every four hours, uncoupling the pipes and moving them from paddock to paddock. There they would spend the next 20 minutes joining together the 10 sections of the pipes that ran the length of a paddock and restart the pump for the irrigation plant to commence the next watering shift.

They were on the job at 4.30 a.m., and by 5.00 a.m. — no later — Joe and Patrick had to dismantle and move the irrigation plant to its next destination before milking began. After breakfast they would dismantle and move the plant again for the 10 a.m. shift, and so on throughout the day to the 6.00 p.m. shift, before turning it off for the night at 10 p.m. Not surprisingly, Fencourt was the only farm in the district to adopt the time-consuming system.

Admittedly, there was a need for the extra grass and pasture that the irrigation provided, but it was costly in human terms and for the extra milk that came out of the bucket. The general opinion was that they were coming out about square, but it certainly impinged on their social life. 'It's my turn — I've got to go and turn off the bloody pump,' Patrick groaned one evening, as he ducked out of the Matangi Hall at 9.30 p.m. It was a maddening chore for a teenager, having to leave the social event of the week — Saturday night's dance, the pub, or a party with friends — to return to the farm and turn off that blasted irrigation pump. Then he would head back to the fun.

The Hautapu Rugby Club was one of Patrick's two focal points of the week, a place where he would make lifelong friends from mates like Bill Taylor, John Warren, Brian Needham and Jim Coventry. Year-round, they knocked about together, driving around in old utes and cars to the next event.

Long happy summer holiday nights were spent at Mt Maunganui beach, going to dances at the Lee Mount — considered the best place for miles around for picking up girls — drinking beer, playing cards, laughing and sleeping in the sand dunes of the beach. And there were the rugby trips — to Hawke's Bay and Northland where, in company with Peter and the Waikato senior team at the end-of-tour party, Patrick ran into trouble with some toheroa; then there was the memorable weekend in Taranaki to support Waikato in its challenge for the Ranfurly Shield . . .

Bill Taylor realised there were two Patricks: one serious and hardworking — almost a workaholic, doing everything at 100 miles an hour — and the other a different person that let his hair down and relaxed, when the Irish in him came out and he enjoyed life to the hilt. Bill admired Patrick for several qualities, but most of all for his ability to think fast on his feet — like the time when they were returning from a big night out after playing for Cambridge juniors at rugby. Patrick was driving, his Vanguard car was packed with four mates, and there was a good supply of beer in the boot. As they hurtled around one bend the car rolled and flipped over into a ditch. Miraculously, all five teenagers clambered out without a scratch and, even more astonishing, after an anxious look in the boot, they discovered that their beer was intact.

'The cops will be coming! Let's hide the beer crate behind the hedge in this farmer's paddock,' Patrick suggested. 'I'm off down the road to alert the neighbours to the accident.'

Why on earth would he want to do that, his friends asked, flabbergasted. Drawing attention to their situation was the last thing in the world they wanted! They scratched their heads as they watched him stride off down the road and through the gates of a neighbouring farm. In response to his knocking, a farmer's wife opened the door. Looking upset, Patrick told her: 'There's been an accident up the road and our car has flipped!'

'Oh dear, are you all right?' she asked in a concerned voice.

'I'm pretty shaken up,' Patrick admitted. 'Could I possibly have a small brandy or whiskey to steady me?'

'Of course, dear,' she agreed, returning a minute later with a glass of brandy.

After downing it, Patrick thanked her profusely and returned to his car and friends. As anticipated, the Cambridge policeman Joe McHugh and another officer had arrived on the scene. 'Who's been driving?' McHugh demanded.

Patrick admitted he was the driver. McHugh moved close, sniffed the air and stated: 'You've been drinking!'

'No, no!' Patrick denied. 'The alcohol you can smell on my breath is a brandy which a kind lady up the road has just given me to calm my nerves.'

McHugh glared, but could do nothing to counter that smart-alec alibi. However, he got his revenge. The following morning when Patrick and his mates went to retrieve their hidden stash of beer, they found the police had arrived ahead of them and commandeered the lot for themselves.

Joe McHugh was the brother of Morrie McHugh, the All Black, which placed him in high esteem in the rugby-mad community. He attended the same church as the Hogans and was an old-fashioned cop who administered his own brand of justice.

Patrick and his friends were good-natured, outgoing kids who meant no harm. They could get away with murder when he chose to turn a blind eye, but McHugh liked to keep a discreet check on their activities — to protect them from themselves, he told police colleagues. Most of the time he knew where the 18-year-olds were, in the patterned society of a small country town, working on the farm all week, at rugby training on Wednesday or Thursday nights, on Friday nights in town walking the streets, looking at the shops and buying a ton of lollies.

Saturday afternoon was rugby and Saturday night was for socialising. They might start the night at the local hotel, going for a drink before the bar closed at 6.00 p.m., then exit by the front entrance before sneaking around to the back door, where the obliging publican, Bill Robb, would reopen the door. They'd laugh at how easily they'd pulled one over old Joe, unaware, until years later, that McHugh knew exactly where they were.

Or they would go to a dance in the Matangi Hall, smuggling their bottles of beer from the boot on arrival and hiding them in a nearby farmer's trough — beer or any other form of alcohol was prohibited at any dance floor or public gathering in the country in the 1950s, but always there were ways to get around a problem. Fresh air was what they needed, Patrick and his friends said to their sceptical dance partners, before escaping out into the night for a refreshing beer, which the forward guard had taken from the trough and had waiting for them.

If there wasn't enough action at the Matangi Hall, they would drive through to Morrinsville or Te Awamutu, or the Starlight Ballroom in Hamilton. Patrick had been to a dance with Bill Taylor one Saturday night and, at about two in the morning, they were back in Cambridge. Bill was the driver and he was keen to see a girl who had obligingly left her bedroom window open. 'Just give me half an hour or so,' he told Patrick as he dropped him off on the Town Hall steps, leaving him with half a bottle of whiskey for company.

Joe McHugh was passing and saw young Hogan was under the weather. He decided he would teach him a lesson. 'Come along with me, Patrick. I'm taking you in for the night,' he said, and drove him to the local jail. Patrick didn't remember much about the night, except that the cell stank and it was a foul way to wake up.

The following morning, McHugh opened the door of the windowless cell and presented Patrick with a hose. 'There you are, hose it out,' he said. Once completed, he dropped Patrick home at Fencourt, but as he walked through the back door, his father was waiting.

'Where have you been?' Tom demanded.

Patrick looked down and said he had missed his ride home and stayed with a mate. 'That's all right,' was Tom's reply, to his son's relief.

And there, Patrick thought, the matter rested. Until one day, months later, when out of the blue, his father confronted him in the paddock and, staring directly at his son, challenged him. 'I thought you didn't tell lies?'

Patrick was puzzled. 'I don't.'

'Well, you told me a lie.' Tom stared at Patrick. 'What's it like in jail?'

It was the worst moment of Patrick's life. He had betrayed his father — the one person on earth that he was so close to, whom he never, ever wanted to let down — by telling a lie.

Close to tears, Patrick apologised. Joe McHugh, Tom explained to his son, had rung him that night, months earlier, saying, 'Don't worry Tom, I'm keeping Patrick overnight in the lock-up. I'll drop him home safe and sound in the morning.'

Was that boy of his hanging around the paddock again with Blueskin? Tom Hogan wondered. As he had done on so many other occasions, he got on the phone to the Lairds, demanding in his strong Irish brogue: 'Send him home where he belongs! Tell him it's time for him to feed the pigs and milk the cows.'

The judgement of Woolf Fisher that afternoon on the Auckland wharf had been spot-on. Blueskin II was an immediate success. Among his first crop he produced those two colts of the year, Bargoed and Blue Lodge. At the conclusion of the 1960 season, both horses were bracketed as New Zealand's joint top three-year-olds along with the Great Northern Derby winner, Stipulate. The Hogans were buzzing with excitement and optimism for the future. Tom's wily horse-sense had done them proud, in this, their first venture into thoroughbred breeding.

With Blueskin II producing progeny of this calibre, there was a brisk demand for his services. Tom Laird's farm was too small for the extra mares that would be coming through the gate to be serviced and, to Patrick's elation, the sensible choice — in Tom's opinion — was to bring Blueskin home to stand at Fencourt.

With horses coming in the front door, the cows and pigs went out the back door, until eventually there were none left.

It was now horses, broodmares and cattle at the farm, and it looked as though Fencourt was going to develop into a full-blown stud farm. It was decided that John, 14 years Patrick's senior, should come home and work on the farm again. 'I'm not getting any younger,' Tom urged his eldest son. John, who was working in Hamilton after a serious back injury had ruled out farming as a career, agreed to join Tom and Patrick at the newly named Fencourt Stud.

Tom introduced a second imported stallion, Final Court, who was also to produce a number of gallopers of high calibre. These included two champion horses from his first crop — Final Command and Fencourt — and, later, the stallions Forearmed and Persian Garden II. (Blueskin II's progeny, like that of his sire, Blue Peter, showed great spring form at two and three, but later were to be mainly recognised as mudlarks, although among his later winners was the 1967 New Zealand Cup victor, Laramie. Tragically, Final Court was to die from colic at a young age.)

With a top stallion and a steady increase in the broodmares being sent to Fencourt Stud to be serviced, life couldn't be any better for a family of horse-mad Irishmen. Tom's yearly trip each January to the National Yearling Sales at Trentham would include Patrick in the future, he told his son. 'You can lead them yearlings around the parade ring for me. I think you'll do a grand job.'

Now that he knew his career was destined for the bloodstock industry, Patrick determined that he and the old Vanguard car he had saved so hard for should pay a visit to his Aunt Kate in Hawke's Bay. From his school days Patrick had loved visiting his mother's sister who worked as housekeeper for a Miss Chambers, the chatelaine of the pioneer Chambers family's magnificent old sheep and cattle station, Mokopeka, at Havelock North. There he rode horses, explored the caves on the farm, helped shepherd huge flocks of sheep at shearing time, and joined in the cattle runs with the Donaldson children, whose father worked on the station.

Mokopeka was totally self-sufficient, making its own milk, cheese and butter, and relying for electricity on its own power supply from Mokopeka Hydro Station, the first private power station in New Zealand. The hydro station was the brainchild of the station's owner, John Chambers, and was completed in 1892 — 115 years later, it is the oldest operational hydro station in the world, having worked continuously since 1892, and is still in good running condition.

Patrick's objective in taking his old car on that long journey through the winding roads over the Ruahine Ranges to Hawke's Bay in 1958 was not just Mokopeka or even to see the aunt he liked so much. He was driving to Havelock North to ask his Aunt Kate if she could persuade Miss Chambers to telephone Tom Lowry of Okawa Stud, and say there was a young man who wanted to have a look at his champion imported stallion, Faux Tirage. It was fitting that a Chambers should be asked to provide an introduction to a Lowry, the third-generation Thomas Lowry to be master of Okawa Stud. As the Chambers were considered to form the top rung of landed gentry in the sheep and cattle world, so too were the neighbouring Lowry family regarded in the social milieu of Hawke's Bay and New Zealand thoroughbred breeding circles.

The massive property that was Okawa near Hastings was established during the 1860s by an Englishman, Thomas

43

Lowry, but it was his son, Thomas Henry, born in 1865, whose passion for thoroughbred horses would bring Okawa its fame and renown. T.H. Lowry, as he was widely known, imported new bloodlines and bred the great mare Desert Gold, and on his death in 1944, Okawa passed to his son, Thomas Coleman Lowry, a former captain of the New Zealand cricket team.

He would be content if he could just look at Mr Lowry's stallion over the fence in his paddock, Patrick anxiously told his aunt. 'I won't be a trouble to anybody.' The call was made to Tom Lowry and the reply given instantly: 'Send the young man out and I'll look after him myself.' Patrick, ever meticulous about punctuality, arrived ahead of time, and was surprised to see Lowry waiting for him. Patrick couldn't remember an occasion when he had felt so nervous — he had never made a visit to a stud farm on his own, and this afternoon there was no Tom Hogan to put everyone at ease, chatting horses and bloodlines.

Faux Tirage, the leading New Zealand sire of the year, was groomed up in his box. Tom Lowry had his groom parade his horse in front of the boy and then, hospitably, he invited him inside his magnificent old home for a chat on horses and a soft drink. It was an afternoon the 18-year-old would never forget — it was a lesson in horsemanship.

Learning from that experience, in his later career as a studmaster Patrick would never turn down anyone who contacted him in similar circumstances.

Life wasn't all horses, though. Ever, in the foreground of his life, there was Justine, the one and only girl for Patrick — the girl with the warm smile and direct manner who had so attracted him from the day they first met at the Cambridge bus stop when he was at Marist and she was at Cambridge High. Unlike Patrick, Justine preferred the quiet life, opting to leave Patrick to do his own socialising with his mates on Saturday nights, while she remained at home with her parents. Whenever they could, however, they got together and, in the baffling pattern of human chemistry, it often happened spontaneously as they bumped into one another in all manner of times and places.

On one blazing hot summer's afternoon, Patrick was driving his brother Peter's tractor to one of his customer's farms and had stopped outside a dairy to buy himself a vanilla ice-cream. Happily licking the sides of the ice-cream, he hadn't gone far down the road when he spotted Justine coming towards him on her bicycle. Of course he had to stop the tractor to have a chat, but what was he going to do with that damned ice-cream? He didn't want Justine to think he was a kid. Driving a tractor was a man's job — only a few nights earlier he had told her he was proud that Peter had entrusted it to his care.

Patrick jumped off the tractor, hiding his fast-melting ice-cream behind his back as she rode up to him. But as the cream-coloured liquid blobs plopped onto the road, he knew his cover was blown. With a smile, Justine asked: 'Why are you holding your ice-cream behind your back? It's melting — why don't you eat it?'

Would she and her girlfriend like to go with Patrick and a mate to the Te Awamutu Show that Saturday? he asked. No, she didn't think they would, Justine replied.

'Pleeaase,' he begged.

'No, we're busy,' came the answer.

A phone call the next day produced the same response, so the boys decided to ask a couple of Te Awamutu girls to accompany them. On the morning of the show, the phone rang. It was Justine. She and her friend had changed their minds and would come with the boys to the show. Tricky! Patrick sucked in his breath as he hung up. They were now squiring four girls — two from Cambridge and two from Te Awamutu, and neither was likely to be enthused with the appearance of the other pair. Well, they just had to go ahead with the arrangement, however awkward, pile four girls into his car, and hope for the best.

At the show Justine and her friend took off, to emerge from nowhere as Patrick sat happily on the grass eating a bunch of grapes and chatting to one of the Te Awamutu girls. Without warning, his grapes were whipped from over his shoulder and calmly downed by Justine to send an age-old 'he's mine, hands off!' warning to her rival.

Sarah Hogan dropped the bombshell in 1958. She needed to talk privately to Patrick about something that concerned him, she said. Patrick was not Tom and Sarah's son, but their grandson, she said. His older sister Biddy was his birth mother, and he had been born at a nursing home in Auckland in 1939. He had spent his first four years living with Tom's cousins, the Coynes, before Sarah and Tom had taken him home to Fencourt to be brought up as their son.

Patrick listened as the words spilled out of his mother's mouth, feeling sick with disbelief. At 19, his world was shattered — and yet, if he was honest with himself, it confirmed a suspicion he'd first had a year earlier when parts of a conversation had drifted in the air about the inheritance of the farm, that there was something different, something apart, about his position in the family.

How did this change things for him, he blurted out, too upset to think coherently. It changed nothing, Sarah replied calmly. Tom was still his father, she was still his mother, his sisters were his sisters, his brothers were his brothers — he was a true Hogan, just as he had always been. It changed nothing, but it changed everything. Why now? Why hadn't they told him as a child? Why tell him at all? Patrick couldn't bring himself to ask the questions that were tumbling around in his head. He had no memories of life before Fencourt, no recollection of any family other than his own.

'Thank you mum,' he managed to say before escaping outside.

He would talk it over that evening with Justine, but even as the first shock waves started to settle, he had resolved a couple of issues. He had no interest in delving deeper into what had happened or in seeing anything change in his life, and he certainly had no interest in discovering who his natural father was. For Patrick, there was only one father, and that was Tom Hogan.

In late 1959 at the age of 20, the legal age under New Zealand Racing Conference rules, Patrick bought his first mare. She was called Nom de Plume, by Gold Nib and in foal to Marco Polo. He bought her from Seton Otway's Trelawney Stud in Cambridge for 450 guineas, paid for with a loan of £150 from Tom, some income from his share of the pigs, and a hefty chunk of his £416 annual wage. From Nom de Plume he got a colt foal that he weaned and prepared for the National Yearling Sales. The colt, Acapulco, was a winner, and Patrick Hogan was on his way.

Generally, he enjoyed going to the races — at Ellerslie, or in the Waikato at Matamata or Te Rapa — with his mates, standing in bars for men only, drinking beer and working out the form, always taking as much money as he could afford to lose, and following the breeds of the horses running, particularly if they had Fencourt bloodlines.

Jenny Kain, who had been a friend of Patrick's from Pony Club days, lived close to the Hogans at Fencourt. She drove a little mini van — the 'Fencourt bus' — that had no seats inside, which was often called into service to take a busload of the friends home at night after a day at the races or a dance. One night after the Te Rapa races, she had dropped off a couple of people and then noticed a car parked on the side of the road, outside the Hogan's farm. 'That's funny,' she thought, then had a closer look and saw a bottom sticking out of a hedge. Jenny looked again. 'That's a familiar backside,' she thought, and stopped her car to see what he was up to. The head shot back through the hedge — sure enough, it was Patrick.

Half-laughing, half-astonished, she asked, 'What on earth are you doing, Patrick?'

He grinned with embarrassment, 'Aaah, um, I'm just checking to see how my mares are.'

Justine and Patrick had known each other for five years and, as usual, Patrick had called in to see her at her parents' home in Cambridge township on his way to his weekly rugby practice. They were sitting in his car in Grey Street outside the Heaths' home when Patrick suddenly blurted out, 'What about we get engaged?'

There was an astonished silence which seemed to last for

ever, then Justine stammered out, 'Oh . . . umm . . . ooh, umm . . . '

'Well, hurry up and make up your mind because I've got to get to rugby practice,' Patrick demanded.

'Oh . . . yes!' Justine beamed.

It was not the most romantic of marriage proposals, he knew, but he was pressed for time. 'Well, I've got to go now. I'm late for rugby practice.' Five minutes later Patrick was at the rugby ground, and when the practice was finished he went home to Fencourt for his evening meal — there would be ample time the following day to sort everything out in the marriage stakes.

Justine confided the exciting news to her mother, who said she was delighted, adding the ritual phrase, 'Perhaps he had better ask for Dad's permission.'

When Patrick phoned the following day, Justine repeated her mother's words, adding cautiously, 'That's what you're supposed to do.' That would mean keeping the engagement quiet from his family and friends until the following weekend when Bill Heath, a trucking contractor who worked at the hydro dams during the week, was home.

The following Sunday, a neatly dressed Patrick presented himself at the Heaths' home. 'Dad's working on the truck out the back,' he was told by his 20-year-old fiancée.

Patrick walked to the section behind the house where Bill Heath was doing some maintenance work on the engine of his truck. The bonnet of the truck was up and Bill, in deep concentration, was stooped underneath it, tinkering with the engine. Standing close to his prospective father-in-law, Patrick cleared his throat. 'Mr Heath, I want to talk to you . . . '

'Oh, yeah, yeah, yeah,' the older man replied without looking up.

'I want to ask you something . . . ' Patrick started his prepared speech again.

'Yep. Could you turn that handle for me? Just turn it slowly, just turn it over.'

Patrick's speech wasn't going the way he had planned, but, as asked, he compliantly turned the crank handle over. He would start again and cut out the preliminaries. 'Justine and I would like to get engaged!'

Without lifting his head out from under the bonnet, a preoccupied Bill Heath replied, 'Yes, yes, yes. Turn that just a little bit more . . . '

Well, he wasn't going to get anywhere with this conversation, Patrick thought. He walked back inside, and described the scene to a laughing Justine. Her father hadn't seemed to pay much attention to what was being said, but at least he had uttered the magic word 'yes'.

On his return home the following weekend, Bill Heath complained to his wife: 'You know I heard that Justine and Patrick got engaged. You'd think he'd have at least asked me.'

'Well,' she told her husband, 'according to Justine he did ask you.'

'No he didn't!' Bill was adamant.

'Well, I did.' Patrick arrived at the Heaths' home as the conversation was taking place. 'I thought you heard me. You told me to crank that handle at the same time that I was asking and you said "yes, yes, yes".'

'I was saying "yes, yes, yes" to the handle going right!' Bill protested.

What did Justine like about Patrick? Almost everything, apart from his driving, which was hairy. He was kind and gentle, and shared her love for animals. She wanted to bring her dog Dulcie to live with them at Fencount when they married, she said.

Better speak with Dad about it, Patrick temporised.

Tom was emphatic. 'You can't bring the dog.'

'OK. I won't come myself. Simple as that,' Justine retorted.

From their first meeting Tom had held a soft spot for Justine, and so there was a hurried conversation between father and son.

'You'd better bring the blasted dog,' Patrick said.

The 21-year-olds were married at St Peter's Catholic Church, Cambridge, on 4 February 1961, on a blazing hot summer's day, with 150 guests and two of Patrick's Hautapu rugby mates, John Warren and Bill Taylor, as his best man and groomsman.

To meet the changed domestic situation, Sarah and Tom Hogan had moved out of the Hogan family home at Fencourt, handing it over to Patrick and Justine. The Hogans senior would live next door in a new cottage which had been built for them.

Justine loved big kindly Tom who had warned her, half-seriously, before they married, 'You will never be able to trust Patrick with horses. He'll just keep buying them and bringing them home.' However, there was an underlying hostility between Sarah, a staunch Catholic, and Justine, who was brought up as a Presbyterian before converting to Catholicism when she married Patrick. Sarah had a good Catholic girl lined up for her son, whom she would have preferred Patrick to marry, Justine suspected.

As a 'townie' she had to adjust instantaneously to farm life and working at Patrick's pace — up at 5.00 a.m. each day, putting up with the practical jokes Patrick and his brother-in-law played on her, being sent to town on nonsense errands, made to leap fences to escape horses which frightened her, getting shocks from electric fences, mowing the lawns, cooking for swarms of people, mucking out the boxes, and helping to watch over the Fencourt horses day and night.

She hadn't seen a foaling before she came to Fencourt and, initially, she was squeamish about having to help with their delivery. Patrick wasn't that sympathetic either, Justine told her mother. 'He'd just say to me, "For Christ's sake, close your bloody eyes if you have to!"' But, Justine admitted, she was already hooked: there was no experience she could imagine to cap the emotion or excitement of bringing a new life into the world — late on a cold spring night, a beautiful chestnut foal slipping into the world under Patrick and Justine's watchful care, Patrick walking the mare gently and massaging her belly to prevent cramping while soothing her with reassuring words, as the mare's 20-minute-old foal with his outsize limbs, wobbled to his feet in search of his mother's milk . . .

And then came the two-legged Hogan babies: Nicola, born on 22 May 1962, and Erin, on 14 October 1963. Both were champion sleepers, and each enjoyed prolonged crying sessions in the early evening. 'Don't worry about it,' said their doctor, 'it's good for exercising the lungs.'

When Patrick drew the night feed with Nicola, he used his own special teat, hiding it from Justine until she went to bed, and then switching his invention for the standard one. It took so long to bottlefeed a baby with a normal teat — 'suck-suck-suck' he'd groan to himself. He would do with Nicola what he did with his calves to speed the process. He took a heated needle, added an extra hole to the teat and was through the feed in no time at all.

'Nicola's got through the bottle in about three great gulps,' he grinned with pride to himself. 'Now there's three great burps . . . a huge amount of air coming up . . . all done in half the time, just like the calves!'

CHAPTER 3

TOMMY'S COME HOME

The Fencourt Stud, Cambridge, advises that both Hermes and Philoctetes are fully booked for the coming season. Both stallions have attracted a wide range of select mares, especially Hermes, who has commanded a most attractive line-up.

— *New Zealand Racing Calendar*, 28 June 1972

Tom Hogan's health was failing. By 1968 the lifelong smoker was in the grips of the lung cancer that would later claim his life. 'I think you boys have got to take over Fencourt and handle it,' he told John and Patrick.

Always the stud's advertising and marketing had been promoted as 'Fencourt Stud — Tom Hogan', but following the death of their second stallion, Final Court, the brothers sought to buy another stallion and, at the same time, signal the new direction of Fencourt's ownership. In future, all promotions and marketing would appear under their joint names. It would be 'Fencourt Stud — John and Patrick Hogan'. The brothers decided they would leave the search for a stallion to their father, whose job it would be to pore through the pedigrees and see what was available in a price range they could afford.

One evening, late in the autumn of 1968, Tom came across a stallion by the name of Hermes who was being quoted by the British Bloodstock Agency (BBA) and the United Kingdom agents for the Hogans. Hermes appealed immediately. 'He will work well for us and do the job,' Tom predicted. But the price put on Hermes was totally outside their reach. What to do? After some deliberation they decided to take the innovative step of syndicating the stallion.

They would take out their 'insurance' by approaching 20 individual breeders to ask them if they would support Fencourt Stud in the purchase of the horse, with a 1/40th shareholding that would entitle each of the shareholders to send one mare each year at no cost for the rest of the horse's standing life, and to share the dividends from the service fees for the stallion. The Hogans would purchase 50 per cent of Hermes and put 50 per cent out in 20 shares in the horse, selling these off to other breeders.

It was a novel concept, although it had been done before in New Zealand. Nancy and Alister Williams of Wairarapa, owners of the fine imported stallions Agricola and Oncidium, had already successfully travelled that path.

Initially Tom baulked at the proposal of syndicating. He did not want to share the ownership of his horse, he said, but his reservations were outweighed by the advantages that his sons spelled out to him. The shareholder support was forthcoming, and a principal of Fencourt Stud now had to fly to England and inspect the horse. Unlike their previous dealings where it had been left to the BBA to check out the stallions, because Fencourt was syndicating Hermes, an on-the-spot inspection from one of the Hogans was considered necessary.

Tom was adamant: 'You two boys had better go, because I'm not going.'

John and Patrick declined. They were working on the farm and couldn't afford to be away from it for a couple of weeks to travel across the world to look at a horse, they said.

Patrick had a brainwave. 'John,' he suggested, 'I think we should cook up an argument between ourselves for Dad's benefit and stick to it. I think Dad should go and look at this horse.' His father wasn't well, but he was well enough to travel to England. However, the compulsion in Patrick's move to get Tom back to the Northern Hemisphere was to give his father a final opportunity to see his family in Ireland.

Tom Hogan had left Ireland when he was 18 and had never returned. Once he had booked his ticket to see his elderly mother, but she had died before he sailed. His ticket was cancelled, and the question of returning to Ireland was never again raised.

The plan was that if John was going to England to look at the horse, Patrick was out. If Patrick was going to look at the horse, John was out. There was only one person who could go — only one person whose judgement both brothers would accept — and that was Tom Hogan. He did not want his sons fighting between themselves, so Tom relented and said he would make the trip, but, as he was unwell, he needed a companion to travel with. And who better to accompany him than Michael Floyd, the 35-year-old bloodstock manager of Wright Stephenson & Company, the Hogans' New Zealand agents.

The company had been involved in the negotiating process and would get a commission from the purchase. It was also a valuable opportunity for Floyd to acquaint himself with the

British bloodstock industry. On arrival in England the BBA would look after them both.

After a near lifetime spent in New Zealand where he had never ventured out of the country, Tom needed a passport — which for some inexplicable reason had to be applied for from Canberra.

'You're creating a bit of problem,' John laughed.

His father looked thoughtful and rather worried. 'I wonder if it's that fishing story?' he muttered nervously. For years, Tom had thrown out hints to his sons about a 'fishing story' but would never elaborate — now was the time for confession. 'The night before I left Galway, I was out with the lads and we were poaching salmon. Then the ranger caught us. I was big and strong, so I grabbed him. The boys got the net out of the river and took off while I pushed the ranger into the river. I didn't worry because I knew I was leaving Galway the next morning,' Tom added quietly. 'You know you can go to jail for poaching . . . '

'No, no,' John reassured his father. 'I don't think after all this time that anyone's going to be bothered about that.'

Then Tom threw another spanner in the works. 'I don't want anybody to know I'm going home,' he said firmly. His wish was to go to England, look at the horse, and then travel alone and unheralded to Ireland where he would surprise his brothers and relatives at his old home in Ballindooley. All right, fine — we'll tell no one, the brothers promised as they booked his flight.

Those were the days when passengers could smoke on planes. Tom was an inveterate smoker — both roll-your-own cigarettes and his beloved tobacco-filled pipe, which he liked to puff as he downed a whiskey. As they flew out of Auckland on a

Boeing 707, Tom leaned over to Michael with his first request for the journey. 'Can you get the girl to bring me a whiskey?' Tom drank whiskey, smoked, snored, coughed and hacked for the entire trip while Floyd, as Hogan's sons had anticipated with a sympathetic chuckle, had a horrific journey.

They arrived in London after an overnight stop-off at Los Angeles and were driven direct to Charing Cross Hotel. Then it was off to the stables at Newmarket, the heartbeat of British horse racing, to inspect the stallion. Hermes was taken out of his box and paraded before the New Zealanders. Tom stared intently at the stallion and ordered the groom: 'Walk him up, walk him back,' then 'Put him in his box. That'll do. We'll take him.'

In less than 30 seconds Hogan had made his decision. However, he wanted 1000 guineas knocked off the price. That could be rather difficult, the studmaster explained. Hermes' owner was sitting in the House of Lords and was not to be disturbed. 'Call him,' said Tom. A flurried call was made to Westminster, a message delivered, a call returned, and the horse was his.

'Well, now you'll be shouting a man a whiskey after taking him off your hands,' Hogan nodded to the astonished studmaster. Half a bottle later, Tom leaned across to Floyd. 'I think we should be getting back to the hotel.'

Hermes would be the goods, Tom knew, though he had cost them more than the sum value of Fencourt farm. His keen eye had never let him down, and now, with Fencourt's business completed, it was time to undertake the second part of his journey and travel to his old home which he hadn't seen for more than half a century.

He was stunned at the changes in Dublin, but he was never

a man for city life. As soon as he possibly could, Tom Hogan was on his way west to Ballindooley.

On a lazy June day in 1968, a taxi pulled up outside Paddy Hogan's pub on Prospect Hill, just off Galway Square, and an elderly man, supporting himself with a cane, stepped out of the car. He entered the pub, looked around with obvious curiosity, and told a young man he would like to speak with Paddy.

The young man — Tony Hogan — indicated an open door that led to a garden and told the stranger that the man he was looking for was outside. The stranger ignored his direction. 'Tell him that there's somebody here who wants to see him.'

Hogan junior trotted outside to his father and repeated the speaker's request. Curious, Paddy Hogan entered the bar. He looked at his visitor and the shock began to register in his face almost before the words reached his ears. 'G'day, I'm your brother Tom.'

With tears rolling down their cheeks, the two men embraced and attempted, through half-finished sentences and gusts of laughter, to catch up on more than 50 years of lost conversation and family reminiscence. The words flowed in English and Gaelic — Tom, the brothers were astonished to discover, had found that he could still speak Irish fluently.

Eventually Paddy got to his feet. 'Come on, we'd better go and see John.'

Unlike his brothers Paddy and Tom, John had remained on the farm at Ballindooley. Tony, a teacher on summer vacation, was the driver. As they travelled across the countryside, memories of his youth almost overcame Tom. Here was the bog bisected by the Clare River, where he had worked as a child, the wide-open space stretching out to the waters of lower Lough Corrib and beyond to the skyline of the Maamturks . . . summer hay, summer turf, summer grazing . . . the pristine whiteness of bog cotton, the green unripe heather, the intoxicating perfume of bog myrtle . . . the bog, always hostile in every season but summer, where they chased the hare and the marshalled troops of salmon running the river, and where Tom had spent his last memorable evening in Ireland with his pals.

They had arrived at their old home. Opposite was Ballindooley Castle which had once been the Hogans' until the English had taken it off them. Paddy leaned across and put a restraining hand on Tom's arm, saying: 'Tom you stay here, I'll go and find John.'

The thatched cottage was still occupied by John and his wife Bridget. They were childless and ageing and, almost as in sympathy with their decline, the outhouses and the house were leaning toward their end. The roof had long since received its last thatching, and the reed-crowded pools that fronted the cottage — from where Tom used to carry water for his mother — had a dark and slightly sinister appearance.

John was at the back of the cottage, bending over his shovel and loosening peat clumps for his fire that evening. 'John! I've got someone here to see you,' Paddy called.

John stood upright and dug the shovel into the ground. Then he looked at Paddy's face and cried out, 'Oh God! Our Tommy's come home.'

Moving more rapidly than he had in years, John led the way back to the car where his young brother was waiting for him. To come home after 50 years — Tom had no idea how much he would cherish being back where he belonged.

60

Unlike the rest of the world, nothing had changed in Ballindooley, Tom discovered. His brother John still rode the bike with one pedal to go down to town, as he had done when Tom was a boy. There was the stone hob facing the empty seat on the far side of the fire, where his mother had liked to sit, stoically nursing her private grief after discovering her husband dead in the stable, with a brood of children and a blind old father-in-law to care for.

Tom was reunited with his brothers and old friends, and met a raft of young relatives for the first time. To his nephew, John Hogan, and the other nephews and nieces, Tom was a larger-than-life, Zane Grey kind of character, with his weather-beaten features, soft felt hat, braces over an open-necked check shirt, boots and a cane. He was constantly rolling or smoking tobacco, fascinating his Irish relatives with his ability to make them one-handed. He was, they discovered to their delight, as argumentative as the rest of the family, and gifted with a wicked and mischievous sense of humour.

That summer of 1968 was 'The Year of Sir Ivor' and the whole country was agog at the achievements of Raymond Guest's Triple Crown-winning colt. John Hogan boasted to his Uncle Tom about the horse's achievements, and opined that the Irish horse was unbeatable. 'I'm not too impressed,' Tom replied. 'There's a horse in France who will beat him in the Prix de l'Arc de Triomphe this October.' (In October, as he had predicted, Sir Ivor came second to Vaguely Noble in the race. Sir Ivor would later play a pivotal part in the Hogan fortunes, as the sire of Sir Tristram.)

The Hogans were enchanted to learn more of their 'down under' relatives from their New Zealand visitor — the poignancy of Tom's Christmas Day ritual in Cambridge where he would lock himself away in his room to listen to Irish music; the episode at the local blacksmith's forge where a group of farmers had watched Tom leaving with his horse, one remarking loudly to his friends, 'That old Irishman always votes Labour,' to which the blacksmith, pausing from his work, had looked up at them and said, 'Yeah, and he always meets his bills by the end of the month.'

Tom stayed with his family for a month and visited the family grave in Castlegar cemetery, where so many members of his family lay. Then it was time to bid farewell — an experience almost too hard to bear, as they knew they would never see each other again.

Hermes arrived in New Zealand by ship in 1969 in time for the stud season. He was a splendid-looking, massively big horse, dark — almost black — in colouring, with a magnificent nature to complement his looks. His dam was Ark Royal and he was named after the World War Two aircraft carrier HMS *Hermes*, but he was anything but warlike — just a great big baby at heart. They could do almost anything with him, they discovered — young children could run around him in the paddock, and the only thing the toddlers need fear was a large lick planted on the side of their faces.

Commercially, Hermes was an immediate success. His first crop were sold as yearlings in January 1970, and created such a favourable impression that they achieved for their sire the distinction of becoming the leading first-season sire on aggregate and average. In the same year, Philoctetes — another Fencourt stallion — had completed one season at stud and had a full booking of mares.

With the success of Hermes and the solid back-up of Philoctetes, John and Patrick's farming partnership with their father at Fencourt Stud was, by the early 1970s, focused on stallions, broodmares, colts and fillies, with a few head of cattle remaining as a second tier of income.

Patrick also took his first step into administration, becoming a committee member of the Cambridge Jockey Club in 1970, where he would serve as a committee man for 17 years and as president for three terms (from 1985 to 1988), and as a life member from 1992. He followed that in 1974 by joining the New Zealand Thoroughbred Breeders' Association, as an industry representative where, in his first term, he would serve until 1982, and as vice president for its latter stages.

In 1926, Wright Stephenson and Company had introduced the New Zealand National Yearling Sales, working in partnership with Pyne Gould Guinness Ltd of Canterbury, a South Island stock and station company who listed on their books many wealthy clients from the established sheep station dynasties of Canterbury and Otago. The pair would eventually become known as PGG Wrightson.

There was a solid tradition of horse breeding in the wealthy southern North Island regions of Hawke's Bay, Wairarapa, Wanganui and Manawatu. It made sense, the two companies decided, to opt for neutral territory in staging the annual yearling sales. Wright Stephenson leased land from the Wellington Racing Club at Trentham, constructed several fairly primitive buildings, as they had no great security of tenure, and launched the Trentham National Yearling Sales, to run at the conclusion of the racing club's Wellington Cup week towards the end of January each year.

Wellington was an obvious choice as a venue and proved to be a good one, with many geographical and social advantages. From the start, it was a party town during the week-long sales, with breeders, trainers and buyers converging from all quarters to buy horses during the day and party long into the night.

As a young man, Ronald Trotter was enjoying his life as the manager of Wright Stephenson in Hastings, when in 1958 he was approached by the company's chief executive and chairman, Sir Clifford Plimmer, and invited to come down to Wellington to become his personal assistant. One of the first things Sir Clifford placed in his lap was to put him in charge of the bloodstock department, complaining that he was too busy to handle it. 'I don't want to have anything to do with people like Jim Fletcher and Tom Lowry and Woolf Fisher — they are always wanting this or that. There's no money in the game.'

With Trotter on the scene, life picked up for the breeders. His father, Clem Trotter, had run Federated Farmers in Taranaki, and Ron's background was attuned to the rural and horsey community. He was in his element, happy to spend time with the breeders, and when they asked 'Why don't you supply the bran, it's not very expensive?' or 'Why don't you supply cut grass?' their needs were met.

When breeders complained that the company hadn't put sufficient investment into Trentham's National Yearling Sales week, Ron concurred and did something about it. Trentham's old inverted wooden banana crate that had been the auctioneers' stand departed, along with the tin shed, pegs and string used to lead the horses around the ring. A new rostrum and more boxes were built, and its facilities were upgraded to be on a par with similar sale rings overseas. Sales improved, prices improved, and breeding improved, along with a more professional approach to the business. As Trotter reported the feedback to Sir Clifford, he smiled: 'All of a sudden they're pretty happy.'

New breeders arrived on the scene, like Patrick Hogan, as well as the established ones, headed by the doyen of the industry, Seton Otway of Trelawney Stud in Cambridge, where super-sire Foxbridge stood and where seven Melbourne Cup winners — Hiraji, Hi-Jinx, Galilee, Silver Knight, Foxzami, MacDougal and Polo Prince — had spent the early part of their lives. (The great Tulloch, considered the equal in Australasian racing history to Phar Lap, Carbine and Kingston Town, was bred and reared at Trelawney, and was sold to the leading Australian trainer T.J. 'Tommy' Smith for 750 guineas at the 1956 yearling sales at Trentham.)

Every young auctioneer is never as good as the old one. Joe Walls, of Wright Stephenson in Hamilton, was in his mid-twenties and working with people twice his age when he faced his debut as an auctioneer at the Trentham sales. It was daunting to be fronted by prominent breeders and asked, 'Oh Joe, which numbers are Peter Kelly doing and which ones are you doing?'

Joe would reply, 'I'm doing 25 to 55,' and they'd give an involuntary grimace and say, 'Uh.' On one of these occasions, Patrick overheard the exchange and rounded on the breeder, saying 'Give this young fellow a chance — I'm putting my horses with him.'

They had first met in 1969 when Joe was 22. He had heard there was a go-getting, hard-working guy at Cambridge called

Patrick Hogan who had started with nothing. They met and became friends. Joe listened to what Patrick was doing with his horses, and they got some sort of repartee going.

The pair caught up again at Trentham. Patrick's horses were considered unfashionable, but, Joe was impressed to see, he managed to sell them all — the Blueskins, the Persian Gardens. Joe and his colleagues generally used to feel rather sorry for him: 'Poor bloody Patrick — geez, he's working hard. One day — one day — he'll strike it rich that fella, he works so bloody hard.'

Year in, year out, the Wright Stephenson boys would see Patrick at Trentham with his horses. They were as immaculate in appearance as their young studmaster, and the 'Patrick Hogan Show' didn't end there. Patrick parading his horses was something to see. Striding briskly into the ring, with horse in step, he'd stop abruptly in front of a major buyer — a Bart Cummings — seated several rows up from the sawdust. Then, another half-dozen strides for man and horse, another abrupt halt to squarely face the next expansive wallet, perhaps Australia's chicken kings, Jack and Bob Ingham . . . Patrick's 'Calf Club Day' performance revamped for the horse market was high theatre, and one of the most enjoyable diversions of the sales.

DEATH OF THOMAS HOGAN

— *New Zealand Racing Calendar*, 28 June 1972
'The death has occurred of Mr Thomas Hogan, a well-known and respected member of the community, and founder of the Fencourt Stud, Cambridge. Born at Balindooley, County Galway,

Ireland, 76 years ago from farming stock, Mr Hogan emigrated to New Zealand at the age of 18.'

After outlining his career and life, the tribute concluded:

'Mr Hogan is survived by his wife, four daughters and three sons, 34 grandchildren and 21 great-grandchildren.'

After Tom's return from Ireland, Patrick observed a marked decline in his father. Going home, reliving the memories, seeing his brothers and the family and the place where he was born, had unnerved him. Without the anticipation of that reunion to live for, he was sliding downhill rapidly and suffering from bouts of acute depression.

Their father had left his heart in Ireland, Patrick told John and his sister, Delia. 'When he dies I want to send his body back to Ireland, because his heart isn't here since that trip. I know it.' But John would have none of it: Tom Hogan's life was in New Zealand, and his family were here, not in Ireland, he replied.

His father's death shook Patrick to the core. Emotionally, it left a gaping hole that would stay with him. He loved his father uncritically — his rough Irish voice, his directness, his mannerisms, his wry humour, his pithy observations, his uncanny sense with horseflesh, his just being there. Justine and their two young daughters, Nicola and Erin, were rocks of strength, and the tributes that poured in brought a bittersweet solace. His father had always wanted for others more than himself, once admitting, 'I'd always be scared to have too much money.'

At Tom's funeral people came from near and far to pay their tributes, many approaching the family to say, 'We'd like to thank your family, because when we were in trouble your father gave us this . . . ' or 'We ran out of stock feed. Something went wrong and Tom brought truckloads of hay around to us and refused to take payment.'

The Hogan family, unaware of much of Tom's quiet philanthropy, shared a warm glow every time another story came to light.

Seated in his pew in St Peter's Catholic Church where a High Mass was being celebrated by Father Frank Quinn for the life of Thomas Hogan, Bill Taylor allowed his memories to roam: the serious and rather shy man he had known . . . Tom's first day back from Ireland, beaming and telling anyone who would listen, tales of how wonderful it was: "Aaah, I think I might charter a plane and send the whole village over to Galway. They can drink a bit you know over there, but I think you can hold your own" . . . and, towards the end of Tom's life, a quiet aside to Bill: 'I don't have to worry about Patrick. I think he can take care of himself.'

It wasn't as though Tom's death was unexpected. The cancer had taken over, everyone knew, as they paid their visits to him in his hospital bed. One afternoon, shortly before his death, Tom made a final request to his youngest. 'Will you promise me something, Patrick?'

Few people warm to an open-ended emotional commitment, and Patrick immediately went on his guard. 'I'll think about it,' he answered reluctantly.

'No! You must promise me.' Tom was vehement.

'I can never promise anything unless I know what it is you are asking,' his son protested.

'I want you to look after John, I don't want you to leave the farm.'

'I'll do my best,' Patrick conceded. 'I'll think about it and I'll do my best.' He would not say yes.

Tom also had a request for John — he'd had a tiff with Frank Quinn and wanted to make his peace before he died. John brought the priest to his old friend's bedside and left them together. 'We buried the hatchet,' Tom smiled faintly, after Father Quinn had left. 'He said a bloody lot of prayers over me!'

In his will, Thomas Hogan left ownership of Fencourt Stud to two of his sons: two-thirds to John, his eldest, and one-third to Patrick, his youngest. His second son, Peter, lived on another farm which was in their mother Sarah's name, and which would later become his own. This was the traditional way, Patrick knew — the oldest son was the heir — but although he and John got on so well together, the distribution rankled. There was a farm the family called Peter's farm and a farm called John's farm, but there was never a farm called Patrick's farm. Well, one day, there would be.

On the surface nothing changed with the new ownership of Fencourt Stud. Since the 1960s, when Tom had first become ill, John and Patrick had owned the stock on the farm and were financial partners in the horses, the stallions and the cattle. However, the broodmares were a different story. This was an area in which the brothers were never able to agree. What John wanted to buy, Patrick didn't, and vice versa.

Matters had first come to a head back in 1961 when Patrick told John he wanted to buy a broodmare. 'She's for tender and I want to bid one thousand and fifty guineas for her,' Patrick said. 'She's called Sweet Wren, in foal to a leading sire, Summertime, and she has a foal at foot by the same sire. She's beautifully bred and she's being sold by the Public Trust under the estate of Mr Moreland. I can't afford to do it on my own — will you stick in 50 per cent of the money for her?'

No, he wasn't interested in going halves in the mare, John replied, and he considered 21-year-old Patrick very foolish to go ahead and spend that sort of money when he didn't have it. His views were echoed by Tom, who infuriated Patrick by pouring cold water on the proposed purchase: 'Don't do it, boy!'

Patrick and Justine were newly married, and although they had saved some money, it fell well short of the amount required. His sister, Pat, was mad on horses — perhaps she would be interested in coming on board? Yes, she would, Pat replied on the other end of the phone, without waiting to hear the price.

'It's not going to be cheap,' her brother warned. 'I may have to go beyond one thousand guineas for it.'

'Whatever you decide, we'll go halves,' Pat promised.

Justine and Pat would own the mare, Patrick said, when he successfully tendered for Sweet Wren. 'She will go in the name of you two girls,' he promised. Then he led the mare and her foal along the country roads from Hautapu to their new home at Fencourt. Sweet Wren's foal was sold at Trentham the following year for 2000 guineas, more than recouping their investment.

In future, Patrick proposed to John, 'The best thing is for you to get the broodmares that you want, and I'll get the broodmares I want. What I get out of them is mine, and what you get out of your broodmares is yours.' It was amicably agreed they should follow this path.

How was Patrick to know what a lucky break this would be? Fifteen years later, when he left Fencourt for Cambridge Stud, Patrick owned eight well-bred broodmares, all ready to go to his new stallion, Sir Tristram.

Justine was 100 per cent committed to Fencourt Stud. From the time they had married she insisted on seeing every one of their foals born, taking it in turns to wait out the night in a tiny wooden shed that was equipped with a television and a rickety bed adjacent to the stud's floodlit foaling paddock. Generously, Jack and Joyce Macky of Pirongia Stud stretched a point to give the young couple a head start by making a couple of bookings with their champion sire, Le Filou.

Sweet Wren had already produced Sweet Time, and from her union with Le Filou came a striking chestnut filly that was born in 1966. Intent on developing bloodstock, because he couldn't afford to get into racing, Patrick phoned Bart Cummings, saying he had a filly who, he believed, had real potential. She would be leased to Cummings if he would take her, Patrick offered, and one-third of anything the filly earned would go back to her owners, Justine and Pat. Yes, the great man agreed, he would add her to his stables where she would be leased to the colourful Ronnie Dabscheck, one of the biggest owners and punters around, Dabscheck's racing partner Jack McDonald, and Geoff Bellmaine.

At Fencourt excitement ran high as progress reports of the classy three-year-old filly, named Gay Poss, filtered back across the Tasman. She had qualified to run in the 1969 Victorian Oaks, one of the highlights of the Melbourne Spring Carnival. Could Justine and Pat afford to go and see their 'baby' run?

Could they *not* afford to be there to experience the huge thrill of their first black-type win if she carried the day? Scraping together their air fares, they flew to Melbourne in a mood of high anticipation, only to find — to their shock — that Gay Poss had been forced out of the race.

The filly had got caught up in a drugs scandal, although she wasn't involved, after an intruder had broken into Bart Cummings' stable and administered dope to several of his horses. Security had been broken and it necessitated Cummings scratching a number of horses from the meeting, including Gay Poss. It was the cruellest stroke of ill luck. Justine and Pat returned home the following day.

They decided that Patrick, as studmaster, should go to Randwick the following April, to network and see Gay Poss run in the 2400 metres Group 1 AJC Oaks Stakes for three-year-old fillies. An added fillip was the presence of Princess Anne, who would make the presentation to the winner. In her honour, the race would be known as the 1970 Royal AJC Oaks.

Tempering his excitement, Patrick faced an embarrassing problem, knowing he would be in the company of a bunch of high-rollers over the coming days in Sydney. Severe restrictions had been applied by the New Zealand government on money that could be taken out of the country, leaving him with barely enough to survive on, let alone buy food.

On the day, after Gay Poss had run a good third in the lead-up race, the Princess Handicap, one of her owners, Jack McDonald, approached Patrick and asked, 'Would you like to put some money on Gay Poss in the Oaks?'

'No thanks,' Patrick replied — he wasn't about to let on that he couldn't afford to back his horse, and nor did he have the money back in New Zealand.

'You should have a bet on her, she'll go well,' McDonald urged.

'No thanks, Jack. I don't want to back her.' And there the conversation ended.

On Oaks day, a fidgeting Patrick arrived early at Randwick, scarcely able to cloak his excitement at the prospect of breeding and owning his first Group 1 winner. At 5–2 odds, Gay Poss was heavily backed to win, with $120,000 going on her in a series of mammoth bets from her Melbourne owners and other big punters. Gay Poss would be ridden by champion jockey Roy Higgins.

Patrick sat in the front row of the stand, looking down on the owners standing nervously in the birdcage with the race fillies parading around them. McDonald glanced up and spotted Patrick who gave McDonald a V for victory sign and a wink.

Guided by Higgins, Gay Poss raced in seventh place until the home turn; then, shooting along the rails, the chestnut filly bolted into the lead at the final furlong and coasted home to win by three lengths. It was a brilliant riding exhibition. Describing his Oaks win, racing writer Keith Robbins in the *Daily Telegraph* on 2 April 1970 wrote: 'Higgins yesterday gave Sydney racegoers a demonstration of his riding ability. He taught some of the locals a lesson on cool, expert horsemanship.'

'Get down here and come to the presentation with Bart and Princess Anne!' The ecstatic owners were waving wildly up at Patrick. It was the best of days, the best of evenings, as the party rolled into the night at the Chevron Hilton where they were staying, hosted by the trainer and master of such occasions, J. Bart Cummings.

The following morning, as Patrick was heading for home, Jack McDonald knocked at his door. 'I've just come to say goodbye and give you the money.'

'What money?' an astonished Patrick asked.

'Your bet.'

'I didn't have a bet!'

'Are you that forgetful?' McDonald stared at him in amazement. 'You put two grand on Gay Poss.'

'No I didn't!'

'Yes, you bloody well did. I looked up and saw those two fingers and I thought, "You bugger, leaving it till the last minute, you could have told me earlier!" and I put the money on.'

'Jack, I gave you the V for victory sign!' Patrick said — he'd better come clean. 'You keep the money, because if that horse had got beaten I wouldn't have had two thousand to pay you. I'd have had no hope — I couldn't have done it.'

'I've got four grand here for you,' McDonald insisted.

Still Patrick refused, and McDonald left.

Ten days later, a bank statement arrived at Fencourt from Australia. The money had been deposited for Patrick at a Melbourne bank. It was unbelievable, a huge windfall for the Hogans, and a thrill that almost matched their filly's win.

And then there was Vicky Joy, a mare that Patrick had bought for $6000. Tom and John had roared with laughter at the sight of her when she first came off the float at Fencourt in 1971, for not only was she pint-sized, she also suffered from grass staggers — but the mare and Patrick were to enjoy the last laugh against the doubters.

Late in 1971, Vicky Joy was put to Sovereign Edition and produced a large, beautiful filly. Patrick leased the filly to Geoff Murphy — a fiery Irishman and a leading Australian trainer, with stables at Caulfield — where her new owner, Ross Ansell, named her Taiona, blending the Christian names of his two daughters, Tanya and Fiona. Taiona was later returned to Cambridge Stud after breaking her tailshaft, which ended her short racing life, but Patrick propelled her into a stellar career as a broodmare.

Twice Taiona was named New Zealand Broodmare of the Year — in 1981 and 1983 — as the dam of some of the great racehorses in Australasia of that era, including Sovereign Red and Gurner's Lane.

In years to come, the descendants of those first mares — Sweet Wren and Vicky Joy — were to reap the stud in excess of $5 million in yearling sale receipts.

BART CUMMINGS AND PATRICK HOGAN

Leading Australian trainer Bart Cummings had contacted Fencourt Stud, telling the astonished brothers he would like to pay them a visit the following day. Fencourt, small as it was, had never featured on the visiting list of the big boys, but Hermes' arrival had put them on the map. There was a Hermes yearling or two at Fencourt, and such was the stallion's reputation that the legendary Bart was coming down to the farm en route to the Trentham sales. Previewing yearlings on their home turf before they were paraded at the Trentham sale grounds was vital for Cummings. He liked to cast a trained eye over them 'cold' for the first time.

They were pretty hick for such a high-powered visit, John and Patrick admitted to each other. Gumboots and old farming gear was the dress norm and, worse, they had no parade ring to lead the yearlings up and down in front of Cummings — considered a must for any self-respecting stud. 'Oh shit,' Patrick muttered nervously to himself after getting off the phone. The 'King of England' in the horse business was about to descend on them.

They ordered a truckload of sand to cover a circular area in front of the cow shed where there was rough old grass growing. There was no time to create a parade ring, but this was the next best thing. The sand arrived and was spread evenly at a depth of about four inches. That looked pretty good, Patrick thought. It would give him enough length to bring the horses out of the stables and lead them up and down on the sand.

The following morning they raked the sand over to give the 'parade ring' a smooth surface and then they waited. Bart Cummings arrived, pleasantries were exchanged, and Patrick led out the first yearling from his box onto their sand pad. The horse sank in the sand as Patrick struggled to lead him up and down.

'Sonny, I'd love to see his pasterns and fetlocks,' Cummings commented mildly to Patrick. 'Hop him off that sand and onto the dirt over there so I can get a better look at him.'

It had taken less than three minutes to realise how naive they were. The Hogans had just been handed a lesson in the art of presentation.

CHAPTER 4

THE SEARCH FOR MR RIGHT

'There is no such thing as the perfect animal and there is no such thing as a perfect horse.'

— Tom Hogan

A CORDIAL RELATIONSHIP EXISTED between the brothers but, after Tom's death, disagreements started to surface in the running of Fencourt. John and Patrick were temperamentally different — John stopped to talk when walking from paddock to paddock, while Patrick strode ahead to save time. John was by nature a gentleman, whereas Patrick was not. John was a traditional, conservative farmer, Patrick a bundle of nervous energy — a flamboyant innovator and go-getter who stretched the boundaries and was prepared to work huge hours to achieve whatever goals he set himself.

However, there was never dissent about their stallions, in particular their star — the magnificent Hermes, easily the best they had got their hands on. His progeny were now performing at a level where he could command good mares on both sides of the Tasman, and by the summer of 1974 the future looked rosy for their 10-year-old stallion and Fencourt Stud. They were about to strike the jackpot, thanks to Tom.

Colitis or horse fever — a deadly inflammation of the membranes lining the intestine — hits very quickly. Patrick had shampooed Hermes for a parade through Cambridge and, on their return, he was stunned to see the stallion shivering and sweating profusely, with rivulets of water running down his coat and leaving great dank stains. Hermes was scouring water very badly and dehydrating fast.

The horse collapsed. 'Get up,' Patrick urged, struggling to get the horse upright again to try walking off the fever. 'Call Bruce!' he yelled across to the yard. The Hogans' vet, Bruce Voyle, worked on the horse into the following morning — the men fighting back tears as they watched his condition worsen.

'Hermes, Hermes . . .' The tears were flowing uncontrollably, and Patrick's voice was choked — a little above a whisper — as he cradled the great stallion's head in his lap as the dying horse lay beside him on the ground. 'Don't leave us, you lovely boy.'

There was a final flicker of recognition from those great beautiful eyes, and then he was gone. For the second time in two years, Patrick felt as though his heart would break in half. Their magnificent Hermes was no more. Thank goodness Tom Hogan had been spared that horror. It was gut-wrenching — absolutely, utterly devastating.

This was the worst of times for the Hogans and the staff at Fencourt Stud who had so loved the handsome black stallion with the wonderful nature. It was certainly the worst of times for Justine and Patrick. Still shattered by the death of Hermes, they then suffered a devastating series of setbacks. Of their five mares who had produced foals that season, they ended up with just one foal. One mare had slipped, another foal was killed, a foal died, and a yearling had broken his leg. 'Let's get out of this,' they would say to each other, 'we're not going to last in this game.' But, by the following week they would be back at it again, working as hard as ever.

The arrival and departure of Hermes affected two of the Hogans more radically than they could ever have imagined. The horse's arrival had given Tom Hogan his longed-for chance to see his home in Ireland once again, whereas for Patrick, the stallion's departure was to pave the way for Cambridge Stud and Sir Tristram.

Hermes' death had opened up a void for servicing broodmares, and to compound their problems the two other Fencourt stallions — Philoctetes and Final Court — also had untimely deaths. If he had to go, Philoctetes died an enviable death, John Hogan smiled. 'He had just served a mare and burst his aorta. Bang! All over. We then lost Final Court to colitis. We had 12,500 guineas in service fees booked to him, and we lost him in the first week in August. So we were stuck with nothing. It was a pretty difficult time.'

Acting on the philosophy that if you put the best with the best, you'll get the best, Patrick decided to send one of his top mares, Acrimony, down to the Wairarapa when she came into season. The day came and Bruce Voyle, having inspected the mare, pronounced, 'Acrimony's ready to go to the stallion now.' They swung into action. Two of Patrick's friends, Barry Lee and Fred Cole, were deputed to put her on the truck and tow her down to the Williams' stud, Te Parae, near Masterton, to be served by their champion stallion, Oncidium — a nine-hour journey over both good and rough roads.

The men arrived at the Williams' home during the evening and their host, Richard 'Buzz' Williams, invited them for dinner, saying that he would get their vet to check the mare while they were inside eating their meal. The veterinarian walked in as they were halfway through the main course, announcing, 'She's not on — she's gone off.'

'She's gone off,' Barry rang Patrick from the dinner table with the bad news. His reaction could be heard by everyone in the room. Patrick was going ballistic. 'She's on! My vet said she was on this morning. She's got to be served! Stick the vet on the phone!'

The exchange raged as the table fell silent, the Williams' vet repeatedly saying 'She's gone off, she's gone off the boil,' with an infuriated Patrick shouting into the phone, 'Listen, if you'd been sitting on your arse all the way from Cambridge to Masterton, you'd have tightened up too! She's ready to serve. Sort it!'

Then he spoke to Buzz Williams. 'If you're not going to get her served, Barry and Fred can put her on the bloody truck right now and drive back through the night!'

Hmmm — that was going to be tricky. They'd downed a few whiskeys, so the group decided to ponder the decision while they had another round. It was late in the evening when they made up their minds what action to take. They rose from the dinner table and walked down to Oncidium's paddock, rousing him by the light of a torch, putting on his lead and taking him to where Acrimony was waiting.

Oncidium covered the mare about midnight, had a bucket of water thrown over him to clean him up, and was led back to his paddock to continue his sleep while, back inside the house, the group resumed their socialising.

The Cambridge men rose early the next morning and loaded Acrimony on the truck for the long journey home. A subsequent inspection from Patrick's vet confirmed that she was in foal.

The unusual 1974 midnight tryst had a stunning sequel, when the filly of that union forced a fast and furious bidding duel at the yearling sales between New Zealander David Benjamin and Bart Cummings. Cummings carried the day — his price of $120,000 was the highest ever paid in the Southern Hemisphere for a yearling thoroughbred of either sex by $20,000, and the biggest sum for a filly in New Zealand by $40,000.

Without Hermes, there was not much to hold Patrick at Fencourt, but he was reluctant to make a move. Then towards the end of 1974, he was given a prod by his brother. Peter had arrived at Patrick and Justine's house one day and tackled them on the issue. 'You've got to regroup and work out what you want to do in the future, where you are heading,' he told the pair.

He had already tried to buy John's two-thirds shareholding in Fencourt without success, as Peter well knew, Patrick replied. What did he have in mind? The death of Hermes was an opportunity for John and Patrick to go their own ways, Peter argued. Both of the partners at Fencourt were married, both had dependent children, and if they carried on as before and shared the purchase of another stallion, they would be stuck together for Lord knew how long. How would they ever prise themselves apart, or find out how successful they could be by going it alone?

Peter's words made sense, Patrick reasoned, so he approached John, who agreed Patrick should look for another property. John would own Fencourt outright, and would pay Patrick for his share of the stud. They shared a stallion in Adios II and it was agreed that Adios would stay with John, while Patrick would buy his own stallion.

The farm was valued, Patrick was paid $90,000 for his share of the property, and the hunt for a new home began. Again, it was Peter to the fore, driving up to Fencourt one afternoon and ordering his brother out the door. 'Patrick, you're coming with me. We're going to see a farm.'

Not realising what he meant, Patrick asked, 'Are you going to buy another farm?'

'No, you're the one who's going to buy a farm,' came the reply.

It was a nice property, a dairy farm of 135 acres at Discombe Road, about five kilometres distant from Fencourt. It had its wet paddocks and it had its dry paddocks — the brothers were invited to inspect the farm as thoroughly as they wanted.

Peter urged him, 'This is what you should buy.'

He was right, Patrick nodded. He had seen enough to satisfy him. Peter would organise the sale details and Patrick would approach the bank and ask for a mortgage of $130,000 which — added to his $90,000 — would pay for the property, which would then become his stud. He was going to name it Cambridge Stud, Patrick said, to mark Tom Laird's former small property of the same name where their first stallion, Blueskin II, had once stood.

Tom, John and Patrick had developed a stud that was now entrenched and respected in bloodstock circles. In 1974, and at the age of 35, Patrick Hogan, studmaster, was about to go it alone. There was one drawback. The farm had a resident sharemilker, with two years left to run on his lease. It was agreed he would remain on the farm and Patrick would stay at Fencourt, working for his brother until the sharemilker departed early in 1977. The sharemilker was happy, he added, for Patrick to come over whenever he liked to fix a few fences for the horses, or start the extensive planting programme that he and Justine had planned.

Nicola and Erin were, by now, weekly boarders at Sacred Heart Convent in Hamilton, which was a wrench for Justine who loved her horses, loved her children and was not one for boarding school. But there were problems in getting them to school in Hamilton, and the two girls were not enamoured of their lifestyle. 'They like our animals, they like what we've got, and they know very well what we've achieved,' Justine explained to friends. 'They just don't like the house being everybody's all the time.'

Patrick should have been euphoric — his own place, 100 per cent, to live with Justine, Nicola and Erin, where he could develop his stud without any fetters to hold him back. By day he was all enthusiasm — he knew what he was going to do, and he made plans, along with Justine, as to how it would look one day. By day, he could visualise everything that was going to happen there. But at night he had nightmares. He dreamed that the whole place was covered in water and there were rice paddy fields instead of grassy paddocks — that no horses could ever go on them. At night he dreamed that Cambridge wasn't going to do the job for him — he dreamed he would go bust.

Those terrible dreams were to haunt Patrick for the next 18 months.

Patrick had secured his property. Now, with that in place, he had to track down the essential element to put him, his broodmares and his venture on the map. He would travel overseas and find the best stallion he could within his tight budget constraints — that's what he'd do — but to achieve it, he needed a hefty cash injection from colleagues in the industry, friends and loyal Fencourt clients who had supported their earlier stallions.

He got on the phone and asked whether they would be interested in purchasing a 1/40th share in a stallion at $4000 a share. Their share price would include a free annual service for one of their mares and the normal dividend arrangements. The deal was that Patrick would buy 20 shares for a total of $80,000, and 20 outside investors would come in at $4000 a head to make up the required amount of $160,000.

Patrick had found more than half of the potential syndicate — many of whom had been in the old Hermes syndicate — but was struggling to find the remaining half-dozen backers when Michael Floyd from Wrightson NMA (the former Wright Stephenson and Company) came to the rescue. Floyd brought in a solid representation of private owners and stud breeders from the lower North Island to add to Patrick's northern contingent. These final 20 investors included an impressive representation of the country's leading bloodstock interests — friends and mentors like Bob Morris who had won the Cox Plate in 1970 with his well-performed grey colt Abdul.

The syndicate was: Mr F.R. Bodle, Whakanui Stud, Cambridge; Mrs J.A. Broome, Hamilton; Mr Kel Cameron, Glenbrook Downs, Tokoroa; Mr C.R. Feisst, Cambridge; Fencourt Stud, Cambridge; Mr J.A. Higgs, Cottonwoods

Stud, Cambridge; Mr O.E. Larsen, Hamilton; Mr J.L. Macky, Pirongia Stud, Te Awamutu; Mr L.A. McCool, Chantilly Lodge, Palmerston North; Mr G.A. Mitchell, Santa Rosa Stud, Palmerston North; Miss J. Mobberley, Hamilton; Messrs R.L. Morris and M. Paykel, Cambridge; Mr J.S. Otway, Trelawney Stud, Cambridge; Miss C.B. Perry, Auchenbreck Farm, Greytown; Mr H.L. Perry, Highden Stud, Palmerston North; Ra Ora Stud, Auckland; Mr C.J. Roberts, Meadowlands Stud, Auckland; Mr E. Ropiha, Fairview Farm, Woodville; Mr and Mrs J.S. Sarten, Auckland; G.D. Shepherd Farms Ltd, Te Awamutu; Windsor Park Stud, Cambridge; and Wynthorpe Stud, Waitara.

The syndicate would be run by a management committee, consisting of Patrick and John Hogan, Laurie McCool of Palmerston North, and Bob Morris of Cambridge, with Patrick as chairman.

In his search for a stallion, Patrick was to be accompanied by Joe Walls, his good friend from Wrightson NMA. What a thrill, Joe exulted. At 28 he'd not been out of the country much, and now he had been asked to help Patrick find a stallion to replace Hermes. This was one great way to be introduced to the Northern Hemisphere via the studs that he'd previously only dreamed of seeing.

There would be a safe pair of hands too, when they arrived. They would be met by Sir Philip Payne-Gallwey of the British Bloodstock Agency, who had visited New Zealand a number of times and was well known to both young men. Sir Philip had posted Patrick the pedigrees of horses he recommended that they inspect. Armed with the pedigree papers, Patrick and Joe flew out from Auckland to Los Angeles on the first leg of their quest for Hermes' successor.

From Los Angeles, Patrick and Joe travelled to the major stables of Kentucky. They saw stallions that were inside Patrick's budget, but none to excite the imagination. They also saw a couple of beautiful horses with price tags of around NZ$500,000, not the NZ$160,000 that was their limit. Time was short — they had just a couple of weeks to find the stallion and so they decided to cut their losses, quit the United States and head for Europe.

Sir Philip collected them at Heathrow Airport and whisked them off to check out a further six or seven horses at the country's top racing centres of Newmarket and Lambourn that lay within his budget. But, as had happened in the United States, nothing jumped out at him. Patrick wasn't panicking yet, though. It was time to pay a flying visit to France.

They were in Deauville, at Haras du Quesnay, the property of the country's leading trainer, Alec Head, and there, in the beauty of the magnificent stud that had been created by a member of the fabulously wealthy Vanderbilt family way back in 1907, Patrick found the horse he was looking for. As the horse stepped out of his box, Patrick beheld another Hermes — a beautiful horse, with great conformation, a great set of legs, beautiful bone below the knee, great hind quarters, withers high, a lovely set of hocks — everything about him was pretty well perfect in Patrick's eyes.

He recalled one of his father's favourite phrases: 'There is no such thing as the perfect animal, and there is no such thing as a perfect horse.' But this fellow, in Patrick's eyes, was as close to perfection as he had seen. However, they were not about to show their hand in front of the trainer and, after thanking him for his time, Patrick and Joe departed.

A phone call to Payne-Gallwey in England dampened Patrick's hopes. Orante, the stallion he had so admired, was totally outside his price range, Sir Philip informed him, and it would be pointless to pursue that channel any further.

They drove on to the horse-racing capital of France, Chantilly, to the stables of Charles Milbank, where, they were told, was a horse who might satisfy Patrick's needs. They had already been to one magnificent stud, and now, after sweeping down an avenue of trees to Milbank's place, Villa St-Denis, they found themselves standing on a wonderfully manicured lawn on a sunny summer's afternoon, facing the boxes of the U-shaped stables.

A groom was mucking out on one side and a couple of horses, with their heads sticking out above their stable doors, stared curiously at the men as a member of Milbank's staff led out the horse for inspection. 'I don't like the pedigree, I don't want him,' Patrick muttered softly to Joe.

His time had run out, and Patrick returned to New Zealand empty-handed. He had done the trip on a shoestring and there could be no second chance to inspect a Northern Hemisphere stallion, so his horse must come through an agent's recommendation. Surprisingly, his spirits were relatively unaffected by the setback, and it was Joe who was the more disappointed of the two. Joe's mood would have been one of desperation in the same predicament, he told Patrick: 'If you have no stallion, you have no income coming in. It's like having a dairy farm without any cows.' Maybe, Patrick replied, but he had his broodmares and had retained his share in John's stallion, Adios, so he wasn't stranded high and dry.

Wrightson's two-year insurance claim payout on Hermes' death was due to expire on 31 March at the end of the 1976 financial year, and it was now January, but technically Patrick still had a year to find a stallion before moving from Fencourt to Cambridge Stud. The word went out.

Three weeks after his return, Patrick received a letter from a previously unknown source, a bloodstock agent in the South Island called Tim Langer, who wrote that there was a suitable horse in France that had been quoted to him. He had heard on the grapevine, Langer added, that Patrick was looking for a stallion, that he had recently been in the Northern Hemisphere, and that he had not succeeded in purchasing anything. 'I have been told,' the letter continued, 'that you have a budget of up to $200,000 landed in New Zealand, including the purchase of the horse, his quarantine period, flying, and getting him to the stud and insuring him. Would the enclosed pedigree of the horse concerned be of any interest to you?'

Seated at the Fencourt kitchen table, as his father had once done before him to study Blueskin's pedigree, Patrick pored over the paperwork that had been sent. It had been well set out. The horse's performance, his pedigree and tabulation were there and, as he made a first cursory check through the papers, Patrick blocked out of his mind the horse's record on the racetrack. He didn't want to know. Well, to be honest he did — he wouldn't have been normal if he hadn't shown some curiosity as to the horse's racing record — but it was the tabulation that was the focus of his attention.

Pedigree over performance had always been Patrick's driver, and he knew that for the price being asked, the horse could not have performed too well on the track. But what a pedigree was unfolding before his eyes! With a racing heart, Patrick checked and rechecked the mouth-watering pedigree tabulations and duplications with his stud books, grading nine generations of tap root mares and stallions, rereading the papers in front of him:

Sir Tristram

Bay. Foaled 1971 at Ballygoran Stud, County Kildare, Ireland.

Sire Line:

Sir Ivor. English Horse of the Year 1969. Champion 2YO of 1967. Eight wins. Grand Criterium, Derby S., 2000 gns, Champion S. and Washington International S. Retired to stud in 1970. Sire of winners of 91 races.

Also in Sire Line:

Man O' War [affectionately known as Big Red, considered by many to be the greatest US thoroughbred racehorse of all time. During his career just after World War One, he won 20 out of 21 races and $249,465 in purses. As a sire, Man O' War was impressive as well; producing more than 64 Stakes winners and 200 various champions. Two of the more famous of his offspring were Battleship, who won the 1938 English Grand National steeplechase, and War Admiral, the 1937 Triple Crown winner. Another offspring, Hard Tack, sired Seabiscuit].

Female Line:

Dam: Isolt. Won in France 2YO. Second in Deauville Prix de Bronville, Saint Cloud Prix de la Bourdaiserie. Daughter of champion Californian racehorse Round Table, a former United States Horse of the Year.

3rd Dam: All Moonshine whose dam was Selene, one of the greatest matriarchs in the Stud Book and half-sister to the great Hyperion (Derby, St Leger, Champion

Sire six times), half-sister to Sickle (twice leading sire in USA). Dam of 8 winners.

Sir Tristram. Race record: France and USA

Age 2. 1973. Two starts for a win and second place.

Age 3. 1974. One 3rd placing.

Age 4. 1975. 14 starts. 1 win, 5 seconds and two third placings.

Stakes won 238,465 frs. New Zealand dollar equivalent $40,313.

Distances won 8 & 9 furlongs.

Raymond Guest, the former American ambassador to Ireland, was living in retirement on his Virginia farm. He had long dreamed of owning a Derby winner and cherished high hopes that his colt, Sir Tristram, was a real prospect for the 1974 Kentucky Derby, a race dubbed the 'Greatest Two Minutes in Sport'. If any icing was needed on this particular cake in this, the race's 100th anniversary, accompanying the winner's prize purse of US$274,000 was a commemorative gold trophy that had been especially struck for the Centennial Derby, which was to be raced on 4 May 1974.

If he pulled it off, 20–1 outsider Sir Tristram would be the first horse that had raced primarily in Europe to win the race. 'I suppose,' mused the horse's assistant trainer David Henderson, in the week leading up to the Derby, 'that there will be many eyes on this horse. If he wins, it might be the start of something.' On Sir Tristram's back was Bill Hartack who was riding for a record sixth Derby victory, a jockey whom local journalist Mike Sullivan described as 'a man whose war of silence with the press is surpassed in sheer audacity only by the brilliance of his achievements in the Kentucky Derby'.

It had been a difficult journey from Chantilly, France, to Louisville, Kentucky, for the muscular bay colt, Guest fretted. His warm-up at Churchill Downs prior to the Derby had left plenty to be desired. 'After he got off the plane in New York,' Guest complained to Sullivan, 'they shipped him by van through the entire city and all the way out to New Jersey for a test. They could just as easily have given the test at one of the nearby tracks. It was a goddamn ordeal.'

The son of Sir Ivor — a former winner of the Epsom Derby who had stood in Ireland before being brought to the United States — had not previously raced in America and, unfamiliar with racing to the left, coupled with handling a sandy course, finished a dull seventh in his seven-furlong warm-up race.

The extra distance of the Derby (a mile and a quarter) would suit him better, Guest and Sir Tristram's trainer, Charles Milbank, assured Sullivan in a newspaper interview, reminding the journalist that Sir Tristram had won his first race at Evry, France, over a mile and an eighth (1800 metres) as a two-year-old, beating a field of 21. Unlike the American pattern, he preferred to come from behind and finish with a long charge, they added. 'I don't say Sir Tristram is going to win the Derby,' smiled Guest, 'but the adventure appeals to me. I think it will be fun. I was just thinking about it all winter and I thought to myself, "What the hell, I might as well take a shot for the 100th anniversary".'

'The race had to do him some good,' remarked Hartack — who had won the Derby a decade earlier on Northern Dancer — to an assistant trainer as he walked off the track after the preliminary race, 'but I don't know if it did him enough good.'

'Was that a good tightener for Sir Tristram, Bill?' a racing writer asked. Hartack, Sullivan noted, 'turned his head slightly as if an insect had buzzed his ear, then looked straight ahead and walked off.'

Guest had wished to go one better than the Epsom Derby wins achieved by his flagbearers Sir Ivor — Sir Tristram's sire — and Larkspur, determining that Sir Tristram should be prepared to run in both the Kentucky and Epsom Derbies of 1974. It was not to be. After finishing 11th in the race, Sir Tristram split a pastern on his return to France, which required the insertion of three steel pins, and his opportunity to vindicate Guest's high opinion of him in the Epsom Derby was history.

As a four-year-old, Sir Tristram ran 14 times in France, winning just once — again at Evry — but placing second or third on another eight occasions before being retired at the close of the 1975 racing season.

The links, the crosses, the powerful mares and stallions, the duplications in the pedigree of Sir Tristram were, for Patrick, mind-spinning. He was easily the best horse he had seen on paper, from the time he'd left New Zealand to the time he returned home. If he could possibly afford him, this was the horse for him.

Patrick lost no time in phoning the bloodstock agent, Langer. 'I'm very interested in the horse, but I've only got a budget of $160,000,' he explained. 'We've done our homework on how much it's going to cost to insure him and fly him out, and I've budgeted at $160,000 landed here. Can we do business on that?'

He continued. 'Oh, and if we're successful, I'll have to split your commission with our agents Wrightson and the BBA in England, who always handle the business arrangements for our stallions. I will need to have our agent, Sir Philip Payne-Gallwey, go and inspect the horse, because I can't afford to go back and look at it myself.'

Langer could not pretend he was happy about an arrangement where, having found the horse, he then had to split the commission three ways and was not given carte blanche to handle the whole deal, but he agreed he would contact the sellers and put the lower price to them.

Then Patrick phoned Joe. 'Can you come out? I've got a picture of a stallion that's been offered to me and I'd like to know what you think.' If he wanted his honest opinion, Joe said later that afternoon, after staring in silence at the photo, they'd seen better on the trip. 'He's not much of a bloody looker, and he's got one of those old-fashioned-type pedigrees. But, quite frankly Patrick, you need a horse quickly, so I suppose he'll do.'

Raymond Guest agreed to sell the horse for $160,000 landed. Now it was over to Payne-Gallwey to check out Sir Tristram at Milbank's stables and, if he approved, to organise a veterinary inspection to check that the horse had two testicles, that 'all the machinery' was in sound working order, and that there was no problem that could inhibit him from becoming a stallion at stud.

'We've already been to Charles Milbank's place!' Sir Philip protested at the other end of the international phone line, 'and you want me to turn around and go back to look at some other horse there?'

'Yes, Philip, I do,' Patrick insisted. 'There's a horse there we didn't see and he's for sale. I think I want to buy him, and I want you to go and have a look at him for me.'

'Righto,' Payne-Gallwey agreed. 'I'll hop across to France and have a look.'

Sir Philip was back on the telephone in his Newmarket office after his brief trip to the Continent: 'Not to put too fine a point on it, Sir Tristram is definitely not the sort of horse I'd recommend to you.'

Patrick's heart sank. 'Why not?' he demanded.

'Well, he's not your kind of horse. If you were here I think you'd say, "Put him back in the box, I don't want to see him any more."'

Feeling sick, Patrick asked, 'What's wrong with him?'

'He's got a shocking hind quarter,' Payne-Gallwey elaborated. 'He's weak, he's got bent hocks, and on the walk from behind one hock rolls out badly. He is a most unattractive horse and, in my opinion, not the horse for you.'

His agent's words should have deterred Patrick. Instead, they rallied the stubborn Irishman in him. 'I'm very, very keen on him,' Patrick countered. 'I've set my mind on him. Everything is spot-on for me, and my father always told me there's never a perfect horse anyway. There's no perfect anything in the world, that anything and everything has got faults — just some are more perfect than the others . . . '

Sir Philip clipped short the protests. 'Well, Patrick, I think this one's got more faults than most. He's far from perfect — I think you should think about it.' Then he relented. 'I know that you are probably desperate for a horse, and I know you haven't got a lot of money. This horse might do the job for you to start off with in your new stud.'

It was a setback, a real blow. Patrick returned to the horse's pedigree in grim mood and set loose the demons inside him, arguing the case for a horse that had been dismissed so cursorily by a respected expert in the equine industry and a man who clearly had Patrick's best interests at heart. But he couldn't tear himself away from that pedigree, drawing circles around the names . . . Selene, the great matriarch; Sir Ivor, described by champion British jockey Lester Piggott as the greatest horse he'd ever ridden; Sir Gaylord . . . Sir Tristram was a fluke in breeding, there was so much prepotency in his bloodline — it was mind-boggling, compelling evidence. Patrick couldn't find a bad horse in the pedigree, either on the racetrack or at stud — he could not find a poor horse in the pedigree for one, two, three, four, even five generations. The duplications were, to him, sensational.

As though chanting a mantra, he repeated the names over and over, visualising the horses in his mind 'Sir Ivor, Sir Gaylord, Princequillo, My Babu, Selene, Round Table, All My Eye, Hyperion, Mossborough, All Moonshine — a beautiful cross to Lavendula . . . ' This was equine aristocracy of the highest order. Probably it was the one chance in his lifetime to buy into this calibre of stallion, and he was not about to give it up.

Two days later he was back on the telephone to Payne-Gallwey in England. 'Philip, I'm still set on this horse. I want you to do something for me, and please don't say no.'

'What's that?' Payne-Gallwey asked suspiciously.

'I want you to go back to France and look at the horse again for me.'

'No! I am not going back to France!' Payne-Gallwey was adamant. He had twice been to Milbank's stables on Patrick's behalf and had no desire to return again, particularly to reinspect a horse he could not recommend.

'I want you to go back, but I want you to be with the horse when you're talking to me,' Patrick persisted. 'I want to ask you about the horse. I want to get a perfect picture of him. You have got to do this for me.'

'Very well,' Payne-Gallwey agreed reluctantly. 'You're the one who is buying him, it's up to you, but all I can tell you is what I see and what I told you in our last conversation. He might do a job for you, but I can't recommend him.'

Fortunately, the telephone line to Chantilly was clear as Patrick fired off a volley of questions to Payne-Gallwey, who was standing alongside the fidgeting horse.

'What are his feet like?'

'He's got good strong, black hooves.'

'Pastern and fetlocks?'

'Sloping pastern, clean-looking fetlocks.'

'The cannon below the knee?'

'Reasonably short.'

'Is it a rough-looking cannon bone, or is it clean and steely looking?'

'I'd say it's hard and clean and steely looking.'

'What's his forearm like?'

'He's got a very good forearm, with a lot of muscle on it.'

'Shoulder?

'He's got a good sloping shoulder.'

'What about his neck?'

'Good rein.'

'Head?'

'Strong head.'

'Ears?'

'Average ears.'

'Eye?

'He's got an average eye. Not a big eye, but he hasn't got a cruel eye.'

'Nostril?'

'He's got a good, strong, short nostril.'

'What's his wither like?'

'He's got a high wither — a sharp, high wither.'

'Condition?'

'He's pretty lean in condition but he's got a reasonable girth.'

'Saddle?'

'A short back saddle.'

'Hind quarters?'

'Terrible . . . weak.'

'Hind leg?'

'Shocking . . . terrible hind leg.' Sir Phillip testily interrupted the interrogation. 'I've explained the hind leg to you before. He's got bad hocks, they're bent. When he's on the walk when you're behind him, he twists one hock out badly. Bad hocks.'

'Well Philip,' Patrick responded, 'from the front of the saddle he must be a pretty good sort of a horse, though from behind the saddle he is obviously shocking.'

'You've got it old man, you've got it,' Sir Philip concurred. 'It's what I told you before . . . '

As they spoke, Patrick recalled the advice his father had once given him. There was no such thing as a perfect horse, but there was one good rule he should follow, and that was 'to get as close as you can to 10 out of 10 from the saddle forward. Out of 10 behind the saddle, if you're going to lose your points there, I wouldn't worry about it, because it mainly follows that the engine's in the front. The front is where the engine is — the whole engine.'

His father's shrewd words resonated in Patrick's ears as he listened to Payne-Gallway's analysis of the horse. 'I'm going to buy him,' Patrick said, his mind made up. 'I'm going to give it a whack.'

Sir Philip was gracious. 'He'll do a job for you, but, you know, it's over to you, boy. I've done my best to tell you as much as I can for you to make the decision. If you are sure that you want to go ahead with it, we'll do the business with Sir Tristram, subject to a veterinarian's inspection.'

How could Patrick admit to Sir Philip that the sentimental compulsion for him to own Sir Tristram was, simply, patriotism? The stallion was Irish. His father, Sir Ivor, had stood his first season in Ireland where Sir Tristram was dam served, conceived and foaled in 1971 and, for the deeply superstitious Patrick, that link to Ireland was a powerful omen. He was intensely proud of his Irish roots, and then there was his allegiance to his father, Tom Hogan. Thanks to that shared Celtic heritage, one large Irish bay stallion was about to leave Europe to embark on a new life at the other end of the world.

Patrick's next phone call was to Sir Tristram's trainer, Charles Milbank. It was amazing, Patrick volunteered, that he was purchasing a horse sight-unseen from stables that he had visited so recently.

Milbank laughed. 'Oh, but you have already seen him! Well, at any rate, the horse certainly saw you because he was the horse in the box with his head over the door, next door to the one we led out. Maybe you don't recall . . .'

'Well I never!' Patrick did recall that horse. How maddening! He had been within metres of seeing and closing the deal on Sir Tristram first-hand, rather than undergoing the convoluted process he had just completed to buy him sight-unseen.

Knowing what he was looking for, why on earth hadn't they shown him the horse at the time of his visit, he queried?

'It's amazing, isn't it?' Milbank continued. 'You've bought the horse that we didn't think was good enough to show you. He was within your price bracket, but coming all the way from New Zealand just to look for a horse, we'd never envisaged or imagined or even thought that a horse like that would interest you. We never thought to show you Sir Tristram because we felt he had no appeal whatsoever.'

Controlling an urge to tell him bluntly what he thought of that decision, Patrick asked whether Sir Tristram was a good-natured horse.

He was, Milbank assured him. 'You'll have no problem with him.'

Well, that was a relief. Now to the next question: did he have a good constitution?

'Yes, he has a good constitution — he's a good eater, not finicky at all.'

'He's not a crib biter is he?' Patrick asked, referring to the harmful habit in which a horse bites the crib and takes in gulps of air, which can affect feeding, digestion and the horse's general well-being.

'No, he's not a crib biter,' Milbank replied, 'he has no bad habits at all. In short, Sir Tristram has all the qualities that are advantageous for a stallion.'

An elated Patrick punched the air as they cordially closed the conversation.

He knew his Achilles' heel lay in his expectations for a suitable stallion. He'd set his sights high — some accused him of setting them too high. The horses they had looked at which he'd liked on his trip had cost too much, and the horses that were within his price range didn't suit him. And now here he was, by some miracle, in March 1976, the owner of a horse that was nearly perfect for setting up shop at Cambridge Stud.

Sir Tristram had a wonderful pedigree, he was within Patrick's price range, he had a great front end — everything checked out. Charles Milbank had just handed Patrick the absolute full confidence he needed, that he would be able to really achieve something and succeed with this magnificent horse when he came to his stud farm.

With the purchase completed, the stallion was sent for a regulation six months' quarantine period in England to the British Bloodstock's Glasgow Stables in Newmarket, arriving on 21 January. But during this time, the BBA sold their stable complex and were required to move their horses to temporary stables to complete the quarantine. On Monday, 24 May 1976, Sir Tristram travelled to Queenswood Stud Farm in Middlesex.

PATRICK HOGAN ON PEDIGREE

On BBC television, Robert Sangster told Peter Aliss in 1986 that the foremost authority on pedigree in the world was Patrick Hogan of New Zealand.

'One of my methods is to work on the tabulation within the pedigree,' Patrick explains, 'with emphasis on the key producing male and female ancestors by way of duplicating them under a system using the Bruce Lowe number that they are given.

'I have a couple of books which I regularly refer to that were written around the time of the 1950s. One of these books focuses on the foundation mares and stallions, setting them out by means of classification under classic categories. That is, they are graded into one to five, under their Bruce Lowe numbers, as the classic families Group 1, which is best. Two would have been graded down — classic families Group 2 and so forth. These were the powerful producers and they were graded on the basis of not only their performance on the racetrack, but their performance on producing champion racehorses.

'This method has been an important part of my plan in breeding successful racehorses, and was applied when I purchased Sir Tristram. I still refer refer to that method today.

'Bruce Lowe was an Australian pedigree researcher in the 19th century, and he categorised all the families. Instead of referring to horses in ancient times by name, he allocated them numbers. The Bruce Lowe numbers went from 1 to 29 — and I always worked on duplicating the Bruce Lowe numbers, which is no different to today.

'You don't find Bruce Lowe numbers very often now, but they do still exist. Our sale catalogues used to have them. If you were ever given a pedigree of a horse for sale, it had to have the Bruce Lowe numbers.

'It was a simple procedure because, for example, Selene's Bruce Lowe number is 6 while Lavendula is number 1. One isn't more important than 6, so the Bruce Lowe numbers weren't allocated to numbers of the best to worst. Number 14 is just as important as number 7. I very much have a liking for the number 9 family. It inherits within it speed, speed, speed.

'Eight generations is probably the ultimate for me to look at a tabulated pedigree and work out what I want to match it to. My favourite key females in a pedigree are:

Number 9	Lady Josephine
Number 6	Selene
Number 1	Lavendula
Number 16	Plucky Liege
Number 2	Feola

From time to time, there are new modern-day key females emerging, such as:

Number 2	Natalma
Number 8	Best in Show
Number 9	Eight Carat (in her own right)

'With male ancestors, I preferably like to see a cross of son and daughter and/or two daughters of that stallion, as opposed to two sons.'

CHAPTER 5

SIR TRISTRAM ARRIVES

'When he paraded Sir Tristram, I've got to admit I was a little disappointed.'

— Sir Tristram shareholder Fred Bodle

QUEENSWOOD STUD FARM, Middlesex — Friday, 25 June 1976. It's close to midnight and the night sky is a blaze of brilliant red and orange columns, the air acrid with the smell of smoke. Inside Queenswood Stud Farm, it's a scene of total chaos — a wild mass of flames and heat and terrified horses whinnying, rearing and careering around the yard. Panicky stable staff shield their faces from the flames as they attempt to free horses that remain trapped in their stables, while others grapple with water buckets and hoses to fight the fire that has broken out in one of the stables.

One mare has taken direct action. In terror, she has broken down the door of the stable and she is followed out by a large bay stallion. Together they hurtle down a narrow pathway to a paddock where other mares have also sought sanctuary.

The stable manager, Mrs Cooper, is frantically trying to bring some order and direction in an attempt to save the horses' lives, ordering her staff in a dozen directions, while her distraught husband is racing to push open doors and gates as escape hatches for the panicking horses.

'We lost five of our own horses in the flames,' Mrs Cooper later told the media who converged on the stud. 'It's a terrible mess. I've never experienced anything like it in my life. Awful . . . dreadful.'

Patrick fielded the call from Sir Philip that evening. There had been the most terrible tragedy at the quarantine stud farm where they had placed Sir Tristram. A fire had raged out of control and five horses had perished. Fortunately, his stallion survived, but at a heavy price.

Patrick's heart almost stopped. What was the heavy price? he demanded.

'Amongst all the chaos, the surviving horses, including the mares and fillies, were herded into one paddock,' Sir Philip spoke slowly, 'and it was all a bit much for Sir Tristram, who actually came close to perishing in the flames. I'm afraid his instincts got the better of him, and in a heightened state of passion he put his mating skills to the test and got badly kicked in the balls by a mare.' There was a resultant swelling of the testicles that could be alarming, Sir Philip added. 'And of course, if that department is impaired, it's crucial to his future career. I will get the vet to call you.'

The veterinarian's words were bleak. 'Sir Tristram has been injured badly in the part of his anatomy that I am sure you have paid a lot of money for. I think things are that bad that this horse may never be able to serve a mare.'

He offered to do a test to see whether Sir Tristram's potency had been adversely affected. However, he warned, this would mean the horse would have to remain in England for a considerable period of time and, as well, there would be insurance issues to consider.

'No,' Patrick replied, 'I'll take the risk. When he's sufficiently recovered, I want him out in New Zealand.'

It was the second piece of damning news that Sir Philip had delivered to Patrick in the space of two months. Another compelling reason for not buying the horse had emerged when Sir Tristram arrived at the BBA Glasgow stables in Cambridge for his quarantine period.

His temperament was a force to be reckoned with and he had learned that the horse already had something of a reputation, Sir Philip Payne-Gallwey told Patrick. Far from being the model of good behaviour as portrayed to Patrick by Charles Milbank, Sir Tristram was a crib biter and feared by those who handled him. He was enormously strong and he had a vile temper.

His strapper, David Henderson, who rode him at track work and had been with the horse since he was a yearling when he was sent to France, described him candidly to Patrick. 'He's a man eater. When Sir Tristram dropped his rider, it was not his knee he planted into the rider, but his teeth! Feeding him one evening, he grabbed me by the waist and threw me against the wall. I had the teeth marks for weeks.

'He's a very strong and bossy horse — a bit full of himself. If you happen to be holding onto the reins a little too tightly, he will slip the reins and pull you straight over his head. The aim is never to let him get into a position to attack you, i.e. by falling off, as he won't run straight back to the stables like most horses. He will straight away go for you. You have to be very careful when you are feeding him, or taking him up.

'Trying to get you off him is something he's very good at, so there are few riders who ask or are asked to ride him. In fact there are only two of us who will ride him,' Henderson admitted. 'It doesn't mean that I'm that much better than the others, but somebody has to ride him, and I like a challenge.'

So there he had it. In Arthurian legend, the Sir Tristram of King Arthur's Round Table had vowed, along with the other knights of this most chivalric order, to 'never do outrage' to another being.

Surely there could be no more bad news delivered to him on the 'outrages' of the 20th century Sir Tristram, Patrick prayed.

The arrival in New Zealand of what was to become one of the world's great equine success stories got off to a very bad start. The stallion looked and behaved shockingly, and he displayed the manners of a street fighter. The scorch marks from the English stud farm fire marred his coat, and someone had cut a fringe on the top of his mane that had left his hair sticking out at right-angles to his head. He was certainly no beauty, Patrick had to admit privately.

But his appearance was of less concern than his temperament. A day after he was delivered to Fencourt on 7 September 1976 he attacked John, sinking his teeth into his jersey and hurling him over a rail into the next paddock. 'I don't want to be involved with this bloody horse,' John stamped off as Patrick arrived on the scene. There was a similar episode with a member of staff, so Patrick decided that if this was going to be the sort of carry-on they had to put up with, it would be in the best interests of everyone's safety if he became the sole handler of Sir Tristram.

He would give Sir Tristram the stable name of Paddy, both for his Uncle Paddy back in Ireland and for the stallion's fiery temper, and allow him a couple of days to settle into his new home before that all-important showing in front of his investors.

Come show day, Patrick paraded Sir Tristram up and down before his syndicate, but he was mortified to experience the one reaction he had never expected, even in his darkest moments. There was utter silence — no comment, no reaction, no nothing. Humiliated and furious at their rejection of his choice, Patrick silently led Sir Tristram back to his box.

It was left to one of his shareholders and a close friend, Fred Bodle from Whakanui Stud, to voice the opinions of the rest, when Patrick rejoined them. 'Look, you know we're pretty disappointed,' he began. 'We think you have made a mistake. We think you've bought a shocking-looking horse.' And it wasn't just Fred giving voice to his personal opinion — three or four other shareholders followed Bodle's lead, telling Patrick they would happily opt out of the arrangement if they could.

Patrick was so upset he didn't know how he retained his composure as he struggled to find the words to defend Paddy and thank his backers for coming to meet their great investment. His dreams had crumbled to dust. Dazed and sick at heart, Patrick somehow got through the evening.

The next morning, after a terrible, sleepless night and with tears pouring down his cheeks, Patrick walked down to the paddock to feed Sir Tristram. He grasped the bit of the stallion who was eyeing him warily, and confronted him. 'Well Paddy, you know, we're in a heap of trouble here,' Patrick addressed the horse. 'It doesn't look like anybody likes you too much, or me either for that matter. We have both failed our supporters. So it's just you and me, and we've got do the best we can together. I'll put my very best mares forward to you,' he promised, 'and in return, I want you to give the best shot you've got for every one of those mares.

'Do that, that's all I ask . . . and I promise that whether you succeed or you are a great failure, you will be in my paddock or on my place or wherever I am for the rest of your life. You will never, ever be removed. You will stay with me for ever, and this will be your paddock and your home until the day you die.' By now Patrick was bawling his eyes out. 'I promise you that, Paddy. I know you are an outlaw, but now we have a bond. We have got to understand each other. We have got to beat the doubters, and we'll do that by becoming as one.'

The following day Patrick prepared his signage and promotional material for the press and bloodstock magazines:

Sir Tristram commences stud duty in New Zealand 1976
Standing at Fencourt Stud. Syndicated Stud Fee (1976) $1500.
Live foal guarantee.

The reaction of the syndicate took his bookings down from 68 mares to 54. Two shareholders opted not to use him at all and, Patrick estimated, about 60 per cent of the remaining shareholders took a sidestep and sent him their poorest-bred mare rather than their best-bred one.

But there was one admirer of the horse. Irascible old Father Quinn invited himself to Fencourt and cast a shrewd eye over Sir Tristram, after checking out his pedigree. 'You've done very well there, boy,' he told Patrick. 'Tom would be proud of you. I think this could become the best stallion that's ever stood in New Zealand — better even than the great Foxbridge.'

Aside from the icy reception handed out to Sir Tristram, this was a time of great celebration at Fencourt. The Melbourne Spring Carnival of 1976 had produced one of the greatest racing doubles on earth for the stud, with wins for Surround and Van Der Hum in two of the carnival's major Group 1 drawcards — the W.S. Cox Plate at Moonee Valley, and the Melbourne Cup at Flemington.

But, coupled with the jubilation, there was poignancy in victory for the Hogan brothers. The winning of their first Melbourne Cup was to be their beloved stallion Hermes' final gift to them.

As part-owners, Patrick and a friend, Colin Stuart, had sent their smart little grey filly by Sovereign Edition and Micheline (a daughter of Le Filou) to Geoff Murphy after he inspected her as a weanling at Fencourt. Cummings had already turned down the filly they called Misty, Patrick told Murphy. 'I don't care what Bart likes — I like her,' Murphy retorted, and took out a lease on the filly. She was to live at his Caulfield stables and be on-leased to an Australian racing syndicate. They named her Surround.

Some horses possess that X-factor which makes them huge crowd-pleasers. Surround had it in spades from the first time she raced, ears pricked alertly forward in response to the storming ovations which came her way from a growing army of racegoers who lined the rails to cheer her on each time she raced. Surround and her jockey, Alan Trevena, were inseparable. An infatuated Trevena told the press, 'If she was a girl, I'd marry her! She's extra special to me because she's my horse. I love her.'

She was a sensation as a three-year-old, winning 12 out of 16 races in top company — 10 of the races straight, to equal the

Australian record for fillies and mares on metropolitan tracks. And as 'Australia's first lady of the turf', Surround got the wall-to-wall treatment when an infatuated carpet supplier had her stable lined with chestnut-coloured carpet.

By the spring of 1976 Surround's stunning performances on the track convinced Murphy he should put her forward for the 2050 metres Cox Plate. The W.S. Cox Plate had first been run in 1922 and was named for Sam Cox, the founder of the Moonee Valley racetrack. From its earliest days, this was one of the classic weight-for-age events of the international racing calendar, and it would become the only Southern Hemisphere race to be included in the World Series.

Tragically for Trevena, he couldn't meet the required 47.5 kilogram weight for the prestigious race and the mount went instead to Peter Cook. Trevena resigned himself to the fact that — for the big one — he would have to be content to watch 'his girl' run from Moonee Valley's birdcage.

Surround was brilliant, but Murphy was not underestimating the challenge that lay ahead for her. If she won, she would be the first filly in the history of the race to be led onto the victory dais, but he need not have feared. Surround it was all the way in the Cox Plate, romping home to win three lengths clear of Battle Heights, Taras Bulba, How Now and Unaware. Surround's record of being the only filly to win the Cox Plate stood until 2005.

Following that stunning performance, Murphy prepared her for the next great challenge, the Group 1 AJC Derby at Randwick. As a build-up she had been entered for the lead-up race, the Princess Handicap, on the Saturday prior to Oaks' Wednesday. Brimful with expectation, Patrick flew to Sydney to see his horse take out the double.

Surround was expected to stroll the Princess — the Oaks would have the tougher field. However, on the night before the race, Geoff Murphy had a quiet word with Patrick. 'Look, I don't want you to be disappointed, I don't want you to be upset, but Surround will not win the Princess tomorrow.'

'Why not?' Patrick demanded.

'She won't win,' Murphy repeated.

Patrick was dumbfounded. 'It's not possible! She'll kill them — there's no one to touch her!'

'Well, what would you rather win, the Princess or the Oaks?'

'The Oaks, of course!'

'Well, let's just leave it at that. Don't go there.'

Foul play . . . it had to be! Patrick was furious and threatened to go to the stewards. 'Drop it,' Murphy urged.

Surround did not win the Princess, but she did win the Oaks. Patrick was told later the 'don't win' edict had been called by a bookmaker who headed the local racing Mafia.

Ten days after the running of 'Surround's Cox Plate', officials at Melbourne's Flemington racecourse conferred at a hasty early-morning meeting. Would they be forced to consider the unthinkable and postpone or cancel the running of the 115th Melbourne Cup? The logistics involved in taking such a step made them shudder.

It had bucketed down overnight. Now, early in the morning the skies had cleared, giving rise to optimism that they could take a risk and go ahead with the 'race that stops a nation'. The Melbourne Cup would go ahead, they confirmed to the media, but shortly after that decision was made, it was raining torrentially again, with the main spectators' lawn lying inches deep under water.

It was dreadful for racegoers, who saw their smart clothes and hats ruined by the driving rain, and dreadful for trainers of entrants in the Cup who did not handle heavy ground well. In these dire conditions the 3200-metre race would be closer to a 5000-metre event, but near ideal for a mudlark from New Zealand and pre-race favourite who was later a hurdler, steeplechaser and qualified hunter.

Van Der Hum, a muscular liver-chestnut horse sired by Hermes, was named after the liqueur by one of his owners, E.L.G. 'Wynn' Abel. Abel was at the forefront of the New Zealand grocery industry and, towards the end of an evening at a grocery conference in Taupo, after the food and wine had been cleared away, he and a couple of colleagues ordered liqueurs. As the waiter poured the tangerine-flavoured liqueur from South Africa into their glasses, Abel made up his mind. 'That'll do for the horse's name. We'll call him Van Der Hum.'

Van Der Hum was trained by a part-owner, Leo Robinson, whose brother Roy — another part-owner — admitted that initially they didn't think that much of him, and that his entry in the Melbourne Cup had come about by chance. As a committee member of the Waikato Racing Club, Roy Robinson had arrived at Te Rapa racecourse to attend a sub-committee function and, as he walked in, the woman behind the desk called to him: 'The nominations for the Melbourne Cup close today. What're you going to put in?'

Astonished, Robinson replied: 'I don't think we've got anything.'

'What about Van Der Hum?'

'Oh. Yes . . . I suppose so. Stick him in.'

Van Der Hum had begun to win some distance races and, fortuitously, from the time he was nominated for the Melbourne Cup, his performances improved markedly. But his New Zealand efforts were as nothing compared with his outings in Australia in preparation for the cup. In his first start, the five-year-old gelding streeted the field by seven lengths in the stayers' Herbert Power Handicap, and followed that with a strongly run third placing in his build-up race, the Group 1 Caulfield Cup. Leading New Zealand jockey Bob Skelton had ridden him in the Herbert Power, and Brent Thomson in the Caulfield Cup, but it was back to R.J. Skelton for the Melbourne Cup.

John and Patrick Hogan were huddled over their radio at Fencourt as the race was called. In the shocking race conditions, Van Der Hum was going out as favourite, but could expect tough competition from Gold and Black among others. The announcer's voice rose to a crescendo as Van Der Hum hurtled over the winning line, closely followed by Gold and Black, and Kythera in third place.

Then as he momentarily fell silent to regain his breath, another voice in the commentator's box broke across the radiowaves loud and clear. 'You fucking beaut!' He was too, the Hogans roared with laughter. Good old Hermes' staying qualities. His son had done him — and Fencourt Stud — proud.

'WORLD EXCLUSIVE!' Australia's tabloid *People* magazine blasted across its cover of 12 May 1977, with an enticer on 'Crocodile Dundee' Paul Hogan, while inside another Hogan, this one from New Zealand, was being introduced to the Australasian reading public.

'"If I sell Surround, I've sold my stud," says the breeder of New Zealand's new wonder horse,' the article's writer, Davinia Jackson, opened. 'Hot New Zealand breeder Pat Hogan — and part-owner of super filly Surround — likes to quote his visitors a saying. It is: "If you put the best with the best and hope for the best, you must come up with the very best." In Surround he has the proof. This three-year-old grey is now the richest filly ever to have raced in Australasia — with 14 wins from 19 starts and $280,000 in prize money behind her.

'She didn't owe them a penny, said Hogan, which was part of the reason why he had recently thumbed away a mind-spinning offer of $1 million for his beauty from a Sydney syndicate. He had turned down the offer after discussion with trainer Geoff Murphy and other members of the racing syndicate.

'"Imagine the amount she's worth to us in promotion and publicity if we put a colt through the ring out of Surround," Hogan said. "We don't like selling our fillies."

'Hogan also considered carefully a US invitation to have Surround race with the world's best horses in Hollywood. Again the money had appeal, but conscious that she has probably run half of her probable track life he turned that down too. "Once she leaves Australia on that kind of trip, you'd have little chance of getting her back," he said. "There's quarantine to worry about, and if she didn't travel well she'd probably race badly in the States."

'Hogan believes the Kiwi climate provides something lacking in Australian horses. He says New Zealand breeders, who supplement-feed later than their trans-Tasman counterparts, produce a cooler-blooded animal that will race longer. "We've never been able to beat the Aussies with our sprinters — but we kill them with our stayers," he says.

The article concluded with another quote from Patrick: "'Misty, as they called her, was nothing special at all. She was not a particularly attractive horse and buckled at the knees. We knew she had the breeding to be a champion, but we never thought she'd make it as an individual," says Hogan. "How wrong we were."

'Their little grey filly Surround — Australian Champion Racehorse of the Year 1976–77, winner of the VRC Oaks, the AJC Oaks, the QTC Queensland Oaks, the Caulfield Guineas, the VRC Ascot Vale Stakes, the QTC Grand Prix Stakes, and the Cox Plate, with 17 wins, two seconds and two third placings from 28 starts — has shown the racing world the face of a true champion.'

In January 1976 Geoff Murphy paid $14,000 for an attractive brown Hermes–Vicky Joy colt, providing some much-needed money to go into the planting of trees on the Hogans' new farm. Wrightson Bloodstock had sent Patrick the cheque for the sale, and the money was rapidly dispersed, also paying for a truckload of rails and posts to fence another three paddocks.

But that satisfaction ended abruptly on a Sunday afternoon, four months later, when Patrick fielded a phone call from Murphy. He came straight to the point. 'Patrick, that Hermes colt I bought off you. We're breaking him in and he's broken-winded, he's of no use for racing. I'm in trouble, because I haven't passed him on. I still own him and I haven't paid for him either. I'm in the crap a bit, and I thought I had better let you know. Had you noticed anything?'

Well, no he hadn't, Patrick said, attempting to grapple with the bad news. 'Geoff, we don't lunge our horses or work them.

They just go to the paddock in the daytime and come into their boxes, so it's unlikely if he was, that we would know anyway.'

'Well, look, I'm in a bit of trouble with him,' Murphy concluded, 'so anyway, I've let you know.'

That $14,000 had been spent. Poop! Patrick got off the phone in a state of shock, unable to remember whether he had promised to get back to him, whether he had said thanks for the information, or whether he had just said sorry about that and goodbye. He relayed the news to Justine, whose response was immediate. 'Well, you would have to take the horse back, wouldn't you? You'll have to take him back and give Geoff his money back.'

She had brought him to his senses. 'You're right,' Patrick nodded. 'You're dead right. Oh damn it, I wished I'd thought of that while I had him on the phone. I'll ring him straight back.' He returned the call within minutes. 'Geoff, look, I'm sorry. You gave me a bit of a shock and I had to think about it. We will refund the money and get the money back to Wrightson's so you don't have to pay for the horse. We don't want the horse back because he's of no use to us. If you want the horse, you take the horse. If you think he can be operated on, it might improve him for racing or give him a chance . . . What about you take half the horse and we'll have half the horse, and you just do everything, but don't waste a lot of money on him, and give it a go if you want to. If not, give him away for some person's pony.'

'Well, that's fantastic,' Geoff replied. 'That's a deal.'

Patrick learned two things from that phone call. He learned from Justine that a deal should be honoured, even if there was no technical reason for doing so. And he learned about the need to scope horses to see if they were gone in the wind. He decided from there on that he would scope all of his horses and he would take it one step further.

Patrick devised a marketing plan that, in future, he would guarantee all of his horses — not to win races, of course, but in the event that in the first three months after buying them, the buyer found something that was identifiably wrong with the horse that either was or could have been a problem before the horse was sold that the stud was unaware of, then Patrick would take the horse back.

There was not a breeder, large or small, in New Zealand who would entertain a thought of emulating that innovative Hogan guarantee. It was commercial suicide, they chuckled. And so Patrick went through the sale rings as a lone ranger in guaranteeing every horse that was sold under the name of his stud. The buyers enthused, and his initiative added megabucks to the price of Patrick's yearlings over the years, helping Cambridge Stud to top the sales for decades to come.

The 'broken wind' story had a sequel. In Patrick's words: 'Geoff came out the next year to the sales. We had eight yearlings for sale and, before any of them went near the ring, he comes to me and says, "I like six of those horses, but I'm not going to buy six. What I'm going to do is try to buy three of those six horses. What I want you to do is tell me how much you want for those six."

'So I said to him, well, what do you want to know that for? He said, "Just tell me what you want for them, I've got a plan." So I gave him the price I wanted on each horse. He said, "Right, that's what you want — now it's up to you to be on your guard, because you know the six horses that I've named, and you've given me the six prices."

'Geoff continued: "The first one, you've got your money guaranteed, because I will take it to the $30,000 that you want. I'll buy it at that. If somebody outbids me, then you're lucky — you've got three more to go. If I buy it, just remember my name's been called out, then you've got two to go." Then he went right through the sale, and just kept pushing the prices up for us. It was unbelievable. He did that for me and Justine, and I reckoned that when we sat down and worked it out, he put $80,000 more in our pockets than we would have expected, because he did get outbid on the first two.

'Afterwards, Geoff came to me and said, "I got my three horses."

'I said, "Yes. Thank you Geoff."

'And all he said to me was, "Well, that's my thank you for what you did last year."

'He turned the $14,000 we gave back to him into $80,000 for us. With this windfall, we just planted more trees and did more fences. That was my good friend Geoff.'

Justine and Patrick shared both a marriage and a partnership — a singleness of purpose, a love of gardening, and a willingness to work punishingly long hours to achieve their dream. They had each other, they stuck together and gave each other the space to develop. 'I'm like Patrick,' said Justine in a rare interview. 'I love work.' They also held fast to another credo — they were, in their own words, 'very particular, extremely fussy' with whatever job they tackled. Cleanliness and tidiness ruled.

They left Fencourt for Cambridge Stud early in 1977 with Nicola, aged 14, and Erin, 12, a skeleton staff, their two stallions Sir Tristram and Heir Presumptive, their broodmares, their fillies and foals, some stock to keep them going financially, and a frighteningly heavy workload ahead of them, in this, one of the highest-risk businesses on earth.

The farm's front entrance was an uncared-for metal drive with, on the right, close to the road, what was to be their home for many years to come — a typical small brick sharemilker's cottage with a corrugated iron roof. The farm's sole redemption visually was a line of ancient oak trees on the left of the drive. But there was no trace of the 25,000 barberry hedge lines, specimen trees, willows, oaks, poplars and the lush gardens that would, one day, come to characterise the stud and adjoining Hogan land.

However, in more serious need of an upgrade than its aesthetics were the farm's fences, which were made of wire. Post-and-rail fences had to be built quickly. As they could afford it, a fencer was brought in to fence each paddock, skirting around individual specimen trees, and to do the fence lines. Their priority was to create stallion paddocks for Sir Tristram and Heir Presumptive, and then they fenced a couple of paddocks with post-and-rails for their weanlings. Every few dollars earned was ploughed back into the stud farm — every sale translated to fencing another paddock to reduce the danger of their horses getting caught up in wire.

They didn't employ architects to design the stable block or have garden planners because they couldn't afford them. Patrick and Justine planted the gardens themselves, with Nicola and Erin popping plants in the holes that had been dug out. They did need experts to tarseal and put in their drive's curving, to plant their avenue of camellias on the right of the drive, and do the stonework, but apart from that it was over to P. & J. Hogan working tirelessly with the horses and on the farm.

They didn't spend a cracker on their house, and they didn't spend a cracker socially. Each time they accumulated a few more dollars, it was saved, and when they had enough, they sank that money back into more bloodstock or another commodity needed for the farm.

First up they needed to build a concrete-block stable block, but, Patrick determined, it wouldn't be anything like the standard Kiwi stable block. Patrick dreamed of something far grander for his horses. He intended to house them in a 1830 square-metre stable of colonial architecture with a high-pitched roof — firstly as a great shop window for showing off his horses, and secondly because the roof would provide better aeration.

The farm was located in a windy area of the district, so he had the stable built with a central race, rather than the standard practice where the doors face outwards; he knew that when they came to mucking out the boxes, if they had doors to the outside, the wind would continually pick up the straw, making it difficult and untidy. He put in attractive windows with shutters on each side, and gave the stable a generously proportioned central entranceway, adorned by an ornamental pitched lower roof supported by a couple of columns. Then Patrick put Sir Tristram in his box in the stable and Heir Presumptive in his. Their splendid stables comfortably housed all the horses they owned — their two stallions, half a dozen broodmares and three or four weanlings.

Patrick nursed a theory that stables which had the appearance of a gracious home would be a great selling point as a shop window to the stud. But then came the criticism. The negative comments had started long before they moved in, vet Jonathan Hope told the Hogans. Some local farmers, who knew Hope did Patrick's work, came to him, saying, 'Patrick is bloody crazy. He's got one of the best dairy farms for land in the Waikato and he's turning it into a horse crush!'

The attacks against the 'Hogan stables' that were circulating about its design and designer percolated back. 'He's built a mansion and he's sticking horses in it . . . it's just crazy to build a stable like this . . . there's no stable in New Zealand anything like it . . . Hogan's got carried away with his grandiose dreams . . . ' and 'Does he think he's an Arab or something?'

His detractors would have drawn comfort from their opinions, when — some years later amid the stud's ongoing success — New Zealand's then Governor-General, Sir David Beattie, came to visit Cambridge Stud. The programme was that he would arrive, have a look at the horses, and then come down to the Hogans' cottage for a cup of tea.

At the appointed time, the Governor-General was driven up Cambridge Stud's tree-lined avenue, vice-regal flag fluttering in the breeze. Sir David climbed out of the car and walked to the entrance of the stables, greeting Patrick by saying, 'Oh, are we having a cup of tea first before we go to look at the horses?'

'No, Sir David,' Patrick replied, 'we're having a look at the horses.'

Astounded, the Governor-General asked, 'They don't live in this house, do they?'

Patrick nodded. 'Yes, they do.'

Not long after Cambridge Stud's stables became a talking point, other stud farms also started to build upmarket-looking stables.

The farm's old farrowing pen was a square brick building to the left of the stables. Patrick decided to keep it, divide it into four equal boxes, and convert it to blend in visually with the new stable. Horses would be housed in three of the boxes, and the fourth would be his office — just big enough to squeeze in a desk with a telephone and a couple of chairs.

'Would it be a good idea if we opened the door?' a visitor would ask uneasily, and Patrick would realise that the neighbouring boxes' smell of horse dung and urine, which he never noticed, was particularly odorous that day.

There was just one thing left to do. Cambridge Stud and all who lived in it needed to be blessed. With Patrick's family present, a priest officiated at a Blessing and Mass in the race of the stable.

NICOLA AND ERIN HOGAN ON PATRICK HOGAN

Nicola: 'On the night when we got a phone call to say that Grandad Hogan had died, it was quite terrifying for Erin and me, as children, to see Dad sobbing. Not crying, sobbing — great loud sobs. We'd never seen Dad cry and didn't know what to do. The only other time I saw him sob was when Hermes died. Later, when Paddy died, the same grief was there, but he bottled it in and became preoccupied and withdrawn. It was like his right arm had gone.

'Erin and I could both cook a roast meal at nine or ten, because Mum and Dad would be busy with the horses. We did all the planting of the hedges on Cambridge Stud — that used to be our school holiday "treat" for about two years. Mum would pack a picnic and off we would go. Dad would dig the hole, Mum would put the seedling in and Erin and

I would pat it down and make sure it was in straight. We thought it was very stink to do that on our holidays, but looking back, I think it was pretty good really — it made you feel part of the place.

'I went away to Canada for a year as an exchange student. We were just an ordinary family then, and when I came back Dad was famous! I always wanted to be a nurse and Dad worked really hard for me while I was away, applying everywhere. He did such a good job, I got accepted for three different places!

'When he was a kid, Dad never had a birthday party or even a birthday cake, and so for his 50th Mum decided to give him a party and invited 12 of his friends. She went into Dad's cellar and got a whole lot of wine and stuck it in the fridge — bottles of French champagne, bottles of chardonnay . . . Mum isn't a drinker and didn't know one from the other. So she's doing the rounds, pouring out $600 bottles of champagne alongside bottles of $5 chardonnay, and people are putting their hands over their glasses, saying, "No, no thanks, Jus," then suddenly recovering their thirst the next time round when they see the label!

'Dad was overwhelmed that he had been given a birthday party and a cake. He later threw a huge surprise birthday party, about 400 people, for Mum's birthday, but she didn't enjoy it much; she's quite shy.

'Dad is such a generous man — he gives so much. People keep asking me if Dad will sponsor them for something, and I tell them to ask Dad themselves. I admire his integrity and generosity, but he doesn't like to be thanked. He just does it.'

Erin: 'I had a great love of the outdoors and the animals — a real little farm girl. One of my fondest memories as a young child was of my mother waking me up very early on a cold and foggy Waikato winter's morning, saying, "If you want to go out on the farm with your father, you had better get up now," which was what I wanted to do. My relationship with my father was very close, as it is today.

'I remember leaving the house with a tummy full of porridge and feeling so wonderful to be close to my father, wearing my little red gumboots, and off we set across the paddock to feed the hay off the old Fergie tractor, all bundled up in our woollens. We did many other things, but that memory sticks in my mind. We would talk about the animals, the family and there were conversations about God too. He told me God was everywhere, and you didn't need to go to church to believe in him — but we still did!

'I remember bird nesting with my father, him lifting me up to look into the bird's nest. I was never allowed to touch, and we would go back every few days to check on their progress. I remember running home and being so excited to tell Mum that there were three eggs, and even more excitement when they hatched.

'I had many different presences in my life and they all contributed. I was close to both my grandfathers. Grandad Hogan lived just across the paddock, so I saw him every day until he died when I was seven. His presence in my life was so strong: he had a stillness about him, gentle and unassuming.

'Forget the sewing and the cooking — I was a tomboy, out with the ponies, the horses, the troughs, catching frogs. What I learned as a child helped me accept the changes our family has since gone through.

'My father and mother's success? I did not cope at all. I was about 14 when they were coming into prominence and I found it very difficult. It was at a time when I was probably trying to develop my own identity. I couldn't go anywhere, or be anywhere without being labelled as "Patrick and Justine Hogan's daughter" rather than as Erin, and being who I was. The essence of my early childhood remained, though, which helped me cope with those changes.

'As an adult I still take with me those earlier solid experiences of family and love, in parenting my daughter Katie. Sometimes I long to go back to my childhood when I was on the Fergie with Dad.'

CHAPTER 6

THIS STALLION'S ON FIRE!

'Make money and stay. Lose money and go.'
— Nelson Bunker Hunt's one-line contract for Waikato Stud

WITH HIS BLACK mane flying, imperious Sir Tristram was charging around his paddock domain and, with the exception of Patrick, farrier Laurie Lynch and the stud's 16-year-old groom, Shane Keating, staff were kept at a wide berth from the uncertainties of handling the stallion. But there was one thing that was never in doubt, and that was his virility.

Paddy, as Sir Tristram was known, had shown impressive stamina from his first introduction to Southern Hemisphere mares, and from among that first crop came a magnificent chestnut colt born in 1977. His mother was Taiona, who had returned from Australia a season earlier, and Patrick was in a bullish mood as he prepared the well-bred yearling for sale.

To his irritation, Wrightson didn't share his high opinion and refused to accept him for the 1978 Trentham National Yearling Sales, forcing Patrick to present the colt at the second-tier yearling sales at Claudelands sale yards in Hamilton. At the sale, Geoff Murphy clearly liked the foal's appearance and picked him up for $6000. It was hardly an exciting price, but the yearling was from Sir Tristram's first crop of babies and the sire was unproven — still denigrated in some quarters, if Patrick was honest. Murphy then told Patrick he was more than happy with his purchase and he already had the right Australian buyers for him. Later, they would name him Sovereign Red.

There was to be a second meeting that afternoon. Walking towards him, Patrick saw Fred Bodle, his neighbour, good friend, drinking buddy at the Cambridge Club on Friday evenings, Sir Tristram shareholder, and the man who rubbished his stallion when he first saw him.

'Fred!' Patrick decided not to beat about the bush. 'What are you sending to Sir Tristram this year?'

'I'm not,' Bodle answered shortly.

As a shareholder, his rights included the sending of one mare to the stallion each year at no charge. In that first 1976 season, Fred Bodle had not sent a mare, then the same thing had happened in the second season, and now here he was in the third season, also rejecting a free service to Sir Tristram. 'Can you tell me why, Fred?' Patrick asked.

'Yes I can,' Bodle retorted. 'My mares are too good for your horse, you should know that. I'm not putting one of my mares to your horse because he's not good enough.'

Miffed, Patrick replied, 'Oh well, if that's the case Fred, if my horse ain't good enough, I think you should sell the share.'

Bodle shrugged. 'If you feel that way, I will sell it. How much are you going to give to me?'

'How much do you want?'

'What I paid for it — $4000.'

'OK. Fine.'

The two men were mates; Fred was wealthy and successful, $4000 was nothing to him — an ice-cream as far as he was concerned. 'But there's a condition,' Bodle continued. 'You have to sell the share by 8 o'clock tomorrow morning or it's not for sale.'

'Right, fair enough.' Patrick knew exactly where to go.

They had enjoyed success in the fishing industry and now brothers Peter and Philip Vela were getting into horses. Peter Vela had approached Patrick two months before this meeting with Bodle, saying, 'If you've got something that's good enough for us to invest in, a stallion or a share in a stallion or something, don't leave us out. Don't forget Philip and me.'

On leaving the sales, Patrick rang Barry Lee, explained the situation and asked him to call Vela immediately to check whether he would be interested in buying a share in Sir Tristram. A condition of sale was that the share needed to be purchased by 8.00 a.m. the following day or it would not be available. 'I want you to be at my office at 7 o'clock in the morning, Barry,' Patrick told him. 'I'm going to give you a change of ownership form, I'm going to fill it in, and I want you to go round to Peter Vela, get him to sign it and give you a cheque for $4000.'

Vela signed, but baulked at paying $4000 on the spot. 'Doesn't that Hogan trust us?' he grumbled. 'Doesn't he think we'll pay our bills? I've never heard of anybody having to pay the account immediately.' Those were his instructions, Barry replied — he had to leave with the $4000 cheque.

Reluctantly, Vela wrote it out and at 8.00 a.m. sharp Lee knocked on Fred Bodle's door, saying, 'Sign here, here's your cheque.' With his bluff called, Bodle was forced to sign the change of ownership and accept the cheque. In what he later admitted was one of the two worst decisions of his life, Fred Bodle lost his share in Sir Tristram.

A year later, Geoff Murphy returned to Cambridge Stud on his way to Trentham. He was playing his cards close to his chest: inwardly he was excited by the potential of Sovereign Red. Was there another Sir Tristram–Taiona foal for him to look at? he asked casually. Well, yes and no to that question, Patrick answered. He really had nothing for Murphy to consider. Taiona had produced a full brother to Sovereign Red, but there were severe problems, he explained. 'As a weaned foal, he got caught in the fence and got his front legs very badly damaged. They were really badly cut about.'

The colt had eventually mended, but he had scars all over him and he had become a chronic crib biter. As things stood, there was no hope that he would be accepted into the sales at Trentham or even at Claudelands. The colt had bony growths, one on his leg in particular that was quite bad, and they had decided that if they were going to do anything with him, he had to have an operation, Patrick explained.

At the time, Jonathan Hope, Patrick's new vet, had suggested there was an innovative technique that could cut a nerve and assist in stopping the horse from crib biting, saying, 'Why don't I tidy that leg up of his, and also do the little nerve operation to see if it would improve his crib biting?'

'Wouldn't it be better if you're going to put him under anaesthetic, rather than do that, just give him an extra lot — give him an extra dose?' Patrick asked hesitantly.

The vet answered curtly. 'I'm here to keep horses alive, not kill them.'

'Well, I don't know what I am going to do with him.' It was a hellish decision to have to make. Patrick loved his horses. This colt was not that valuable but he had top parentage and, anyway, he loathed the idea of putting down a healthy young horse. Half-apologetically, he justified his stance. 'I can't have horses running at the back of the farm — we haven't got that many acres. What am I going to do with him? I'm not going to give him away because he probably won't get looked after —'

'I refuse to put him down,' Hope repeated.

'Well, do the operation but while you're there you might as well nick his neck, tidy up his leg and cut his nuts out,' Patrick agreed reluctantly. 'You might as well do a three-in-one. And Jonathan . . . give him a bit of extra stuff if you think things aren't going well, because I don't know what use this horse is to me. He's a disaster.'

The colt was frisking around the paddock as Patrick recounted his troubled history to Geoff Murphy. To his amazement, Murphy looked closely at the yearling and said, 'I'll give you what I gave you last year for his full brother.'

'What, $6000?' Patrick was astounded.

'Yes.'

'It's yours!' he exclaimed, and they shook hands.

Shortly afterwards, Patrick received another Australian visitor who introduced himself as a Mr Needham from Queensland, and asked whether he could have a look at Taiona, the colt's mother. Certainly, Patrick replied.

'I understand she's for sale for $50,000 or $60,000,' his guest said.

She was, Patrick confirmed.

'I'm a bit interested in having a look at her.' After checking out the mare, Needham promised, 'I'll be back in touch. I think I've got someone in Queensland who will buy her.'

Justine tried to persuade her husband not to sell Taiona, saying her first progeny by Sir Tristram hadn't yet hit the racetrack, and she found a surprising ally. A week later, Patrick received a phone call from Geoff Murphy. He had heard, he said, that Taiona was for sale and he was offering to buy her. 'You don't own broodmares! What would you want to buy Taiona for?' Patrick asked in amazement.

'Because you and I are good friends,' Murphy replied. 'I don't buy broodmares, but I'm going to own one for the first time.'

'Oh well, I suppose so, if you want her.' Murphy's decision was incomprehensible. 'I've had one guy who said he'll come back to me, but he's not back yet, and he didn't ask for an option,' Patrick added.

'Don't sell her!' Murphy's voice was sharp. 'Don't sell her! That's why I've rung you. I'll be straight with you. I don't want to buy her. I don't own broodmares, but I'll make a prediction. Sovereign Red, Taiona's foal that I bought from you last year, will win the VRC Derby — nothing will beat him — and he'll win a Group 1 race before that as well, maybe the Ascot Vale. I repeat, don't sell her!'

Patrick thanked him and withdrew Taiona from the market.

His Aussie-Irish mate, Geoff Murphy, was, as usual, on the button. Sovereign Red handed Sir Tristram his first Group 1 winner in taking out the 1600 metres Caulfield Guineas. And, as Geoff Murphy predicted, he won the VRC Derby and the Ascot Vale, becoming Australia's Champion Three-Year-Old, winning in all six Group 1 races.

Sovereign Red was a top, top horse — his performance in the early 1980s was only eclipsed by that of his 'disaster' of a younger brother who had come so close to being put down, and who Murphy had bought from Patrick for $6000. That colt would become known to the world as Gurner's Lane.

Gurner's Lane would become one of a glorious, rare breed to achieve 'the champion's double' by winning both the Caulfield and Melbourne Cups (1982). Other triumphs for the gelding in his illustrious career included the AJC St Leger, the VRC St Leger and the Newcastle Gold Cup.

Between them, the Sir Tristram–Taiona brothers — Sovereign Red and Gurner's Lane — who had been bought for a total sum of $12,000 would amass stake earnings of A$1,107,950. And, following Murphy's sound advice, Patrick's mare Taiona would continue to prosper in New Zealand by producing top colts and fillies. She was named the New Zealand Broodmare of the Year in both 1981 and 1983.

From the inception of Cambridge Stud and the arrival of Sir Tristram, Patrick had used his formidable marketing skills to target the Australian market at the Trentham yearling sales. The profile his stud would enjoy from selling his horses to the Tommy Smiths, the Bart Cummings, the Geoff Murphys and the Colin Hayes, and having them compete in the great Group 1 events across the Tasman was what he had dreamed of since the heady days of Gay Poss.

But, remembering his own start in the industry, it wasn't only the big guys he targeted to get the best price he could. One afternoon he fielded a call from Matamata trainer Dave O'Sullivan. 'Patrick, my boy Paul and his mate Paul Moroney have just reared their first foal and they want to sell it at the yearling sales at Claudelands. I said I knew the best person to parade their horse to fetch a good price, and I promised I'd give you a call. Would you be prepared to do that for them?'

'Sure,' Patrick agreed.

'He did an amazing job for you,' Dave told his 17-year-old son after the sale. 'He probably got far more for you than the horse is worth.' (Thirty years on, Paul O'Sullivan is a top trainer in Hong Kong, while Paul Moroney is in partnership with his brother, Mike, in a successful trans-Tasman training operation.)

Racing commentator Keith Haub publicly credited Patrick with raising the tone for yearlings: 'Hogan is setting the standard for the rest of New Zealand. Even when he's struggling to make it, he feeds his horses better, he grooms his horses better, and is marketing the New Zealand horse across the board better than anyone else. He's studied his competitors, noting their strengths and weaknesses, and he's had the enviable gift of learning to acquire the former while avoiding the latter.'

Sir Tristram continued to be a handful. Patrick remembers one particular occasion: 'In a flash he picked me up and held me. I was literally hanging under his neck. It was probably only a few seconds, but it seemed minutes to me. He dropped me — fortunately I landed on my feet. I picked up the lead, led him out of the barn back to his paddock, and let him go without indicating to him in any way that it had even happened to me. Once I let him go and took three steps away from the paddock, I started to shake.'

Patrick had allowed his guard to slip for an instant when he had taken his eye off the horse. For the stallion's other

133

principal handler, groom Shane Keating, there was never to be any let-up in his vigilance when handling Paddy after one early experience.

Shane was the fourth generation of his family to be involved in the equine industry, starting with his great-grandfather, Fred Smith, one of New Zealand's leading trainers of his era, who notched up 112 black-type winners. When his daughter and son-in-law were killed in a road accident in 1944, Fred undertook to rear his three-year-old grandson Peter Keating, Shane's father, who spent his childhood revelling in the heady, topsy-turvy world of racing at his grandfather's stables in Auckland.

Roughies winning, sure-fire winners losing, race tactics played out by the hour with little lead horses on a table top, cheeky apprentice jockeys having the kid on . . . life was never dull, Peter later told Shane. 'They were exciting times. From about the age of ten I was expected to be up for riding exercise in the mornings, and when I came home from school I'd strap the horses.'

He was passionate about horses. As soon as he could leave school Peter went to work at Woolf Fisher's Ra Ora Stud. Then, in 1963 he saw an advertisement for the position of manager at J.A. Mitchell's Santa Rosa Stud at Palmerston North, applied for it and got the job. This was a wonderful horse 'homecoming' for Peter, as the champion former Fred Smith-trained filly Passive and her Derby-winning son Sobig were at Santa Rosa; after J.A. Mitchell's death, the horses were sold up.

By chance, the Texan oil billionaire Nelson Bunker Hunt was visiting New Zealand for his first and only time, buying up a host of broodmares and yearlings at the Trentham sales. He was looking for a stud manager to run his new enterprise, and the name of Peter Keating was recommended. 'I was told Mr Hunt would like to see me in Matamata, which was about 300 miles away,' Peter recalled, years later. 'I only had an old car and my two children, Shane and Emma, but eventually I got there. I found his motel, knocked on his door and out came this huge Texan. He showed me the farm he had bought and asked me to set up everything for him, which I said I would.

'After that I took him to Auckland to the airport where, before flying out, he told me I had a one-line contract: "Make money and stay, lose money and go." That farm became Waikato Stud.'

Shane grew up at the Matamata stud, having 'no desire to stick my backside on a horse', but loving the lifestyle. How could working with horses ever be considered a job when he was enjoying it all so much? As his father had done, Shane was out of the school door as soon as he could, going to work at Cambridge Stud for a six-month trial period, as a groom during Sir Tristram's second season.

It didn't take long to feel completely at home. In Justine, known to all the staff as 'Mrs H', Shane saw a woman whom he admired more than any woman he knew — apart from his mother. The first time he met her she was sweeping out the stables and shed. Justine was a rock — astute, blunt and tough with no grey areas, kind, compassionate and with no ego. He greatly respected her for that. But with Patrick, the relationship was different. Shane was to have an ongoing, emotionally volatile father-son relationship; the pair would be embroiled in an angry spat one minute, and five minutes later the closest of mates again.

The Hogan family were like staff in their own place — Patrick drove a little Morris 1100, and they were content to live in a sharemilker's cottage. Shane found he was amongst good, down-to-earth people. Everyone was body and soul committed to the enterprise, unlike other places he knew where staff numbers were higher and the workload was lower. He was less enthused about the stud's pride and joy, Sir Tristram, muttering that he was 'a dirty, stinking mongrel' after the horse had tried to savage him one afternoon as Shane was leading him from his paddock.

The first time Shane had handled him, the horse had grabbed him by the chest and shaken him. 'He scared the living shit out of me!' an ashen-faced Shane confessed to another stud groom.

Staff were expected to work huge hours during the season, six days a week, from four or five in the morning to around seven or whenever the day's work was complete, but the junior groom appreciated the fact that his boss never asked anyone to do anything more than he was prepared to do himself. As long as Shane kept pace with him, Patrick was happy. He was a hands-on boss, with the relentless energy of 10 men, thoroughly immersed in every aspect of his operation. Patrick, along with Justine, was happy to spend countless sleepless nights delivering foals during the four-month birthing season.

By day, Justine worked for stable manager Errol O'Brien around the farm, doing the gardens and mucking out the stables. At night, when they heard the gate click at their cottage and there was a tap on the window, the couple would grab their clothes and dash out for the next foaling. They would wait until the foal was on suckle then they would go back to bed, a sequence of events that could happen up to six times a night. Then they would get up in the morning and start all over again, doing all the usual things. However, Justine would never watch a mating. It didn't interest her, she said.

Patrick's goal was never just the money — it never even seemed to be an issue. That was quite a surprise really, Shane thought — a family enterprise like this, with everyone working God-knows-what hours, and money was never discussed, never even touted in the 14 years he would come to spend at Cambridge Stud. What Patrick did want — and he made it very plain — was to be the best. To do that, he had to get his horses to Australia — and to do that, he had to have good horses.

The stud's manager, Errol O'Brien, was leaving. Patrick asked Shane, 'Do you want to have a go at running Cambridge Stud?' At 18, he'd been junior groom and general dogsbody around the place, and now he, a teenager, was being asked to manage the place!

What an honour, but was he up to it? Yes, of course he was, he chivvied himself, and yes, of course he wanted the job. Sir Tristram was coming on line and, with Patrick alongside, it couldn't be that hard running Cambridge Stud, Shane rationalised. What sort of things could go wrong? He had spent his entire life around horses, and was aware that if you are dealing with Mother Nature, you can have every crisis imaginable hurled at you. His fervent hope was that Mother Nature would ease back for a while, at least until he was well settled into his new job.

The boss demanded perfection. It wouldn't matter if Patrick lost an argument as long he achieved the objective that was set. Now it was to be Shane's job to ensure that perfection was achieved wherever possible. He had heard his father say, and probably his great-grandfather before him, that man controls about 10 per cent of a horse's destiny; the other 90 per cent the horse does on its own.

At Cambridge Stud they had to do that 10 per cent very, very well. If they wanted to compete in the top end of the market — which in New Zealand was the export market — they had to stand out above the rest.

Wearing protective jerkins and crash helmets, Shane and Patrick are in the service barn, grappling with Sir Tristram in the serving of a mare. They know what a risk he is and they have learned how to manage him. Safety is paramount — they don't have the luxury of back-up staff. They have to do things differently with him to stave off potential danger.

It's the middle of the four-month breeding season, the veterinary work on the mares has been done, the foals that needed attention have been treated, and now they have enticed Paddy out of his paddock with food rewards, simultaneously putting on his lead and two bits into his mouth to give them extra control.

They are talking to soothe him as he's led to the service area: 'Hey Paddy, old boy . . . we've got a lovely mare for you tonight . . . just your type . . . we'll have you back in your paddock before you know it . . .'

Ten days after the birth of her last foal, the mare is in season again and ready to be served. If Sir Tristram is as potent as he usually is, the odds are she will be in foal by the end of this day, for a gestation period of approximately 11 months and 11 days before her next foal is born.

Paddy is trying to bite Shane's hand. 'Look after me, Paddy!' Shane berates him. 'Don't be a ratbag!' Shane is attempting to forget a recent six-hour ordeal in the barn with the stallion trying to eat his face off.

Sir Tristram has only been at Cambridge for a couple of seasons and already he's built himself quite a reputation on the ladies' front. He'll enjoy playing his little party tricks on you, Shane has been warned by groom Russell Warwick. 'He'll pin you up against the wall if you are not careful, or he will drop his head over the other side of the mare to make things difficult. He's playing around with you . . . that's just his nature and his way of looking at life. I guess it keeps things from being boring for him.'

Sir Tristram is choosy. He doesn't like overweight mares, or mares that won't stand still. He doesn't like competing with tail hair, so the mare's tail is neatly wound around with a soft blue tape. He has an intense dislike for foals and, in the breeding barn, they have to be moved well clear of this dominant male. Putting a stallion like Sir Tristram to a mare is never easy.

The mare is separated from her foal, her lower legs are strapped with the blue tape, and protective soft 'overshoes' are put on her hind feet in case she lashes out at the stallion. To further keep her under control, they have a soft clamp on her lip. In case Paddy decides to attack the mare, they always have an emergency plan. In a crisis the aim is to slip the mare out of an escape hatch and straight outside where the stallion can't go.

This is no romantic encounter, but today Sir Tristram is prepared to play ball and serve her. With a primeval noise, halfway between a snort and a roar of excitement, he mounts the mare. Another happy owner is contacted 42 days later, when Jonathan confirms a positive result. Now Shane returns the stallion to his paddock until the following morning when the same scenario will be re-enacted with another mare.

Stud groom Peter Stanaway was never tall, but he reckoned he was getting shorter and dumpier by the day through one of the jobs he did around the place. Each day it was his task to gather up the horse droppings from the paddocks — 'and Paddy's are real whoppas both in size and weight' he complained — stick them in a big chaff sack, then sling the sack on his back to recycle his load as manure, which he would shake around the base of the young specimen trees and plantings on the stud.

There were no farm bikes, no utes or any other form of transport at his disposal — not even a spare horse. He walked it. If the weather was kind, the sack was still heavy enough, but on a winter's day with the rain pouring down, the sack piled high and sodden, that horseshit was enough to shag his back for good, he grumbled.

Farrier Laurie Lynch knew the way to Sir Tristram's heart. The stallion had an endearing vanity — he loved having his feet attended to. He wasn't being fanciful, Laurie thought, in holding to an inner belief that there existed some sort of horse-man bond between the two, though he was never reckless enough to let his guard down. The empathy had been there from the start, when both had arrived in the Hogan fold within three months of the other. 'I can do anything with this horse,' Laurie would say proudly. 'He's never bitten me and he never will.'

It seemed to settle the horse, having the no-nonsense, bluff farrier give him his usual curt greeting — 'G'day Paddy' —

accompanied always by a pat, before grabbing a leg for shoeing in exactly the same way and sequence as he had done the time before and would do again on his next visit.

When Laurie arrived in his red ute, along came the farrier's inseparable companion, his black Labrador dog Nick, who would run over to the stallion and receive a big, sloppy lick from the horse. If the grooms had trouble catching Paddy, they'd yell, 'Come and back up your truck, Laurie!' Recognising the ute, the horse would walk over to the gate and allow himself to be caught.

'I'm going to get something done with my feet.' You could almost see the pleasurable thought flashing through Paddy's mind. And so Laurie would oblige and play around with his feet — putting another nail in a shoe, or whatever. The stallion was happy to stand still for as long as it took. Seizing the moment, other members of staff would take advantage of the stallion's preoccupation to apply a head collar or perform some other work on their recalcitrant charge.

The real wonder in the dynamics of the place was that Patrick and Laurie were working together at all — what would eventuate into a 30-year-plus working relationship could scarcely have got off to a worse start.

Laurie was just 16 and at the Trentham sales for the first time — an apprentice farrier who had been thrown into the scene at the deep end. His childhood had been spent at one of New Zealand's oldest studs, Grangewilliam Stud in Wanganui, where his father worked. They travelled north to Matamata and, by the age of 15, Laurie was eagerly anticipating his future career as a farrier — that is, when he was able to gain a coveted five-year apprenticeship to take up the trade.

After six months of waiting for a vacancy, the boy secured a job with a local farrier, Merv Paget, who was only permitted to employ one apprentice and one journeyman. Eight months later, Paget had a heart attack and could no longer work — 16-year-old Laurie was instantly promoted to the position of farrier, with his boss standing over him, breathing down his neck, criticising every piece of work that was not absolutely to his satisfaction.

Laurie learnt the hard way: working in the forge, crafting horseshoes in the mornings and going out to shoe the horses in the afternoons. Each horse has its own size, and some horses — like humans — have different-sized feet, with one bigger than the other. Young horses always take a bigger size in front because the back feet are slower maturing, and like a human's fingernails, horses' hooves have to be trimmed every month — shoe off, trim the foot up, and stick the shoe back on again.

Life at Trentham was an eye-opener for the country boy. By day, he was flat-out shoeing horses for racing in Wellington's Summer Racing Carnival. Pre-race, he would take the horse's shoes off, replace them with racing plates and, after the race had ended, reverse the process, receiving his fair share of kicks and rips to the body from jittery horses that had just performed on the track.

By night he was off larking up at the nearby Taita Hotel with his mates and other junior staff of the racing mileu, who slept dormitory-style on mattresses lined up in rows in the hastily converted public bar. Trentham was the greatest place, Laurie thought. It was exciting stuff, mixing the races with the horse sales. Everyone was hyped up, spending like princes when the money held up, cutting back to the bone when it ran out.

Few farriers bothered to travel with their horses to Trentham, however, under Merv Paget's instructions and his own initiative, Laurie was there from the start as a service for clients. Their clients' stricture was to have their horses' feet right for the sale — a detail that many sellers did not worry about.

One day at the sales, Laurie's mate Barry Young asked him to shoe one of Patrick Hogan's yearlings for him as a favour. Head bent in concentration, Laurie saw Patrick from the corner of his eye, coming around the corner.

'What's he doing?' Patrick asked abruptly, pointing to Laurie. 'I don't want him shoeing my horses,' he instructed.

Right. Fine. Laurie completed his shoeing and walked off to his next client.

As the only farrier there for the week, he was not altogether surprised a day later when Patrick approached him, asking him to shoe a yearling. 'Bugger off,' Laurie said.

Sir Tristram had sired 37 foals in his first 1976 season, giving him an excellent fertility rate of 80 per cent. Then his first and second crop obliged on the track, without a great deal of fanfare in the autumn of their two-year-old careers, and by 1980 it was all on.

One minute, Patrick reflected, they had yearlings in the paddock that were worth anything from $8000 to $12,000 and now, less than four years later, they were staring down the barrel at yearlings that, he believed, could fetch anything between $60,000 and $80,000. It was breathtaking.

Suddenly Wrightson wanted Sir Tristram's foals out of Taiona. Suddenly everyone in the Australasian thoroughbred world realised that Sir Tristram was the hottest property on four legs. The stallion was on fire.

'I had a horse with Bart Cummings at his stable in Sydney, and Bart rang me up and said, "I've got bad news for you. We lost your horse — we had to put him down."

'It was a blow. "Yes, it is sad," I said, "but there's nothing we can do about that, Bart. I'll get you another one sometime."

'That was all that was said. About twelve months later, I sent Bart another horse to train and the first account I got from him had on it a charge for a new rug and head collar. So I rang him up and said, "Bart, I've got your account and I want to query it. You've charged me for a rug and head collar."

'And he said, "Well, your horse has to have a rug and a head collar."

'Yes, but I said, "JB, don't you recall that I lost a horse at your stable? A horse that had a rug and had a head collar. Don't you recall that?"

'He said, "I do, but I'd like to ask you something. Do you blokes in New Zealand bury your dead naked?"

'It was worth the price of the rug and the head collar!

'Bart's one-liners are something else. I think one of his best was when Darren Beadman gave up riding. He was a champion jockey, but then decided to go into the ministry, telling journalists, "I had a calling from God." Bart was there at the time, and, quick as lightning, he chipped in, "Well, I think you'd be very wise to get a second opinion."'

The Hogan family farmhouse in Ballindooley, Ireland.

Tom Hogan aged 17, Ireland 1913.

Toddler Patrick Hogan.

Calf Club Day — Patrick with Neatness.

Patrick (third player from left in middle row) as a Cambridge Junior Rugby Representative. Two of his future groomsmen were also in the team: John Warren (third from left in front row) and Bill Taylor (extreme right in front row).

Blueskin II with Tom Hogan and Tom Laird, right.

Patrick, left, with Bill Taylor and Tom Brown kitted up to party on one of the Hogan draught horses at the Cambridge A & P Show.

Eighteen-year-olds Patrick and Justine at the Starlight Ballroom, Hamilton.

The bride and groom — Justine and Patrick on their wedding day.

Patrick's parents, Sarah and Tom Hogan, at the wedding.

Patricia Kelly and Justine with Sweet Time and her colt by Hermes.

Hermes.

Hogan's Bar, Galway, Ireland.

Surround, 1977 Australian Horse of the Year, won five Group 1 races including the MVRC Cox Plate, pictured above.

First promotional publicity for Sir Tristram.

Sir Tristram at Churchill Downs for the 1974 Kentucky Derby with strapper
David Henderson and trainer Charles Milbank.

Patrick takes centre stage at the Trentham Yearling Sales.

The front entrance to
New Zealand Bloodstock's
Karaka Sales Complex.

Patrick shows Cambridge Stud's scanner machine used for pregnancy testing to the ruler of Kuwait, Sheikh Hamad al Sabah.

Sir Ron Scott, Robert Sangster, Patrick and grooms Shane Keating and Russell Warwick with a champion pair of mares, Surround and Taiona, at Cambridge Stud.

Her Majesty Queen Elizabeth II with Justine and Patrick at Cambridge Stud.

Her Majesty Queen Elizabeth II with a foal at Cambridge Stud. The foal would later be named Queen's Choice.

Patrick Hogan.

Zabeel and Sir Tristram.

A day at the Te Rapa races: Justine with rock star Rod Stewart.

Another day at the Te Rapa races: Patrick with movie and TV star Joan Collins.

'Bro' Mark Vince leads Sir Tristram to his twenty-fifth anniversary birthday cake.

Evans' cartoon on Sir Tristram's death. (*New Zealand Herald*)

BUCKINGHAM PALACE

23rd May, 1997.

Dear Mr. Hogan

The Queen has asked me to write to say how saddened she was to learn of Sir Tristram's death. Her Majesty recalled visiting your stud to see Sir Tristram, and knows how much of a loss he will be to you and the New Zealand racing industry.

The Queen wanted me to say that her thoughts are with you at this time.

Yours sincerely,

(SIMON GIMSON)

Mr. Patrick Hogan.

A letter of condolence from Her Majesty Queen Elizabeth II on Sir Tristram's death.

Sir Tristram's headstone in the forecourt of Cambridge Stud.

AUCKLAND RACING CLUB

Auckland Cup winner Irish Chance, owned by Sir Patrick Hogan (partly obscured) and Sir Michael Fay, trained by Colin Jillings and Richard Yuill, jockey Noel Harris. At extreme left is Bart Cummings Junior, at right Lady Hogan.

Empire Rose, ridden by Tony Allan, wins the 1988 Melbourne Cup by the closest of margins from Natski.

CHAPTER 7

SERIOUS MONEY
AND HORSES

*'All you've got to do, son, is feed your horses better than
anybody else and you'll have the edge on all the others.'*

— Bart Cummings

I N MAY 1980, Michael Floyd received a phone call from the
Auckland merchant banker Michael Fay, of Fay Richwhite and
Co. Would he be available to come to a meeting in Fay's office
to discuss some bloodstock issues in relation to New Zealand's
current taxation laws? Floyd, who was by now the managing
director of Wrightson Bloodstock, had recently moved his base
from Wellington to Auckland and accepted Fay's invitation,
taking with him to the meeting his offsider, Michael Otto.

Fay came straight to the point. He had, he said, some
knowledge of the racing industry, but not much direct
involvement. 'Why can't I do with horses what I've done with
films? How would I go about it?' Fay Richwhite was looking
into anything, Fay continued, where New Zealand had an
advantage, where it was competitive, where they thought they

could see a profit by being involved at an early stage of an investment.

They were interested in a number of industries which included horticulture, deer farming and thoroughbred breeding. New Zealand had a particular advantage with horses, he noted. 'We grow very good horses!' His meeting with Floyd and Otto was part of a process of speaking and visiting everyone within the breeding industry, Fay added, to evaluate who would become their partner.

Fay Richwhite had financial expertise and capital to invest, and the company was looking for an industry partner. They knew where they thought the profit opportunities might lie: it was through tax, an important component of the investment, as horses were categorised as a depreciating asset. It was not a risk-free investment — probably it was set at about the right level of tax write-off, for what was being bought and the risks that were being taken.

Bloodstock investment was definitely attractive — getting tax write-offs out of those partnerships which the investors could use and make profits more attainable. And, at a personal level, Michael Fay had always liked horses since his father had taken him to the races as a kid. As a merchant banker, he judged the people his company planned to invest with or partner — in particular, who was going to lead them through an industry. In Fay's eyes, Patrick was an absolute stand-out.

Under a financial arrangement with New Zealand's National government, led by Sir Robert Muldoon, there had existed long-running tax advantages for racing. But, all of a sudden, the rest of New Zealand — because they had a lot of money in their pockets at the start of the affluent 1980s — woke up to the obvious advantage there was to be had by investing

146

in the thoroughbred industry. It was a bit like film-making partnerships. Seeing tax loopholes, the big operators moved in on the scene.

Bloodstock interests were given huge tax write-offs, gaining a complete tax write-off when a broodmare became 15 years old. Syndicates or individuals could buy 15-year-old mares for anywhere between $50,000 and $300,000 and then write it off completely in that one year, safe in the knowledge that they could expect at least another four or five years when the mare would continue to produce progeny. (Horlicks, the winner of the 1989 Japan Cup, produced a healthy foal to One Cool Cat at Cambridge Stud in November 2006 at the ripe old age of 24.) A stallion carried a higher risk on return and had a lesser timeline advantage — he could be written off in three years.

It was very tax-effective and made every kind of sense in a climate witnessing the freeing-up of investment options. Michael Fay was the trailblazer, and the industry soon saw public companies listed on the Stock Exchange, with the sole purpose of putting together intricate bloodstock investment schemes.

Fay approached Patrick, using tax write-offs as an incentive for investors, for the proposed partnership. They had a sizeable advantage, as the first to buy mares at prices ranging between $100,000 and $150,000 for perfectly legitimate tax write-offs.

Fay Richwhite's pioneer Saratoga partnership made their first purchases, buying 16 mares in 1981. In an interview with Adrian Blackburn of the *New Zealand Herald*, Patrick said he couldn't see a better type of investment. 'Look at the mare Free Gold in our Saratoga partnership. We bought her for $150,000 and were considered crazy, as she was reckoned to be worth only $100,000. But she was in foal to Zamazaan when we bought her, and that yearling made $80,000.

'Her next foal cost the partnership $15,000 in stud fees and as a yearling made $400,000. Another mare we bought for $150,000 was in foal to Sir Tristram. That foal sold for $250,000. Every filly you have by a top stallion has to be worth what its dam's worth. Say you have four fillies out of one mare and retain one — you have trebled your investment.'

However, it was becoming a less attractive exercise for their successors. Later syndicates who opted into similar schemes had to pay a higher premium for their broodmares — $200,000, even $300,000 and more.

From the outset, the nature of bloodstock investment was high risk and needed all of the right elements at play for a real chance of success. With any one of the key components missing or of dubious quality, that chance of success would evaporate.

Author Ian Wishart would later describe some of the shady operators in the Australasian bloodstock investment schemes in his book *The Paradise Conspiracy* (Howling at the Moon Productions, 1995).

> These partnerships had been set up essentially as investments with promises of profits and — at least initially — apparently enormous tax benefits, in the days when governments gave incentives to produce movies and the like.
>
> In the bloodstock partnerships there was a hidden element, allegedly not disclosed to the investors in

the prospectus or anywhere else. It was a secret company controlled via Hong Kong called Zorasong, which was acquiring horses from overseas studs and allegedly flicking the nags on at vastly altered prices to New Zealand investors in the bloodstock partnerships.

In one example highlighted in a High Court Statement of Claim, Zorasong allegedly purchased five horses for just over $791,000 but onsold them to the bloodstock partnership for $1.7 million on or about the same day. To add to the confusion, the money trail was wending its way through a string of offshore entities in tax havens and financial centres around the globe . . .

Wishart interviewed ex-pat New Zealand journalist David Hellaby, who described some Australian bloodstock syndicates. 'These businessmen would each put $100,000 in, form a syndicate, and be told, "Right, you've got all this breeding stock — some in New Zealand, some in Australia, some in Ireland" — that sort of thing.

'Now some of it actually existed and was available for them to go and inspect, but of course the other stuff was over the other side of the world and it didn't exist. The papers existed — the horse was even in the stud books. What they did was when a stallion serves a mare you have to put in a service return, then you've got to put in a certificate of pregnancy. So they would get that, and then they would get a situation where a top stallion served a top mare, but then the foal slipped or died at birth. They wouldn't put in the death return — they would put in a live foal return!

'They already had the first two pieces of paper, now they put in the third piece of paper and they created a fictitious horse. Beautiful! Entered in the stud book, they leased the horse, and, of course, it would eventually die. A guy was sent to England from Adelaide to find horses valued at $44 million. He found $4 million worth — the rest didn't exist and never had.'

Years later, Michael Floyd reflected: 'I read Ian Wishart's book and was absolutely fascinated. At Wrightson Bloodstock we were a bit to one side of all of this. We kept well clear of all these mad schemes, but many people lost an awful lot of money.

'I have to say that Patrick was always straight up and down — totally honest and fair in all of his dealings. We weren't involved with the partnerships, but we were involved with the syndication of Sir Tristram — we were involved in the syndication of most of the stallions. Patrick's were the most successful syndications, because he bent over backwards to be fair. Some of the syndications we did were a nightmare.

'Not many years after Sir Tristram's service fees were first set at $1500, we were selling his service nominations for $100,000 and reselling the odd share in him for $500,000! It was quite unbelievable. Those Sir Tristram shareholders were making seriously big money.'

In the spring of 1980 Sir Tristram served 109 mares. No fewer than 88 of them held on one service, and a further 10 were subsequently found to be in foal, giving him a staggering 90 per cent fertility rate.

Answering media questions as to his stallion's raging fertility, Patrick replied that aside from Sir Tristram's natural proclivity, there was a meticulous management regime at Cambridge Stud for the horse that was rigidly adhered to. And his equine star was not the sole beneficiary of that regime, he added. He made it his business to inspect every horse on his property at least twice a day, and he believed strongly in providing his horses with a quality balanced diet, which, he said, was a crucial part of producing top mares, stallions and foals. Bart Cummings had once told him, 'All you've got to do, son, is feed your horses better than anybody else, and you'll have the edge on all the others.'

Patrick told journalists he imported all of his grain, hay and lucerne for the stud. Lucerne and red clover hay were brought in from Hawke's Bay, meadow hay from the Taupo area, and oats from the South Island, which, he considered, were the best in the country. 'Grass is the only fodder grown on the property that my horses eat — by looking all over the country for my feed, I am striving to get the best out of all areas.'

By adhering to that theory, he could acquire balanced nutritional needs, he explained to Don Wright of the *Southland Times*. 'The dressing of grain is of the utmost importance. Tins of rubbish and dust can be sieved and extracted from oats, the most important brand of feed for a young horse, who will later have to eat more of that grain in training than any other form of food.'

However, as top chefs are loath to share their recipes with the world, Patrick admitted he jealously guarded his exact diet for young horses at their various stages of development. It had cost him thousands of dollars, he said, to research the diet by calling in nutritional experts.

Patrick's passion for soil management had sprung from the early Fencourt days when the Hogan family had the good fortune to have Tom Wallace as their vet. He lived on his family's dairy farm and could be out of bed and into the Hogans' foaling paddock, if needed, in seven minutes flat. A thoughtful man, Wallace was invaluable to them, having spent time working at the Ruakura Research Centre — a world-respected animal husbandry centre near Hamilton — before setting up his own veterinary practice in Cambridge.

He believed there was a significant selenium deficiency in the soil at Fencourt, Tom Wallace told Tom Hogan one day after inspecting a sick foal. And it was not just that foal. The same condition — thick rigid necks, swollen pads over their stifles and an inability to suck — was causing a serious clinical problem in a number of Fencourt's newborn foals.

'I think it's white muscle disease,' Wallace had pondered to Tom. 'I've seen this in lambs and pigs, but never before with foals. I'd like to send a sample or two to the diagnostic laboratory at Ruakura.' A few days later, the results confirmed his analysis — it was white muscle disease.

The foals were given injections of selenium and Vitamin E and most were saved. Tom's wife, Sarah, became the expert spotter of the condition, reporting to Wallace any onset of symptoms in the newborns which were promptly dealt with. A regime of injecting every newborn foal with selenium was instituted and complete control was established.

On another occasion Wallace saved the Hogans' bacon when their yearlings being prepared for the Trentham thoroughbred sales suddenly sported enlarged thyroid glands a fortnight before, which would have made them unsaleable. Panic stations! There was a possibility, Wallace said, that the problem was caused by the feeding of a daily ration of cut pasture, which was a new planting of H1 ryegrass. Again, he contacted his colleagues at Ruakura, who told him that particular strain of ryegrass was oddly deficient in iodine. Therapy was required, with two or three iodine salt intravenous injections to the youngsters, and all was well in time for the sale.

Pasture management to provide good nutrition for mares and foals was a subject under constant review at Fencourt. Under Wallace's guidance, they were made acutely aware of the problems created by the grazing habits of horses — producing closely grazed patches and leaving long lank areas — and as experienced dairymen they understood only too well the need to manage their pastures well to obtain nutritious foodstuff for their precious charges. The answer was to have cattle grazing to clean up the pastures before those patches appeared and to maintain an even sward.

Patrick was on the council of the New Zealand Thoroughbred Breeders' Association and the highest flyer in the industry, but as his fortunes rose, he never failed to protect the little man. It was one of his most likeable qualities, according to his mate Joe Walls.

'Patrick looked after the little people in the bloodstock industry. He was always a great champion of the small guy — the types who were so prevalent in the 1970s and the early 1980s. The farmer and the little breeder down the road with a couple of mares . . . they'd flock to him. At any one time he'd have 15 or 20 of those people.

'They'd say, "Oh, we'll send the horse to Patrick because he'll look after it, and if I get it wrong . . . " His attention to service was near-perfect.

'If someone had a mare and sent her to Patrick and something went wrong, or the foal died, and that person wasn't deserving of a refund, he'd still give them one. He'd ring them up and say, "Look, you had a bit of bad luck there. I'll fix that. Send the mare back next year and I'll cover it for you. Don't worry about it."

'I respected him for that. There wouldn't be a fairer person in the business than Patrick.'

Cambridge Independent
OBITUARY, 3 FEBRUARY 1981

Sarah Margaret Hogan. Loved wife of the late Thomas Hogan and loved mother and mother-in-law of Vern and the late Eileen Whiteman, Margaret and John Dunn, John and Jean Hogan, Pat and Arthur Kelly, Peter and Jewel Hogan, Delia and Michael Bibby, Patrick and Justine Hogan.

Aged 84. Requiem Mass will be celebrated at St Peter's Catholic Church, Cambridge.

Mrs Hogan's main interests were her family of seven and the farm. She was active in Fencourt district affairs, St Peter's Catholic Church and the Women's Division of Federated Farmers.

The loss of their mother was a time of sadness and reflection for the family. John cherished a memory from his childhood: 'I remember one year, when it was the time of the annual A&P Show in Hawera. Everyone had the day off school and went to the show in their nice clothes. Dad was showing his Clydesdales, but a couple of weeks before the show, Mum said: "I can't go."

'Dad said, "Why not?"'

'She said, "Because I've got nothing to wear."'

'She had about two frocks which she wore day in, day out. He'd never noticed that, and she had never sought to have any money spent on her. He gave her £5 and she went off to town and came home all dressed up in her new frock and a hat, and us kids — the three of us — couldn't get over how beautiful our mother was.'

Sarah had always unquestioningly supported Tom, Patrick mused, as they worked together, side by side, throughout life — Tom up front and Sarah content to remain in the background. Her world had revolved around her family, the church and the local Women's Federated Farmers, while for social contact she and Tom liked nothing better than to play the odd game of cards with close Irish friends like the Lynchs or the Johnsons.

Sarah was happy to look after her brood and cook good plain meals, including pikelets to die for, or do the washing. She had been a good and dutiful mother to him, but Patrick could not pretend to feel the same overwhelming grief that he had when Tom died.

Perhaps, with him, she had always felt there was a small cross to bear. A lingering resentment at having Patrick landed on her, 18 months after her sixth and 'final' child, Delia, was born, had subliminally percolated through their relationship. (In 1982, his Uncle Paddy in Ireland showed Patrick a letter he had received from Sarah when Delia was born: 'After six children I've told your brother Tom that the gate is shut from now on.') Perhaps it was the later tension that existed between Justine and his mother, who didn't get on. Nevertheless, Sarah had done much to make his later life possible, and he was deeply grateful for that.

Cambridge Stud had opened for business with 135 acres just four years earlier in 1977, but the outstanding success of Sir Tristram and the increased demand for the stud's services necessitated another purchase of land. Conveniently a further 30 acres came up on the next-door property and Patrick's obliging bank lent them the money for the purchase. It was inadvertently topped up by Bart Cummings who had promised Justine one summer's afternoon — en route to the Trentham sales — as he pointed across to the paddock: 'That filly over there . . . I am only going to buy her if Patrick promises to build you a new house.'

The filly was duly purchased by Cummings in the sale ring for the record price of $130,000 on behalf of Sydney's Amco jeans king, Cliff Vincent, but as soon as Patrick got his hands on the cheque it was ploughed straight back into the farm and extra land. The following year Cummings arrived at Cambridge Stud again and said to Justine, 'Are you going to take me and show me your new house?'

'Yes,' she said, 'I will. It's down in the paddock, running around.'

While the success of Sir Tristram was common knowledge in the Southern Hemisphere, news of the deeds of his progeny had not yet travelled to the United States. Late one night Patrick had a call from an Australian bloodstock agent, Jim Shannon, who asked if he would be interested in purchasing the full brother to Sir Tristram. He was a foal weanling, and unproven in every regard, but knowing that Patrick had bought Sir Tristram he decided to give him a call to sound him out.

The foal could be bought in the United States for the very reasonable price of $30,000.

Yes, he would definitely be interested, Patrick replied, but before he could buy the horse, he would have to apply to the Reserve Bank and seek approval to take the funds out of New Zealand. Was the purchase he was making coming back to New Zealand? Reserve Bank officials asked Patrick. 'No,' Patrick admitted, 'he has to be weaned off his mother and he needs time up there to prepare. It might be 12 months before he gets down here. Or he might race in the United States before I get him down.'

That's no good to us, Patrick was told. The application was rejected.

Patrick rang Parliament and spoke with his good friend and Prime Minister, Rob Muldoon, telling him what had transpired with the Reserve Bank. 'What are you going to do with this horse?' Muldoon asked him.

Patrick explained: 'He's only a foal so he'll have to stay there and race up there. If he's any good, he can come down here to New Zealand as a stallion and serve at Cambridge Stud along with his full brother Sir Tristram. The intention is that he will come here.'

'Give me two hours and then get back to the Reserve Bank and it will be approved,' the Prime Minister promised. Two hours later, Patrick was back on the phone to the Reserve Bank and was told his application had been accepted.

Ten days later, Patrick got a second call from Jim Shannon, saying that Laurie Connell in Perth had heard on the grapevine that a full brother to Sir Tristram was up for sale as a weanling and had contacted them. 'Would you sell it?'

'How much?' Patrick asked.

'What would it take to buy him?' Shannon countered. 'Give a cheeky price and see what happens.'

'$100,000,' Patrick replied.

'Agreed.'

What a brilliant deal, for no work at all! Then he remembered. He'd already said the horse was coming back to New Zealand; the money had already gone out of the country and now the horse wasn't going to happen. He rang straight through to Rob Muldoon. 'Look, Rob, I'm in a bit of a fix with what's happened. That horse I bought may not come back to New Zealand.'

'Why not?'

'Well, I've had an offer for him for $100,000 from Western Australia.'

Muldoon chortled. 'Grab it! We've got a hundred grand coming into New Zealand. The Reserve Bank will be thrilled to bits!'

Justine had always retained a special fondness for the first mare she had bought with her sister-in-law Pat in 1961. Then, Sweet Wren had arrived at Fencourt with a little chestnut filly at foot who they called Sweet Time, and who later would become the mother of the champion mare Gay Poss. Now, in 1981, at the advanced age of 21, Sweet Time was enjoying her post-foaling twilight years grazing in her paddock at Cambridge Stud, nearby to her daughter Gay Poss who had returned to New Zealand for a career as a broodmare.

Gay Poss left a lot to be desired in that department, Patrick and Jonathan Hope concurred gloomily one afternoon in the yard as they examined the mare. The teaser stallion was next door to them, and the one that was the hotter of the two was her mother, Sweet Time, the men laughed. 'Bring Sweet Time into the crush and we'll see whether or not she's ready to serve,' Jonathan grinned.

'Oh, we wouldn't dare,' Patrick laughed. 'Mrs H wouldn't be happy with that. She's not allowed to have any more babies. I'm under orders there.'

They led Sweet Time round to the service barn, joking as they went. 'She must be wanting sex — she's out there hotter than her daughter! Let's give the old girl a thrill and put her to Paddy.'

They thought no more of it — just laughed from time to time, saying, 'Well you know, she might be out of the stud book, she'll never have another foal, but she's had some sex anyway . . . a last fling with Paddy, the dear old soul.'

Nothing could come of it, Patrick was confident. Justine would slaughter him, he knew, if 'her girl' became pregnant. She had insisted that Sweet Time's breeding days were over and that she be retired. Patrick had promised her that that would be the case.

A few months later Jonathan said to Patrick, 'You'd better bring that mare in and make sure that she's not in foal.' Well, they couldn't believe it — the mare showed up positive. Sweet Time was in foal.

Holy shit! Suddenly, the joke was no longer funny. 'Nobody's allowed to say anything about this to Mrs H,' Patrick ordered the stable staff and Jonathan. 'With a bit of luck she might slip her foal and we'll be off the hook.'

But as foaling time loomed, Justine became suspicious. 'What's Sweet Time doing in there with the mares in the foaling paddock?' she asked Patrick.

'She's just being a mate for Gay Poss,' her nervous husband replied.

A couple of weeks later, when Gay Poss had foaled, Justine confronted him again. 'Why is Sweet Time still in the foaling paddock?'

Patrick was panicking. 'Aah . . . uumm . . . she's being a very good nursemaid to the other mares.'

It was a Saturday morning and, as usual, Justine and Patrick were taking turns for foaling duty, standing near the day paddock with Jonathan and their old friend, Fred Cole. 'There's a mare foaling out in the paddock,' Fred said, staring into the distance. 'Who is it?'

The two words were dragged out as slowly as Patrick could manage. 'Sweet Time.'

'WHAT?!' Justine swung around on her husband, so furious she could barely get the words out. 'Right, that's it! I'm packing my bags and I'm going to find a unit in Hamilton and I'm shifting. I'm moving. I'm leaving you. If you've done that to Sweet Time after I said I wanted her to have no more babies, that is IT! If anything goes wrong, if Sweet Time dies, if she dies having this foal, you know you are going to be in a lot of strife!' Fuming, Justine stormed off.

Dear God, he was in deep trouble now. He knew she adored Sweet Time, but he'd never expected her to go so bonkers about a horse.

'Shit, we'd better make sure that she and this foal live,' Patrick murmured to a subdued Jonathan, as they tramped over the grass to the mare. Everyone else around the place who had witnessed the altercation was running for cover, and he couldn't blame them.

The foal was a little chestnut filly — the smallest, ugliest little filly one could imagine. 'Oh, what a trollop!' Patrick exclaimed, inadvertently naming her in the process.

'Don't say that near Justine,' Jonathan advised nervously — he was still awestruck by the force of her outburst. As he glanced up, there was Justine approaching the two men, her mare Sweet Time and her newborn foal.

'Well, I've rung the land agent in Hamilton and he's showing me a place by the lake tomorrow . . . ' Her opening words were not promising, but then, as Justine crouched on the grass to look closely at the foal, her demeanour changed. 'Oooohhh, she's so beautiful . . . she's gorgeous! I'm going to call her Sweet Rose. And don't you ever do anything like this to me again!' she added vehemently.

Sweet Rose, stable name Trollop, was born with a club foot and could never race. She became Justine's special pet, and lived out her life at Cambridge Stud as a much-loved addition to the team.

At a Matamata race meeting in August 1981, John Costello, the racing editor of the *Auckland Star* and its weekend edition, the *8 O'Clock*, was heading through the birdcage towards the stairs up to the pressroom when he saw a group which included Patrick and Steve Brem, the then chief executive of the New Zealand Thoroughbred Breeders' Association. 'Gidday Patrick, Steve,' John chirped cheerily, without slackening pace.

Steve shuffled his feet and, Costello thought, looked a tad embarrassed, as though they had just been talking about him. Patrick, his expression stony, looked straight through him.

As he sat down in the press box Costello shook his head in disbelief. He hadn't experienced being 'cut dead' before. He had always got on pretty well with Patrick and . . . uh oh! He remembered the article he had written in the *8 O'Clock* the week before. Costello's column had criticised the decision of the New Zealand Thoroughbred Breeders' Association to split the 1980–81 Broodmare of the Year title between Taiona of Cambridge Stud and The Pixie, a fine old broodmare owned by the Dennis brothers from Southland. Costello had stated he thought the award should have gone to The Pixie.

Taiona was represented by Sovereign Red, a multiple Derby winner and the best three-year-old in Australia, and his younger brother, Gurner's Lane, whose career after one notable win in Queensland had yet to really come onstream. The Pixie was represented by three individual black-type winners in that single season from the performances of her splendid daughters, The Twinkle, The Fantasy and The Dimple. Costello was rattled that Patrick seemed to have taken the article so personally, but put it aside and got back to work.

Just before the last race there was a knock on the pressroom door. As it happened to be Costello's turn to be chairman of the pressroom — as president of the Racing Writers' Association, the luckless holder of that office was also 'chairman of the pressroom' — he answered it. It was Patrick.

'Cos!' said Patrick, with a beaming smile as if the incident earlier in the day had never happened, 'I'm glad it's you. I've just got word that Sir Tristram has won the Dewar Trophy by a few thousand dollars from Rangong. I'd like to shout the pressroom some bubbly, if that's all right.'

It was very all right indeed. The Dewar Trophy, awarded to each year's leading sire for combined Australian/New Zealand progeny earnings, was certainly something to celebrate. The mainly Auckland-based pressmen drove home that night after the races awash with joie de vivre and Veuve Cliquot.

As he had downed his first glass of champagne that afternoon, Costello had shaken his head with admiration, recalling the stony reception he'd received earlier in the day. He speculated that, as he walked away from the studmaster, Patrick would have thought to himself, 'That was dumb. The media can be a lot of help, so why antagonise a pressman?' The sensational news about Sir Tristram had allowed Patrick to mend a briefly broken fence with the journalist.

The incident would stick in Costello's mind as a telling example of Patrick's complete professionalism. If you think you have made a mistake, fix it straight away — even if you privately think that bumptious, half-bred Kiwi/Irish plonker of a journalist got it all wrong and you hope the rest of his hair falls out . . . which it pretty well did over the years.

The New Zealand Thoroughbred Breeders' Association judges did make a Solomon-like decision in splitting the title for the first and only time in the Broodmare of the Year award's history, Costello reflected years later: 'The early 1980s was the period when commercial imperatives were beginning to play a dominant role in the breeding industry, with Patrick leading the charge. Australia was — and continues to be — our main market, and in marketing terms the Australian deeds of Taiona's son, Sovereign Red, perhaps had more impact than The Pixie's threesome at home. A shared award could certainly be justified.

'For me, as a racing writer on a daily and weekly newspaper, the main focus of my work and interest was the racing scene, the horses and the people who actually provided the race day drama and excitement. The breeding sector was secondary at best, if not peripheral. It wasn't until I became editor of *New Zealand Bloodhorse* that breeding became a primary focus for me.

'I had seen the broodmare tussle between Taiona and The Pixie as simply another contest between two thoroughbreds, and I went for the "form horse". Though there was certainly nothing personal in it, in hindsight I could imagine how upset Patrick would have been by an article that questioned the deservedness of Taiona's award. For me, it was just another opinion piece, but for Patrick it was prestige, future value, dollars and cents.'

Meanwhile, on the track Sir Tristram had produced his first New Zealand Group 1 winner and star in Noble Heights. She was born out of the stallion's second crop in 1978 by Gold Heights, and had barged into a water trough before the 1979 yearling sales, requiring extensive stitching on her body. Although it was unsightly, it shouldn't impact on her performance, Barry Lee assured the Vela brothers who had expressed interest in buying her. But as everyone knows, looks count. The stitches were off-putting and the Velas picked her up for a good price.

Then she began to show impressive form under the training regime of Laurie Laxon. At two, in her only start, Noble Heights won the Waikato Racing Club's 1981 Kindergarten Handicap. She came into her own throughout the 1982 season as a three-year-old, showing her ability and versatility by winning at distances ranging from 1200 to 2400 metres.

Noble Heights took out the Group 1 New Zealand Guineas at Riccarton, the Group 2 Auckland Racing Club's (ARC) Royal Stakes, the Group 3 Hawke's Bay Jockey Club Gold

Trail Stakes and Masterton Racing Club's Lowland Stakes, as well as a second placing in the Levin Classic and a third placing in the ARC Ladies Mile.

From just eight starts in 1982 she had four wins and two placings to amass earnings of $65,345. Noble Heights was named the New Zealand Filly of the Year for the 1981–82 season.

Patrick saw Fred Bodle's car swinging up the drive at Cambridge Stud. It was springtime in 1981 and the stud's gardens were immaculate, its specimen trees were taking shape, and the former rudimentary surroundings were beginning to show the landscaping charm that would improve by the year.

It must have taken some doing by Bodle — a serious swallowing of pride. 'I want to put a mare to Sir Tristram,' Fred opened the conversation.

'Oh, do you?' Patrick gave him a non-committal smile.

'Yes, I want to put a mare to him,' Fred repeated.

'Well, that's not going to be very easy, Fred.'

Bodle looked amazed. 'You're not going to NOT let me have a mare to Sir Tristram, are you?'

'Well,' Patrick said, 'I am.'

'You're selling his services, aren't you? On what basis can't I breed to him?'

Patrick had waited four years for this moment. 'Your mares aren't good enough for my horse. I couldn't possibly take one of your mares, because they aren't good enough.'

Fred Bodle laughed. OK, joke over. He regretted telling Patrick back in '78 that his precious stallion wasn't good enough for his mares. 'What's it going to cost me?'

'It'll cost you what he stands at — $100,000.'

'Whaaat? You want me to pay $100,000 to breed one foal when I had a share for $4000 and I could have had that for the rest of the horse's life?'

'Yes. It's $100,000 or nothing.' Patrick was adamant.

Fred was a good mate. They were close friends and Patrick could have wished this hadn't happened to him, at a time when the horse's price was skyrocketing, but still he was cheeky enough to say that Fred's mares weren't good enough for his stallion. That comment of Fred's had rankled.

Fred Bodle duly sent his mare, Summer Fleur, to Cambridge Stud and handed over his cheque for $100,000 to breed a foal, who emerged in the world as a big beautiful chestnut filly. If receiving the $4000 cheque for the sale of his share in Sir Tristram was the worst racing decision Fred Bodle had ever made, the $100,000 he paid out for this foal would surely be his best.

CHAPTER 8

THE SANGSTER CONNECTION

'Hogan is a quality man and everything bears his stamp of excellence. His operation is fantastic . . . as a one-man organisation, he's the best in the world.'

— Robert Sangster

IT WAS SERENDIPITOUS for the fortunes of New Zealand and Australian racing interests that soccer Pools magnate Robert Sangster jetted into Sydney on a Sunday evening. He had arrived for a meeting the following day with media mogul Kerry Packer to discuss the setting up of Pools in Australia, to be run on similar lines to Sangster's Vernons Pools family business in the UK.

At breakfast in his hotel on that Monday morning, Sangster glanced through *The Australian* newspaper before turning, as he always did, to the racing section. To his astonished delight he saw three pages devoted solely to thoroughbred breeding news, a Monday weekly feature of the paper. What a contrast to England where the main quality racing paper, the *Daily Telegraph*, gave thoroughbred breeding an eighth of a page, if the industry was lucky!

A country with barely a third of England's population giving such expansive coverage to bloodstock matters had to be all right, Sangster thought. It could be worthwhile setting up part of his racing empire 'down under'. He'd talk with Packer, an astute businessman and huge personality of a man, whose racing plunges were the stuff of legend, and then do some research of his own.

Robert Edmund Sangster was born on 23 May 1936, the son of Vernon Sangster who founded the Vernons Pools empire. He had grown up accustomed to wealth — a condition ideally suited to a big-spending man who embraced life with equal dollops of gusto and urbane charm, and who had a deep passion for horse racing.

From the humble beginnings of Swettenham, a small stud in Cheshire which he bought into in 1961 at the age of 25, Sangster became the first person in Britain to own racehorses as a successful commercial venture. However, it took another six years and a partnership with two Irishmen — John Magnier and Magnier's father-in-law, the legendary trainer Vincent O'Brien, who prepared Robert's horses — for that enterprise to be transformed into an empire.

The trio was to experience great success in their plan to develop commercially successful sires from the horses they raced. They became a major presence, buying many horses in America — their patronage of the great sire, the Canadian stallion Northern Dancer (the former winner of the United States' classics the Kentucky Derby and Preakness Stakes) and his sons — was particularly auspicious.

Their partnership, which included the Greek shipping

billionaire Stavros Niarchos and Californian businessman Danny Schwartz, in its early stages, would develop Coolmore Stud of Ireland into the world's biggest breeding operation. Of their English partner, O'Brien said, 'Robert is a true visionary whose large-scale investment in the best American-bred yearlings in the 1970s was one of the principal factors in establishing Ireland and Coolmore Stud as major forces in the bloodstock world.'

Within two decades of buying into that modest enterprise in Cheshire, Sangster's thoroughbred racing and breeding empire extended beyond his native England and Ireland to the United States, France, Venezuela, Australia and New Zealand — his racing colours of emerald green tunic with royal blue sleeves and white cap with emerald spots becoming a familiar sight on the great racecourses of the world.

He developed his own extensive stud in Australia, combining with trainer Colin Hayes to win the 1980 Melbourne Cup with Beldale Ball — a Southern Hemisphere jewel to add to the Sangster crown that would come to include two Epsom Derbys, four Irish Derbys, two French Derbys and three Prix de l'Arc de Triomphes.

Robert Sangster was a brilliant businessman, a racehorse owner and breeder *non pareil*, but it was the romantic goings-on of his high society and racy lifestyle that provided the juicy fodder that was meat and drink to Britain's tabloid media, and guaranteed to rivet the papers' readers — particularly its women. In 1978, Sangster left his first wife, former model Christine Street (by whom he had four children — Guy, Ben, Adam and Katie), for an attractive and stylish Australian blonde, Susan Peacock, who was previously married to the deputy leader of the Australian Liberal Party, Andrew Peacock.

It was the stock of Sir Tristram that influenced Sangster's decision to extend his racing interests to New Zealand. One of Sir Tristram's daughters, Mapperley Heights, had scored an eye-catching win on debut at Te Rapa, and as word got back to Sangster, he decided to buy a half-share in the filly from her owner, Mark Davison of Mapperley Stud in Matamata, who had purchased the horse for $150,000 at the 1981 Trentham National Yearling Sales.

Mapperley Heights further stamped her mark as an exciting young galloper in winning the 1200 metres sprint Leopard Classic at Avondale in April 1983, when, as on her debut race, she came from a tight position at the turn to steadily lengthen her stride near the winning post.

'So deceptive is the massive two-year-old in her galloping action that one can only describe her as a horse that is doing nothing, but at the same time simply killing her opponents,' enthused the *Auckland Star*. 'Yesterday's win had many old-time racegoers staring in disbelief by the manner in which she took out the prestigious event.'

Her trainer, Dave O'Sullivan of Wexford Stables in Matamata, described Mapperley Heights as having almost freakish qualities: 'I've had a few good ones in the past, but she takes the cake.' His apprentice son Lance, who rode the filly, agreed. 'One minute she's giving you nothing and then, by some means, when she sights that winning post, she just gives a little more each stride until she's got control. She's just too fantastic for words.'

With Mapperley Heights destined for an Australian campaign later that year, O'Sullivan was stunned to be told that Lance would not be needed on that trip as he was considered too young for such a tough undertaking. That anger was compounded when the O'Sullivans were later informed by Davison and Sangster that 'their girl' was to quit their stable. Mapperley Heights was transferred from Wexford to the stable of top Australian trainer Colin Hayes in preparation for the lucrative AJC Oaks in April.

The O'Sullivans had lost their star, but there was another well-performed horse in the Wexford stable who could put up a good showing against her old stablemate, they believed. La Souvronne in the hands of Dave, Paul and Lance O'Sullivan would represent New Zealand interests in the Oaks.

At Randwick, Robert Sangster, Colin Hayes, Dave and Paul O'Sullivan exchanged the briefest of courtesies before a nervous wait as their well-backed fillies paraded around the birdcage. The two horses, who had once done their track work together, now entered the race with Mapperley Heights as favourite.

In the hands of Lance O'Sullivan, La Souvronne, a notoriously slow starter and standing the leaders almost 20 lengths into the straight, burst through the wall of horses 200 metres from the finish line to take the lead and hang on grimly as a determined Brent Thomson on Mapperley Heights challenged . . . The result was an upset win in the AJC Oaks to La Souvronne, by a long neck from Mapperley Heights.

After the race, a gracious Robert Sangster approached and congratulated his former trainer: 'That you would entrust the riding of this race to an apprentice, your son Lance, is a great credit to you both.' It had been a bold decision by his father, Sangster added. Lance was the first apprentice to win the AJC Oaks since World War Two.

Robert Sangster arranged a meeting with Patrick Hogan in Melbourne towards the end of 1982. Previously the pair had met only casually at the races. He wanted to purchase an interest in Sir Tristram, Sangster said. Were there any shares available? 'He's the Northern Dancer of the Southern Hemisphere,' Sangster enthused. His glowing comparison with the most successful thoroughbred sire in the world had the desired effect, and Patrick promised he would see whether something could be arranged.

The two had hit it off famously and, as always, Sangster concluded their proposed deal on the shake of a hand. The traditional gentleman's agreement was ever his code, as Patrick was to discover.

There were no shares available in Sir Tristram, but Patrick was acutely aware that if he could form a business relationship with Sangster and his broodmares in Australia, it would provide a unique opportunity for the stud.

After some to-ing and fro-ing between the men, it was decided that Sangster would send up to 30 mares — the bulk from the Northern Hemisphere and the remainder from his stud in Australia — to Cambridge Stud where they would remain, producing their foals under the stud's care.

In the process of the discussions, Patrick and Robert had also become close friends. On learning that Patrick and Joe Walls intended to travel to Ireland in 1982 to inspect a colt sired by Northern Dancer called Danzatore — an equine resident at the stables of Coolmore Stud — for future stallion duties at Cambridge Stud, Sangster invited the two Kiwis to visit him and his wife Susan at their home on the Isle of Man.

They arrived for a three-day visit and were treated royally. However, the following morning Robert surprised Joe and Patrick by saying he had to head off to the United States later that afternoon. They were more than welcome to stay on with Susan. Then Sangster had a discreet word in Patrick's ear. 'You are very welcome to remain here, but I'd suggest that you might like to make yourself scarce after tomorrow morning, because it's likely that the American press is going to break the story that I'm in the States to see Jerry Hall!'

His Lear jet was available to fly the men anywhere they wished to go, he added. 'Europe, London — wherever you like.' The pair took his sage advice and made themselves scarce, flying in Sangster's plane to London for the weekend, just hours before the story broke that Sangster had formed a relationship with the leggy Texan model who later married Mick Jagger.

Danzatore, which Patrick held in partnership with Sangster for the huge sum of $8 million, did not bring the bonanza his owners had hoped for. The highest-priced stallion ever to come to New Zealand was never a raging success.

Danzatore's credentials couldn't be faulted. He was rated the equal third-best two-year-old in Europe in 1981. He was by the exceptional Northern Dancer, and his dam was a Group 3 winner by Raise a Native, creating a 3f x 3m cross to the legendary Native Dancer. Patrick had disagreed when Sangster warned him that he had chosen a horse that was too good for the local market. However, Patrick was later forced to admit that the horse only realised moderate commercial and racing success, at best.

Patrick kicked himself. He had acquired Danzatore for all the wrong reasons. He was seeking tax relief from the 58 cents in the dollar he was currently paying to the Inland Revenue

Department — by buying a pricey stallion who he could write off in three years, he would at least see some return for his taxes.

Despite the fact that Danzatore was crowned Champion First Season Sire for Australia/New Zealand combined in 1987–88, he was onsold to Kentucky interests and sent to the United States to further his stud career, where he would flourish as a sire of fillies and mares.

From that initial meeting in Melbourne, Robert and Patrick were to have a long and enduring friendship. Sangster relished the Australian and New Zealand lifestyle, its people, the antipodean sense of humour and, above all, the racing scene. And, as his mares came to produce a phenomenal number of Group winners from Sir Tristram — far higher than the average from other mares sent to Paddy — it was to provide the icing on the cake for both Sangster and Hogan. Sangster raced many of those horses in Australia and, as the results came through, the Sangster connection gave the stallion a huge profile, both there and internationally.

Socially, the two men enjoyed the banter together. Robert loved jousting, and the pair would shadow-box after a few beers until one or two blows connected. Like Patrick, Robert had a passion for winning and getting the upper hand in equine matters. Beneath the trappings of wealth, both men were, at heart, addicted horse traders. Robert Sangster's motto was 'every horse, no matter how successful, has its price'.

When he moved to Sydney in the early 1980s, New Zealand trainer Graeme Rogerson was living in the plush Southern Cross Hotel, where he was joined by some of his old pals, including Bob Morris and Patrick Hogan, for the annual Sydney yearling sales. It had been a long day, and turned into an even longer night. They were all pretty drunk, they agreed, at some advanced stage of the evening — time for bed.

After a few hours, Patrick woke. Nature called and he needed to make an urgent trip to the bathroom. He climbed out of bed and, half-asleep, opened the door — not to the bathroom as he had intended, but the door adjacent, which promptly closed and locked behind him, leaving him standing naked in the hotel's corridor.

Sobering quickly, Patrick banged on his mates' neighbouring doors, but all were dead to the world. What to do? He couldn't hang round the corridor for the rest of the night and he couldn't get back into his bedroom, so he did the only sensible thing. He caught the lift down to the ground floor lobby and, with his hands cupped over his crown jewels, strolled up to the reception desk to ask as nonchalantly as he could for a bath towel and a duplicate key to his room.

Hoteliers are trained to react to human foibles with sang-froid. However, the young male receptionist who had drawn the graveyard shift reacted sharply when, after handing a towel over, he was invited by Patrick to accompany him back upstairs, so that he could return the towel immediately. 'No way!' (It is reported that the manager of the Southern Cross Hotel cherishes the video of that episode to this day.)

Grosvenor (Sir Tristram–My Tricia, by Hermes) was locked in a triangular contest with Veloso and Cossack Prince, but trainer Geoff Murphy was confident that the handsome bay colt, to be ridden by Mick Dittman, would notch up his stable's third victory in six years in the prestigious 1600 metres Caulfield Guineas of 1982.

Murphy, who had previously captured the Guineas with Surround in 1976 and Sovereign Red in 1980, said he believed the champion three-year-old would go into the classic race with important advantages over his rivals. 'I think the home track advantage will be a big factor in his favour . . . he has done well since he's come back from Sydney. Grosvenor is such a relaxed horse that he shouldn't give Mick Dittman too many worries getting over from his No 13 barrier. Whatever happens, Veloso, Cossack Prince and the others will know they've been in a race against him.'

Grosvenor was going into the race as favourite, with Veloso at 4–1, while the odds for Cossack Prince had firmed to 5–1 third favourite. The Guineas would continue a fascinating three-way struggle between the horses, which had begun six weeks earlier in the Peter Pan Stakes at Rosehill.

In that race Cossack Prince won, Grosvenor finished sixth and Veloso eighth. It was Grosvenor's turn at their next outing in the Gloaming Stakes at Rosehill two weeks later, when he defeated Veloso by a long neck, with Cossack Prince third, one-and-a-half lengths away. Veloso then decisively turned the tables on his two rivals on 25 September 1982, winning the 2000 metres AJC Spring Champion Stakes by three-quarters of a length from Grosvenor, with Cossack Prince a half-neck further back.

Meanwhile, in Queensland, four-year-old Dalmacia (Sir Tristram–Gay Juss, by Persian Garden II) was also turning heads, improving with every race he ran, and shaping up as an outstanding middle-distance performer. He had been purchased at the Trentham National Yearling Sales in 1979 for $28,000 by

Brisbane trainer Eric Kirwan, and was later transferred to the stable of Neville Begg. Named by his Brisbane owners after a beach resort area on the Adriatic Sea, the bay horse was going into the rich Epsom Handicap with top form and Ron Quinton on his back. If Dalmacia won, this would be the first Epsom victory for the trainer-jockey combination of Begg and Quinton in 17 years of trying.

Who would believe it? Within the space of one dizzy month — from the start of October to the first Tuesday in November 1982 — three of Sir Tristram's progeny set the racing world alight.

First up, Grosvenor won the $140,000 Caulfield Guineas from the tail of the field, edging out Veloso by a long neck, with Cossack Prince coming through in third place. Just days later, it was the turn of Dalmacia to take out the $120,000 AJC Epsom Handicap with ease. After the race, the jubilant part-owner and businessman, Jack Lustica, confirmed that the partners had been offered close to a million dollars for Dalmacia as a stallion.

Gurner's Lane followed by winning the VATC Caulfield Cup, and then Grosvenor surged back into the limelight. After finishing a close second in the Cox Plate, he triumphed in the Victorian Derby at the end of October, with two other of Sir Tristram's horses, Cossack Prince and Dynamo, coming home in second and fourth places respectively.

Patrick was in Melbourne during this incredible run, meeting with Robert Sangster. There was just one race left to go, and one of his horses left to run — Gurner's Lane in the Melbourne Cup. Incredibly to his Aussie mates, Patrick opted to fly back to New Zealand on the day of the race. 'I need to go home, there's too much work to do.' It sounded a bit of a lame excuse, they shrugged, but each man to his own. Patrick's vet Jonathan Hope could have supplied them with the answer: 'He's such a superstitious Irish bugger, he wouldn't go near the racecourse in case his presence cast some kind of hex on the horse!'

Patrick flew out from Melbourne to Sydney and on to Auckland airport, dashed to his parked car and drove on the speed limit to Cambridge. He walked in the door at 5.08 p.m., two minutes before the start of the race, to join Justine, Nicola and Erin and the entire staff who were clustered around the television.

On 2 November 1982, Gurner's Lane achieved the rare pinnacle reserved for the best of the best, in following his Caulfield Cup win with victory in the Melbourne Cup. He had looked gone for all money at 500 metres from home, with Kingston Town having the run of the race, but — miraculously — jockey Mick Dittman found the gap by the inside rail for Gurner's Lane to bolt through, catching Kingston Town on the final stride. A mighty cheer erupted around the cramped living room as Cambridge Stud recorded another milestone — its first Melbourne Cup.

And it wasn't just this star trio who performed outstandingly in that month-long winning spree — in the same period Star of Knight took out the Queensland Guineas, Cossack Prince won the Hill and Peter Pan Stakes, while Trissaro was making headlines back in New Zealand.

International reaction to the sire's outstanding results was swift. On 19 November, the New Zealand Press Association (NZPA)

reported that Patrick Hogan had turned down $30 million for his share of Sir Tristram. The offer had come from a New Zealand bloodstock agent on behalf of a Californian client, it said, following the Gurner's Lane win in the Melbourne Cup. He would not sell his stallion at any price, Hogan replied, telling the agent he was just not interested. 'I turned down another American offer of $16 million a few months ago, and that buyer was so keen he wanted to have it put in writing so that negotiations could be started.'

A week before the Melbourne Cup win and the $30 million offer, Patrick spoke at length with Jack Petley of *NZ Truth* explaining why he had turned down the $16 million. 'Sir Tristram will stay here until he is retired! No money in the world will get him off this property. He's a once-in-a-lifetime stallion and he'll die here. Breeding is my life. If I sold him, what the heck would I do? I've had American enquiries to breed him in the Northern Hemisphere and also enquiries from England and Ireland. They are from people who have racing interests in Australia and who want bookings to our time.'

In all New Zealand breeding history, Petley wrote, no stallion had made such an impact in such a short time. 'His oldest progeny are only five. Yet already he is being hailed as the greatest sire ever to stand in this country.'

The worth of the Sir Tristrams, Petley said, was their ability to go any distance, act on any type of footing, and stand up to solid and hard training. 'Sir Tristram is an almost light liver bay with wonderful black markings on his legs. And what a build. He's big in the shoulder and like brick from the back — a studmaster's dream.'

Les Carlyon, writing on Sir Tristram in Melbourne's *The Age*, had this to say: 'The worst thing you can do with any horse is bury it in superlatives; anticipation then runs ahead of events as so often happens with the million-dollar two-year-olds.

'So let's just inflict one label on Sir Tristram. He's a freak, the most freakish stallion we've perhaps seen since Without Fear in 1975–76. My advice is that if you see anything by Sir Tristram in the Davis Cup, back it!'

By not selling Sir Tristram, Patrick ensured a great boost for the New Zealand thoroughbred breeding industry, which, he told media, was of vital importance. 'It's given our industry just what it needed — worldwide recognition and the opening of some new markets, like Mr Sangster.'

In the wake of Dalmacia's success, Clyde Conway of the *New Zealand Herald* reflected on the export dilemma faced by New Zealand breeders in an article headed 'Sir Tristram Continues to Reign Supreme'. Conway wrote: 'Bred in New Zealand to be raced in Australia — it is something we have had to accept for the past 30 or more years, and there must be regret that such blood cannot be developed and raced here. Yet, to maintain a buoyant market for our breeders, it is essential that our recognised top blood should continue to enjoy regular success in the big-name races such as the AJC Epsom Handicap . . . The lines of Dalmacia would have to represent peak appeal. Goodness knows what would be the value of a younger brother, or sister, on the current market.'

Goodness knows indeed. Hard on the heels of that dazzling succession of wins, it was announced that for the upcoming 1983 National Yearling Sales at Trentham, three top Sir Tristram progeny would go under the auctioneer's hammer.

The three yearlings with the impeccable credentials that so excited the industry were a filly out of Taiona and a full sister to Gurner's Lane and Sovereign Red; a colt out of Surround; and another colt, a full brother to Grosvenor, out of My Tricia. Steven Brem, national secretary of the New Zealand Thoroughbred Breeders' Association, predicted that each of those three could top the million-dollar mark. 'In January 1982, yearlings sold over the two days at Trentham fetched $10,197,000 of which Cambridge Stud collected just under two million. However, there is little doubt that the stud will do much better in 1983 with an offering of 12 yearlings by Sir Tristram, 12 by Marceau and 11 others by an assortment of stallions.

'Hogan's success at Trentham is due to his meticulous preparation and uncompromising effort,' added Brem in an interview with the *Auckland Star*. 'He is a remarkable man in the bloodstock industry. He may not be the most eloquent of spokesmen about what he does, but there is no doubt that he thinks things through and is ahead of the rest.'

To Jack Petley of the *NZ Truth* Patrick admitted: 'When I was selling Persian Garden's progeny for three or four hundred dollars, I thought, "One day I'll get a big price for one of my yearlings." At that stage I'd set my heart on $40,000. It seemed to me to be like a million dollars.'

Six months later in 1983, at a time when everything was ticking over sweetly for the New Zealand bloodstock industry, New Zealand's Prime Minister Robert Muldoon dropped a bombshell. He ruled a line through bloodstock taxation exemption in New Zealand, saying, in effect, 'This has gone far enough. We are now not going to have these rules that apply to bloodstock.'

Ironically, at the same time, Australia's government was studying the New Zealand model and deciding, 'We need those tax advantages that New Zealand is enjoying.' As New Zealand's National government reversed its previous stance, the Australian government decided to adopt their trans-Tasman neighbour's policies for the industry.

Muldoon's decision would do almost irreparable damage to investment in New Zealand thoroughbred breeding, while for the next couple of decades the Australian industry would continue to forge ahead, unimpeded by being forced to compete against their nearest neighbours.

Cambridge Stud became a much sought-after work experience for young people from New Zealand and overseas, who were taken on each year to learn the ropes. In October 1984 one of those applicants was a fresh-faced 18-year-old from England — Adam Sangster, the third son of Robert Sangster. 'I want you to toughen him up and teach him how to work hard,' Sangster had said on the phone to Patrick, asking him to take on Adam for six months. 'There's only one place anywhere in the world that I would want to put Adam for a season, and that's your place at Cambridge Stud, because it is the most professional,' Sangster added.

Adam arrived, sporting fashionably ripped punk-rock jeans from London. 'Right, we'll have lunch and go straight to work,' Patrick told the boy. It probably wasn't the coolest thing to admit that he hadn't actually touched a horse before on a stud, Adam thought. He'd keep his own counsel and hope his Pony

Club days as an eight-year-old, before he was sent off to prep school, would stand him in good enough stead to muddle through until he picked up the gist of what was going on.

Patrick led Adam outside. 'Take this mare and go and put her down in the paddock.' All right so far . . . he followed the instructions and was back at the office within a few minutes to report the job done. Which paddock had he placed her in? Patrick asked.

'Well, as I was leading her down there, I looked over and saw a paddock that only had one horse in it, and I thought it must need some company. So I opened up the gate, put the mare in and . . .'

'You put the mare in where?' Patrick interrupted.

'Umm . . . I put it . . . down there . . .' As Adam described where she was, he found himself addressing thin air. Patrick had shot off in the direction of Paddy's paddock. Fortunately the mare survived, but she was moved out very quickly.

The horse world had always been there for Adam. At his famed old public school, Harrow, the standard reading matter for pupils was — as it had been for generations past — the *Racing Post* or *Sporting Life*. Break time came at 11.00 a.m., and Adam would always take the period before off so that he could retire to a place called The Hill where he would sit down with his carbon copy book and hand out chits to schoolboys who came in wanting to have a bet. It was a great little gambling den.

His father's highly publicised life had always been there too. His father's closest friend, Ross Benson, was a leading gossip columnist on Fleet Street who worked for the *Daily Express*, thus ensuring a plentiful supply of stories. At Ludgrove, his prep school, his mother Christine Sangster would phone the headmaster to seek his cooperation. 'Any time there is something written about Robert, could you please cut out that page?'

She was used to reading about her husband rather than seeing him, because he was, in Adam's words, 'always gallivanting around', but it was a different matter where her sons were concerned. With them she was protective, knowing if there was nothing in the newspaper, the other pupils couldn't rib the Sangster boys about their father.

You will never have to work harder than I do, Patrick had promised Adam on arrival — this was his motto, he said. Well, that was true. It was hard — the hardest work Adam could imagine. It included mucking out boxes, raking the gravel, running around from dawn till dark, surviving primal initiation ceremonies with Patrick as gleeful ringmaster — the sort that would amaze even an English public schoolboy — along with being on the receiving end of practical jokes handed out by Shane Keating or grooms Russell Warwick and Marcus Corban. But there was also the hearty breakfast dished out by 'Mrs H' for the unmarrieds every Tuesday morning to enjoy, and getting to know the horse-breeding business — as was his older brother Ben, who had also been sent on a learning mission to Colin Hayes' Lindsay Park Stud in South Australia.

But, best of all in those early weeks, Adam experienced at first-hand the miracle of birth. Two of his father's mares, the incomparable Eight Carat, and Biscalowe, were in foal to Sir Tristram, and both were due to deliver their foals. Maybe it was pre-ordained by the Gods, given the parallel racing futures of the two glamour Sangster colts, because they arrived within minutes of each other on the same night. Adam was there to help foal the first to emerge, an attractive black foal with four white socks, who he would later name Kaapstad, while across the paddock Biscalowe's foal, Marauding, also shot into the world.

It was the most incredible feeling in the world to watch a foal being born, Adam enthused to Russell Warwick, who suggested he should capitalise on his mood of euphoria by phoning his father to see whether the foal could be leased. Robert agreed to the proposition and, barely four months out of the classroom, Adam found himself a 50 per cent owner of the lovely foal he had brought into the world. Of the other 50 per cent, 40 per cent was shared between Shane Keating and Patrick, while the remaining 10 per cent went to Robert's racing manager who had pushed the deal through.

Adam's six months' stint in New Zealand was at an end, and en route back home he stopped off in Cape Town (or Kaapstad in Afrikaans) where he chose his foal's name. He had revelled in working first-hand in the racing scene and, on returning to England, he applied for a job writing for the racing publication *Timeform* that was established in the dour Yorkshire town of Halifax.

To his deep chagrin, Adam failed the interview. His mother suggested that instead he should make his career in banking, suggesting, 'Why don't you try the City?' That comment led to seven years with Capel's investment bank in London, before he decided to head off to Hong Kong to further his career as an investment banker.

But the lure of racing and horses was too deeply ingrained. After three years spent working in Hong Kong he told his mother he had decided to make his career in the thoroughbred industry, working for his father's Australian Swettenham

Stud, an hour's drive northeast of Melbourne. His time spent at Cambridge Stud, he said, had shown him the life that he wanted to pursue.

Christine Sangster, who had often warned her son there was nothing worse than horse bores — 'All they can talk about is horses, booze and sex . . . it's as boring as golf or cars . . . women hate that. You'll never pick up a woman!' — then confessed that she had rung the man at *Timeform* in Halifax and told him not to give Adam the job.

Adam crossed the room, kissed her on both cheeks, and said, 'That was the best thing you have ever done.'

CHAPTER 9

THOSE HEADY DAYS
AT TRENTHAM

*'Through the 1970s and into the '80s, Patrick led most of
the Cambridge Stud yearlings through the Trentham ring
himself, and there was no better sale ring presenter.'*

— John Costello, racing editor of the *Auckland Star*

T HE RAIN THAT teemed down on the Trentham National
Yearling Sales in January 1985 reflected the bittersweet
mood of many. The free-spending spirit was still there, but the
end of an era — so cherished by many of its participants — was
looming on the horizon. The decision, under the driving force of
Michael Floyd, the general manager of Wrightson Bloodstock,
had been made. Trentham was to lose its hosting right for the
National Yearling Sales.

Trentham's annual yearling sales which, combined with the
Wellington Cup meeting at Trentham racecourse, had set the
scene for a heady week in the capital city for close on 60 years,
were to be relocated to the Auckland area within two years.
Predictably, the Wellington community and southern breeders

187

were greatly upset by the news. Deputations from Wellington City Council, the city's restaurants, hotels, racing industry and southern stud farm interests urged Wrightson Bloodstock to reconsider and keep Wellington as its venue. The city depended on the income from the annual sales, they said. Floyd remained unmoved by their pleas.

Northern thoroughbred breeders, including Patrick Hogan, were the prime instigators of the move. Inexorably, the heartland of stud farming had moved north — principally to the Waikato region — and they objected to hauling their horses on the lengthy and winding 12-hour journey by float. Theirs were valuable cargoes, and the longer the journey, the more vulnerable their precious charges were to being injured, they argued. Somewhere around Auckland, at just two hours' drive from the location of the bulk of the Waikato studs, was the obvious choice.

A northern breeders' delegation approached Wrightson Bloodstock and, in Joe Wall's words, 'held a gun to our heads. They said to us, "If you don't build a bloody sales complex in Auckland, we will." Then they went to Michael Fay. He was in for anything in those days and he said, "Yeah, I'll do it," so we had to do it.'

And if further argument was needed, Wrightson Bloodstock now faced a threat to their monopoly of the business from the old stock and station agent company Dalgetys, who had entered the bloodstock business in the early 1980s, building a number of stables at Te Rapa in Hamilton where they commenced the sale of yearlings at the Claudelands Showgrounds.

In anticipation of the move north, Michael Floyd had shifted his office from Wellington to Auckland in 1980, commuting between the two cities throughout the first half of the 1980s while preparing the ground for the change of venue. First, Floyd had to find what he considered to be the right spot for the sales complex, and then he had to ensure that the new home of the National Yearling Sales would be of a design, style and ambience that could foot it with the best in the world.

Of one thing he was certain: at the new venue he planned to adopt many of the innovations that Patrick Hogan had introduced to Trentham — marquees, hospitality tents, fine food and refreshments, quality table cloths and napkins. On the national scene, he would apply the same attention to hospitality detail that had long been the stamp of the Cambridge Stud.

Trentham had stood for so many things to so many people within the industry for as long as they could remember. The genial Hawke's Bay brigade would arrive for the duration, with well-stocked picnic hampers in their car boots; they'd clubbily group together behind their cars to enjoy a gin and tonic, a beer, or freshly cut sandwiches while chatting over the detail of the day's sale. Farmers and breeders from the South Island, from Manawatu, Wairarapa or Wanganui, would converge on Wellington, the men to enjoy the racing and yearling sales, their wives to relish a week's shopping or browsing at the quality department stores of the calibre of Kircaldie and Staines or the D.I.C. (Drapery Importing Company).

To top up the magic, there was the well-heeled and party-loving Australian cluster of buyers, breeders and trainers who would come to do serious business on the buying front and then join the fun when the day's work was over. Convivial nights at the James Cook Hotel were common, where the liquids flowed and the piano was called into action with 'The Princess' — aka Jane Lowry — singing in inimitable style.

There would also be the fun of a couple of days at Taupo en route, where Patrick took his client friends for some fishing on the lake in Olympic coxswain Simon Dickie's launches. Bart Cummings would drop a crate of champagne in at the water's edge, and Phil Vela would cook fresh-caught trout over the fire on some beach where the boats had pulled in for a late lunch, the aroma of newly baked bread and an ice-cold beer or two wafting over the water — food for the Gods. It was the larrikin stuff of a few days' break from a tough industry.

'Tell you what, let's give The Commander something to chew over,' Geoff Murphy suggested one year to one of his Aussie mates, using one of the 'titles' that Patrick was known by in the industry. 'Let's mark his entries on my sales catalogue with a bit of rubbish. Then we'll leave it lying around and see if he's a snooper!'

Methodically they trawled through the pages, scribbling 'No good' . . . 'No!' . . . and similar comments alongside Cambridge Stud horses, while pumping up yearlings from other breeders: 'Bid high' . . . 'Yep' . . . 'Go to $500,000' . . .

As they readied themselves to drive down to Wellington early the next morning, The Commander gave both Aussies a cool reception. 'He's read it!' Murphy exulted.

Along with their colleagues in the industry, Trentham was the highlight of the year for the staff at Cambridge Stud. In the words of Cambridge stud groom Peter Stanaway: 'Everyone loved going down to Trentham. Twenty or thirty of us would get down there the night before the sales began, staying in the old

Taita Hotel, which was pretty rough — mattresses set out row by row in the bloody bottom bar that would be open all night, people rolling over in beds, hopping down the fire escapes, jumping on the train to go into town when you weren't supposed to. Patrick paid all the bills, but he didn't pay for any alcohol, ever!'

And from farrier Laurie Lynch: 'At Trentham, one day a bloke came in holding a black satchel. He had jandals on and was wearing shorts — he was a scruffy-looking bugger. He wanted to see the yearlings! He looked as if he didn't have two bob to rub together — we all ignored him, thought he was a waste of time.

'He said he wanted to buy one of Patrick's horses — that black satchel held nothing but cash. He bought himself a Sir Tristram yearling, probably for at least a couple of hundred grand, and then he had to count the money out from that old black satchel! Dunno how the horse went later . . . '

For Joe Walls, the reason why Trentham worked so brilliantly was because there were no stud farms in the area. 'It was almost neutral territory. Everyone stayed in the same hotel — the old James Cook — and it was like party town for a week. All the breeders, all the overseas guests — it was a lot of fun and a great race meeting. Auckland's Karaka would later provide a far better complex, but there was something missing. Wellington had real atmosphere.'

The former racing editor of the *Auckland Star*, John Costello, recalls: 'Though the National Yearling Sales had a 40-year history at Trentham when Patrick began to make his mark on the scene, it's probably accurate to say that, for most of those decades, the spring breeding season was the focus of attention for most studs, and the stud fees their stallions generated was the main income stream.

'The Trentham sales were, for many, a great social scene — though, of course, also the stage where the progeny of the stallion put the spotlight on their sire and, through the prices they fetched, brought greater or lesser patronage to him in the coming season.

'The young Patrick Hogan had a different approach. Though stud fees for outside mares were, of course, important to him, Patrick focused his attention on the yearling sales from the time he set up Cambridge Stud. The Trentham sales were, as he would later say, his Melbourne Cup. And he attacked them as if it was a military operation. Staff were bussed to Trentham, their individual tasks and responsibilities clearly delineated.

'In those days many yearlings were led through the Trentham sale ring by handlers whose appearance ranged from smart to downright scruffy. The Cambridge Stud staff were not only required to be smart — they wore Cambridge Stud uniforms. Patrick may not have been the first vendor to have a hospitality tent out by the stables — rumour has it that he hauled down the old Hogan family tent used for their holidays at the beach in those first few years — but he and Justine and the family, including his sister Pat, certainly adopted that aspect of the sales with enthusiasm, with the usual Hogan thoroughness and on the usual Hogan scale.'

Innovation on the hospitality tent front belonged to David and Masey Benjamin of Field House Stud (later Fayette Park) who were the first people to take marketing to the racing fraternity. But Patrick was a fast learner. The following year he produced brochures, staff sporting Cambridge Stud monogrammed polo shirts, a lean-to campervan and tent, tablecloths, napkins, fine food, flowers and wine — Cold Duck and Barossa Pearl, soon to give way to better wines — for his invited guests. Later it would become silver service, a show-stopper that almost halted the sales.

'What's he doing all that for?' people snorted. Hospitality was unknown on this scale, said Joe Walls' wife, Wendy. 'Patrick got the edge with his marketing. For a person who hadn't seen a lot of the world it was quite remarkable — all natural thinking.'

John Costello concurs: 'He was a masterly promoter and marketer, and much of his work had already been done prior to the sales (through inviting and hosting potential buyers at Cambridge Stud on a previously unprecedented scale) or outside the sale ring. Through the '70s and into the '80s, Patrick led most of the Cambridge Stud yearlings through the ring himself, and there was no better sale-ring presenter. As smart and well groomed as the young thoroughbred he was leading, he would always move the horse briskly round the ring — no slovenly amble for horse or attendant — and he knew exactly where the potential big buyers were . . . Tommy Smith, always in that corner there; Bart Cummings over there by the exit; the Foysters or the Inghams (or whoever the new and perhaps temporary big boys on the bench might be), up there, six rows back. And he would stop in front of each of the big players, presenting the colt or filly right in their face.'

But to win them, you've first got to woo them. Patrick introduced a classy catalogue of Cambridge Stud yearlings, and personally spent up to $300,000 a year to fly over 20 or more Australian trainers to the sales, where they were treated as royalty from go to whoa. They responded by buying up large, and familiarising themselves with the top New Zealand bloodlines and their hosts in 'the Shaky Isles'. Patrick reckoned he also did the Aussies a big favour socially, 'because when we block-booked the seats on the plane from Melbourne to Sydney, we had all these blokes — who had only previously nodded to each other at racecourses — sitting alongside each other, staying together at all the hotels and partying up large at Taupo before or after the sales. Many of them ended up becoming good mates.'

In close to 30 years, gun Australian trainer Bart Cummings had never missed a New Zealand National Yearling Sale. He was a big spender on his equine purchases, but never an incautious one and was wised-up to most of the tricks in the book where horses were concerned.

In the mid-eighties, the then current fad for buyers was to measure a yearling's heart rate to gauge its potential racing ability, but at the 1985 sale Cummings' preoccupation had broadened to include that of horses' girths. The first Patrick knew about this was when Cummings' son, Anthony, and one of the regular Cummings entourage arrived at the Cambridge Stud stable block at Trentham, saying: 'We want to measure the girths of your horses if we can.'

'Certainly, that's OK,' Patrick shrugged.

Patrick's job would be to hold the horse in the box while they slipped a string — marked with lengths on it — over the girth of the horse, they explained. Ha! That's what Bart was after, Patrick grinned when he looked at the string marker. They were looking for big girth horses —big girth, deep bodies, bigger heart. Well, he would help that process along if he could. Instead of holding his horse on the near side to the two men, as was usual, Patrick slipped around to the other side, putting his hand under the string to give the horse an extra half or three-quarter inch girth.

The trio repeated the process through the rest of the Cambridge Stud yearlings, an artful hand providing a valued extra notch on the marker. Anthony Cummings and his colleague left with thanks. 'I bet I've got the biggest girth horses on the show ground, so we're going to crop the best,' Patrick grinned. He'd put a good one over Bart.

The following morning, Patrick received a second visit at the stables, this time from Bart Cummings, who came straight to the point. 'Sonny, I'd like to measure those horses of yours again, the girths, and I'll be doing it myself.'

They went into the first box. Patrick stood on the other side and Cummings said, 'Sonny, would you come round this side, please?'

'But J.B.,' Patrick protested, laughing that he'd been caught out. 'I can't slip my fingers in behind on this side.'

'No you can't,' retorted Cummings. 'I knew there was something. Your girths were far too big.'

One of the regular big-spending Australians at Trentham was Nick Columb, a Melbourne businessman, horse owner and breeder. He first met Patrick in the late 1970s in New Zealand at the Trentham sales. This is Nick Columb's story.

'New Zealand racing was really flying in the late 1970s through to the mid-eighties. It was party place and that's why we went there! All of these bloodstock investment companies, like Troy Corporation, were involved — they were picking their favourite clients and flying us over at their expense.

'They would pick us up in limos and fete us in Taupo, with fishing on the lake, large dinners, and so on. We'd process down the country from Auckland via the studs. I liked to travel with my trainer Ross McDonald, who looked like a sumo wrestler, and my vet Jack Sewell, a giant of a Scotsman who always wore a green and red tam-o'-shanter. I was the little one. We would go to see the horses before they loaded them on the trucks, because it was interesting to see how the trip in the float affected them.

'We always stayed at the James Cook which was a den of iniquity. We had a lot of fun — there was a lot of drinking, and a lot of running around late at night. When we got to the James Cook, invariably our booking wasn't there, so we'd give the guys behind the desk some money and they would mysteriously find that booking! Every year we went through the same process with the barman, of keeping the bar open until four or five in the morning, by just continually giving him money! Everything was available for a price at that time.

'Patrick was a young cheeky fellow — very cocky. He had an answer for everybody on anything. He always wore a pale blue denim shirt — they were the Cambridge colours in those days. That's how I first remember him at Trentham. What got me at first was that he was the boss of Cambridge Stud, which at that stage was not well known or marvellously popular.

'I had the habit of going to New Zealand during the year to inspect the foals after weaning, and when they turned one. Then, if I liked something, I would buy it at the January sales so I'd already seen them a few times. I used to drop in and see Patrick quite a bit. I vividly remember one occasion in 1980 when I arrived unannounced. Justine and Patrick were in the kitchen of their little house on the right of the entrance to the stud (everyone used to think the stables was the house, because their house was a little brick shack). They had a laminex table which was covered with all these papers.

'They had just worked out that they had a $6000 overdraft, and they couldn't work out how they could get rid of this debt to the bank. That's how close things were. Paddy's first crop had just come through. After that, as they started to perform, all those worries disappeared.

'I loved Trentham — the racetrack and the atmosphere — but it was a pain in the bum going way out there with a hangover. We always looked forward to seeing Patrick because he was the little general. You would arrive there and the troops would be organised, the food was organised — he introduced a luxury and an ambience that would encourage sales.

'He would see you coming and he knew what you were looking at, so the game was always to trick Patrick a bit. If we were interested in THAT one, we wouldn't look at it — we'd look at it when others were looking at it. His horses would go for 200, 300, 400 thousand dollars more than we would pay.

'I think that my horse Tristarc, a filly of Sir Tristram, was the one that slipped under his guard. I paid NZ$130,000 for her at Trentham. I'd seen her in the paddock earlier in the year at Cambridge Stud and she was little, but she was mean — I could see she was just a scrawny little thing. She was a bay and she looked tough — a bit of a scrapper. I liked her dam, Renarc, and Sir Tristram was the sire, so when Tristarc came into the ring, I couldn't believe that he'd sell her, but he did.

'Patrick used to lead them into the ring, which was an event in itself, and he could hardly keep her feet on the ground — she was rearing. I bought her and Philip Vela, who was standing behind me, said, "What did you buy that bloody thing for?" and I said, "To beat you one day, my son!"

'She came back to Australia to live on my farm on the Mornington Peninsula. I reared her there and broke her in. She had 14 starts before she won. She showed some promise, but she was hopeless in her races. We persevered; she was just ratty in the head. With her it was more a mental thing — she needed all the little marbles to fall into place.

'In 1985 I sent her to Adelaide to an old jockey called Glynn Pretty for his opinion on her, because all the track riders were telling me she was sensational, but in 14 runs she couldn't win a race, even the bush races. I needed to get somebody I trusted, and I trusted Glynn Pretty's opinion. When he got on her, the first thing he said was, "This will win on Saturday." He rode her in an 1800-metre race in Adelaide and she won. It wasn't anything flash, about three rungs up from a maiden, but all the marbles had fallen into place and she knew how to win.

'Then after that she only ever won five other races, and they were all Group 1s! She was unbeatable. We discovered she had an amazing tolerance to pain — she could sprint for 1000 metres.

'Her second win was the AJC Derby which, for a three-year-old filly, was rare because it was such a demanding race, and she followed that with an all-the-way win in the Queen Elizabeth Stakes at Randwick in April, beating some very good horses on the way. Then she came back in the spring as a four-year-old and won the Underwood Stakes, the Caulfield Stakes and trumped her four previous Group 1 wins by taking out the Caulfield Cup.

'Her jockey was a fellow called Wayne "Smokey" Treloar, who had been a top apprentice, and had been with Tommy Smith, but had later fallen on hard times. I saw him one day at the Werribee races and said to him, "Look, I've got a couple of nice fillies. Do you want to come and ride them in work?" and he said, "Oh, yeah."

'They called him Smokey Treloar because he always used to stand around with a smoke in his mouth. We rejuvenated old Smokey. On the AJC Derby Day I had to send my wife to pick him up because I knew he wouldn't turn up. She had to find him — he was hiding. He didn't want to turn up, because he didn't think Tristarc could win. The other reason was that he was very angry with me.

'I had two three-year-old fillies, Tristarc and Centaurea. In Adelaide, I put the great English jockey Lester Piggott — who happened to be touring Australia — on Centaurea and they won the 1985 Australasian Oaks. I had put Piggott on and taken Treloar off. Then in Sydney I put (Mick) Dittman on Centaurea, because I thought that I had the AJC Oaks organised for her, and I would run Tristarc in the Derby.

'I booked Smokey for Tristarc and he was very reluctant. We had forced him to come up to Sydney for the Derby, and he was bitching and blueing all morning. He got on Tristarc, went out and won the Derby, and he looked at me as I was leading her in after the race and said, "You're a bloody freak."

'Then after that, we couldn't get him off her. It rejigged his career. He won the five Group 1s on her, including the 1985 Caulfield Cup, the richest race of its type in the world. To show you how good Tristarc was, in the lead-up to the Caulfield Cup, Smokey had been wasting all week with spas and saunas. His toes had cracked, an infection had got in and gone up his lymph system, and he had this huge swollen leg. 'At three in the morning on Caulfield Cup day, he rang my trainer, Ross McDonald, who was in Epsom [Victoria], and said, "I can't ride her. I'm crook, I've got a fever." So Ross jumped in his car and went over to him, made him put his jodhpurs on, put the boots on and stood over him, saying, "You're riding."

'Caulfield Cup day was terribly hot that year. When Smokey came out into the mounting yard I was absolutely boiling, and he's shivering and rubbing his hands up and down his body. So I said to him, "Jeez, it's cold isn't it?"

'He said, "Do you reckon it's cold?"

'"Yeah," I said, "it's freezing!"

'He said, "Oh good, I thought it was just me."

'In that Caulfield Cup, which is considered the roughest and toughest 2400-metre handicap race in Australia, Tristarc had drawn barrier 16 and, before the race, when Smokey was still on the same planet, we made a decision that she should be dropped out to last.

'As it turned out we didn't need to say a thing. Tristarc took it into her own hands — she went around every horse in the field, took off at the last 1000 metres to make sure she had enough time to get to the post, and then she barrelled them down. You could ride her in front, behind — didn't matter one bit to her performance.

'Smokey was in another world. He couldn't remember the ride at all. He went past Our Sophia who came second, yelling, "See ya later, Harry" to her jockey [Harry White], which he also doesn't remember, and won the race by a neck.

'He was unconscious when we pulled him off Tristarc. Somehow we managed to get him into the weigh-in room and then he was straight off to hospital in the waiting ambulance.

Smokey couldn't go to the celebration, couldn't do anything — he was gone.

'I then made the greatest mistake of my racing career — I didn't race her in the Cox Plate the following week. We were hoping to be invited to Japan for the Japan Cup and we weren't. It was then too late to get her into the Cox Plate, so we missed out — the horse that went on to win the Cox Plate had come fourth to her in the Caulfield Cup. She then ran fifth in the Melbourne Cup in bog conditions which she hated.

'Finding Tristarc was probably the greatest thrill in my years of racing, but she never mellowed. When we walked onto Caulfield, a strapper for my trainer Ross McDonald led her in — at that time the owners used to have to queue up at a booth near where the horses walked in. A fellow who had come across from South Australia to see his horse run that day was just standing there, mild as could be, and Tristarc walked in and double-barrelled him — no reason! She caved the poor bloke's head in. He ended up in hospital, and didn't see his horse run — Tristarc had fractured his skull.

'She was bad-tempered like her father and difficult, but she had this tremendous will to win. Tristarc just had to have her way. On her day she was unbeatable.

'Tristarc came after a small lull for Sir Tristram and proved to be one of his best. She earned about A$880,000 in stakes earnings, which was enormous money then. But, no doubt to me, her greatest performance of the five Group 1s was the Caulfield Cup, because she won from the outside in a large field, carrying a barely-conscious jockey on her back. She dictated the terms of the race and won it through sheer willpower.

'Tristarc was bad-tempered, skittery and so small. We were lucky — in those days we could use steroids to build her up. It was legal then, and that's what got her through her training. These days she probably wouldn't win a race.'

Sir Tristram had produced 'a couple of chips off the old block' in his two incredibly gutsy daughters who were to be the talk of the 1985 Melbourne Spring Carnival — Tristarc in the Caulfield, and Koiro Corrie May, the New Zealand grey mare, in the Melbourne Cup a fortnight later. Nobody in their right mind would have given Koiro Corrie May a bolter's chance of taking out the most prestigious race in the Southern Hemisphere. Even her trainer Dave O'Sullivan had — for the only time in his life — opted to remain behind in Matamata, leaving her in the care of the co-trainer, his son Paul.

Her Australian campaign had begun promisingly. Koiro Corrie May easily won the Geelong Cup to qualify, shoving her opposition aside with disdain. Then just four days out from the running of the Melbourne Cup, Paul phoned home to report that Koiro Corrie May had developed sore front feet and was a far-from-certain starter for the race. He was attempting to fix her using an old Australian bush remedy that someone had told him about and was putting cow dung on her feet. Dave was sceptical.

'Put me onto Lance,' Paul asked. His younger brother could fly over and take a punt that she could come right by Tuesday. 'It might be your one chance to ride in a Melbourne Cup,' he advised.

Koiro Corrie May was declared a race runner on the morning of the Cup, two things having worked in her favour. The cow dung remedy had worked, and a heavy fall of rain overnight had given the mare her preferred conditions underfoot. But unpromisingly, she had qualified in the number 24 slot, the cut-off figure for Cup runners, and had drawn an outside barrier at 18.

Koiro Corrie May was beaten in the final two strides of a magnificent race — she missed winning the Melbourne Cup by a short head to the aptly named What a Nuisance, ridden by Pat Hyland. She had tried her heart out, staggering over the line and cannoning into the running rail five or six strides after the winning post. Both horse and rider couldn't have done any more.

They had given the race their all and he was delighted with their second placing, Lance O'Sullivan told the waiting media as he dismounted. 'I've ridden her for most of her career and she's a lovely animal to ride, my old grey mare. I'm really quite fond of her. She is always tough in a tight finish and she just raced out of her skin today.'

Koiro Corrie May had previously broken down twice in her career, and now the demanding Melbourne Cup run had finally done for her. Koiro Corrie May was immediately retired to stud while Tristarc was to die while foaling at Cambridge Stud, three years later.

Michael Floyd was under heavy pressure from many players in the industry to build the new National Yearling Sales complex in the grounds of Ellerslie racecourse, home of the Auckland Racing Club, that was located just minutes from the heart of the city, but he was adamant he would not let it go there.

When asked his reason why, Floyd had a standard reply. He had lived with the constraints of Trentham being on the

Wellington Racing Club's land and he did not want to have a landlord again. 'I want a place that is surrounded with lots of green fields.' He was shown a number of potential sites, including one on Auckland Racing Club land at Takanini in south Auckland, but there was always some drawback.

Finally, in desperation, he hired a helicopter to fly over the Auckland environs and, at rural Karaka, near to State Highway 1, he found exactly what he was looking for. It was perfect from the air, and it was ideal when inspected on the ground. Karaka, on the border of Auckland and Counties, it was to be, and now that the purchase was complete, Floyd had to come up with an attractive and suitable design.

In September 1985 he had taken a young Wellington architect, Rod McDiarmid, overseas for a three-week tour to inspect sales complexes around the world. For Floyd, one of the great advantages in choosing McDiarmid was that the architect had never been to a horse sale in his life, so there were no preconceived ideas to battle with. It was not surprising that at each sales complex they visited they found something of note to emulate — from Saratoga in upstate New York, through Ireland and England, and finally to Deauville in France. The design of each had its own advantages, but the one that the pair were to get the most inspiration from was the Deauville sale ring, which they so nearly missed.

They were in England at the end of their travels, and it was suggested that they should take a flying trip to France to check out its design. Deauville was closed, but an obliging worker there let them inside and, within minutes, both were enthusiastically swapping opinions on what elements could successfully be adapted for the New Zealand scene. What they found to be almost the most interesting was the flat wall behind the auctioneer's stand, unlike most sales complexes where people crowded around the auctioneer's rostrum. That would be something to adopt for the Karaka complex, they agreed.

On returning to New Zealand in late September, McDiarmid told Floyd: 'You won't hear from me for four to six weeks. At the end of that time I won't bring you design drawings. Instead I'll bring you a model of the complex I visualise, so that you can take something tangible around the country to show your people.' And thus, in December 1985 McDiarmid produced his model of the Karaka auction ring complex. It was brilliant, Floyd enthused, as did other leaders of the industry. The only modifications required were two small alterations to the toilet and office blocks.

Karaka was to be built at a cost of $17 million for Wrightson Bloodstock, with Michael Floyd as general manager. McDiarmid became project manager, seeing the enterprise through to its completion at the end of 1987, in time for the first National Yearling Sales in January 1988. The Karaka Sales Complex was later recognised as the finest equine sale ring in the world.

Michael Floyd retired in 1992 and his colleague Joe Walls took over the reins. However, Walls says, Karaka's book cost of $20 million, coupled with the downturn in the New Zealand economy during the early 1990s, created major problems. 'We couldn't make the thing pay because I couldn't get that kind of return on investment.' Fletcher Challenge, the owners of Wrightson Bloodstock, also ran into financial difficulties, and the Karaka complex was onsold to the Vela family at a heavily reduced price. (In 2007, in a salute to the ambience of those heady Trentham days, the addition of a one-day Carnival

Sale was introduced at Karaka to coincide with the Auckland Racing Club's Auckland Cup week in March.)

GAI WATERHOUSE ON PATRICK HOGAN

'My first memory of Patrick was when I was a teenager being taken by my father [T.J. 'Tommy' Smith, the great Australian trainer] to the yearling sales and seeing him leading the horses around at Trentham. Patrick was always at the forefront then, and he has been ever since.

'When I did the "TJ" room at Tulloch Lodge I wanted it to capture — in a small Federation home — the achievements of my father. It's very much like that when you go to Cambridge Stud — the place is all about what Sir Patrick has achieved for New Zealand breeding. It just hasn't been for his generation, it's been for many generations, and he's still going strong. If Patrick doesn't go to Hong Kong or Australia or somewhere, Marcus [Cambridge Stud's general manager, Marcus Corban] will go in his place. Recently Laurie [Lynch] came over here from Patrick's stud and he's having such input in a major Australian racing stable.

'It's so funny — when I buy lots of horses from Cambridge Stud, the relationship is much healthier. If I'm not buying horses from Patrick, it's very terse and he gives me no end of an earful down the phone! He's very proud — and rightly so — of his product. As my husband Robbie, who has been a bookmaker for many years, says, "Be very mindful of the suffix NZ." Once a horse has that behind it and you get to a mile (1600 metres) plus, the difference is quite remarkable. Up to a mile, the Australian horse has a great advantage, but from a mile plus the New Zealand horse is so much better.

'It's a very tough world and Patrick has sharpened his teeth against the best. I wouldn't care whether he was in New Zealand, Siberia, or running a stud in England or Kentucky, Patrick would be supreme — he'd be the leading studmaster wherever he was.

'He's just got a remarkable ability to rise to the top, and he has this uncanny ability to choose a stallion — Sir Tristram, Zabeel and now Stravinsky . . . as every decade unfolds. He's a remarkable man.'

Gai Waterhouse Racing Stables
Tulloch Lodge, Randwick, 2007

CHAPTER 10

THE BIG CRASH . . .
AND EMPIRE ROSE

'To be successful as a breeder and a trainer, you have to have the feel, the love, the dedication to horses. As far as an investment goes, you have to clearly understand the value of a horse.'

— Patrick Hogan

THE BULLISH ECONOMIC mood sweeping New Zealand in the early months of 1987 was near-irresistible in its momentum. Sober citizens mortgaged their homes to the hilt in order to reinvest their capital in the stock market darlings — Brierley Investments, Judge Corporation, Chase or Equiticorp — and their actions were reflected in racing circles, where Trentham's swansong sales year reached dizzy new heights.

In January 1987 the yearling sales extravaganza produced a staggering 34.7 per cent increase in the sale aggregate over that of the previous year when 400-odd yearlings had sold for a total of $44,114,000. Presiding over the all-time-high total, one stud and one stallion utterly dominated.

Cambridge Stud's contribution was a net $11,640,000 of

which Sir Tristram grossed a massive $9,457,000 through the sale of his 39 representatives. Fittingly, the closest challenge to his supremacy came from another of Cambridge Stud's stallions, Danzatore, while third in the stallion stakes was Grosvenor, a son of Sir Tristram, who stood at Field House Stud.

As was becoming an increasingly familiar pattern, a record price was also set by a Sir Tristram yearling. A smart-looking bay filly by Sir Tristram–My Marsellaise (a three-quarter sister to Grosvenor) fetched $800,000 and went to Arthur Williams, a Wellington buyer, who fought off a stern challenge from Perth's Laurie Connell. However, in the big stakes, honours went to Tommy Smith, the legendary Australian trainer, who took home 38 yearlings at a cost of $4,113,000 — his purchases being headed by two Sir Tristram colts and a Danzatore colt.

Summarising the sale, journalist Mary Burgess wrote: 'Cambridge Stud was certainly out on its own in the race for highest grossing vendor. Having witnessed Cambridge's domination of the number one spot over recent years, the repetition of this feat should not provide more than a passing touch of déjà vu.

'The 1987 sale, though, was different. In 1986 Cambridge had amassed $6.1 million from the sale of 44 yearlings, and Haunui Farm, in second place, grossed $3.1 million. This year Cambridge opened up a huge break on the remainder of the country's breeders, earning $11.6 million from their 58 yearlings sold. With 26 yearlings on offer, Ra Ora Stud reclaimed the runners-up position with $3.2 million, while Haunui's 40 sales raked in a touch over $3 million.

'Cambridge also topped the vendors' averages with $200,689 (selling 58) followed by Blandford Lodge who sold 10 for an average of $178,500 . . . '

Asked by a newspaper reporter what he recommended for producing top thoroughbreds, Patrick replied: 'To be successful as a breeder and a trainer, you have to have the feel, the love, the dedication to horses. As far as an investment goes, you have to clearly understand the value of a horse. You have then got to work out what it's going to cost you for the stud fee to rear it, market it and then, before you market it, you have to look at the opposition.'

Patrick had once commented to his brother Peter, at Fencourt: 'I think the old man's losing his marbles. He's putting 80 mares a season to Blueskin! That's a ridiculously high number.' Thirty years on, similar accusations were now being levelled at Patrick, by those claiming that the astonishing fertility of Sir Tristram could only be explained if Patrick and his vet, Jonathan Hope, were practising artificial insemination (AI) with the stallion — an illegal practice within the thoroughbred industry.

How else, they asked, was it possible for any one stallion to serve a rumoured three mares a day without it affecting his fertility? That could total upwards of an incredible 140 mares per season! Even John Magnier of the famed Coolmore Stud in Ireland, who had a totally full booking of mares, worked on the premise of 60 mares per stallion. Anything more was impossible, the thinking went, even if the stud was losing money hand over fist.

Veterinarian Hope was forthright in countering such disbelief. 'We do not practise AI on our stallions! Through Sir Tristram, Patrick is the first person in the world to realise that a stallion can serve at least three mares a day without it affecting his fertility — and can do it three times a day for the X number of days that you've got in the total stud season. There is no reason why a stallion should be limited to 60 mares per season.'

Hope would explain that Patrick had gone to Ireland to discuss the subject with Magnier a couple of years earlier. 'How on earth is it possible to have a successful 95 per cent fertility rate?' they queried. Patrick talked Magnier around, said Hope, and convinced Magnier that 'the world's your oyster — you can do an unlimited number of three times a day.'

Magnier opted to take the risk and adopt the concept, and with the month-longer breeding season that operated in the Northern Hemisphere, his stallions were, in future, able to successfully serve a phenomenal number of mares — anywhere from 180 to 200 per season. What had once been deemed impossible by factions within New Zealand's breeding industry later became standard practice.

Sir Tristram was cleaning up all round. By 1987 he was Champion Sire of Australia four times during 1980–87 and the first stallion to earn in excess of A$4 million in one season. He was Champion Sire of New Zealand for the 1986–87 season and the comprehensive winner of the Dewar Trophy for Australia/ New Zealand combined earnings from 1980–81, and after that each successive year from 1982 through to 1987.

In February 1988 at Wrightson's first National Yearling Sales at Karaka, Sir Tristram's sire average for sales topped the table, both in volume (47 yearlings sold) and price average of $256,277, while Bletchingly, in second place, was a distant $175,000. *New Zealand Herald* racing writer Wally O'Hearn had written in 1986 that the fee for the outstanding stallion had increased by $40,000 to $100,000: 'That makes Sir Tristram the most expensive sire standing at stud in the Southern

Hemisphere. Standing at $60,000 last season, Sir Tristram served 94 mares and his fertility rate was 92 per cent. There were 423 applications for nominations for him for this year.

'Sir Tristram, at 17 years of age, has left 43 individual Stakes winners from six-and-a-half crops. In all he has left 34 individual Group winners, 21 individual Group 1 winners, 32 individual Stakes placegetters, eight Derby winners and three Oaks winners. His progeny has amassed total stake earnings of about $8.3 million. The original outlay for a share in Sir Tristram was $4000. Those lucky enough to have taken up one of the 40 shares have received a cash dividend in the vicinity of $53,000 since then.'

At home, grazing or charging around in his paddock, Sir Tristram was the star turn at Cambridge Stud, attracting a steady stream of visitors from far and wide, including one from the president of Ireland, Dr Patrick Hillary. The horse was often to be seen with his little friend Niggy, Patrick's black cat, who Justine, Nicola and Erin had brought from Fencourt and who liked to run dog-like in Patrick's wake as he strode around the farm, sometimes leaping onto a horse's back to get a ride home.

Niggy was something of a feature around the place —he was fond of sitting on the stallion's back, lolling on one of his paddock's fence rails, and perching up high as an interested spectator to watch Paddy 'perform' with the mares.

But Paddy's manners with the human race had not improved one iota, in spite of the increased exposure and admiration he was receiving. On one memorable occasion, he turned his back and farted loudly on a delegation of well-dressed men and women from the local Chamber of Commerce who had enthusiastically anticipated their afternoon with the famous horse. 'In the wild, Paddy would have been the King of the Forest, the king of the herd,' Patrick liked to describe him. 'No doubt about that. He totally dominated other horses.'

And no doubt at all that at Cambridge Sir Tristram was the king, albeit of one large tree-lined paddock bounded by black post-and-rail fences and a good-sized box in the stables. A king who, aside from Niggy, tolerated no one intruding on his patch — including the sparrows who had the temerity to land on his ground.

Young Cambridge accountant John Ryan had first come into contact with the Hogan family in 1956 after receiving a phone call from Tom Hogan one afternoon at his office. 'I'm having a bit of trouble with them tax boggers. Can you come and see me at my farm tomorrow?' he asked. Then Hogan added: 'I've just bought a horse called Blueskin and I want you to do the accounting for it.'

Nothing could have been closer to the heart of horse-mad Ryan. As a boy in Wanganui he had gone to his first race meeting at the age of 10, and began serious betting a year later at the ripe old age of 11. This was the sort of client he could relate to. The following day, as requested, he drove out to Fencourt and, in Ryan's words, 'This fine-looking young man, who was introduced as Patrick, led this horse out, and that's how I came to start doing the Hogan books.'

More than 20 years after that first meeting with a Hogan stallion, Ryan encountered Sir Tristram standing in his 'flash box' at Cambridge Stud. Conversationally, the accountant nodded in the horse's direction: 'By God, you're a long-backed bugger.' Then, says Ryan, 'This horse turned around and looked me straight in the eye and the force of that look almost set me back ten feet.

'I've never had an experience like it in my life. I thought, "Whew. We've got a bloody handful here . . . the guys who handle him must be very brave men." I went home and said to my wife, "I've just struck an enormous personality and it's a horse!"' After that initial meeting, it was never to surprise Ryan that the stallion threw such quality horses because of the strength of character he possessed.

Naturally, the Sir Tristram phenomenon and the rise and rise in Cambridge Stud's fortunes were mirrored at the modest first-floor office of Ryan's accountancy practice, located a street away from the township's main road. 'The whole thing just blew up like a balloon and so our work increased accordingly,' Ryan later reflected. 'People were coming at us from all directions, trying to get shares in Paddy. The money that was changing hands was simply incredible.

'From being just one of my clients, Cambridge Stud grew so rapidly that it was taking more than 20 per cent of our time. I had a young girl, Corrina Holmes, working in my office who, by 1985, I assigned full-time to Patrick's work. I spent a lot of time on Patrick's stuff as well — it was growing like Topsy. There was just so much happening.

'One day Patrick came to see me, and I said, "I know what you've come here for! You want to shift part of my office to Cambridge Stud and have Corrina working for you there." So that's what we did.'

Corrina Holmes started work at Ryan's office straight out of school in August 1977, and in that first season she entered the returns for Sir Tristram's stud fee at $1500. The following year the figure had risen to $6000 . . . then $12,000 . . . $25,000 . . . $40,000 . . . and when the price freeze was implemented, everyone went to tender, and the fees shot through the roof. Now she was to shift to the hub of action at Cambridge Stud where she would share a pint-sized office with Margaret Fife, a keen young horsewoman who had come to work at the stud from Putaruru in south Waikato. Margaret's job included typing the stallion returns on an old typewriter, with no latitude for error. 'There was no way of correcting anything and going back,' she told Corrina.

By this time, Patrick was employing a dozen or more full-timers on his farm, a number which expanded to 45 during the foaling season. Many applied, few were selected. People came to him for work — he never had to recruit. He employed skilled, loyal, hard-working people, the bulk of whom were to remain with him for 20 years or more.

Marauding and Kaapstad — the two Sir Tristram foals who were born on the same night at Cambridge Stud in 1984 and were bred and owned by Robert Sangster — were set to race each other in the 1987 Golden Slipper, the world's richest horse race for two-year-olds held during the Autumn Racing Carnival in Sydney.

The Golden Slipper, run over 1200 metres at Rosehill Gardens near Parramatta in western Sydney, and the magnet for the crème de la crème of the nation's youngsters, carried a weight limit of 54 kilograms for colts and geldings, and 51 kilograms for fillies, and a total prize purse of A$1 million. Trainer Colin Hayes was looking to run both Kaapstad and another of Sangster's horses, Midnight Fever, in the Slipper, while fellow trainer Brian Mayfield-Smith wanted to run his colt Marauding.

According to Adam Sangster who owned 50 per cent of the lease on Kaapstad, his father was sitting at home in the Isle of Man and was on the phone to the two rival trainers on the eve of the big race. 'Dad said, "Right lads," to Hayes and Mayfield-Smith, "I've got a coin in my hands, and I'm flicking it — heads Brian, tails Colin . . . Heads it is — Brian, you've won, so Marauding will race and we'll scratch Kaapstad."'

Patrick had flown to Sydney with the expectation of watching Kaapstad — with whom he shared the lease with Adam Sangster — in the rich race, and went through the roof when told by one of Sangster's Australian managers, David Cole, that the classy colt had been a late scratching. 'A decision made on the other side of the world on a damned toss of a coin!' Patrick fumed. 'This is a huge race with huge stake money. Kaapstad has a pretty good chance of winning and I've flown over here to see my horse run! I'm very bloody upset.'

Cole told Patrick that there was a sound reason — as well as Robert's whimsical action in tossing the coin — for Kaapstad's withdrawal. If Kaapstad, who was considered the main danger, or any other horse in the race beat Marauding, his proposed sale as a future stallion for John Kelly of Avon Park Stud could be in jeopardy.

Patrick phoned Adam. 'Whose side are you on, your father's or mine?' he raged.

'Yours, but . . . '

'Yes, yes . . . I understand.' Patrick calmed down. 'Of course, you can't go against your father.' There was nothing further to be done.

Reluctantly, Patrick took himself off a couple of days later to Rosehill, to see how the other of Sir Tristram's sons would fare in the Slipper. Nothing else mattered now that he was sitting in the stand, waiting for the start of the big sprint race. Recriminations over Kaapstad faded into the background — more than anything he wanted the foal that he had once brought into the world to win.

With a thundering heart he watched as Marauding came from the back of the field to fly down the straight, bowling aside the opposition, and in the hands of Golden Slipper specialist jockey Ron Quinton, get up in the last stride to catch Lygon Arms on the post. Patrick's eyes filled with tears for his big wonderful, difficult, intelligent fellow Sir Tristram, who had become the first New Zealand-based stallion in 30 years to sire the winner of the Golden Slipper Stakes — his son Marauding. For Robert Sangster the thrill was every inch as great at Patrick's in winning his first Golden Slipper. 'It would be hard to better this,' he said.

Three days after the running of the Slipper, it was announced that Kaapstad was to be retired to stud at the end of his three-year-old season and that the colt had been bought by two New Zealand companies for $3.5 million. The NZPA reported that 'the purchase from international magnate Robert Sangster was announced at the weekend, with further details released yesterday by Kieran Moore, Australian manager of Australasian Breeding Stables Ltd.

'Mr Moore said the purchase had been completed by his company in association with Troy Corporation Ltd. However, he added that Kaapstad was to be syndicated into 50 shares at $70,000 and would remain in Australia. "It seems that the leading breeders to whom we've spoken agree with us that Kaapstad is the most exciting stallion prospect in either Australia or New Zealand at present," Mr Moore said. "Of Sir Tristram's 27 Group 1 winners, only this colt, Grosvenor and now Marauding have been successful in Group 1 two-year-old races at set weights. That's an elite group indeed.'"

In the 1986–87 season, which closed on 31 July in both New Zealand and Australia, Sir Tristram had amassed an incredible line-up of results:

- captured his fourth general sires' premiership in Australia — the past three in succession — and his first in New Zealand, becoming the first stallion since Beau Pere 40 years before to hold both the Australian and New Zealand titles;
- claimed the Dewar Trophy for combined Australian/New Zealand earnings for the sixth time, the past five in a row;
- earned just short of $4 million in prize money, doubling the previous earnings record of $1,982,215 which he set in the 1982–83 season;
- boosted his lifetime stud earnings to $14 million (just $5 million short of Northern Dancer's career total);
- became the first New Zealand-based stallion in 30 years to sire the winner of the Golden Slipper Stakes and win the Australian Champion Sire title for two-year-olds, his fourth sires' title for the season;
- appeared as a significant sire of broodmares;
- was represented by his 28th individual Group 1 winner, beating (by two) Northern Dancer's world record at the highest level of competition;

- at the January yearling sales his 39 yearlings fetched a staggering $10,654,000 — 25 per cent of the total turnover for 403 lots sold.

Assessing Sir Tristram's performance, Tony Arrold wrote in *The Australian*: 'With the death last month of Europe's finest stallion, Habitat, and the pensioning off from stud duties in April of the North American wonder, Northern Dancer, New Zealand may now make claim to having the world's best living, active thoroughbred stallion.'

It was too good to last. On 20 October 1987 the New Zealand stock market crashed, following the events of Black Monday on Wall Street, New York. Share prices fell by 59 per cent over a four-month period, and bloodstock shares, which had been so fashionable, went the way of the other glamour investments — down, down, down.

In the early days, commentators had regarded the drop in prices as a temporary correction in an overinflated economy, and urged the country's shareholders to keep their collective nerve and not panic. 'Don't sell! Strong bluechip shares will rise again,' they urged. *Personal Investor: New Zealand's Money Magazine*, in its November 1987 issue — which had gone to print before the stock market crash — had, ironically, chosen as its theme 'Shares Special', profiling in particular 'Kiwi companies with offshore profits', 'Hot Asian stocks' and 'Bloodstock winners'. Patrick Hogan was featured on the cover, holding the reins of his new stallion, Gold and Ivory.

The article's writer, Helen Vause, who had visited Cambridge Stud, put a conservative estimate of $40 million on the three grazing stallions — Sir Tristram, Danzatore and Gold and

Ivory — in the stud's front paddocks. In the article, Patrick spoke critically of many of the bloodstock syndicates that had been set up to gain tax advantages being offered by special partnerships, saying, 'Many investors have got their fingers burned. Frankly, many syndicates paid far too much for mares, and investors went into syndicates without having any hope of being able to realistically assess their return. They were not getting value for money.

'I am certain,' he continued, 'that of the approximately $100 million that has gone into special partnerships in the last couple of years, at least $70 million of it was very unwisely spent. What these investors bought was simply not worth the money.'

However, on the next page, in an article titled 'Blue blood stocks: If you cannot afford a racehorse, the next-best thing may be a share in his progeny', Lynda Thompson wrote: 'There is still strong interest in partnerships managed by such listed bloodstock companies as Allegra Corporation and Troy Corporation.'

'There were many ordinary people, excited at having the chance to experience the heady thrill of owning racehorses, who were badly burned financially by those partnerships,' said racing journalist David Bradford. 'By 1988 and beyond there was a whole army of disillusioned people — some of those people had families who saw what happened, and that probably took the gloss off the whole thoroughbred industry for the next decade and more. However, there were a few breeders who ran family businesses — like the Andertons in Dunedin and the Fells in Palmerston North — who hadn't got caught up in all the hype and they weren't too badly affected.

'When Patrick's syndicate with Fay Richwhite terminated, Patrick did the decent thing and bought into quite a good number of those mares himself. He didn't suffer too badly because — thanks to Sir Tristram — he was already strong enough to ride out the storm. He was probably better positioned than anyone else in New Zealand for the resurgence when it did come.'

Australia faced the same problems in 1988, Bradford said. 'However, they went about it in a different way. Melbourne got behind the racing fraternity in developing their Spring Racing Carnival, which was to became immensely popular.'

While optimists in the industry might hope that 1988 and beyond would see everything bounce back to normal, at Cambridge Stud they were taking no chances. 'We have to work harder, even harder,' Patrick urged his troops. 'We could be in for a long and rough ride.'

A New Zealand/Australian trainer and a good friend of Patrick's, Graeme Rogerson, had a top horse by Star Way in the late 1980s; he was entered for the Sydney Cup.

'There's no way in the world he'll win the Sydney Cup, Rogey,' Patrick said.

'I think he will,' Rogerson agreed to disagree.

'I will run naked up the main street of Cambridge if you win the Sydney Cup,' Patrick scoffed. 'And I will eat my underpants!'

Rogerson's horse won and that night, at a celebration party at the Southern Cross Hotel, he arranged with a girl to telephone Patrick in New Zealand, saying 'I'm Carol from Australian television. We have organised the TV cameras and they will be with you at eight tomorrow morning to see you running naked through your town and eating your underpants at the same time.'

It was late at night. Patrick and Justine were in bed when the telephone rang. As Patrick was saying, 'Oh no! . . . Who? . . . What?! . . . No, NO!' Justine woke and heard a girl's voice talking at the other end of the phone.

'What's going on Patrick? Who's that?' she demanded.

They telephoned him from Sydney the following morning at quarter to eight, but Patrick was not to be found.

Ask a racing man whether he would rather be granted eternal life or to produce a winner of the Melbourne Cup, and he wouldn't hesitate for a second. One of those 1988 optimists — whose optimism centred around a large and expensive chestnut mare who he had bred and reared at his stud — was Fred Bodle, a highly successful businessman and the owner of Whakanui Stud.

A decade earlier, he had famously relinquished his $4000 share in Sir Tristram, and had then been forced to pay $100,000 in 1981 to have his mare, Summer Fleur, served by Sir Tristram. This coupling produced a chestnut filly in 1982, who Bodle registered as Empire Rose, a name linking Whakanui's 'rose family' — Rosemere, Summer Rosa, Summer Fleur — with her size, because 'she's as big as the whole bloody Empire,' Fred laughed.

From the outset she was huge, always needing to have her food intake severely curbed to prevent her from becoming too heavily overweight. But she needed the feed, because she was growing like nothing the Bodles had ever experienced before. And here came an unexpected godsend. Fred Bodle had considered recouping his investment by selling her at Trentham, but after a visit from Patrick, who said, 'There's no way that she will ever get to the yearling sales: her epiphysitis [a knee problem associated with rapid growth] is so bad,' Bodle had changed his mind.

Fred and his son Tim, a veterinarian, immediately put her out into the paddock at Whakanui for a year, with no feed restrictions imposed on her diet. Empire Rose never stopped growing, recalls Tim Bodle. 'When she was a two-year-old she was nearly 17 hands high — she was huge! We were a bit worried, because not very often does a big horse come through. They say that size is everything, but when you get a horse of that size and with those knees, you can get chip problems. We weren't hoping for great things — we thought maybe she was too big.'

They decided to keep their concerns to themselves, break her in and see what transpired. Empire Rose was sent out to Cambridge trainer Laurie Laxon to do some preliminary work before returning her to Whakanui — the Bodles telling him they didn't want to push it too hard at that stage because of her problems.

Eventually her knees settled down and by the time she was a three-year-old she had grown into a great strapping mare. Now was the right time to send her into training with Laxon, Bodle decided. After her first gallop Laurie rang the Bodles in buoyant mood. 'This filly is something out of the ordinary!' he said. 'Even though she's big, she's got a fantastic stride and I think she's going to be all right.'

She had her first barrier trial at Tauranga over 1200 metres and won. She would never handle the wet well, but in her first test she won convincingly in the rain. Laxon swung around to Tim Bodle as she bolted past them, grinning. 'I told you she was pretty good.' She was, too. Tim sent a happy message to

223

his father: 'Empire Rose has won the trial — and daylight was second.'

Then she had her first race at Matamata. 'We were very confident,' Tim recalled. 'In the same race, Dave O'Sullivan had a horse called Haig running, and there was another horse called The Cowboy. I saw Dave before the race and asked him if he had a horse running.'

Yes, and he's pretty good, came the crisp reply.

'Oh well, we've got a horse running in this race and we think she's pretty good,' Tim retorted.

'You won't beat my horse,' O'Sullivan was confident.

Haig won, The Cowboy came second, and Empire Rose finished third. Whakanui's connections were deflated. However, it transpired that there were three very good horses competing against each other on that occasion, with Haig later winning 12 races and The Cowboy 10.

They took Empire Rose to Hamilton for a start at Te Rapa in a 1600-metre race. She led all the way, won in the fast time of 1:34 and from then onwards she was in full stride with Tony Allan, the apprentice jockey for Laxon, who rode her throughout her campaign. She travelled to Ellerslie to compete in the Group 1 Royal Stakes where she was to run against another of Sir Tristram's daughters, the well-performed Royal Heights, and came second to her. However, Empire Rose was later disqualified after giving another contestant in the race a hefty bump as she came hurtling around the bend, causing the other horse to almost disappear from the track, after being catapulted 15 horses sideways.

The filly's next outing came at the Wellington Racing Club's Group 1 New Zealand Oaks where, again, she took on her rival, Royal Heights. They fought all the way along the straight, with Royal Heights beating Empire Rose by a nose and Eau d'Etoile coming home in third place — Sir Tristram horses finishing one, two and three. Later her breeder, Ross Douglas, told Bodle this was the race that finished Royal Heights. 'She never recovered after that. She had given it everything and Empire Rose had pushed her all the way.'

Five years on from that race, Tim Bodle bought Royal Heights as a broodmare. The two daughters of Sir Tristram — Royal Heights and Empire Rose — who had been born just weeks apart, were to share the same paddock for the rest of their days. 'They had fought each other on the track, then they became the best of mates until they were well into their twenties,' Bodle said. 'They were only parted by death.'

The Bodles decided to send four-year-old Empire Rose to Bart Cummings in Australia, but she did not handle the stable environment well, partly due to her size. One problem the mare battled with throughout her career was a proneness to corns on her big, flat feet. Despite this, Cummings got her up to the stage where she came second in the Dalgety Handicap, which qualified her for the Melbourne Cup.

She ran fifth in the 1986 Melbourne Cup which, the Bodles considered, was not a bad effort for a four-year-old, because she was still quite weak, said Tim. 'We decided that with all the problems in her feet and her corns we would bring her back home to Laurie. She lived out on the paddock and everything was a bit more settled.

'In that year it was a very wet spring, and we couldn't get any races into her — I think we had a 2100-metre race at Te Rapa and she came 15 lengths last! That was a week before the Melbourne Cup. Laurie couldn't work out what had gone wrong — she'd been training well — so we got a heart scan. One vet said, "Put her straight in the broodmare paddock, she's got bad eurhythmia in the heart," but our vet, James Blakely, did another heart score on her and gave a different opinion, saying, "It's just a temporary thing. She'll be all right."'

Laxon made the decision, saying, 'We'll keep working her and see what happens.' She looked pretty good to him, he said, the following day, and the Bodles agreed. They took her to Australia a couple of days before the Melbourne Cup and she performed brilliantly, coming second to Kensei.

Following that stirring performance she was flown from Melbourne direct to Christchurch where she won the 1987 Lion Brown New Zealand Cup the following week — this, despite a split off-fore hoof, suffered in the Melbourne Cup, which needed constant attention from a young Cambridge blacksmith, Garry Carvell. Such was Carvell's devotion to Empire Rose that he flew to Melbourne before the Cup to nail huge 45-centimetre plates to her feet barely minutes before she lined up. A week later at Riccarton he hammered on her size eight plates — an average horse wears size four or five — only 20 minutes before the field left the starting barrier.

The Bodles truly did have the champion they had long dreamed of. With some confidence, they could now aim their campaign for a 'third time lucky' crack at the Melbourne Cup in 1988.

Empire Rose arrived at the 1988 Melbourne Spring Carnival to compete in the Group 1 Mackinnon Stakes, with odds of 66–1 against the crowd's hero, Vo Rogue. 'The Vo', as he was known, was as popular as he was able. Nevertheless, Empire Rose came from last and won it on her ear. Afterwards, an Australian commentator said he had been talking to Laurie Laxon before the race. 'Laxon said to me, "She just needs a good blow out." 'Well,' the commentator opined, 'if that's a blow out, on Tuesday it's going to be an explosion! She will win the race by as far as you can kick a football on a windy day.'

In the wake of her outstanding performance, an elated Fred Bodle paid for his family to fly over to watch the Melbourne Cup. Empire Rose was starting as favourite. Luckily for her, the weather was good and she was relaxed — in typical pre-race mode she put her head down and had a nap. Like others of Sir Tristram's progeny, she was relaxed before a race but very aggressive during it, and never hesitated to kick other horses after a race or push people around. She would intimidate other horses because she was so big, said Tim Bodle. 'She'd just look them in the eye or she'd give them a bump. Wow, she loved racing.'

Empire Rose had drawn barrier 23. Laurie Laxon took 20-year-old Tony Allan for a walk around the track before the race and told him the race tactics. 'Tony, you've got to get up handy — one back, one out — and just chug along. Keep her as quiet as you can.'

The media, interviewing Laxon prior to the race, asked, 'What are your tactics for the Cup?' Laxon shrugged: 'Well, I've drawn 23, so we're going to get her up handy and drive her along the straight, one back, one out . . . '

The pressmen were incredulous. 'Why are you telling anybody your tactics before the race? Some of the other runners might start doing the same.'

Laxon grinned. 'Have you seen the size of Empire Rose? She's 17.1 hands high and 635 kilograms in weight — probably

100 kilograms heavier than any other horse in the race. No horse is going to bump her out of the way, because we're going to be right up there.'

Laxon got exactly what he wanted. Tony Allan had her tucked in behind the leading horse, then she took the lead on the turn and forged ahead down the long Flemington straight, beating the fast-finishing Natski, ridden desperately by Mick Dittman, by a whisker.

Speaking to a huge throng of press after his mare's triumph, an excited Laxon admitted that his horse could have lost the race if Natski had not drifted in on her in the closing stages. 'What won it for Empire Rose was that Natski ended up alongside her. When he ranged up to her girth, she started fighting him. If he'd stayed out wide, he probably would have beaten her. It's simply that she wanted to race him.

'She's a real fighter — when horses are wide apart it's not the same. She's very aggressive, especially when she's had a hard fight and won. If anything runs up her backside pulling up in a race where she's had a fight, she'll lash out and kick them.' By contrast with her mood when racing, at home Empire Rose was the perfect lady, he added.

Asked what he remembered of the race, Tim Bodle admits, 'It's a blur. I was in such a daze, Natski was actually in front of Tony Allan when they crossed the line, but Empire Rose's head was in front of Natski and her body was behind. So her size had triumphed! For the family to watch our big girl win the great Flemington race was like an amazing kind of dream. We all went off to the big Cup dinner that night on cloud nine.'

Australians had also taken the chestnut mare to their hearts, none more so than Therese Glennon who lived on the Gold Coast, loved roses and was a strict Catholic. At church she prayed for Empire Rose to win the Mackinnon Stakes, then backed her prayers by staking her all — $2000 at odds of 66–1 — on the New Zealander. She watched the race on television with her heart in her mouth, and realised that, for the first time in her life, she was a wealthy woman.

But while 99 per cent of the human race would have happily pocketed the A$132,000, Mrs Glennon was made of sterner stuff. She returned to church the following day, prayed once more for the horse with 'rose' in its name, then plunged her entire winnings on Empire Rose in the Melbourne Cup at $3.50 for the win. Empire Rose had not let her down in the Mackinnon Stakes, she said — she won't let me down in the Cup either.

Therese Glennon won nearly half a million dollars, enough to form a family trust for her children to go to the schools that had always been beyond her financial reach. From that day onwards, she sent a large bunch of roses to Peg Bodle every year on the day of the Melbourne Cup.

After her Melbourne Cup win, Empire Rose was invited to compete in the Japan Cup, but the Bodles declined as they thought it was too far for her to go. (It took another six-year-old New Zealand mare — Horlicks — that travelled to Japan the following year, 1989, to win the world's richest race in world-record time.)

Empire Rose returned in triumph from the Australian spring campaign to compete at her favourite New Zealand track, Trentham, in January 1989 — she was never to win at Ellerslie, preferring the big free-running left-handed tracks. Naturally the 'big rose' started as favourite for the Wellington

Cup. Richard Holden, the head of Foster's beer who were sponsoring the race, was so confident she would win he had a special victory rug made for her, emblazoned with the words '1988 winner Melbourne Cup and 1989 winner Wellington Cup'.

The huge mare became an even hotter Wellington Cup favourite when she won the first-day Trentham Stakes by five lengths. But she failed in her bid to add the Wellington Cup to her trophies cabinet.

It rained before the race — they should have scratched her, but they didn't — and Empire Rose was beaten. 'You may as well keep the rug as a souvenir of what never happened,' Holden laughed. 'Take it home as a memento,' which is exactly what they did.

Four months after winning the Melbourne Cup, Fred Bodle suffered a massive heart attack in March 1989 and died the same night.

In 2007, Tim Bodle reflected: 'It was sad, but, knowing Dad as we did, it was a great way for him to have gone out — on top of the world and with the goal of his lifetime achieved.'

Empire Rose never amounted to much as a broodmare. Once, in desperation, Bodle put her to Pentire, a small stallion, to try to breed a medium-sized foal. Clearly, with Empire Rose's height, there was a need to think outside the square to achieve success on this front. Whakanui Stud staff dug a two-foot-deep hole for Empire Rose to be served, but even with this aid, Pentire could only get one leg over. 'The other leg was left dangling in the air!' Bodle laughed. The combination produced a large 17-hands-high colt that was bought by Bart Cummings.

Great good may have come from Fred Bodle's decision back in 1978 to opt out of his share in Sir Tristram, Patrick believed.

'Had he not gone down the track he did, Fred may never have bred Empire Rose. It ended up so beautifully, because he got a Melbourne Cup winner out of it at the end. And we were both so happy for one another.'

A decade later, Patrick and Tim built the Prince Albert Hotel in Cambridge as a commercial investment, and today Hogan is a trustee for Tim's children. 'We've carried on the friendship,' smiles Bodle. 'Patrick's looking after me, like Dad once looked after Patrick when he was a cheeky young guy.'

TONY ARROLD ON PATRICK HOGAN

'Sir Patrick stands alone in the world of breeding in one sense. I don't think there's anyone who can touch him in the modern days of breeding when you consider his situation.

'He's a hands-on stud guy who has developed a rampantly successful stud operation, and continues to run it as a family operation. He's there every day doing that. Look at the success he has had — the mere fact that he has had two world-class champions stand there, and one which came as the consequence of the first one — Sir Tristram and now the reigning champ Zabeel.

'When you look at Sir Patrick from a worldwide situation you will find that there will be very, very few major organisations, breeding-wise, that can touch him. You look at Coolmore and even that was started up by three multi-millionaires, and probably none of them — apart from John Magnier — would have spent a day at the stud. Even in America, all those big families have just passed it on from generation to generation.

'Hogan's situation is so completely unique in terms of where he sits every day, looking out over his own property, running his staff, running an organisation that you would have to say has been one of the best in New Zealand, full stop. I just marvel at the guy — what he's achieved over all these years and how he's managed to keep repeating it. What was the last result out of Karaka? He's had 26 consecutive years as the leading vendor. You just don't get stats like that anywhere — anywhere! And you're talking about first-class bloody products here.

'To achieve what he did with Sir Tristram was quite bloody amazing, and then to turn around and secure a horse like Zabeel when he had so many options to choose from. He waited and then he zeroed in on Zabeel — a decent chip off the old block.

'One of my early visits to the stud, when Patrick had just been there for a year or so, was when he had Surround on the property. Surround had just had a foal and I was prowling round — I was doing the Air New Zealand Stakes — and I didn't have a camera. Here was this legendary mare with her first foal, and I was desperate for a photo, so Patrick organised someone to come out from Hamilton and take it, and then shipped it over to Australia for me. That's marketing for you!

'I don't want to overindulge in the fellow, but I would go so far as to say he is unique in the world today. In all the studs around the world, he wins it by the length of the home straight.'

Editor, thoroughbred section, *The Australian*
Sydney, 2007

CHAPTER 11

WHEN THE QUEEN CAME TO LUNCH

'We hosted the Queen for lunch at our home, and from time to time I still think, "Was she sitting at our table or not?" That to me is the greatest award. It is recognition greater than the CBE.'

— Patrick Hogan

THEY FIRST MET in 1986 on the royal yacht *Britannia*, at an Auckland luncheon hosted by the Queen. On receiving his invitation, Patrick assumed he was one of a couple of hundred guests attending the event, and was astonished to see a handful of people waiting to board the yacht.

Then H.R.H. Queen Elizabeth II arrived, direct from Ellerslie racecourse after attending a rally for schoolchildren where an activist had flung an egg at her. She immediately went to her apartment on the ship to change. Her guests were told, 'Her Majesty will be with you in a few moments, but as you go through, would you please familiarise yourselves as to where you will be seated for lunch.'

Then came a hell of a shock. Patrick saw that he was sitting to the left of the Queen, while on her right was Sir Tom Skinner, head of the Federation of Labour. 'There were 12 of us seated at this huge table,' he told Justine later that day. 'To my left was the Queen's lady-in-waiting. When we sat down, the Queen turned to Sir Tom and spoke with him.' That was quite a relief, Patrick confessed to the lady-in-waiting — he was so nervous, he didn't know what to say. 'I've got news for you,' she replied with a smile. 'Her Majesty is very good at these things. You will both get half an hour to speak with her.'

Thirty minutes later, the Queen turned to Patrick. Naturally, their conversation was horses, horses and horses. To his delight, Patrick found the Queen was very well briefed on Sir Tristram, and she knew about the other horses he had at Cambridge as well, far more than he knew about her horses at the royal stud farm at Sandringham. 'She broke the ice beautifully with me by saying, "Don't you think you're a bit greedy, sending so many mares to your stallion?"' he told Justine.

'I said I didn't think so and explained why, but I had one up my sleeve too. I said, "Well, you know, you've got an exceptional stallion yourself, ma'am. I see that he's served some 50-odd mares and got 50 in foal. That's unheard of for a stallion to be so highly fertile," and she came back at me, quick as lightning, saying, "Well, I've got an Irishman as a studmaster!"'

Things were ticking over smoothly until dessert arrived. Patrick was horrified to see brandy snaps, with cream protruding from each end, on their plates. 'How on earth am I going to deal with this?' Anguished thoughts raced through his head. 'I'm a noisy eater, or so everyone tells me. How can I avoid making great crunching noises in the Queen's ear? Worse, what say I take a bite, and the cream shoots out of one end and spurts all over my clothes?'

The Queen, reading his mind, leaned towards her guest. 'I'd give the cream a short sharp poke if I were you.'

'Oh, right.' With relief, Patrick got the handle of his spoon and pushed the cream to the middle. The Queen then followed suit.

As their allotted time was drawing to a close, Patrick said, perhaps cheekily, that he was 'quite disappointed' the Queen hadn't come to Cambridge Stud when she visited neighbouring Middle Park Stud to see the great Balmerino, who had raced so successfully in the Northern Hemisphere, adding, 'If you happened to notice that face peering through the boundary fence, ma'am, it was me!'

The Queen answered that she did not get to choose where she went — that decision was left to the Department of Internal Affairs, although the Palace had to approve it.

'It would be great if you could come and visit us on your next trip to New Zealand,' Patrick suggested. And there the matter rested.

More than three years later, in October 1989, Patrick received a call from a man claiming to be from the Internal Affairs department in Wellington, informing him that on her upcoming visit to New Zealand in February 1990 to attend the Commonwealth Games festival and officially open Ellerslie's new grandstand, Her Majesty Queen Elizabeth would be pleased to pay Cambridge Stud a visit.

'Yeah, yeah, Philip Vela, I'm not that stupid that I can't recognise your voice,' Patrick laughed, 'I know you're having me on.'

He was most certainly 'not having him on' the man replied.
'Oh, go on, of course you are.'

'No, no,' the man protested, 'I am telling you the truth, and I would like you to ring this number to verify it.'

'Phil, I'm not ringing any phone numbers for you! Goodbye.' And with that, Patrick put the phone down.

Within minutes, the telephone rang again, with a different voice asking Patrick to please call a certain number urgently. Hmmm . . . the number given certainly started with the 04 code for Wellington. What if the caller, whom he had just rubbished, a flustered Patrick thought, had actually been for real?

The phone was answered on the second ring. 'Mr Hogan,' the voice at the other end of the phone volunteered, 'I'm the person who has just called you about the Queen's proposed visit.'

He was truly sorry and apologised for his reaction, an abashed Patrick explained. 'I, um, thought it was one of my mates playing a joke on me, because I honestly thought this could never happen.'

Her Majesty the Queen had made a special request to see Cambridge Stud on her visit, the official said, and details of the procedure involved would follow by letter. Patrick got off the phone in a state of dazed shock. The Queen of England was coming to visit them at Cambridge Stud!

The itinerary and schedule arrived through the post shortly afterwards. The Queen was to visit them on 4 February 1990. Would they be happy to host Her Majesty for lunch? 'We are going to have the Queen sitting down at our table in our house for lunch —' Justine repeated incredulously on hearing Patrick's news. 'Good grief!'

At the time it was, in Patrick's words, 'all go' at Cambridge Stud, with the foaling season in full swing. The yearling sales were coming up in late January, and the Queen's visit would follow a few days later. Although the gardens at Cambridge Stud were looking a picture, they had to be improved by 50 per cent, the perfectionist Hogans decreed. No question about that, and no question about 'instant gardens' doing the trick — Justine and Patrick would commence their planting programme the following day.

As the news got out, Patrick told a journalist he saw the royal visit giving the racing and breeding industry a tremendous boost that could prove timely after the recent downturn in the yearling market.

The security procedures they had to go through were surreal to the New Zealanders, who were used to a relaxed, security-free lifestyle. 'We had to submit a copy of every passport of our staff who happened to be working for us at that time,' Patrick later recalled. 'As usual, we had a number of young people working for us — Irish, French, English. We had lots of people at the stud from the Northern Hemisphere and they all had to be checked out.'

The visit was to be on a Sunday, coinciding with the Hogans' wedding anniversary, and the Queen was to travel from Auckland after attending morning service at the Anglican Holy Trinity Cathedral in Parnell. Later, Patrick was told confidentially that the Queen had asked the Dean — the worldly and genial Very Rev. John Rymer — to keep the sermon short as she was travelling down country directly after the service 'to see my animals'.

From Cambridge Stud she was to be driven further south to Otorohanga, for an afternoon stop at the Ferdon Jersey

Stud. The farm's co-proprietor, Warren Ferguson, told media: 'About 80 per cent of the Queen's Windsor stud farm have the bloodlines of Ferdon stock,' adding, 'We have been exporting cows to the Royal Windsor Stud for 15 years.'

The Hogans were requested to submit a choice of menus offering different alternatives — including wines — to Internal Affairs which they would send onto the Palace for the Queen to make her choice from. ('No brandy snaps!' Patrick ordered their regular stud caterer, Ian Metcalfe of Hamilton.)

In the build-up to the royal stopover, the stud, which had grown into an equine paradise of 600 acres, and their attractive new home, across from the stud in Discombe Road, were put through a painstakingly thorough security sweep. A day before the Queen was due to arrive, the police brought sniffer dogs and searched the place from end to end. They planted a dummy bomb in Patrick and Justine's bedroom, and had one of the dogs find it. They combed the ceiling, the house, the environs of the house and the farm. On the following morning — the day of the Queen's visit — the routine was repeated. Then the entire property was ringed by a contingent of eagle-eyed British and New Zealand security police.

It was swelteringly hot at 27 degrees Centigrade as, on schedule, the royal entourage arrived at the stables. The Queen climbed briskly from the car, smiled and said to Patrick, 'We've met before,' immediately putting him at ease as he introduced her to Justine and their family — daughters Nicola and Erin, and toddler grandson Patrick. They, along with staff at the stud, had been briefed before her arrival that the Queen was to be addressed as 'Ma'am to rhyme with ham, not ma'am to rhyme with farm'.

As they walked through the stable area, then onto the service barn and crush area, Patrick felt a huge sense of relief sweep over him. The Queen was so relaxed. There could be no reason, by anything that she was saying, for him to be nervous. She was down to earth and 'fantastic'. At eight paces behind, Justine had a slightly more uncomfortable time of it, being told in a peremptory tone, 'Shhh! I'm talking,' by the lady-in-waiting.

Then followed an equine parade in front of the stables, first by their new sire, Gold and Ivory, closely followed by the stud's foundation mares, Taiona and My Tricia, with foals at foot. A little chestnut filly, by Sir Tristram out of Taiona, captivated all hearts when she timidly approached the Queen and licked her hand. Instantaneously, Patrick knew what the name of that filly would be. For her future racing career this filly would be known as Queen's Choice.

Then came the moment . . . 'Please, PLEASE, Paddy, behave . . . ' Patrick prayed silently as stud manager Shane Keating led out Sir Tristram. His stallion, sensing the occasion, was on his best behaviour, exchanging a regal glance with Her Majesty. As she patted the stallion's neck, the Queen recalled their 1986 conversation on the *Britannia* when she had jokingly chided Patrick on how many mares Sir Tristram serviced, saying to laughter all round, 'Well, it's not done him any harm.'

She was deeply interested in the horse, particularly in view of his age — 19 — and that he had served 85 mares that season. Also, she said, she was very taken by Sir Tristram's condition and physique, and that 'he runs out day and night and is not housed'.

'Mr Hogan praised the Queen's quick eye and expertise,' wrote the *Waikato Times*. "I had earlier pointed out that Sir

Tristram's conformation was always untidy behind," Hogan said, "and later — when the Queen saw his foals — she was quick to say he had not thrown that characteristic to the young progeny.'"

Patrick made one faux pas, which the Queen remarked on several days later, when they met at the opening of Ellerslie's new grandstand. He had instructed the bevy of cameramen attending the event to stay together on one side of the parade area, telling them they were not to move, so that when Paddy came out of the stable area, he would be facing them and they could get good photographs.

Obediently, the photographers remained rooted to the spot and, in the excitement of the moment, Patrick faced the horse the opposite way, so that the cameramen were looking at his back end as he was led up to the Queen, who patted his neck. When the photographs were published they showed the rear view of both.

Before the Queen's visit, Patrick had asked: 'Can we offer the Queen a horse? A foal?' and was told by her officials, 'No. Her Majesty thinks it is bad policy to accept presents of horses. The reason is that more often they would be unsuccessful than successful, and that makes it rather embarrassing.' However, Patrick did present the Queen with a horse as they posed for photographs in the gardens of Cambridge Stud — a bronze of Sir Tristram which had been commissioned from the Hamilton sculptor Rick Lewis.

It was time for lunch. With some hesitation, Patrick escorted the Queen through the front door of their home. As her host and after a two-hour plane and car journey, plus stud visit, the question needed to be asked, but how? 'Do you want to use the bathroom?' . . . 'Ma'am, would you like to go to the . . . ' For days he had mentally rehearsed different ways in which he should couch the question to the Monarch. Nothing sounded right. But the Queen read his thoughts. 'Yes, I would like to use the bathroom.'

On her return, Patrick asked whether she would like to have a drink before lunch — yes, she would like a gin — and then with their other guests, including Ross Finlayson, the chairman of the New Zealand Breeders' Association, the group walked through to the dining room.

Artfully, Patrick had planned the seating so that he and the Queen would sit facing outwards to see — beyond the dining room's glass sliding doors — an attractive tree-lined green paddock occupied by three mares and their foals. He instructed staff that, close to the paddock's rails and facing the dining room, they were to spread a generous portion of oats as he and the royal party were touring the stud, so that as they ate lunch the Queen could see mares and foals peacefully grazing, in her direct line of sight.

It fell into place beautifully. Partway through the luncheon the Queen volunteered to Patrick: 'You have something I do not — I can't look out of my window and see what we can see here.' Patrick smiled and thought to himself, 'Well, that worked!'

It was a relaxing, lovely lunch. The Queen set the pace from the outset by using their Christian names, kicked off her shoes under the table, and told Justine that on the *Britannia* she had been impressed when Patrick had spoken to her of the number of mares Sir Tristram had serviced, adding, 'I knew then that I would one day sit down at Cambridge Stud.'

Later, Justine told media that the visit was 'absolutely fabulous. Never in my wildest dreams could I have hoped that it would be better. From start to finish, everything went perfectly.' She had been 'terribly nervous' beforehand, Justine admitted. 'There was so much to do on the planning front. We were also given a list of things we couldn't talk about, i.e. the family, but there were subjects we could talk about, like children and horses. She was terribly pleasant . . . so lovely with Patrick, interested in everything.' Some days later, Justine was placed alongside Prince Philip at the races. 'Ma'm really enjoyed her lunch with you,' he said.

The brief visit, which had run so smoothly and happily, came to an end. The Queen presented her hosts with a signed photograph of herself, and as the royal party drove away, Patrick and Justine were left with a delightfully, homely memory of H.R.H. Queen Elizabeth II — her head out of the royal car window and her body swivelled around, snapping a photograph of the Hogans with her camera.

Three-year-old Sir Tristram filly Tristanagh had been named New South Wales Racehorse of the Year in 1989, her outstanding record of seven Group wins and two second placings from nine starts for trainer Bart Cummings winning her the award by a single vote from Victoria Derby winner Stylish Century. Earlier, a historic moment was captured in the 1989 *New Zealand Thoroughbred Racing Annual*, showing a beaming photograph of two men.

Its caption read: 'Cambridge Stud's Patrick Hogan congratulates Japan's Hyakutaroh Kobayashi on the purchase of

New Zealand's first million-dollar yearling — the $1.2 million Sir Tristram–Surround colt sold at the Karaka sales.

'Kobayashi said he would have gone higher to buy the top-priced colt, whom he fell in love with four months before the sale. "I saw the colt at Cambridge Stud when in New Zealand for the Horses In Training Sale the previous September, and was always going to be the one to beat in the bidding duel."

'Bart Cummings also paid one million for a Sir Tristram–Winter Folly colt.' (A year earlier Cummings had gone to his 'absolute limit' in paying $750,000 for a Sir Tristram–Eight Carat filly.)

It was an event that bucked the post-crash trend. The following year's annual reported a decline of nearly 50 per cent in trade value at the 1990 National Yearling Sales, which saw turnover fall to 1984 levels.

The state of the New Zealand and Australian economies, the tightening of credit facilities by the auctioneers Wrightson Bloodstock, and a drop in the quality of entries were all contributing factors to the most pronounced problem — old faces absent, and those old faces who did attend buying less. The exception was Ingham Bloodstock, the company led by brothers Jack and Bob Ingham, who saw fit to increase its activity by 38 per cent, paying $3,822,000 for 26 lots.

The publication also detailed a controversy that had erupted at the sales between Patrick and Wrightson Bloodstock:

> The love affair between Cambridge Stud's Patrick Hogan and Wrightson Bloodstock became tense and stretched at the Karaka National Yearling Sales. Hogan was openly critical of Wrightson's dramatic credit cutbacks for potential buyers. The action came

as no shock to many in the light of the bloodstock company being left in the lurch for unpaid millions on purchases from the 1989 sale.

For Hogan, the company's move was responsible for a good part of the dramatic drop in sale prices, claiming that Wrightson employed poor business practices by cutting the credit line from 30 days to 14 days. 'Having only 14 days to pay is ridiculous,' Hogan says. 'I'm not suggesting they give a whole lot of credit to anyone, but there are good clients who have played the game all along the way. Wrightson is saying because there are a few bad guys, the good clients have to sit in the sinbin with them. I'm certainly not saying I'm disappointed with my sale; but there are many smaller breeders taking a hiding who would have got better prices for their stock if Wrightson had had a better attitude.'

Wrightson general manager Michael Floyd's initial reply was one word: 'Rubbish.' He went on: 'Nothing has changed. We have never guaranteed credit. Admittedly we have put in the conditions that buyers are required to pay within 14 days, but that will be fairly loose.' The real tightening, said Floyd, was that half a dozen or so bad payers or non-payers from the previous year's sale were advised that if they attended the sale, their bids would not be accepted.

Part of the cooling of the relationship emanated from Hogan splitting his top drawer draft between Karaka, the Gold Coast Magic Millions sale, and

Sydney's Australian Easter sale. [The rift was repaired later when Patrick confirmed he would be consolidating his full strength behind the 1991 Karaka National Yearling Sales to the exclusion of the Magic Millions.]

The Karaka offering was down 30 per cent in terms of quality, but Hogan has no truck with those claiming he helped to sink the ship at Karaka. 'I accept no responsibility at all,' he said emphatically. 'If you want to survive in this business, you must be prepared for change. I judged 12 months ago that there would be sticky times ahead because of a tremendous oversupply of horses. At the same time, preparing and marketing 60 to 70 horses for sale, as I did last January, was becoming too much for the one sale. For that reason Cambridge Stud decided to select yearlings best suited for the three major sales in Australasia.

'Cambridge Stud sold 40 yearlings at Karaka's premier session and they accounted for 30 per cent of the aggregate from a catalogue of more than 500. So it is simply being unrealistic to lay the blame, even part of it, on the stud.'

Sir Tristram was the least affected by the downturn of the leading stallions, but that wasn't to say he had an uneventful season. Patrick was forced to put a temporary halt to the superstar's activities in September 1990 when a mare the stallion had been serving lashed out and caught him flush on the head.

Sir Tristram went down for the count, but like a true champion got up off the canvas and five days later resumed serving the blue bloods. 'It wasn't critical, but it certainly hurt him,' said Patrick. 'It wasn't serious enough to call in the insurance companies, but we did have him on round-the-clock treatment for 48 hours.'

Mike Dillon, editor of the *New Zealand Thoroughbred Racing Annual*, lamented in his editorial: 'It's a crying shame racing is so inextricably tied to the state of the economy. The lifeblood of almost every other sport or recreation does not depend on the economic health of the country. Rugby fans will still abound at a test match, regardless of any economic downturn. But it is an inescapable fact that if there is not a spare dollar in the punter's pocket, the punter doesn't bet.

'When the harsh realities of the New Zealand recession hit home through 1990, racing began to suffer in the hands of an alien force over which it had absolutely no control. It was the final nail in the coffin for some aspects of racing which were already taking the strain . . . '

As an example, Dillon profiled two disastrous plunges by racing clubs — the Avondale Jockey Club's venture into night racing, and the Auckland Racing Club's $25 million grandstand, which had been opened by the Queen in February 1990, claiming: 'The disastrous factor was that the parlous state of the economy kept people from both attending race meetings and betting off-course, which, coupled with crippling mortgage interest rates, placed the two clubs in a financial squeeze.

'Budgets, made by necessity several years earlier, were unable to be kept to. Those budgets were calculated in buoyant times when attendances were rising, if not spectacularly, and there was no suggestion of a stock market crash or general downturn.' Avondale Jockey Club's on-course turnover dropped from $13 million in 1986 to $7.6 million in 1990, Dillon reported. 'Clearly with attendances and turnover dropping, the club could not service its debt.'

As patron of the New Zealand Equine Research Foundation, formed in 1976 and based at Palmerston North, Patrick was outspoken on the need for awareness and responsibility in the field of equine research. 'The world has become so much smaller,' he told thoroughbred breeders. 'We're part of the globe now, with many of our horses being exported and imported.

'There are countries which have more problems than we do, and we have to have in place the systems to counter these problems if they ever reached New Zealand. We have a responsibility to support the research foundation, especially as we're growing so fast. It's always been a business, but never a bigger business than it is today, and it has to have the back-up.'

He criticised a local lack of support for the development of equine research, and said that his concern reached across the whole equine spectrum — for sport horses, work horses and racehorses. 'They're all built the same,' he said. 'It only makes sense to approach them that way.'

Dr Brian Goulden, a member of the foundation, who had been seconded from Massey University's veterinary faculty and who was internationally known for his work in a wide range of equine fields, concurred with Patrick's comments, adding: 'Mr Hogan's involvement is particularly appropriate for the foundation because of his prominence in New Zealand's most visible equine sphere and his support of other disciplines.'

Shortly after delivering that speech, Patrick was back in the headlines, declaring that professionals were needed in the racing industry. He was, he said, concerned by the number of young people entering the racing industry who believed they could gain job promotion on the basis of their practical experience. He admitted that he had made it to the top by learning from his mistakes and having some good luck. But, he said, people could no longer rely on experience at 'the university of hard knocks' to get them through the ranks.

'Twenty or thirty years ago, a young bloke could make a decent living through knowing his horses and having the gift of the gab,' Patrick declared. 'A farmer could turn his property into a thoroughbred stud and become an owner-operator. But those days have gone.' There was no shortage of young people who were good with horses, he said, but there were nowhere near enough with business skills.

He said he would be right behind any move in New Zealand to establish an intensive business and horse management course, similar to the one provided by the Marcus Oldham College horse management course at Geelong in Victoria. 'We need training that will give us young people with business skills and the ability to deal with clients, public relations, accounting and staff management.'

The course at Marcus Oldham College covered a broad spectrum of stud and stable management, farriery, fencing, welding, mechanics, pasture and plant management, real estate, stable construction, equine health and nutrition, law, bookkeeping, public relations, taxation, marketing, insurance and staff management, he said. As well, two three-week study tours of New South Wales and New Zealand were held during the course, and the students spent a day each week visiting various businesses for hands-on experience.

Cambridge Stud had joined forces with Waikato and Blandford Lodge studs to sponsor a young woman from North Canterbury for the year-long course, Patrick said. Another horse management student from Cambridge was also being sponsored by eight standardbred studs.

In 1991, Patrick received the BMW Award for Outstanding Contribution to Racing Excellence, and was awarded the CBE (Commander of the British Empire) in the New Year's Honours list for services to racing and the community. *Waikato Times* racing editor Phillip Quay, after outlining his services to racing, then wrote of Patrick's extensive activities and generosity within the community.

'Recently he held an open day at Cambridge Stud, raising $162,000 for a Life Education Trust mobile classroom to teach children the dangers of drugs, after watching the ravages of drug abuse kill one nephew and ruin another. Mr Hogan said if his efforts could help save just one child, it would be worthwhile. He and his wife donated $80,000 to the trust.

'Mr Hogan is patron of the Waikato branch of the Epilepsy Society, patron of the Cambridge Chamber of Commerce, a trustee of both Tourism Waikato Incorporated and Waikato Sports Foundation, and supports the Air Ambulance service. Last year he "called up a lot of favours" to meet a $12,000 shortfall in an appeal on behalf of a Cambridge infant, Charlie Rainer, who needed a liver transplant.'

There was another group in the community — and intrinsic to the hopes of Waikato rugby supporters — who also benefited from Patrick's generosity. In 1988, Patrick, Nelson Schick, Tim Bodle and Alan Jones — described as 'Cambridge "horse men" and passionate Waikato rugby supporters' — were among those who became major sponsors of the Waikato Rugby Union's R & R Club, an initiative that aimed to help out financially and retain the province's leading players.

The province had seen proud days in its history, but by the end of 1985 the unthinkable had happened. Waikato was relegated to the second division of the national competition for 1986, and avoided the same fate for the 1987 season by just a single point, winning the second division decider against North Harbour 13–12 thanks to a hair-raising last-minute try.

It was time for action. A player on the brink of All Black status was given financial support by the R & R Club to buy his first house; another was encouraged to travel north to play for the province. By 1989 Waikato was again a force to be reckoned with, back in the first division, and the province finished second in 1990, its best-ever placing.

Waikato All Black Matthew Cooper said that support from the R & R club made a huge difference to players' morale. 'When we went down to play Southland, a handful of the R & R boys came along too, which we all thought was great. Patrick was appointed our "water boy" and he rushed on and off the field with all the enthusiasm of a little kid!' In 1992 at Rugby Park in Hamilton, before an emotional team of R & R supporters and 32,000 cowbell-ringing fans, Waikato — bristling with stars and an All Black front row in Richard Loe, Warren Gatland and Graham Purvis — went on to win its first-ever first division NPC title, demolishing Otago 40–5.

'Such is the esteem Patrick Hogan is held in in this country that his name cropped up in speculation as a contender to become Governor-General some years back,' wrote Cambridge journalist John McMenamin. 'His bearing and leadership qualities are such that he would not be out of place in high office. Amongst the most striking features of one of Cambridge's favourite sons — outside of his outstanding success as a thoroughbred breeder — are a rare dignity, humanity, modesty and utmost integrity.

'Cambridge owes a great debt to Mr Hogan and his wife Justine for the care and loyalty they have shown this community. The local racing fraternity have good cause to rejoice in the special recognition given to Patrick Hogan, CBE.'

The *New Zealand Herald* wrote: 'The CBE awarded to Patrick Hogan in the New Year's Honours (1991) recognises the achievements of a man who has brought a new approach to the New Zealand thoroughbred industry.

'Mr Hogan has opened up new dimensions in the marketing and promotion of thoroughbreds, traditionally the realm of sheep or cattle farmers with time and money to spare . . . He is the complete professional, renowned as one of the most astute and effective businessmen in the industry worldwide. He has become a role model for other breeders striving to present the same professional image and achieve the same degree of commercial success.

'He has developed Cambridge Stud into Australasia's most successful thoroughbred nursery, with its land and bloodstock holding conservatively valued at $20 million . . . In the New Year's Honours list, he receives one of the top awards, becoming a Commander of the British Empire.

'"I feel deeply honoured and extremely proud," he said. "I have always striven to do the job right and am extremely proud of the standing that Cambridge Stud has attained. But it's not only the personal recognition; it's the recognition of our racing and breeding industry that has thrilled me. This is an award for which all New Zealanders involved in the thoroughbred industry can feel proud."

'Mr Hogan still rates the visit of the Queen to Cambridge Stud as the highlight of his career. "It was a tremendous thrill to receive a request from Her Majesty to visit the stud," he said. "We hosted her for lunch at our home, and from time to time I still think, 'Was she sitting at our table or not?' That to me is the greatest award. It is recognition greater than the CBE."'

CHAPTER 12

ZABEEL — THE 'PRINCE OF HEAVEN'

'Our passion for the sport of thoroughbred racing, as much as anything, stems from an understanding of the animal, which has been passed from father to son, for over 150 years.'
— Sheikh Hamdan bin Rashid Al Maktoum, Deputy Ruler of Dubai

ACROSS THE TASMAN, as Dr Grace was cutting a swathe through all-comers in the manner of his illustrious cricketing namesake, another outstanding son of Sir Tristram was preparing to reverse the trend and return home to the two horses' birthplace at Cambridge Stud. Both had been born in 1986, both were bred by Robert Sangster, both were sold at the first yearling sale at Karaka in 1988, and both enjoyed great success on the racetrack.

'If you want Derby winners, you've got to go to New Zealand. There are only two horses coming up at these Karaka sales who could possibly give you a second Derby win,' New South Wales trainer Dr Geoff Chapman said to Sydney businessman John Denoon on the eve of the sales. 'I'll buy you one or the other.'

The first of Chapman's two choices raced to $650,000 in the bidding, more than $200,000 over the Denoon price limit, while the second — Dr Grace — sold to Chapman for $210,000 in the bargain of the decade.

By the age of four, the fine-boned Dr Grace was firmly established as Sydney's glamour galloper. Bred from an Australian mare of Sangster's, English Wonder, who resided at Cambridge Stud and who had been a classy and versatile galloper in her prime, Dr Grace was to have a glittering career, chalking up victories in a series of Group 1 races: the Chipping Norton Stakes, the million-dollar BMW International, the Underwood Stakes, the Chelmsford Stakes, and — the race his owner most coveted — the AJC Derby.

Dr Grace had started third in the betting for the 1990 AJC Derby, with Stylish Century, the punter's choice, setting a cracking pace. At the 700-metre mark, jockey Jimmy Cassidy gave Dr Grace a light flick with the whip and, in a lightning move, the horse pounced, moving easily into fourth position. At the bottom of the Randwick straight, Stylish Century was in front by three lengths, with Dr Grace closing. The 'Doctor' then wore the favourite down, stride by stride, in a soul-stirring effort to win by half a length and render John Denoon near-speechless with emotion.

'I apologise, my voice has gone . . .' Denoon croaked to the crowd from the winner's podium. He, whose racing interests had always lain with distance or classic racing as being the true test of a horse, was the proudest man on Randwick racecourse that day — maybe the proudest man in the world.

He had owned the champion Myocard, bought from Sir Henry Kelliher and raised on Puketutu Island in Auckland, who Chapman had singled out for him at Trentham and who had won Denoon the Derby in 1987; and now another Kiwi, Dr Grace, had presented him with a magnificent double — victory in the 1990 AJC Derby. The magnificent Dr Grace would record 12 wins, nine second placings and seven third placings throughout his stellar career, amassing winnings of $2,762,681.

However, it was the second of those two Australian four-year-olds who was the focus of Patrick's attention. He had long been concerned that Cambridge Stud needed to find a suitable successor to Sir Tristram who, at 20 and despite his continued fertility, was clearly in the twilight of his career as a stallion. A son of Sir Tristram's was his ideal . . .

When Zabeel was born to Lady Giselle, a French-bred mare by the leading sire Nureyev, who Sangster also kept on a long-term stay at Cambridge Stud, Patrick felt an instant empathy with the foal. He was, in Patrick's opinion, 'lovely, with a beautiful head, huge eyes and an aristocratic bearing.' He was horse royalty to the bone.

He lacked the fractious temperament of his sire, but aside from that, the colt was his spitting image. Perhaps that explained Patrick's attachment — perhaps it was just that uncanny Irish second sight that drew him to the foal. Whatever — he loved the little fellow. 'If only he can be a good racehorse too,' Patrick sent up a small prayer.

At 16, Sir Tristram was getting on, and Patrick knew that within the next four years he would have to hunt for a replacement: he would keep his eyes open and ears to the ground in preparation for the next stallion to jump through the gate. But from the foal's birth, he'd had an irrational gut feeling that Zabeel would be the horse that would some day stand at Cambridge Stud towards the end of Sir Tristram's reign.

Patrick had taken an absolute shine to Zabeel's pedigree, as he had to his sire's, but these days one needed more than pedigree. It had been acceptable in Sir Tristram's era, when New Zealand breeders knew that they couldn't afford both pedigree and performance, and were prepared to forgo on the performance side. These days, in a more competitive business climate, performance was the key factor.

However, in a surprise move that shook Patrick to the core, the foal and his mother — along with all of Sangster's other mares and their offspring — were shortly to be moved off Cambridge Stud. Robert Sangster and his business partner, John Messara of Arrowfield Stud in the Hunter Valley, now jointly owned the Sangster mares, with Arrowfield having bought into 70 per cent of Robert Sangster's holdings. Without Patrick knowing what was happening, John Messara went to the Isle of Man and did the deal.

'It took months to actually document,' Messara recalled years later. 'When we finally got the deal done, we fronted Patrick with the news that we now owned control of all these wonderful mares of Robert Sangster's that were resident at Patrick's, as well as a share of those 14 breeding rights to Sir Tristram that Sangster had originally bought. Patrick was genuinely surprised by the whole thing and, naturally, he was not best pleased at losing the mares, who we moved to Ra Ora Stud in Auckland, which we had bought off the Sir Woolf Fisher estate.

'Inexorably, we were tied together for a period as major investors in Sir Tristram, and there was a bit of tussling over what 14 breeding rights meant because the deal was done at a time when Sir Tristram was serving X number of mares, and subsequently he was serving X plus Y number of shares.'

Those 14 breeding rights became worth less and less with the more mares that were served, according to Sangster and Messara, who put forward the proposition that they ought to be involved in the number of mares that were being served. 'Eventually, he agreed that that would be fair,' said Messara. 'Patrick was pretty good-natured about it all really, and from that moment on, I don't think we ever exchanged a cross word again.'

At the Karaka sales, the rich-coloured bay colt was purchased by Sheikh Hamdan bin Rashid Al Maktoum's bloodstock agent, Angus Gould, for $650,000 (the other of Dr Geoff Chapman's two options) and taken to South Australia for training at Colin Hayes' superb Lindsay Park establishment. In accordance with the Sheik's wishes the colt was named Zabeel, a name famous in Dubai, with the royal palace and premier stables bearing the name Zabeel.

Sheikh Hamdan bin Rashid Al Maktoum — a senior member of Dubai's ruling family — had developed his future passion for thoroughbred racing while attending Cambridge University during the late 1960s. In the spring of 1967, Sheikh Hamdan and his brother, Sheikh Mohammed, attended their first-ever race meeting — at nearby Newmarket — but it was not until 1980 that Sheikh Hamdan's famed blue and white silks began their rise to prominence.

Widely respected as a philanthropist for his people in the United Arab Emirates state, and as one of the world's foremost authorities on breeding, Sheikh Hamdan had the good fortune to possess an almost photographic memory of pedigrees and bloodlines — a wonderful advantage when later developing the family's global racing operation Godolphin into the richest operation on earth. Sheikh Hamdan had the extraordinary ability of being able to identify animals from a brief video of them as foals or yearlings. Sometimes several years later, he would see the same horse and identify the animal and its parentage from memory.

Zabeel the racehorse lived up to his looks, competing with distinction for Sheikh Hamdan and Hayes, who rated him as good potentially as his champion stablemate, Better Loosen Up. 'He's poetry in motion,' Hayes enthused. Zabeel won one race from three starts as a two-year-old, then showed his true classic form at the age of three. Outclassing his rivals, he captured the Group 1 Australian Guineas over 1600 metres, with his regular jockey, Michael Clarke, allowing the colt to produce his withering finish in the home straight to score a three-length win over Ark Regal.

He added further lustre to his record by defeating Dr Grace and the Golden Slipper winner Courtza in the Group 2 Moonee Valley Stakes over 1600 metres, and carried his class to 2000 metres, defeating the VRC Derby hero Stylish Century in the Group 2 MVRC Alister Clark Stakes, smashing the course record by 1.4 seconds into the bargain.

Further Group success came for Zabeel with his win in the Group 2 Craiglee Stakes as a four-year-old, before breaking down in the running of the George Ryder Stakes at Rosehill, forcing his premature retirement from the track. His race record showed seven wins and five placings from 19 starts, while his earnings, when he retired during the 1990–91 season, stood at A$1,138,400.

Years before Zabeel's shock early retirement, Patrick had spoken with Peter Kelly, the head auctioneer and agent for Wrightson Bloodstock, who was also a close friend of Colin Hayes. 'Peter, will you keep your eyes open if ever an opportunity comes up for Zabeel as a replacement for Sir Tristram?' he asked.

Patrick had done his arithmetic and worked out that when Zabeel finished racing, Sir Tristram would be at least 20. He had long determined that he would not stand another such stallion at Cambridge Stud until Sir Tristram reached an advanced age, because he refused to insult Paddy by standing a son against his sire, then having to head both lots of progeny off to the sale grounds for buyers to make invidious comparisons: 'Oh, his son's outdone him.' But, if he could buy Zabeel when Paddy was 20 or so, by the time his son went to stud and his babies went into the ring two years later, Sir Tristram would be at least 22, and that would be acceptable.

Kelly came back to Patrick on a number of occasions, saying the horse would not be sold. When Zabeel's career ended as a racehorse, he would be standing at Lindsay Park. It was deeply disappointing. Of all the other stallions by Sir Tristram that were available, there were none that came near to Zabeel in Patrick's eyes. Kaapstad was a magnificent-looking horse and he had been offered the opportunity to buy him, as he had with Grosvenor, but in both cases the timing was out. It was too early — his inner promise to Paddy, not to pit him against his son in the sale ring, was the brake.

Imagine, then, Patrick's astonishment when he was approached at the 1991 Magic Millions sales in Queensland by Sheikh Hamdan's racing manager Angus Gould, who opened up their conversation by saying, 'I'm surprised you've never shown any interest in Zabeel.'

'In what way?' Patrick queried.

'Well, the boss [Sheikh Hamdan] is looking for a home for Zabeel to stand at stud as he's finished racing. He's looking to sell the horse.'

Patrick had come to the sales with the notion that he might buy into the Sangster/Messara broodmare band, which had — somewhat surprisingly — been put up for sale. Now here he was, receiving an offer out of the blue to purchase the one horse he wanted more than any other!

He was absolutely amazed by Gould's comment — floored, in fact. 'I've long shown an interest through Peter Kelly and Michael Floyd to see if I could have a chance to buy the horse,' Patrick answered, 'but I was told that he would be standing at Lindsay Park, and there was no hope that he would be for sale.'

'Well, he is for sale and the boss has asked, would Cambridge Stud be interested?'

Would they? Absolutely!

Gould continued: 'He doesn't want to put him to auction. He doesn't want to hawk the horse around, but if you're interested, he's there.' He commented that Colin Hayes had also expressed an interest in buying Zabeel and would be putting in a rival bid. 'What I'd like you to do is put your bid in an envelope and I'll collect it in the morning. I'll do the same for Colin. I'll let you know straight away.'

It was awkward. Colin was Patrick's mentor and friend, and he had modelled himself on Hayes because he thought he was a terrific horse businessman — Hayes not only had a leading racing stable, but he also ran a superb stud farm. However, this was Zabeel. Patrick submitted his bid.

At the Sydney sales Angus came up to Patrick, put his hand out, shook the New Zealander's hand, and said, 'Congratulations, you own Zabeel. The boss has accepted your bid, which was the higher of the two.'

He was elated, aside from a niggling feeling of guilt. Patrick went straight to Colin and said, 'I'm awfully sorry, because he's more your horse than mine. You trained him and he's lived with you for the past few years.'

Hayes was magnanimous in defeat: 'No. I'm happy for you. Congratulations.' Then he added, 'I think he will be a very good stallion, because I've had three horses with enormous turn of foot at the end of a race. The best of them was Dulcify, and the other two were Better Loosen Up and Zabeel. I'd probably put Zabeel in second spot, because he and Dulcify were colts, Better Loosen Up was a gelding. I predict that you are going to have an enormously successful stallion.' There was another hand shake. 'Congratulations. You got me by $50,000.'

They were in Queensland, the horse was at Lindsay Park in South Australia, and Patrick needed a veterinary check immediately. He spoke with Matamata vet Jim Marks, who was with them, and asked, 'Look, what are you doing tomorrow, Jim?'

'What do you want me to do?'

'I've just bought Zabeel subject to vet checks,' Patrick explained. He needed a vet quickly for insurance purposes and soundness for breeding.

'What time?' Marks asked.

'As early as you like, just get the plane booked.'

The following morning the men met in Adelaide and drove to Lindsay Park. They took a cursory look at Zabeel; then

Patrick, too nervous to wait around, nodded to the vet. 'You get on with it, and I'll go for a wander.'

On his return, Marks had disturbing news. 'He's fine, but there's just one problem — he's got a murmur in his heart.'

'Oh, shit. Is he not insurable?'

'I'd say he's insurable — I would pass him. He's got a murmur in his heart, but he's probably always had it and probably always will have it.'

Hmmm. He had to admit that he was pretty worried. 'Will he be no good as a stallion?' Patrick asked again.

Marks turned to Patrick: 'Listen son, he don't fuck with his heart. The other part looks all right to me. Buy the horse.'

Patrick could have cried with relief. He was so lucky to have a vet as practical as Jim. Another more conservative-minded vet could have prevented the sale, warning Patrick that Zabeel had a heart murmur, and perhaps cover himself, by adding words to the effect, 'I'm a little bit shaky on this, I can't guarantee you.' It could have put him off realising the dream he had nursed for years.

He was indebted to Marks for his words, Patrick enthused. 'You've got a free service to Zabeel whenever you want. Probably it's not worth much now, Jim, but take it if the horse is any good,' and he handed him his fee.

From the arrangement that had been brokered between the two men almost a decade earlier, Robert Sangster had acquired four champions in Kaapstad, Marauding, Zabeel and Doctor Grace. He had done brilliantly out of the deal, but in turn — out of all of that — Patrick had won back his 'jewel in the crown' in Zabeel, who would turn out to be worth a fortune as a successful sire.

Fifteen years later, Adam Sangster added an intriguing detail to the Zabeel sale episode, saying that Colin Hayes had confided to his father Robert that he 'was gutted to miss out on Zabeel,' but having told Sheikh Hamdan what he considered the horse's value to be, Hayes could not then lose face and offer more.

Zabeel had inherited all the wonderful virtues of his father. Sir Tristram possessed a great ability to pass on some real genetic qualities which came through in spades with Zabeel, especially heart, lung capacity and brain — the three essential ingredients for a top-quality racehorse. Interviewed on his purchase by Australian journalist Alan Groves, Patrick said he believed Zabeel had the credentials to make as large an impact at stud as he had on the track. 'He is from a sire line that is well-proven in this part of the world and has an international pedigree.'

There was to be no shortage of takers for the syndication of shares in Zabeel. Joe Walls had completed the deal with Patrick at Lindsay Park Stud, and then speedily organised the syndicating of 40 shares, of which Patrick would retain 20. Asked for local reaction to the news, Joe answered: 'It would be fair to say he has been oversubscribed.'

Groves reported: 'Every leading stud and breeder in New Zealand has taken a share in the horse, as well as Robert Sangster's Swettenham Stud, ANZ Bloodstock and prominent Brisbane breeder Roy Thompson. "The original shareholders in Sir Tristram were given first option on the shares," Hogan said. "This is the strongest syndicate ever put together in New Zealand."

'Hogan has been scouting for a stallion for 15 months, and said that Zabeel was the best available. "This is the horse that best suits my situation, and that the industry in New Zealand needs." Hogan said the "timing was right" for Cambridge Stud to stand a son of Sir Tristram, who is now 20 years old.'

Cambridge Stud's new sire attraction had wasted no time in settling into his new environment, his proud studmaster reported: 'He's made himself right at home, and in the wake of the Sir Tristram experience, I'm pleased to say that when I led him out, there was not one of the shareholders that didn't like Zabeel!'

A week after the horse's arrival from Australia, Patrick spoke with Phillip Quay from the *Waikato Times*. Quay wrote: 'You can't help but be impressed by his looks. "He has an exceptionally good head and eye, and is a rich bay which makes him very attractive," Hogan says. "He still has a look of a racehorse about him, but I am sure he is going to let down into a terrific stallion. He is more short-coupled than his sire, Sir Tristram. His pedigree is a lovely blend of some of the finest bloodlines in both hemispheres, and he has excellent racetrack performance to match."'

'People talked about Sir Tristram and what a real handful he was,' said Jonathan Hope, defending the horse to a group of vets. 'He has taken us through the boom years of the 1980s and the collapse of the industry in the wake of the stock market crash, when his fees had dropped from $220,000 a service down to $35,000 today.

'Without his $35,000 for a service through these lean years we wouldn't be here today. He's kept the whole show on the road, even though he's coming up to the twilight of his career. And, for what it's worth, to my knowledge Patrick was the first studmaster in New Zealand — possibly in the Southern

Hemisphere — who kicked out the handlers of the stallion and did the job himself, because of Sir Tristram's aggression. He was probably the first person who put himself at risk to look after the staff and, in the process, broke every occupational health and safety rule in the book.'

'When Sir Tristram retires, so will I,' Wrightson's Michael Floyd liked to joke, as a tribute to the stallion's financial contribution to the breeding industry in the post-crash era. In 1992, when Floyd did retire, prepotent Sir Tristram was still going strong, producing 10 Stakes winners in New Zealand and Australia that season — more than any stallion in either country.

Sir Tristram's line was set to continue at Cambridge Stud with Zabeel. Patrick could now sleep easy, and turn his attentions to the state of the New Zealand breeding industry.

They were back to a more common-sense situation in the whole industry, Patrick told Tim Greene in a major profile in *Bloodhorse* magazine in July 1992. A new era had emerged from the extravagant eighties, the industry had bottomed out and stabilised, and was now on a more even plateau. Consequently, the nineties should be tackled with a totally different attitude and approach, he believed.

'We are in the business of producing horses to race, and we are heavily reliant on an export market. If we don't perform, we will have no export market and we will not survive. Australia is still our biggest market and we need to tap into it even more these days. At the same time the Australian industry is now competing better for export markets than they have ever done, and so we, as an industry, have to place more emphasis on marketing, cooperation and promotion of our product.'

It was a well-worn theme of Patrick's — marketing, promotion, exporting — and to practise what he preached, he said he had agreed to return to the council of the New Zealand Thoroughbred Breeders' Association for a second stint as an industry representative.

He had been under a lot of pressure to join the council in recent years, but did not feel it was appropriate in the middle of the boom, he said. 'It would have been difficult to convince the smaller breeders, the majority of the association's membership, that with the success of Cambridge Stud and the manner and techniques of the way I sold horses, any decision I was party to would be made for the benefit of that industry and not for Patrick Hogan.

'In that regard, I won't deny Cambridge Stud did prosper, but on the other hand, you will not convince me that the industry as a whole did not gain very real spin-off benefits from the success of the stud, Sir Tristram, and Patrick and Justine Hogan.'

He believed the CBE he was awarded in 1991 was more of a tribute to the industry as a whole than to any one individual in it, Greene added, with the comment that racing had benefited directly from Hogan's largesse. 'He sponsors two Group 1 features, the WRC Cambridge Stud International and the ARC Sir Tristram Railway Handicap, as well as the Group 3 Sir Tristram Fillies Classic.'

'There has been criticism of the present council over recent years,' Patrick commented, 'but people have to realise the council consists of volunteers elected by members. I go along with the contention that those with the biggest investment in the industry should put themselves forward and give a hand. To be honest, some of the major players have lacked a bit of responsibility in sidestepping the requests from the industry to go forward to these positions.'

He was looking forward to the future, Patrick said. 'It is now a very exciting time to get involved in the industry. Investment levels, unlike the early to mid-1980s, are relative to profit potential. For example, today if you paid between $30,000 and $60,000 for a broodmare, you can have a very good chance of an excellent return and making the investment work.'

While Cambridge Stud was home to more than 120 mares, he was continually looking for new blood to upgrade his mares, Patrick told Greene. 'We have mares at the bottom, middle and top of the range, and are constantly trying to mate mares to get the best result. Because of the wide spectrum of mares I have, I can occasionally put a moderate-value mare with a good pedigree to a sire like Sir Tristram.

'It's a risk I can afford to take because, if it doesn't come off, it can be absorbed within the overall operation. If it does work, it can increase the young mare's and her family's value for the rest of their breeding life. By upgrading a mating for a young mare, a decision can be made on her potential as a producer that much earlier.

'It is something I have always done, and have the likes of Surround and Gay Poss to back it up. I have not improved our mares with Sir Tristram alone, and in fact never want more than 20 per cent of the broodmare band by him. Otherwise I will end up competing against myself in the sale ring by having too many similarly-bred progeny. There is no answer to breeding champions, and all one can hope for is from time to time to breed a top-class horse.'

Being at the top of any sphere in these parts brought with it more than its share of criticism from below, wrote Greene in concluding the *Bloodhorse* profile. 'Patrick Hogan has had this [criticism] for years, yet it has never dampened his enthusiasm or caused his stride to falter. Despite what the niggardly may think to the contrary, Patrick Hogan's contribution to the breeding industry in the next few years will be as valuable as it has been over the last decade.'

A driver in Patrick's commitment to come aboard with the Thoroughbred Breeders' Association a second time around was to help steer through changes in the racing industry, which he considered were not only desirable, but vital for its long-term health. Along with fellow Cambridge studmaster Nelson Schick, he was elected at the association's annual meeting, saying that he had previously stood down when Cambridge Stud was starting out, and that now he could give a fuller contribution which would benefit all in the industry.

Progress was taking place, the industry was beginning to move in the right direction, new boards were being installed; but the critical voices remained a force to be reckoned with. 'The association must be aggressive in its future approach to marketing,' he told the council. Patrick was also a strong believer in the concept of tiered racing so that punters — the industry's customers — could follow horses through the system. But to set this in place, in his opinion, there needed to be a greater degree of cooperation than had existed in the past, and less parochialism from racing clubs.

He exhorted those who were prepared to listen to bury their differences for the greater good. 'Racing is a business and has a responsibility to the total population within New Zealand. One of the problems we will always have here in New Zealand is our very spread-out population. However, the industry must cater for all those within it and encourage new participators.'

Patrick insisted that there was still a place in the industry for smaller-scale breeders. 'If it wasn't for the little man with a mare or two, the whole industry would become too monopolised. Besides, it's not always the big breeders that produce the best racehorses. More often than not, top horses come from small establishments and are not bred in the purple. Look at Bonecrusher for instance.'

In 1993 Patrick was elected president of the New Zealand Thoroughbred Breeders' Association to serve a three-year term.

The dual Group race-winning two-year-old filly Tristalove (Sir Tristram–Diamond Lover) was proof of trans-Tasman cooperation, in her transfer from the O'Sullivans' Wexford Stables in Matamata to those of Bart Cummings in Melbourne, according to Auckland bloodstock consultant Rob McAnulty, later that year. 'The shift is by mutual agreement between Dave O'Sullivan, Bart Cummings and me,' he said. 'We think she'll be a spring filly, and there are many good reasons to have her in training in Melbourne then, not least of which is the number of suitable races with big stakes.'

Tristalove was unbeaten in three starts in New Zealand, including the Group 2 Matamata Breeders' Stakes. In her two races in Sydney, she won the A$200,000 Group 1 AJC Sires' Produce Stakes and finished second in the Group 2 Magic Nights Stakes. Tristalove later added a further five Group wins to her tally, including the Group 1 Australasian Oaks.

In consecutive years, Patrick had introduced two new Australian-raced sires at Cambridge Stud — Zabeel in 1991 and Centro in 1992, the latter a Group 1 Guineas winner from Victoria.

As well as being a consideration for Sir Tristram's advancing years, there was also a practical requirement for new blood. Explaining his reasoning in purchasing Centro, Patrick said: 'We have something like 30 of our 120 broodmare band with Sir Ivor blood, most of them, naturally, by Sir Tristram, so in looking for a new horse I wanted to swing right away, yet find a horse that would complement those mares and that blood.

'When looking to buy a stallion, you are controlled by two major factors: how much money you have, and what horses are available. In Centro I am confident I have the best horse available. He appeals because he is a strong bay, standing at 16.2 hands, with a lovely head on him, good rein, with a strong sloping shoulder, a deep girth, short cannon with plenty of bone, good hocks and a very good hind quarter. I am looking to Centro as a sire to produce classic horses.'

There was a more pragmatic rationale for acquiring Centro. Patrick had decided that Cambridge Stud would in future mate their most commercial mares with Zabeel and Centro in a bid to establish the new sires before Sir Tristram was withdrawn or died. He would, Patrick admitted privately, have preferred to acquire a stallion from the Northern Hemisphere to add appeal for the new Northern Hemisphere markets of Hong Kong and Asia that were growing so rapidly — also for South Africa, a destination he was keen to target.

Patrick had his two new sires to complement Sir Tristram plus Gold and Ivory at Cambridge Stud, but he was ever-keen to have a stake in a Northern Hemisphere stallion. And so, when Robert Sangster approached him in 1993, suggesting they might pool their financial resources and look for a replacement stallion to Sir Tristram from the Northern Hemisphere, Patrick lost no time in accepting the offer.

Buying the world's leading bloodstock was becoming prohibitive. 'It costs millions of dollars to bid on the leading Northern Hemisphere prospects,' complained Robert, who was second only to the Arab sheikhs as the largest bloodstock owner in the world, 'but I have faith in the New Zealand breeding industry. We should aim to have a suitable stallion here this winter, ready to begin serving mares this stud season.'

After that mission was accomplished, Robert said, he would perhaps find the time to read his recently released book, *Horse Trader*, that covered the bloodstock boom and crash periods experienced during his time in the industry, and the manner in which he cornered the market in so many parts of the world.

No super Northern Hemisphere stallion materialised from that venture, but Patrick need not have troubled himself about hunting for a replacement that would be as fine as his Paddy. He already had one, sitting under his own nose. Once again, his intuition had proved spot-on, confounding those in the Australian and New Zealand racing industries who expressed little enthusiasm for Zabeel as a sire.

By the conclusion of the 1993 season, when Sir Tristram had picked up his ninth and final Dewar Trophy for Australia/New Zealand combined earnings, Zabeel had sired progeny from his first and second crop who were destined to set the son's name up there, right alongside that of his sire. They included Cronus, who performed brilliantly in three countries; Jezabeel, a future Melbourne Cup winner; Octagonal; Mouawad; and Might And Power; the latter three were all destined to become Australian Champion Racehorses of the Year.

'There's a lot more to making a stallion than just putting up a sign and saying, "We're open for business." It's about ensuring that the produce goes into the right hands. The follow-up — what I call the after-sales service — is underrated by a lot of people, but not by Patrick.

'Of course his great marketing ability also comes to the fore — he's got a terrific power of persuasion. He's able to persuade the right people to buy them, and of course the progeny get the chance to see what they can do. Horses can be good and get lost in the wrong hands. It's his ability, not only as a breeder, but also as a marketer to produce some good stallions. But, like all of us, he turns up the odd dud. That's genetics, and no one's got the key at this stage — that might spoil the fun!

'I don't look on him as a rival, simply because he operates in another country. I think of him more as a colleague than a rival. While we had some rivalry in the '80s, through the Sangster business, that's entirely faded with time, and now we try to help each other where we can.

'Patrick's significantly responsible for putting New Zealand on the world map as a breeding country. I think New Zealand has a lot to thank him for. He's very sure of himself . . . optimistic . . . which you need to be in this business; he's very much at the helm. I first met Patrick back in the late 1970s when I came over to New Zealand looking for broodmares to buy. Barry Lee, who was an agent I was using, took me down to meet this fellow, Patrick Hogan, who, Lee said, "has got a few mares he's looking to sell".

'That might have been the biggest mistake of my life — I went to see these mares and they're all in foal to this horse called Sir Tristram. I said, "Who's he?" and they said, "Oh well, he's a new sire. We're very confident about him, but he's not proven yet." He wasn't an imposing animal to look at, but some of those mares I looked out turned out to be the dams of some of his best-known Group 1 winners! They had a hefty price on them, but in the end it wouldn't have been a hefty price.

'I might have landed one or two of his best broodmares, if I'd been a bit more gung-ho then! He's sending mares to us now, because we've got Redoute's Choice, and we send some mares to him, because I know he will do them justice. I'm always happy to accommodate him because he'll do such a good job.

'People say a great horse can change your life and I think it's true for Patrick, and for me with Danehill and Redoute's Choice. The Irish eventually took Danehill back, so I went looking for his sons — Flying Spur, Danzero and then Redoute's Choice. Probably his three best.'

Arrowfield Stud
Sydney, 2007

CHAPTER 13

PADDY

'Sometimes, I don't think Patrick knew the difference between himself and Sir Tristram. If the stallion was firing, Patrick was firing. If the stallion was going through a lull, so was Patrick.'

— Australian owner and breeder Nick Columb

A T 23, THE prime worry with Sir Tristram was not his age but his feet, which had deteriorated alarmingly from the drugs he had been given after a mare had kicked him in the serving barn. He required heavy drugs to recuperate, and whilst some horses can absorb these drugs, others can't. Paddy was unfortunate in that they had a detrimental effect on him — once the drugs were in his system, his feet went.

Normally, that spells history for a horse. Normally, he would have to be put down. But, miraculously, Paddy was to be given a new lease of life courtesy of the American space shuttle programme. Farrier Laurie Lynch had read an article in an American magazine which described a new wonder glue that had emerged from experiments revolving around the space shuttle. It was worth a try, Laurie thought, and so he phoned through to the United States and had the glue sent out, which he then used successfully in a trial with two broodmares. Laurie was quietly jubilant — 'I think I've got a winner here' — and he felt sufficiently confident to use the glue to relieve Paddy's feet troubles.

It was early February 1994, and Patrick and Justine were about to leave home for a week to walk the Milford Track. Laurie had kept Patrick informed about the effectiveness of the new glue on the two mares, and while Patrick was interested he was unconvinced, approaching Laurie shortly before they left and emphasising, 'You don't know how much the horse is worth.'

Laurie snorted: 'Well, we'll know how much the horse is worth if this doesn't work.'

'OK,' Patrick conceded, 'but I'll only let you do one foot, and I don't want a phone call from you.'

'No, that'll be all right,' Laurie agreed.

The day he put the glue on was the day that Justine and Patrick began their southern trek. Laurie did one foot, then he looked at the horse and said to the boys, 'I'm gonna break his rule because he's not here to see it — I'm going to do the other front foot.' When Laurie was finished, the stud grooms returned the horse to his paddock, then quickly retired. They couldn't intrude further — that was the stallion's territory — but there was nothing to stop them watching Sir Tristram from the safety of the other side of the rails, testing out his two new plastic front feet.

He galloped around and around his paddock for the first time in months — instant relief. To see him so happy and mobile again brought a grin to every face. Perhaps he would phone Patrick to tell him the good news, Laurie thought, but then decided, no — he might wait and let the boss witness 'the 'miracle' for himself, which Patrick and Justine duly did when they returned home from the South Island.

A month later they did his back feet. It was only possible to do one foot at a time as there were three tubes in each foot that heated up when the glue was applied. Stoically, Paddy stood immobile without a restraining lead, as he had done a month earlier, not flinching at the treatment.

He was a brave old chap, Laurie said. He knew, too, that Sir Tristram had brains and understood the farrier was there to help him — like the time when Patrick and Laurie were forced to return early from the Karaka sales, after receiving a mobile call to tell them that the stallion had gone lame. Mark 'Bro' Vince was waiting for them outside the stables, and as Laurie slammed on the brakes, Bro said: 'Paddy's laying down there in the middle of his paddock and he won't get up!'

'Oh, is that right?' Laurie drove his ute straight into the paddock. There was Paddy, lying on the ground, and Justine hovering nearby, looking deeply worried. Was he dead? Laurie climbed out of the ute and called out to the horse, 'What in the bloody hell have you done?' Sir Tristram looked up at the farrier, raised his head and lay back down again.

As Laurie walked over to him, Paddy lifted his sore foot in the air for Laurie to inspect — 'Just like a little kid saying "it's sore, Mum",' Laurie later told Bro. It was going to be awkward to fix with him lying down, Laurie thought, as he knelt down to remove the shoe. There was very little of Paddy's old foot left — the rest was glue.

Laurie had to remove several layers of glue to find where the infection was lodged, and Paddy behaved superbly. Knowing that Laurie was working for him, he accepted the treatment, allowing the man to cut out the old glue and infection. Laurie glued the foot back up again, put drain holes in the glue, and put his shoe back on. 'Well, it's done now. Are you going to get up?' Laurie asked Paddy.

'He sort of half-pie looked at me, as much as to say, "Do I have to?"' Laurie later told staff who had missed seeing the action. The busy farrier couldn't hang around for long, and as he put the gear back in his vehicle and went to open the ute's door, Sir Tristram got to his feet. Watchfully eyeing Laurie, he tentatively patted the ground with his new hoof, to ensure that it was better before his friend left.

Laurie nodded reassurance. 'That looks OK. Now you're going to have to walk over to the gate, because we're going to have to bathe your foot.' Sir Tristram obediently followed the ute out of his paddock and across the yard, where they bathed his foot in hot water, which he loved. The following morning, as Laurie walked up to his paddock, Sir Tristram greeted him with a large whinny and a show-off careering gallop around the grass and the paddock's central oak tree.

The space-shuttle glue was a vital factor in keeping Sir Tristram alive, and it enabled him to enjoy a good life once more. One day, some time later, Patrick said to Laurie, 'I've got a recurring dread that he will have to be put down because of his feet.'

'I don't think so,' Laurie replied. 'Not now. We've got this glue down to a fine art. That glue is one of the great inventions in the history of the horse.'

In a 1994 interview with Barry Lichter of the *Sunday-Star Times*, after Sir Tristram, at the advanced age of 23, had again topped the sires' list at the national sales at Karaka, Patrick said he had just one more favour to ask of his old friend. 'I often say when I'm working with him, "You've done everything right so far — when it's time to go, please just drop dead." I'd hate to nurse him and not know whether to put him down or keep him alive. If I had my wish, I'd find him dead. That would be a lovely way for him to go, and then everything would be perfect.'

At that same two-day sale at Karaka, bloodstock buyer Rob McAnulty committed $700,000 of the $1,475,000 he spent on three Sir Tristram colts, expressly because of the stallion's age. 'My Sir Tristram colts were selected for their residual value as stallions,' McAnulty explained. 'And they were steals. Sir Tristram's not going to be here for ever, and if one of these colts can win a Group 1 race, they're worth $2 million.'

That season, Sir Tristram won the 1993–94 Dewar Trophy for the ninth occasion in one of the closest-ever finishes for the award. The title fight went right down to the wire, with Sir Tristram heading off his son Grosvenor, and Noble Bijou. The final Australasian earnings for each stallion were: Sir Tristram $2,103,525, Grosvenor $2,011,971 and Noble Bijou $1,979,913.

'I had a bird on my shoulder when I bought him,' Patrick said of the horse who had started life as a stallion with a $1500 service fee. Sporting number plates 'Sir T' on his Range Rover, he added, 'No animal will ever take the place of Paddy.'

A 25th birthday — a quarter of a century — is worth celebrating in anyone's language, even that of a horse. Patrick decided he was going to give his Paddy a magnificent day to mark the event, with a large gathering of friends and family to share in the celebrations.

His champion stallion would also have a large horseshoe-shaped birthday cake with green candles, Patrick announced. There would be no expense spared for this, a never-to-be-forgotten event in the life of a most remarkable horse.

'PADDY'
SIR TRISTRAM
25th BIRTHDAY
9 February 1996

We are at Cambridge Stud with hundreds of invited guests and the Cambridge Stud family gathered together on a wonderful hot day, tables set under spreading oak trees on the lawn, with green, yellow and white balloons flying over the stable entrance, and television cameras and media photographers at the ready.

Master of Ceremonies for the event, Joe Walls, is on the microphone and invites those present to take a glass of champagne from one of the long white-damask clothed tables dotted around. 'We invite you all to share with Sir Tristram in a very, very special birthday celebration. We are going to pay tribute today to a horse who has become a phenomenon — this is a day to honour Sir Tristram, affectionately known to his friends as Paddy,' Joe begins. 'He has been an unequalled sire of Group 1 winners, with his progeny earning over $40 million to date.

'On the big screen in front of you, his birthday celebrations will feature famous victories by Empire Rose, Dr Grace, Gurner's Lane, Marauding, Tristalove, Romanee Conti, Isolda, and the outstanding colt Octagonal, by his son Zabeel, in tribute to the success and the depth of Paddy's breeding dynasty. It will take you on a journey covering the life of Sir Tristram to date, from Ballygoran in Ireland, through Chantilly in France, the United States and finally to Cambridge Stud, here in New Zealand.'

To a background of Irish music, the story of Sir Tristram unfolds on the giant screen. There are video clips of a foal gambolling with his mother in the misty green setting of Ballygoran farm, then a switch to Raymond Guest's property in Virginia, his widow lamenting that the Sir Tristram experience 'taught us a lesson. If ever we sell a horse, we should keep two shares!' Then it's off to the Villa St-Denis at Chantilly and Charles Milbank in reminiscent mood: 'He was a very strong, tough horse, but because of that split pastern and perhaps because of going to Kentucky, he never reached his potential for a French classic campaign.' Next is Sir Philip Payne-Gallwey of the BBA admitting to coming away from that initial inspection 'rather depressed . . . but he did have a wonderful outlook about him.'

Next stop is the horse's arrival at Cambridge, where his turbulent personality is revealed. A young Patrick in a checked Swanndri jacket is seen grappling to control the rearing stallion. 'He got more than what he bargained for,' Joe breaks into the commentary. Now there's a clip of the late Fred Bodle, which brings laughter as he recounts the saga of selling his share, then breeding Empire Rose, and concluding, 'As far as Patrick is concerned, I've forgiven him!'

Next is a video clip of Tommy Smith, the legendary Australian trainer: 'Sir Tristram stands out like a neon light above the others,' Smith says, before the film jumps to Robert Sangster: 'He's terribly versatile. If you had 20 mares and you had the availability to use them, you would send them all to him,' and on to Bart Cummings: 'He and Patrick have been wonderful servants of New Zealand and also for Australian racing.' Then there's a jump in time to the Queen's visit in 1990, where Her Majesty is shown stroking Sir Tristram's nose and conversing with Patrick in the gardens of Cambridge Stud. Finally, a display of Sir Tristram's nine Dewar Trophy awards swamps the entire screen. 'Ladies and gentlemen, can you move back a little in the forecourt,' Joe requests. 'Bring the old boy out!'

To loud applause, the birthday boy is led to the front of Cambridge Stud by his groom, Mark Vince. True to form, Sir Tristram neighs and rears up with a wild roll of the eye. As he has done for the past 25 years, he is wearing his old fawn-coloured halter that has been removed only twice during that entire period — once for the governor-general and once for Robert Sangster — when, on both occasions, his halter had been taken away for restitching.

'He was a bastard when it came to taking off his halter,' veterinarian Jonathan Hope says in reflection, watching the stallion's entry. 'He didn't want it removed — like a dog with canker in its ears.' A decade earlier, Jonathan had travelled to Lexington in Kentucky and brought home a fine new American halter with a vertical ring. 'I've bought a present for Paddy and you've got to have it,' Jonathan had urged Patrick. 'The vertical rings will make it easier for the grooms to control him.'

No, no, Patrick demurred. Paddy's old one was fine.

'The reason why you always want to keep Paddy's original halter on is because you're so damned superstitious!' Hope had laughed, and Patrick had nodded in agreement.

It's now time for Andy Ryan to sing the first of two evocative musical tributes to Sir Tristram, specially composed for the

281

occasion by John Costello. As he sings, the cameras switch to Justine, holding the hands of two of her grandchildren, and the Hogan daughters, Nicola and Erin.

'Now, folks, I would like you to raise your glasses and toast Sir Tristram,' Joe proposes. 'To Sir Tristram . . . Sir Tristram . . . to Paddy . . . Paddy . . . ' the voices murmur, as hundreds of glass flutes are raised aloft. Joe leads the toast: 'Happy 25th birthday, Paddy.'

A misty-eyed Patrick toasts his horse. 'Paddy, it will be exactly 20 years since you came here on a wing and a prayer, and while there were many times that we nearly didn't make it, your achievements went way beyond our wildest dreams. You have brought good fortune to many people, and in one way or another you have touched the lives of thousands, not only in New Zealand and Australia, but right throughout the world.

'Paddy, we are all proud, and thank you for the great opportunity that you have given us all. Look around you, everyone — what you see here is what Sir Tristram has provided. For this, your 25th birthday, we raise our glasses to you, and drink a toast to you that you may continue to enjoy good health, have good mares, and carry out the rest of your days contented in the paddock.'

'Ladies and gentlemen,' Joe continues, 'meet the gentlemen who have handled Sir Tristram at Cambridge Stud.' As the star of the show tosses his head restively, Joe introduces the staff. 'Right now he is being handled by Mark Vince who has done so for the past five years in a very, very capable manner. Mark understands well the temperament and antics of Sir Tristram . . .

'Also here is Laurie Lynch who has been the backstop of this horse for almost his entire career. He has looked after him, which is even more of a feat these days. Today, Laurie is acknowledged as probably New Zealand's greatest blacksmith. Laurie, please step forward.' Reluctantly, Laurie faces the limelight and buries his head behind a large bear hug that he gives the stallion.

Sir Tristram, in calmer mood, is led by Vince over to his large white birthday cake, rather like a huge lump of sugar, flanked with tall green candles. Laurie symbolically cuts the cake and the photographers swoop to find their best angle; then, led by rising New Zealand tenor Shaun Dixon, the guests sing 'Happy Birthday'.

It is customary to have a reply to the toast, Joe says. 'We knew it was going to be difficult to capture this on video, but we have managed to get the old fellow to say a few words to us . . . ' The big screen beams into Sir Tristram leaning over the rails of his paddock, addressing his well-dressed audience, in gruff bog-Irish tones.

'Hullo there! Ladies and gentlemen, eh, if you don't moind I'd like to sey a few words meself. Yes, it's me! It's not bloody Mr Ed with an Irish accent! No! Well, the Boss, y'know, has all these ideas about me being difficult, but I tell you, Irish and all, he's not the easiest bogger himself, y'know!

'Anyway I never wanted to be a racehorse in the first place. They pushed me into trying to win the Kentucky and the English Derby, and it's never been done before. So why me? I knew all along what I wanted to do . . . I seen what was going on in the stables in Ireland and I can remember thinking, "That's for me!"

'I got me first taste of it in England the night the house burnt down. I knew I had it in me. Then the Boss spotted me and brought me to this fantastic bloody harem in Cambridge!

Blondes, brunettes, big ones, little ones . . . Eh, Boss, if I might say so we've made a great team. You got the money and I got the girls!! Anyway, I've enjoyed me work and I'm proud of all me kids. Thanks for coming along everybody, and let's have a party. Have a pint on me!'

'Thank you, Paddy,' Patrick says, 'how did you enjoy that?'

'Meself, I enjoyed it, but I was a little hoarse!' Whinnies of laughter.

It's interview time for an upcoming video, 'The Promise', that will mark the event. First up, it's Tom Williams of Wairarapa, who's followed by bloodstock consultant Peter Kelly and former champion jockey Linda Jones, who says, 'This birthday is a wonderful thing for the horse and he definitely does deserve it! He has just been wonderful for New Zealand racing and the world. Basically it's put New Zealand on the map.'

There isn't a dry eye as Shaun Dixon delivers a stunning rendition of the Irish classic 'Danny Boy' to lyrics written by John Costello — 'The Ballad of Paddy Boy'. What a voice!

Formalities over, Sir Tristram is returned to his paddock as the guests tuck into a lavish luncheon buffet, seated at their tables under the trees. Patrick sits there, swamped with emotion and pride — this is one of the happiest days of his life. He and his horse are two fiery Irishmen — two stubborn characters. Between them, they have forged an extraordinary partnership built on dreams and a promise, and have succeeded beyond their wildest of dreams.

Too late for his party, even greater acclaim was to come Paddy's way. In June 1996, towards the end of the 1995–96 season,

Dupain (Sir Tristram–Best Image) won the QTC Brisbane Cup by six lengths to create a new world record of Group 1 winners for Sir Tristram.

The flood of colts and fillies had by now dwindled to a trickle, but Sir Tristram's 'autumn leaves' included two by the champion mare Horlicks — Bubbles, and the 2000 Melbourne Cup winner Brew. In addition, Tristachine, Starina and Diamond Cashel were all class, producing wins and placings in Australasian Group races into the next century.

However, eight months after the momentous birthday party, attention at the stud had shifted from a progeny of the old sire to one of his son, Zabeel. For, as his older full brothers Octagonal and Mouawad were creating waves across the Tasman, a highly valuable Zabeel–Eight Carat foal, born in late 1996, had the roughest of entries into the world and, Patrick knew, would be lucky to survive.

The brown colt was born without a blemish, but he was paralysed. He had bacteria in his blood, and would have to be treated for septicaemia — the feared blood poisoning — using an innovation that Patrick had recently introduced to the stud, if he was to have any chance of survival. Foals get brain damage from the infection, but, if the treatment is right, they are capable of getting over it. Jonathan Hope was called in immediately to work with Patrick and Marcus Corban on an intensive care regime to try to save the foal.

Staff were rotated on a round-the-clock watch over him, while his mother Eight Carat was lodged in the adjacent box to whinny at her baby to encourage him to survive. The foal was placed on a water bed, where he was to remain without standing for three weeks. And, as he lay on his water bed, he was put on intravenous therapy and high-dosage antibiotics plus oxygen.

He would require much intensive care to bring him through that, Jonathan believed, without suffering damaging after-effects.

After a fortnight, they were relieved to see that their treatment was working, and as he started to improve the colt was put onto oral milk and electrolytes to maintain his body functions. Finally, there was the rehabilitation. He was lifted up and down and encouraged to raise himself up on his own four feet and walk unassisted.

Finally, to the elation of Patrick, Marcus, Jonathan and the exhausted staff, the foal, now named Colombia, made a complete recovery and, subsequently, a brilliant sale at Karaka in January 1998, where he went for $1,600,000 to Roselands Stud in Victoria, Australia.

'Patrick was the first person to put in an intensive care unit for foals that also served as a neo-natal unit for weak or premature foals,' Jonathan said. 'He was the first to realise that with these valuable foals being born, the success rate would be far higher if you had a decent facility on the property. The saving of Colombia's life, who was unable to race because of an injury but later became a very fine stallion, would probably never have happened without that.'

Towards the end of his life, Sir Tristram — the stallion who had served literally thousands of mares — fell head over ears in love. The Cambridge team were amused to see him so smitten with a broodmare who lived in a neighbouring paddock.

She wasn't much of a looker, Marcus and the team agreed, but each to his own . . . They marvelled that even when she wasn't in season, Sir Tristram would still go nuts for the mare, standing for an entire day just looking across at her, or running around his large paddock trying to impress her.

On Wednesday afternoon, 21 May 1997, a sick little girl called Michelle Callagher, aged 13, was granted her wish: the chance to visit her heroes Sir Tristram and Patrick Hogan. From her hospital bed she was taken to Cambridge Stud, where she struggled out of her wheelchair onto crutches for the first time in more than two years and, unaided, took a couple of steps towards the stallion. 'I wanted to be able to stand up to pat him,' she explained, crying with delight as she leaned on Sir Tristram's shoulder. He had never seen the horse look so well, his handler Bro thought.

But just three hours after that visit, Inga Schiffer, a German stud worker in her fifth year at Cambridge Stud, was on the radio-telephone to Patrick: 'There's something wrong with Sir Tristram!'

Fighting down his panic, Patrick rushed to the stallion's paddock. What he saw confirmed the worst. There was his Paddy standing still, his foreleg swinging unnaturally. Calling for two vets from the local veterinary practice in the absence of Hope — John Hunter and Paul Frazer — he told them to drop everything and get over to Cambridge Stud as soon as they could.

Hunter, a family friend, shook his head after making a brief inspection. 'Patrick, I'm afraid to say that Sir Tristram has broken his femur bone. Nothing can be done to save him. He'll have to be put down.'

Oh Paddy, why didn't you just do the decent thing and die in your sleep? Better still, why couldn't you have stayed alive just a little longer? The tears welled up in Patrick's eyes; he couldn't bear the pain of what he was about to live through. He called a shocked Justine and stud staff and asked them to join him immediately at the paddock to make their own goodbyes to Sir Tristram — their Paddy.

Patrick gave his horse a final cuddle and a hug and then he cradled Sir Tristram's head in his arms, murmuring, 'Thank you, Paddy. Where would I have been without you?'

Mark Vince, whose job it had been to give Sir Tristram his breakfast every morning, had one final task to perform for his 'rogue and hard old bugger'. It was his arm that Sir Tristram bit into as Hunter ended the stallion's life with an injection. That bite mark was almost a badge of honour, Vince said.

Nobody had seen Sir Tristram fall and break his leg that afternoon after he had received the visit from Michelle Callagher in the forecourt. Perhaps, everyone thought, he was playing around or kicking up his heels to impress the mare. If that was true, then Sir Tristram had died as he had lived — a ladies' man.

For deeply superstitious Patrick there lurked an irrational inner horror that it was he who had put the hex on his horse, after Paddy had served his final mare on 13 January that year. He was being retired, Patrick had told Paddy at that time. 'You've done your job. You won't be used in '97.'

Everyone always claimed that the horse was half-human. Had he understood? Had he maybe thought, 'I'm not required any longer. I've got to step aside now.' He would not have wanted to hang around in the shadows of his son Zabeel.

But the grief of it . . . Remembering a promise he had once made to *Waikato Times* racing editor Phillip Quay, Patrick picked up his office phone at 7.30 p.m.

Four top Irishmen. From left, New Zealand Prime Minister the Right Honourable Jim Bolger, Patrick, the Prime Minister of Ireland Albert Reynolds, and Sir Tristram at Cambridge Stud.

Patrick and Justine with Eight Carat.

Octagonal being led back to scale by his proud owners, brothers Jack (left) and Bob Ingham, after winning the 1996 WFA Mercedes Classic.

Octagonal's brother Mouawad, after winning the George Ryder Stakes, with Patrick.

Might And Power strides to victory in the Caulfield Cup.

The Hogan brothers, from left, John, Peter and Patrick.

The 1998 Melbourne Cup. A New Zealand quinella for Cambridge Stud as Jezabeel on the rails heads off Champagne in the final strides of the race.

Patrick with his star sprinter Diamond Lover following her win in the Group 1 Railway Handicap.

Arise, Sir Patrick. Sir Patrick Hogan is knighted by the Governor-General of New Zealand, the Right Honourable Sir Michael Hardie Boys, January 2000.

Patrick with the Princess Royal, Princess Anne, at Sir Tristram's resting place, Cambridge Stud.

At Cambridge Stud, Horlicks and her foal by Maroof are led out by Michael Fleming for inspection by members of the 2003 Asian Racing Conference.

Bart Cummings. Zabeel.

The joy of victory. Jockey Michael Walker, in Cambridge Stud colours, is jubilant as owner Sir Patrick leads Smiling Like back to scale after winning the Wellington Cup. This was Michael's first Group 1 victory.

Trainer Gai Waterhouse and Dr Percy Sykes at her Tulloch Stables, Randwick. Percy has been a veterinarian at Tulloch Stables for more than 50 years, working first for Gai's father, the late T.J. 'Tommy' Smith.

Waikato Times billboard, 14 June 2003.

Patrick Hogan, the gardener.

Adam Sangster.

Demi O'Byrne.

Sir Patrick Hogan
with Tik Tik
Trinidad in the
Cambridge Stud
complex at the
Karaka Yearling
Sales.

Left: Tristarc, multiple
Group 1 winner and
champion.
Above: Nick Columb,
Tristarc's owner.

Gurner's Lane winning the 1982 Melbourne Cup following his triumph in the Caulfield Cup. Another champion son of Sir Tristram.

Emirates Melbourne Cup Tour day at Cambridge Stud, 2006.

Joe McGrath from the Victoria Racing Club at Cambridge Stud on Melbourne Cup Tour day.

Fencourt and Cambridge Stud's seven Melbourne Cups on display. From left, Van der Hum (1976), Gurner's Lane (1982), Empire Rose (1988), Might And Power (1997), Jezabeel (1998), Brew (2000) and Ethereal (2001).

Broodmares grazing peacefully at Cambridge Stud.

Farrier Laurie Lynch, with visiting Irish groom Emma Hartigan, his broodmare Sapphire Blue and her hour-old foal. Cambridge Stud, November 2006.

Chairman of New Zealand Bloodstock and head auctioneer Joe Walls, centre, is flanked by Guy Mulcaster (left) and Michael Kneebone during the auction of the $2 million Sunline–Zabeel colt at the 2007 Karaka Yearling Sales.

Cast in bronze. Zabeel (right), sculpted by Nichola Lewis, and Sir Tristram (below) by Rick Lewis. (*Jenny Kain*)

An aerial view of Cambridge Stud.

The stables at Cambridge Stud.

Sometimes he's Paddy, sometimes Sir Tristram . . . the stallion's presence remains part of daily life at Cambridge Stud.

Zabeel at Cambridge Stud (above) and with Sir Patrick (below).

A knight of the realm on an upturned bucket. Co-trainers Debbie Rogerson and Sir Patrick watch over Katie Lee (above) prior to the running of the 2000 Guineas at Riccarton, 2009 — and celebrate her victory alongside jockey Opie Bosson (below). (*Trish Dunell*)

Sir Patrick with his honorary doctorate from the University of Waikato in 2013. (*University of Waikato*)

Sir Patrick leading the last Zabeel colt through the ring at Karaka, 2015. (*Jenny Kain*)

The Hogan family, 2016: Jed Casey, Katie Livingston, Erin Hogan, Sir Patrick Hogan, Justine, Lady Hogan, Nigel Steel, Nicola Steel, Patrick Hunt, Kristen Hunt, Liam Hunt and James Hunt.

The permanent staff at Cambridge Stud, 2016. From left, Jenny Kain, Corrina Holmes, Marcus Corban, Lloyd Monehan, Bevan McCallum, Ken Potter, Mark Vince, Peter Stanaway, Jan Mitchell, Mallory Phillips, Mark Fox, Tracee Soti, Julian Corban, Margaret Fife, Ken Tsunemoto, Barry Lee and Keri Gore. (*Jenny Kain*)

The big story in New Zealand racing had always been 'What if anything should happen to Sir Tristram?' That's what the editors wanted — that was the story any racing journalist would die for. It would guarantee front-page treatment with any newspaper in the country. 'Would you please ring me first if anything ever happens to Sir Tristram?' Quay had once begged Patrick.

And so it was that Quay was sitting at home having his dinner when the phone rang. 'It's for you, Dad,' Quay's daughter said. 'It's Patrick Hogan on the phone.'

Patrick's voice was choked with emotion: 'You asked me to ring you if ever something happened to Sir Tristram . . . I'm ringing you because I'm keeping my word to you. You've got till tomorrow morning — no one else will know — and you can tell the whole world.'

The following morning the *Waikato Times* led with the story that one of racing's and the province's most esteemed sons — a horse so famous that he had put Waikato on the map for visiting dignitaries, had been honoured by New Zealand Post with his image on postage stamps and was currently the subject of a high-priced investment phone card release — was no more.

They held a funeral service for Sir Tristram and buried him in the central garden of the stud's courtyard — in accordance with the dictates of international tradition — in a standing position with his back to the rising sun. At Cambridge Stud, that would have Sir Tristram facing the stables. The philosophy of the tradition, dating back to ancient China, was that to bury your famous and noble in that way would ensure that good fortune, good health and good luck would continue to flow on.

And, in death as in life, Niggy the cat, who had slept with the stallion every night and who had died just months earlier at the age of 19, was laid beside the body of the horse. Sir Tristram's old mate was dug up from his little cardboard-box grave in the garden. Ashes had replaced the substance of the cat and they were transferred to a small concrete Chinese urn which was placed alongside Paddy, so that the two friends could remain together for ever.

There was so much grief and emotion to weather on that fittingly grey and soggy winter's day. Patrick and Justine, their arms locked around each other and heads bent, fought back the tears while Nicola, with a single red rose, placed her tribute to Paddy on the earth mound of his grave, alongside a wreath of green — to honour Paddy's Irish origins — which had been sent from the Graeme Rogerson stables in Sydney. Shane Keating hugged his young son Jack.

The Hogans' close friend Bob Morris, who had been with Sir Tristram from the outset, reflected on the 21 years he had been involved with the horse as he cast a flower onto his grave as a final act of respect. Yes, like others in the syndicate, he had made a couple of million dollars from being a shareholder for the 'Sir T' duration, but the loss he felt that day was far closer to the heart than any sort of monetary consideration. It was the horse's spirit that Bob would miss.

Laurie was away from the stud when Sir Tristram broke his leg and returned immediately on learning the news. He had offered to perform a last favour for the horse who'd had a passion for having his feet tended to and who Laurie had loved so much, saying he would be the one to dig the hole where Paddy would lie. To Laurie, there had never been a horse like Paddy and there never would be. In 2007 Laurie admitted, 'I still look in his paddock to see if he's there.'

Random thoughts circled through Marcus Corban's head as he stood solemnly beside the mound. Paddy had a quite unnerving awareness of his own importance — maybe they had made him that way because he was so important to the stud. And then Marcus allowed himself a small smile, at an irreverent reflection of Paddy in the serving barn. The stallion was always choosy about which mares he wanted. He preferred his ladies mature — he wasn't partial to a skittish maiden — and there were some mares Paddy would refuse to serve. When that happened they would bring in a teaser mare to get him excited, then whip her away and put the original mare back when he was totally sexually aroused and had got to the stage where he couldn't help himself.

It was exciting all right hanging onto the mare — you had to be really on the mark. Would he miss those particular adventures, Marcus wondered? Probably not, but he would certainly miss Paddy. The thought of his empty paddock was almost unbearable to contemplate.

Standing alongside, Mark Vince was grief-stricken. 'I'll never look after another horse like this guy. He was awesome,' he said.

How many horses are accorded a burial service with full rites and a priest to officiate? But then, how many Sir Tristrams are there? Father Desmond McCarthy had imparted dignity to the brief burial ceremony, and now — in closing — he offered a prayer of thanksgiving.

It was then left for Patrick to bring down the curtain on the ride of a lifetime with the incomparable Paddy. 'The family held a Mass in the stables when the stud started,' Patrick explained, fighting back tears. 'Sir Tristram was blessed at his arrival and it is appropriate that he should be at his departure. Sir Tristram has been no ordinary horse. It's a sad day and I've lost a good friend. Without him we would have all been the poorer.'

He then read out a farewell tribute to Sir Tristram from himself, Justine and the staff at Cambridge Stud:

The record books will tell the tale
Of records set and smashed
They'll place you on a plateau high and rare
But they won't tell the story of the horse we came to love
And the day that left your paddock bleak and bare.

Non-horsey folk can read the words
And marvel at your deeds
They can see your breeding influence in the charts
But they won't understand that you were more than 'just a
  horse'
Or know the place you held in all our hearts.

The green sward, trees and post-and-rails
At Cambridge Stud, your home,
Owe everything to you and your success
They stand as your memorial
Yet still tell half the tale
Of the human lives you touched, and changed and blessed.

Your temper was notorious, your ego super-sized
A moody king upon your hard-earned throne
Yet somehow that was part
Of the legend that you built
Of the character that made you stand alone.

Your life was long, your gene pool vast
Your influence, so strong
Will last for many generations yet
It was a privilege to know you, Paddy
To be part of the legend.
Here at Cambridge Stud, we won't forget.

Two days after the stallion's death a letter was sent from Buckingham Palace to Cambridge Stud. It read: 'Dear Mr Hogan. The Queen has asked me to write to say how saddened she was to learn of Sir Tristram's death. Her Majesty recalled visiting your stud to see Sir Tristram and knows how much of a loss he will be to you and the New Zealand racing industry. The Queen wanted me to say that her thoughts are with you at this time. Yours sincerely, Simon Gimson.'

The death of Sir Tristram was the subject of interviews, local and international television coverage, newspaper features, editorials and a superb cartoon by the *New Zealand Herald*'s cartoonist Malcolm Evans. Patrick hired a documentary crew to film the stallion's story and ordered a handsome black granite headstone for the stallion's grave, on which these words were engraved:

'Paddy'

SIR TRISTRAM (IRE)

BAY HORSE
SIR IVOR–ISOLT BY ROUND TABLE
7 April 1971 – 21 May 1997

'The greatest thoroughbred stallion to ever stand in the southern hemisphere.'

For two decades Sir Tristram cast his giant shadow
over Cambridge Stud, changing forever the world of
thoroughbred breeding, marketing and racing in Australasia.

Through his veins coursed the blood of champions of all
ages, champions not just of today but of generations of
thoroughbreds to come. The Sir Tristram dynasty, fuelled
by his prepotent sons and daughters, grandsons and granddaughters,
will remain with us forever as his powerful living legacy.

By every standard — Group One winners, Stakes winners
and progeny earnings — Sir Tristram was the greatest.

'With the sun on your back and the wind at your feet
Call your harem of mares to pastures so sweet
Enjoy rest dearest Paddy, the cycle's complete
As you drink from clear waters of a swift flowing stream
Lift your head and remember — no it wasn't a dream
In a world of great stallions, only you reigned supreme.'

Over the years you shaped many people's lives
You helped make many dreams become reality
To us, you were the inspiration, to become the best that we could
In a profession we love

We'll never forget you Paddy.

(Words by Paddy's handler Russell Warwick)

No other stallion would be permitted to grace Sir Tristram's
paddock until the year 2000.

The Ballad of Paddy Boy

An ode to the great sire Sir Tristram, fondly and gratefully known by those closest to him as Paddy, sung to the tune of the Irish classic 'Danny Boy', with lyrics written by John Costello.

Oh Paddy Boy, the pipes, the pipes are pumping
From mare to mare
And then . . . a few mares more
But now they've gone, and life is dull and boring
You hang your head
And dream of days of yore.
But come ye back
When spring is in the meadow
And when the mares come dancing down the lane
You'll lift your head
Your crest will rise, your nostrils flare
It's breeding time
And Paddy rides again.

When you were young, you knew the European tracks
You loved to run, for racing was your game
They even planned
That you'd run for The Roses
But injury

Cut short your chance at fame.
Then came Patrick, looking for a sire prospect
He looked at you
And then he looked again
He brought you home, to faraway New Zealand
To Cambridge Stud, the place you'll never leave again.

♣

There were some breeders
Didn't like the look of you
They thought your stock would be too big and slow
There were some breeders
Wouldn't use your services
I wonder where those sceptics have gone now.
For when your oldest progeny were three-year-olds
The winners came like rushing flood-waters
The Group wins came
From sons and from your daughters
And people knew
A champion had arrived.

♣

Remember when
That pretty shy Taiona
Came to your court and then she came again
The foals were born and both of them proved champions
First Sovereign Red and then came Gurner's Lane.
Your fame spread far, spread all around the racing world
The list of Group 1 winners still unfurled

Then came the day
That you passed Northern Dancer
And you became
The greatest sire in all the world.

Oh Paddy Boy, the years have swiftly flown
Your time must come
As nature takes its course
You've left a mighty hoofprint on the breeding world
But the Reaper comes, to human as to horse.
But you'll live on
Through sire sons and through daughters
Through generations
Distant, not yet born
Yes, you'll live on
While racing folk have memories
Oh Paddy Boy, your name
Will never ever die.

CHAPTER 14

HEAD TO HEAD WITH
THE RACING CHIEFS

*'I don't think a title suits me. But if you want it, that's
fine by me.'*

— Justine, Lady Hogan

IN 1998 PATRICK and Dave O'Sullivan prepared for political
battle in Wellington with the chiefs of three separate boards —
New Zealand Thoroughbred Racing, the Racing Industry
Board and the Totalisator Agency Board — as they fronted the
case for RaceO, a lottery-style game that, it was claimed, would
be the salvation of racing. Dave and Patrick had first come up
with the idea five years earlier, in 1993, after discussing the
impact of Lotto at a race meeting. How could racing compete?
How, the two men pondered, could their industry become more
competitive and attract a wider New Zealand market to racing?

'This Lotto really gets down your throat,' Dave grumbled.
'Why does so much money have to go into Lotto every week?
They're only just marbles! Why can't we have a Lotto game for
horse racing, which would be far more exciting to watch?'

Patrick's mind forged ahead. 'We could offer prizes of up to one or two million dollars, with the profits ploughed back into the racing industry. That will give us higher stakes for races and be a stimulus to the whole industry.' Before the arrival of casinos, poker machines and Lotto — introduced by the government and the Department of Internal Affairs — New Zealand racing had received the bulk of the discretionary gambling dollar, which was now being eroded at an alarming pace by their new rivals on the scene.

They knew nothing about technology or computers. That would be the domain of the project's developer Berri Schroder — a whiz with computer technology — who agreed to join the pair for a beer or two at a meeting held in the living room of the O'Sullivans' home at Wexford Stables in Matamata. They outlined to Schroder what they had discussed previously.

'I could put something together that runs along the lines of Lotto and be the ticket,' Schroder nodded. 'In fact, there's another idea that I've got and that's a tracking system, which tracks the horses around the course while they are racing. The jockeys have a little chip on their helmet which relays the horse's name or number on the screen, so that people who find it difficult to follow their horses in a race can keep up with the play. With this tracking system, it would be easy.'

They would stick their money where their mouths were, Dave and Patrick agreed after the meeting, and invest in Schroder's Lotto-style concept — the tracking system might have to wait. They also agreed to present a united front on the project. Whatever Patrick invested financially in the project, Dave would equal, and whatever Dave said publicly on the subject, Patrick would go along with. They were 100 per cent committed to the idea and prepared to put whatever time and effort it needed to get it off the ground.

When Schroder returned with the concept of RaceO, a user-friendly online game in the development stage, they were enthusiastic. RaceO would operate on similar lines to Lotto, Schroder said, by selecting eight winners and with each race limited to only eight possible outcomes. Expert analysts would give each RaceO runner a level of ranking — and the likelihood of it winning — and any horse not in the top seven would be bundled into a group called 'the outsiders'. If a punter bet on one of those outsiders, the entire group would run for him.

Players didn't need to know anything about racing to enjoy the game, he said, and the odds were better than Lotto. For a stake of, say, $2, people could decide whether they wanted to choose their own numbers on the horses' form, or take a lucky dip. It was not another form of Pick Six, Dave explained patiently, RaceO was a little more scientific than that, but it would provide top prizes, it would be simple to operate and would be fun to play.

Functioning properly, this could earn the industry tens of millions of dollars, the trio believed. 'With RaceO on board, we can be in the situation where we will be racing for real money again,' Dave said. 'This has great potential for the industry.'

Of course, they knew they would have their fair share of enthusiasts and knockers, but even they were disconcerted by the blinkered reaction they received from some prominent green-eyed colleagues in the racing industry. 'Here's these two successful buggers who have made a quid in the industry, now they're want to make a quid out of the gambling dollar,' the gossip went.

Yes, they were shareholders in RaceO, Dave and Patrick argued, but this was going to help them all, for God's sake! Where was the problem in going head-to-head with Lotto, for the benefit of racing? Look at the income Lotto generated — racing could have the same.

It took five years for the prototype to be finely honed and ready to present to the three boards for their consideration. Early in 1998 a trial run was staged with the Auckland and Counties Racing Clubs, using phantom tickets, and it went well. 'This is well worth having a look at . . . we'd support it . . . it's great,' they said typically. Armed with that support and with spirits high, Berri, Dave and Patrick flew to Wellingon.

Berri was to present the case along with his experts before the three boards, while Dave and Patrick would attend one — that of the influential Racing Industry Board. To their irritation, they and RaceO were not to be given the time of day, being placed — they noted — at the worst possible time for each of the board meetings. However, because the Racing Industry Board was dealing with a presentation by the combined forces of Patrick Hogan and David O'Sullivan, the country's leading breeder and trainer respectively, they could not be dismissed out of hand.

Dave and Patrick were called into the meeting for their presentation of RaceO and the tracking system at about 4.30 p.m. A dozen or so members were present, representing gallops, trotting and greyhound interests. Four excused themselves immediately: 'Sorry, we're unable to be with you. We've got a plane to catch to go home.' Another said, 'Sorry, I've got another appointment.' The chairman gave them, in Patrick's words to Dave later, 'no time of day whatsoever'.

They could sense the aggro in the air, almost see their thoughts written on their faces: 'These guys are not going to play the big shots round here!' Aware of the hostility, Dave and Patrick offered: 'You can have it — the whole thing — because, as far as we are concerned, this is for the racing industry.'

They had been treated with disrespect and 'a total lack of courtesy' said Dave as they left the room. It was an insult to be treated in that manner, Patrick fumed. 'If they had said, "We'll look further into it," that would have been great. If they had said, "It's not a goer for us at this stage, we don't want to go down that track at the moment," that would have been acceptable. They could have said, "Sorry we've stuffed you up, but it's late in the day after our board meeting — please be brief and just give us an outline." If they had looked at it properly and made a decision one way or the other, that would have been OK.'

'We've spent five years working on this for the benefit of the industry and they rubbish us like that. None of those boards wanted a bar of it, they didn't even want to know about it,' Patrick raged. 'As representative boards they have a responsibility to consider everything that's put in front of them. To me, they have failed as board members representing the whole industry. They were not professional!'

Berri Schroder had been full-on in his enthusiasm — perhaps a little too enthusiastic, Dave wondered uneasily, as he had glanced at the frosty faces across the table.

An American investor later showed interest in the project — too much interest. He developed his own software, copied from RaceO and the tracking system, after signing a confidentiality clause, and was made to pay compensation.

Schroder and his company, Racing Lotto Limited, were forced to move offshore to develop the game. RaceO UK was invested in heavily by some influential backers and brought to life on the Internet in September 2006. Within weeks, the number of hits on the website soared as the jackpot climbed from £400,000 to £1 million.

RaceO was finally introduced to New Zealand in February 2007 as an online betting game and launched on 24 February for the Matamata Breeders' Stakes Day, with Henrietta, the Dowager Duchess of Bedford and a director of RaceO UK, seeing it launched for the race she sponsored, the Breeders' Stakes. Fourteen years after the idea of RaceO was born, the dream had become reality.

Today, Patrick and Dave retain a small 10 per cent shareholding in the enterprise, hoping that RaceO will take wings. Dedicated European punters could be the answer — RaceO comes in the middle of their night and faces no local competition.

In February 2007, Patrick met an official from the Department of Internal Affairs, who volunteered, 'You know that idea you had in the 1990s for a tracking system on jockeys' helmets? Well, if that tracking system had got up and running, you would have had the jump on a huge amount of technology that is now being developed around the world, doing exactly that. It was a really brilliant idea.'

Berri Schroder had seen the big bucks in RaceO, more so than in the tracking system. Patrick and Dave had decided that RaceO was the simple one to develop — the tracking system could follow — but after the insulting rebuff they had received in 1998 to their initiative, Patrick and Dave cooled to the idea of pursuing the tracking proposal.

The aggravation Patrick experienced over the 1998 RaceO episode and a publicised spat with Rob McAnulty that had surfaced at the yearling sales was, as ever, tempered by his wonderful Zabeel. The 'spitting image' stallion son had done so much to help ease the ongoing anguish of his loss of Sir Tristram. Uncannily, and on cue, Zabeel had fired up to fill his father's shoes.

On the track, the performances of Zabeel's progeny in 1997 and 1998 were sensational — little short of sublime. Let us reflect on just five of these horses . . .

Might And Power (Zabeel–Benediction) was purchased by the Sydney vegetable merchant Nick Moraitis for just A$40,000 at the 1995 Easter Yearling Sales in Sydney. He would go on to earn A$3,596,510 from a string of Group 1 victories and titles, including Best Racehorse in Australia 1997, International Stayer of the Year 1997 — the first time any such award had been given to a horse south of the equator — and in 1998 and 1999 the Australian Horse of the Year.

In a meteoric 12-month period during 1997 and 1998, the bay gelding swept all before him, winning the Caulfield Cup, the Melbourne Cup and the Cox Plate, becoming only the second horse after Rising Fast to win the three big races of the Australian turf.

Trained by Jack Denman and ridden by the flamboyant Jimmy Cassidy, Might And Power raced to one of the most emphatic victories ever seen in the Caulfield Cup. Riding against instructions, Cassidy took Might And Power to the front and allowed him to stride along freely. Turning for home he was well clear and raced away to win by seven lengths in record time.

Betting markets for the Cox Plate and Melbourne Cup were hastily rearranged, with Might And Power being installed as a short-priced favourite for both events. But, as it turned out, Might And Power had to wait another 12 months for a Cox Plate run, because Denham and Moraitis decided to go directly to the Melbourne Cup without another run.

Might And Power had received a 3.5 kilogram penalty for the race after his win at Caulfield and was now carrying 56 kilograms. Despite the quality field, on Melbourne Cup day several large bets were wagered on Might And Power — at the time of the start he was established as the 7–2 favourite.

During the race Cassidy again took Might And Power to the lead, and, in an extraordinary display, the horse withstood three distinct waves of challenges from Crying Game at the 1600-metre mark, Linesman on the home turn, and Doriemus over the final 200 metres. Might And Power shook off Linesman and was leading by more than two lengths with 300 metres left to run with Doriemus closing strongly. Edging closer and closer, Doriemus — the 1995 Melbourne Cup winner — appeared likely to cause the upset, but Might And Power found again in the final strides, with the two horses crossing the line too close to separate. Greg Hall on Doriemus waved his whip in salute, but the photo showed Might And Power had held on for victory.

A year on, in 1998, Might And Power, now dubbed the 'People's Champion', led throughout the Cox Plate to win in spectacular style, setting a record time of 2 minutes 3.54 seconds and returning to scale to a massive ovation from racegoers. 'I just idolise this horse,' his owner Nick Moraitis beamed, and so did Australia. In all, the mighty Might And Power would win 15 Group 1 and 2 races.

And then there were the brothers. 'What might the autumn racing season of 1997 have been without Octagonal and Mouawad?' pondered Tony Arrold in *The Australian* under the heading: 'Oh brother, what a double!'

'As special as they are as individuals, what has made this pair unusually rare diamonds is the fact that they are full brothers (Zabeel–Eight Carat) separated by one year in age. Both first saw the light of day on the grounds of Patrick and Justine Hogan's Cambridge Stud in New Zealand.

'Four-year-old Octagonal and his year-younger brother Mouawad teamed recently for a rather special feat from mid-February to the third week in March alternately to win a Group 1 race on six successive weekends, over distances ranging from 1400 metres to 2400 metres.'

Jack Ingham and his younger brother Bob were familiar figures at Trentham and later at the Karaka National Yearling Sales. They had bought their share of winners over the years, but none was to match their pride and joy, their 'very special' Octagonal — 'Big O' or 'Occy' as the crowds who would flock to see the glamour horse liked to call him — who the brothers had purchased, on behalf of their Woodlands Stud Syndicate, at the 1994 yearling sales.

The Inghams and their new trainer, John Hawkes, checked the yearling 'about ten times' over a period of three days before purchasing him for $210,000. 'We kept going back to him. He just had that eye and that look about him,' Bob recalled later. 'It was the first season of Zabeel and he was unknown as a stallion, so the breeding was a big factor. With Johnny we had what we classed the "A's" to look at, and he was right up there. This was a stand-out horse. We thought we would probably have to pay half a million for him — there was no better salesman than Patrick! In saying that, he was always the perfect gentleman, even if we did have to pay more for our horses!'

The Inghams' gut instinct was spot-on. In 1995 as a two-year-old, Octagonal had his first Group 1 victory in April at the AJC Sires' Produce Stakes, and capped that on 28 October when, ridden by Shane Dye, he won the Cox Plate by a neck from Mahogany.

Off the track, Octagonal was an endearing character, greeting visitors by sticking his head over the box for a stroke, or putting out his tongue to have it tickled. On the track, it was a different story. He showed the classic traits of a Sir Tristram heritage — all aggression and heart, and with the habit of stopping in his tracks to eye-ball his opposition before they reached the starting blocks for the race.

But his style of racing made Octagonal heart-attack material for the Ingham brothers who watched his every race, Jack always sporting a hat, Bob bare-headed. The horse's trademark performance was to come from the back to win in the final strides of the race. On so many occasions, the brothers thought: 'He can't pull it off this time,' but he always did.

Between 1996 and 1997 Octagonal won the Group 1 Canterbury Guineas, the Rosehill Guineas, the Mercedes Classic, the AJC Derby, the Underwood Stakes, the Chipping Norton Stakes, the Flemington Australian Cup, and the Rosehill Mercedes Classic for the second time. On that particular Golden Slipper race day, a helicopter had flown overhead, adorned with a banner in the Ingham colours of cerise pink and just two large words — 'Big O' — whilst the crowds, decked out in cerise-coloured caps to match their favourite horse's colours, continued to chant the same words long after the race had finished.

Octagonal was Champion Horse of the Year as both a two-year-old and a three-year-old. But, of all the races in that glittering career, there was one that stood out for the brothers — the 1996 AJC Derby, where 40,000 racegoers were treated to the finest Derby ever. At the 600-metre mark the people's champion 'Big O' looked to have no hope, with only three runners behind him. Up against the likes of VRC Derby winner Nothin' Leica Dane, Bart Cummings' star Saintly and the brilliant Filante, jockey Darren Beadman applied the pressure and Octagonal shot forward to win by a long head from Saintly. The crowd erupted and Jack's joy was almost beyond words: 'He never looks as though he's going to get there . . . ' he enthused to his brother Bob. Their Occy had pulled off the impossible, yet again.

Octagonal was retired to stud as the greatest stakes earner in Australian racing history, amassing A$5.89 million. A decade on from those stirring events, he stands at the Ingham's Woodlands Stud at Denman in upstate New South Wales — his own stallion legacy secure in the reputation of his brilliant son Lonhro and a magnificent successor to the Sir Tristram/Zabeel/Octagonal tradition.

Through the deeds of Lonhro, Octagonal the stallion would become the only Australian Horse of the Year to sire an Australian Horse of the Year.

Opposite the first stallion yard at Woodlands are some carefully tended rose gardens. They flank a fine, bronze, life-sized statue of Octagonal that greets visitors as they approach the entrance of the biggest racehorse owners in Australia — possibly the second biggest in the world after Dubai's Sheikh Mohammed Al Maktoum — along the two-kilometre drive from the front gate.

In 2003 a dying Jack Ingham had one final request for his brother Bob: 'When I die, I want my ashes buried alongside the statue of Octagonal.' Man and horse, together for ever.

Both equine brothers had started their careers as brilliantly as the other, with an almost identical level of peak performance, but whilst Octagonal went on to a glorious retirement, there was to be a tragically different outcome for Mouawad.

Bob Emery's involvement with Mouawad began when Rob McAnulty approached the Cambridge breeder and friend of Patrick's at the 1995 Australian Easter yearling sale after McAnulty had bought the colt. He was looking to syndicate the yearling, he said to Bob. 'Look, I've bought a Zabeel colt, and I've got a share available for $50,000. Do you want it? You should take it.' Not realising that he was Octagonal's brother, but relying on McAnulty's judgement, Emery agreed.

He was a beautiful dark-brown colt and this was a real fun syndicate to belong to, Bob thought. The Kiwis in the Easter Syndicate got in the habit of hopping on a plane for Australia on Friday to watch their colt run over the weekend, with never any thought about him not winning. It was exhilarating — the headiest time any of them could ever recall from owning a horse.

In a racing career that lasted less than a full season and with just eight starts between October 1996 and 15 March 1997,

Mouawad achieved the hat-trick, winning three successive Group 1 races in the Autumn of 1997 — the VRC Australian Guineas, the VATC Futurity Stakes and the George Ryder Stakes — as well as the Listed VRC Moet & Chandon Stakes, the Sandown, the Canterbury and the Rosehill restricted, prompting Sydney's *Daily Telegraph* form analyst and ratings expert Mark Read to predict the sky was the limit for Mouawad. 'He has the best rating pattern of any horse I've assessed in Australia and New Zealand in the past ten years. We still don't know for sure just how good this horse is.'

Whatever the future may hold for the pair, said Read, 'the big brothers O and M are fast cementing an indelible place for themselves in the history of Australian racing.' With seven wins from just eight races, Mouawad crowned a golden season, being named the Australian Champion Three Year Old for 1996–97.

Big M had burst, comet-like, on the racing scene and was to depart from it as abruptly. Mouawad was forced into a premature retirement after the syndicate weighed up the options of a long rest for a suspected leg injury before resuming racing, against that of a lucrative stud career. Tragically, that was never going to be an option. Mouawad the stallion was infertile.

There were two differing opinions within the syndicate on what should be done with the horse. It was 'not a great time to live through' admits Emery, who was in hospital having surgery at the time when the other syndicate members were debating the options. The insurance company paid them out and Mouawad was auctioned off to a Hong Kong buyer, who took him to China to try and improve his fertility.

And then what? China, concrete floors . . .'It was not successful,' Bob's voice drops almost to a whisper. 'It's a sad story. Mouawad was something else.'

In 2007 a large framed photograph of the handsome Mouawad hangs on the wall of Bob Emery's office, alongside that of his champion mare Champagne. His smile broadens as he talks fondly of 'his girl'.

Who could forget the 1998 Melbourne Cup with two New Zealand mares — Jezabeel and Champagne — both the daughters of Zabeel, slugging it out to the line? Patrick and the Cambridge Stud staff roared and cheered the pair to the line. Who would win? Who cared? 'They're ours!' Patrick yelled.

Mike Dillon for the *New Zealand Herald* and Phillip Quay of the *Waikato Times* were two Kiwi journalists at Flemington on that historic occasion when New Zealand came first and second. 'It was such a huge highlight because New Zealand horses hadn't won the Melbourne Cup for ten years — the last was Empire Rose. Not only were Jezabeel and Champagne mares, but they were New Zealand bred, owned and trained,' said Phillip Quay. 'It was a very proud occasion for us.'

And, as the only two mares in the 3200-metre race, they would ensure that Zabeel's sex appeal, current service fee of $40,000 and bank account would be sent sky-rocketing.

'I first saw Champagne at Karaka in Patrick's draft and fell in love with her,' Bob smiles. 'I was looking to buy blue-blood fillies in particular, with the idea of racing them and then breeding with them. I had my vet, Douglas Black, with me and my trainer, Laurie Laxon. We'd go round day after day and look at hundreds of yearlings and I found this filly, on my own, and I said to Douglas, "Go and look at this filly. I love her." He came back and said she was everything I'd want.'

Emery then took Laxon to inspect her. He was not as impressed — she was going to be too big: 'She'll probably be racing as a maiden as a four-year-old!'

Go back and have another look, Emery urged.

She came through the ring and Emery bought her for $100,000. Zabeel was just starting his stud career, and not everyone was complimentary that he had spent so much on a Zabeel horse out of an American broodmare. 'Laurie soon changed his opinion about her when he got her on the track!' Bob noted happily a few months later.

Champagne came out in the spring as a three-year-old and won at her first start. Then, ambitiously, they sent her down for the 1000 Guineas at Riccarton, where she ran fifth. Rob McAnulty phoned him after the race. 'You have got an exceptional filly on your hands.'

'Which one?' Bob asked. 'The filly who'd come fourth or the other filly who came fifth?'

'Champagne. I believe she's exceptional,' Rob replied.

Bob had always respected Rob's judgement and her next few races proved he wasn't too far off the mark. She came back from Christchurch and started winning good three-year-old filly races.

Bob had a plan for her. He decided to bypass New Zealand and try for the big money in Melbourne and the Australian black type for her pedigree. They took her to Melbourne in February for the first race and she won. Thereafter, she ran only in Group races in Melbourne and Sydney as a three-year-old, and was in the money every time.

The last race they gave her in Australia was against older horses to see how she would go. She came second. They brought her home and rested her, and then got her ready for the Melbourne Cup. Her lead-up form wasn't that great, Bob and Laurie fretted, but she was racing in Group 1 races.

Champagne's first sign of form came in the Caulfield Cup, alongside Jezabeel, where both were nearly put over the running rails by the winner of the race, Taufan's Melody. He had cut them out of a chance of winning and should have been disqualified, the two Kiwi camps stormed.

Four days prior to the Melbourne Cup they had set Champagne up for the weight-for-age Group 1 Mackinnon Stakes. For anyone racing a filly with the idea of breeding, that race was considered the ultimate. Champagne romped home, winning by six lengths. It was one of the greatest moments of Bob's life and all he wanted to do was to pack up and go home, he told Laxon. Forget about the Melbourne Cup, she had done them proud. No, no, Laxon convinced him, they must run her in the Melbourne Cup: 'These opportunities don't come often.'

As the horses came out and paraded in front of the crowd on Cup day, Bob was standing beside Bart Cummings, the 'Melbourne Cup legend'.

'Your mare looks fantastic. Just fantastic,' Cummings said. Bob thanked him and, as he was walking away, Cummings added, 'By the way, I think she'll win.' Well, that's come from the legend himself, Bob thought. Maybe she has got a big chance.

Champagne hit the lead at 300 metres, put up a brilliant fight and lost by a nose to Jezabeel who was ridden by Chris

Munce. Bob was so proud of her, he could have burst! He had never thought she was a leading chance — she had never won beyond 2000 metres previously and here she was, pipped at the post in a 3200-metre race!

She was being stabled at David Hayes' Flemington stables, and Bob went round to see his mare at about 9 o'clock that night. There she was, standing with her head down between her legs. 'She was absolutely buggered.' Bob's distress almost matched that of the horse. 'I stroked her and made her a promise that I would never, ever put her in a two-mile race again.'

Champagne injured herself in training in late autumn 1999 and Bob retired her immediately, to reign supreme as the queen of Bob's stud farm in Cambridge. 'Sometimes I think she's a king!' he says proudly. 'She has a lot of the characteristics of a stallion.' At the time of writing this book, Champagne is in foal to Australia's premier sire, Redoute's Choice.

That biggest of punters, Kerry Packer, had placed $1 million on Might And Power to win the 1997 Melbourne Cup and, along with his friend and sometime racing partner, billionaire Lloyd Williams, he stuck with the winning Zabeel formula for 1998, plunging an estimated $5 million on Jezabeel to win.

In taking the Melbourne Cup, Jezabeel would become the first horse to win both the Melbourne and the Auckland Cups, while her breeder Jeanette Broome would also have a double distinction, that of breeding the winners of the world's two greatest races — the Grand National at Aintree and the Melbourne Cup at Flemington. 'I stopped the Northern Hemisphere for about six minutes and I stopped the Southern Hemisphere for about three-and-a-half,' she laughs.

A remarkable mare and a remarkable woman . . . Jeanette Buchanan was born in Ross on the West Coast, where her father was the postmaster, and later moved with her husband Jack Broome to Lower Hutt in 1963 to work with his parents who ran the Olympic Hotel. Here Jeanette met hotel guests attending the annual yearling sales at Trentham, and made contacts who would spark her interest in thoroughbred breeding and racing.

In 1973, Jeanette and Jack bought 97 acres at Eureka, a hamlet 13 miles east of Hamilton, and Jeanette began to pursue her now full-blown passion for horses under the name of Loch-Haven Thoroughbreds. She bought broodmares and became a committee member of the Waikato branch of the New Zealand Thoroughbred Breeders' Association.

Seagram, a chestnut gelding bred by Jeanette and trained by David Barons in the United Kingdom for Sir Eric Parker, won the 1991 Grand National — an ironic gift for the race's sponsor, who had turned down a previous offer to buy the already named horse. That year, Jeanette won the inaugural BMW New Zealand Breeder of the Year title and, 26 years on, remains one of only three women to win the award in her own name. And then came Jezabeel, bred and sold by Jeanette to the Cambridge trainer Brian Jenkins for Adrian Burr and Peter Tatham.

The contribution of Jezabeel and Champagne was officially recognised across the Tasman in 1999, with Jezabeel being named the BMW Champion New Zealand Stayer of the Year, and Champagne the BMW Champion Weight-for-age Performer of the Year.

In 2004, sales and advertising guru John Singleton, one of three part-owners of the Magic Millions, spoke of the oddball circumstances in which he later became the owner of Jezabeel. Singleton had owned Jezabeel for several years, he said, with the mare foaling down three thoroughbreds by Danehill, one by Carnegie, and she was currently in foal to Danehill's champion son Rock of Gibraltar.

How did he come to own Jezabeel? an Australian journalist asked. It was widely known that Melbourne businessman Lloyd Williams had bought Jezabeel as a broodmare investment after her 1998 Melbourne Cup triumph. 'I have had a number of business dealings for many years with Lloyd and I became Jezabeel's new owner after finalising one, challenging him to a toss of a coin to settle the account, which he agreed to,' Singo recalled. 'I won. As a matter of interest, I also own another of Lloyd's former top mares, the Golden Slipper winner Merlene.'

When Bloodstock Update, the statistical arm of the Victoria Racing Club's computerised Racing Services Bureau, published the final figures for the 1997–98 racing season in Australia, Zabeel had toppled the great Danehill for the stallion's title. He'd done it by the shortest of short heads — $7,434,690 to Danehill's $7,421,682 — but as every punter knows, that's enough.

Patrick, who had been named eight months earlier in the *National Business Review*'s Rich List as having an estimated worth of $35 million, then turned down an offer of $22 million to sell his super-stallion. 'Go away,' he said.

Towards the end of 1999, Patrick received an official letter addressed to 'Patrick Hogan, CBE' at Cambridge Stud. The

Department of Internal Affairs had written to tell him that his name had been put forward for a knighthood for services to thoroughbred breeding and racing. They would be delighted if he would accept. However, he was to keep the contents of the letter confidential, even from his wife, he was told.

Well . . . Patrick had certainly had his ups and downs in life and in the industry he loved, but the conferring of this honour blew him away. The hardest part, he knew, would be to follow the instructions in keeping it from Justine, until closer to the announcement date.

In mid-December and a fortnight before the publication of the New Year's Honours list, he told her. In future she would officially be known as Justine, Lady Hogan, he said. 'I don't think a title suits me,' Justine replied. 'But if you want it, that's fine by me.'

PATRICK HOGAN ON EIGHT CARAT

'The sale of Cambridge Stud's Zabeel–Eight Carat colt for $1.6 million to a Victorian stud on the opening night of the 1998 National Yearling Sales at Karaka marks the highest point in New Zealand yearling sales for the past 50 years, says vendor Patrick Hogan. For Hogan, who has made top price at the annual yearling sales 14 times, this year's $1.6 million record is "a quantum price leap" on his previous record price of $1.2 million paid in 1989 for a Sir Tristram–Surround colt.'

— *New Zealand Export News*, February 1998.

'It's really quite odd that my standout stallion, Sir Tristram, came originally from Ireland, and my most outstanding mare came from England — both Northern Hemisphere horses of

Irish origin. Robert Sangster had made a successful bid to buy Eight Carat — whose deeds on the racetrack were nothing to write home about — from her previous owner in England, and then he sent her over from Australia to Cambridge Stud, to be covered by Sir Tristram.

'That union produced a magnificent-looking colt in Kaapstad and I later had the chance of buying Eight Carat (Pieces of Eight–Klairessa) from Robert for $850,000 which was a substantial sum at the time. I leapt at it because I loved her pedigree and the duplications in that pedigree.

'People talk of the outstanding sires' performances. I would like to have that of Eight Carat's put right up there alongside that of Sir Tristram and Zabeel. Her career achievement was comparable with that of a highly commercial stallion. Eight Carat, who was called the Queen of the Stud Book, won the New Zealand Broodmare of the Year a record-equalling three times from 1995 to 1997, largely due to the deeds of Octagonal and Mouawad.

'She was the dam of five Group 1 winning champions — Diamond Lover, Kaapstad, Mouawad, Octagonal and Our Marquise — and when you consider that a broodmare is likely to produce about ten foals in a lifetime, that record is simply outstanding.

'Kaapstad and Octagonal in turn have sired Group 1 winners, including the great Lonhro, winner of 11 Group 1 races (Octagonal) and Tall Poppy (Kaapstad) with six Group and listed wins in New Zealand.

'Eight Carat's daughters have also thrown Group 1 winners, including Danewin, Peruzzi, Don Eduardo and Tristalove, and her granddaughters have produced equal performers in Viscount, Viking Ruler and Shower of Roses.

'She was a lovely mare to have around the place and when she died in 2000 we had her buried close to Sir Tristram on the Cambridge Stud forecourt — a fitting final resting home, we felt, for a wonderful broodmare.'

CHAPTER 15

THROUGH THE ROOF
AT KARAKA

'He's got everything.'

> — Tik Tik Trinidad, bloodstock manager at Gooree Stud,
> New South Wales

EIGHT CARAT'S FIRST Group 1 winning daughter, Diamond Lover, and Zabeel had combined to produce a colt who would send the Australasian yearling record into the stratosphere — a colt judges would rave over as 'outstanding . . . stunning . . . a smasher' at the 2000 Karaka National Yearling Sales.

'The description I really liked, though, was a bloodstock agent's assessment of the colt as a "Comaneci", the perfect 10,' wrote Tony Arrold, editor of the thoroughbred breeding section for *The Australian*. He picks up the tale: 'A very formidable field of players lined up when Sir Patrick Hogan's masterpiece entered the arena. The noise level inside the packed auditorium dropped to a hush. Kieran Moore started the ball rolling at $800,000 and was soon joined by Graeme Rogerson after he had taken proceedings to $1.7 million — over the existing New Zealand record. Bart Cummings waved the white flag after going to $1.8 million, leaving just two principals to continue.

'In a corner of the press box high up in the auditorium, Gai Waterhouse sat beside Dr Shalabh Kumar Sahu, manager of the Emirates Park Stud at Murrurundi, New South Wales . . . to their right, further around in the public sector, Tik Tik Trinidad from the Philippines leaned against a column support, holding a mobile phone in his hands. He was speaking to Eduardo Cojuangco, head of the Manila-based San Miguel Corporation and operator of the Gooree Stud in New South Wales.

'The Waterhouse party lodged benchmark bids of $2 million, $2.5 million, $3 million and $3.5 million. Trinidad's mobile had gone dead with the bidding at $3 million, leaving Cojuangco's private trainer, adviser and friend over many years to fend for himself. He decided to stay in the intensive two-way duel and his $3.6 million bid went unchallenged — he had won. As thunderous applause broke out with the fall of auctioneer's hammer, Trinidad re-established contact with Manila and was given the okay from Cojuangco. "I think that [$3.6 million] was to have been my last call," a relieved Trinidad said afterwards.

'Cojuangco had jetted into Auckland five days earlier with Trinidad to inspect a select group from the catalogue, and Trinidad confessed he had been struck by a bolt of lightning when he saw the Diamond Lover colt. Cojuangco had departed, leaving Trinidad in charge of doing his own bidding.

'Trinidad was lost for words when asked for his thoughts of the colt in his pre-sale inspection. "He was just . . . " But the rolling of his eyes skywards and a beaming smile said it all for him. "He's got everything. We hope he will make the grade as a racehorse, then he can go off to be a stallion.'"

Trinidad's expectations were later fulfilled when the colt, Don Eduardo, racing in the red and black stripes of Cojuangco's Gooree Pastoral Company, was named top of the 2001–02 Australasian three-year-old classification. He was retired to stud in 2003 after winning the Group 1 AJC Derby.

'On conformation, I rate him the best I have ever bred,' Sir Patrick said within minutes of the hammer falling on his colt, his voice quavering from the emotion of the moment.

New Zealand Bloodstock chairman Peter Vela admitted to being swept up in the electric atmosphere as the two-party bidding duel proceeded from $2.1 million in increments of $100,000. 'It was real theatre . . . awesomely exciting. There will be a tremendous spin-off internationally for this sale,' Vela said. 'I am reliably informed this colt is the sixth-highest-priced yearling to be sold anywhere over the past 12 months, so the message will be that New Zealand is no backwater of the racing world, and that this sale is no Mickey Mouse show.'

How many $3.6 million yearlings would it take to match the price New Zealand Bloodstock gave the ailing Wrightson Bloodstock for its showcase Karaka Sales Complex just four years before that day? Arrold said the popular figure thrown around at the end of 1996 was $7.2 million — precisely double what this colt had fetched — but Peter Vela was not buying into any of that.

'What I can say is how delighted I am that we've grown our business in four years for the premier session from $21.6 million to $55 million,' he said.

The rags-to-riches Vela story begins in Croatia in the early part of the 20th century, when the poverty-stricken fishing family's sons are sent to the four corners of the earth to seek their fortunes and return some of those proceeds to the family at home. One of those sons ends up in Nelson, New Zealand, working as a fisherman and producing two sons who will become horse-mad — Peter and Philip.

As a family, the Velas spent their holidays with a family who had racing interests. Peter loved being around the thoroughbreds. He loved seeing them and looked forward to the day when he could race and own one. From Nelson College, Peter went to Waikato University, graduating with a Bachelor's degree in Social Science and Economics and a Master's in Politics and Sociology. He worked on the starting gates wherever races were run in the Waikato for about $13 a day, and became a fisherman on his father's boat in the university holidays.

Philip came on board when Peter started racing in the early 1970s, racing horses they had bred at their farm at Te Kowhai. Then the brothers decided they needed a strategy — they would acquire fillies that were well bred and breed from them. They hit the jackpot with their first. Noble Heights was sold by Cambridge Stud at Trentham to the brothers and, years later, Peter Vela said she was something else.

'We haven't had one as versatile since, for the distances she could run. She could run 1 minute 10 seconds at 1200 metres, and she ran a record time at 2400 metres — quite incredible! We've had wonderful success with the Sir Tristram breed. It was the best thing that ever happened — that $4000 share in Paddy — and we were very fortunate. We ended up filling the farm with Sir Tristram fillies with which we had incredible luck and success.'

Richebourg, a Vice Regal filly, bought as a yearling on Joe Walls' recommendation, would become the cornerstone of Vela's Pencarrow Stud's most exciting family — Group champions all. Richebourg left Romanee Conti, Romanee Conti left Ethereal, Richebourg left Grand Echezeaux, who left the brilliant Darci Brahma (purchased at the 2005 yearling sales by David Ellis of Te Akau stud for a sale high of $1.05 million) . . . 'It's pretty compelling,' Vela says. 'Then there's the likes of Riverina Charm, whose mother was covered by Sir Tristram. She was quite special and virtually unbeatable at 2000 metres, winning the 1000 Guineas at Caulfield in 1988, the Rosehill Guineas, the Canterbury Guineas and the Group 1 Air New Zealand Stakes.' And, typical of her bloodline, she was strong-willed, with a burning desire to be competitive.

Vela beams with pride. 'She would do anything to ensure success, even at a training gallop. It wouldn't be beyond a Sir Tristram filly to turn and try to have a piece of the thing she was working with! But on the ground, we never had one that had a bad attitude. That's what set them in great stead as broodmares.'

The brothers had their stud farms, but their bread-and-butter income lay in the fishing industry. That was until the Velas decided to sell their domestic fishing distribution business in 1986 and buy it back — following the stock market crash in 1989 — as a much bigger animal than the one they had sold. They were now the owners of Wattie's fishing interests to add to their original company, and commensurably richer.

Almost by chance, Vela became the purchaser of the Karaka Sales Complex. In the last week of November 1996, he took a call telling him that it was up for sale — Fletcher Challenge had decided it was a non-core business for them and they were keen to divest it. There had been a group of New Zealanders who had tried unsuccessfully to put a group together, his caller added. 'It seems as though it will be sold to William Inglis in Australia. Would you think about taking it on — even if only in a caretaker capacity?'

He would consider it, Vela promised. A couple of weeks later, he ran into Patrick at the Hong Kong Cup and told him of the proposal. 'What's your feeling on it?' Vela asked.

'If you'd step up to the plate and buy it, you would do us all a great favour and you'd have my support 100 per cent,' Patrick pledged.

They did a quick due diligence and, a few days before Christmas, the Vela brothers announced to Karaka staff that they had bought the sales complex. The vendor was keen to sell prior to the next yearling sale in January 1997, they added, and so the changeover would be swift.

On moving into Karaka, Vela realised that he was the inheritor of a complex mess and, in coming to grips with it, his background as a thoroughbred breeder would prove to be invaluable. 'There were many things as a breeder I felt we needed badly and it wasn't happening,' he said. 'It was a matter of addressing a number of areas to get a more stable business.' He had lived through the problems that others encountered — the availability of finance and stallions, what it was like to try and sell yearlings when there were no buyers, what it was like to try finding homes for them when there was no finance available — and, as a bonus, he had been a prominent buyer at sales around the world and knew how the auction system worked.

In his first six years at Karaka, Peter Vela worked tirelessly to get the right systems going so that it could be left secure in the hands of a hand-picked team, including his lawyer daughter

Petrea and Karaka's marketing manager. 'To get the really critical things in action took four or five years, but I never despaired that we would turn it around. In terms of return from funds employed, it's still a long way from being very profitable — it's not that sort of business. There's a fair bit of sentiment attached.'

Most professional buyers who spend their lives travelling from sale to sale would agree Karaka is the finest complex in the world, he claims with pride. 'Demi O'Byrne, the buyer for Coolmore Stud and the biggest buyer in the world, says Karaka is, undoubtedly, the finest complex in the world today. This is really the only purpose-built complex in the world, where they've started with a bare piece of land and said, "We want the best we can get," and come back and created, pretty well, a dream.'

Today Vela's life is divided between Switzerland, Portugal and his Pencarrow Stud in Waikato. 'The really sad thing about breeding,' he reflects, 'is that it's so exciting, when you do a mating, that you are just wishing for time to pass quickly — you're always waiting for a mating to become a foetus, a foetus to become a foal, a foal to become a yearling, a yearling to become a racehorse, and a racehorse to become a Group winner . . . '

In one foaling paddock at Pencarrow Stud, there's Romanee Conti, Grand Echezeaux and Romanee Conti's daughter, Ethereal — the Cambridge Stud-sired winner of the 2001 Melbourne Cup. That was the experience every owner hoped for. 'She was just tremendous, as was her mother, Romanee Conti, a little Sir Tristram mare who tried her heart out anytime she was set a task, and had won for us the Hong Kong Cup at Sha Tin,' said Vela. That had been a wonderful thrill — and then, to have Ethereal, who turned out to be even more stroppy than her mother and impatient about life, but who was a beautifully tractable race filly that an experienced jockey could do anything with in a race.

Ethereal had won the Caulfield Cup by a nose and then drawn number 13 for the Melbourne Cup — in life and racing, an incredibly lucky number for the Vela brothers. Peter was standing with Jack Ingham at the draw and the first horse called out was Ethereal. Ingham said, 'Oh, no good there, son.'

Peter replied: 'First out, first home, Jack!'

Ethereal raced wide in the field, but her jockey Scott Seamer had walked the track and was confident of his charge. Godolphin Stud's Give the Slip went six or seven lengths clear, but Ethereal ran him down and got him in the last few strides. It was the most wonderful moment for Vela.

Late that night, he returned to the hotel to find a letter under his door from the Prime Minister, Helen Clark, offering congratulations: 'What a great achievement for you and for New Zealand.' It made him realise he had done something pretty good for his country, Peter told his family.

'There is nothing to compare with the joy of victory, as long as you never forget the deeds of the horse,' Vela says. 'If you wander through my farm, you will see horses we sold as yearlings that have ended up racing in Singapore, and that we have flown home because they were going to end up going to the zoo.

'With every paddock where we have three or four foals weaning, we will have a horse just like that — an old broodmare that's retired, or a horse we've sold that has come to the end of its racing life. Our broodmares have a place on our farm for as long as they live.'

Aside from their $3.6 million colt, there were two other great events on the horse front for Patrick in 2000.

Brew, a gelding sired by the ageing Sir Tristram from the champion mare Horlicks, won the Melbourne Cup, setting the record at six for Fencourt and Cambridge Stud. As significantly, it was a world-record 45 individual Group 1 successes for Sir Tristram — and made him the sire of three Melbourne Cup winners in Gurner's Lane, Empire Rose and Brew.

The media started calling, just moments after Brew's win, and the calls ran long into the night from both sides of the Tasman. What many were not aware of was Patrick's first reaction after watching the race on television. As Brew crossed the line, he walked outside, grabbed his gardening snippers and placed two red roses on Sir Tristram's grave. 'Thank you, Paddy,' he murmured. The following morning his red roses were joined by a bunch of yellow lilies from an unknown admirer.

'The New Zealand thoroughbred industry is as elated as Brew's owners, trainer and Cambridge Stud,' said Michael Martin, chief executive of the New Zealand Thoroughbred Breeders' Association. 'This is the result we all wanted.'

The concept of using the services of a shuttle stallion had been suggested to him years before by Michael Fay. 'Why don't you bring in those stallions from overseas? They only work six months there.' He saw the picture straight away, Fay said later. 'It took a long time for it to happen, but it did happen because Patrick is very focused, very energised. It's fun to be around someone like that, and Justine, of course, is the calm in the storm.'

Stravinsky — who would become worthy of second billing at Cambridge Stud behind Zabeel — commenced stud duties in New Zealand in 2000, his duties as a shuttle stallion 'down under' agreed to on a handshake. His owner, John Magnier of Coolmore Stud in Ireland, had given Patrick the breeding rights to Stravinsky in the Southern Hemisphere for half of each year.

If he had failed to nail Stravinsky, Patrick said, there was another stallion whose services he was keen to acquire. His name was Cape Cross; he stood in England at a stud owned by Sheikh Hamdan bin Rashid Al Maktoum, and was a Group 1 winning miler from the Northern Dancer line. What appealed, probably most of all, though, was that his sire was out of a Sir Ivor mare. Through Cape Cross Patrick would have a breeding link to Sir Ivor, the sire of Sir Tristram.

'I've got to go and look at this horse,' Patrick told Joe Walls, who had accompanied him on his European trip. He loved the champion two-year-old stallion on sight. He was black, he was beautiful and it was indicated that he was for sale and could be bought for one million sterling, which the New Zealanders agreed to. There was a condition though, Joe told John Ferguson, Darley Stud's manager — the buyer's name was to be kept confidential.

However, as events transpired, Cape Cross would not be sold. He would become the second shuttle stallion at Cambridge Stud, standing there for four years before being transferred to Darley's farm at Aberdeen, New South Wales. But New Zealand breeders would continue to benefit, with Darley transporting mares free of charge to Australia to be covered by Cape Cross and other Darley stallions.

His title — Sir Patrick Hogan, Knight Companion of the New Zealand Order of Merit (KNZM) — had been won for him by a group of determined friends, including Fred Cole, John Ryan and Sir Ross Jansen, who had begun their campaign back in 1996. One of his backers, Rob Feisst, an original shareholder in Sir Tristram, began his letter to the then Prime Minister, Jenny Shipley, on 17 August 1999:

'About three years ago I was privileged to join a group of people who wished to nominate Patrick Hogan for higher honours. Naturally, I have, along with a large number of people, been disappointed to see that our nominee has not received the number one position in the draw. The great [racehorse] owners are known worldwide and are highly influential people. New Zealand does not have the great owners now. However, we do have a breeder of thoroughbreds whose deeds and achievements rank him with the world's best.

'Patrick Hogan has achieved recognition of his feats on an international basis and has highly enhanced our reputation as a producer of quality stock. I cannot emphasise enough what this international goodwill does for New Zealand as a whole.'

After referring to Patrick's assistance to many charities, Feisst concluded: 'I am firmly of the opinion that if it had not been for the standards set and achieved by Patrick Hogan, the entire New Zealand thoroughbred industry would have languished so far behind the Australian industry so as to cease to count on the international stage.'

Ross Finlayson, president of the New Zealand Thoroughbred Breeders' Association, would write to Fred Cole in support of their bid, saying 'He [Patrick] has been a quiet man of charity. I am not privileged to know of his full generosity but from a horse industry point of view, Patrick is always first to commit.

'Just as one small example he recently purchased the Thoroughbred Library compiled by the late Bob Stead and donated it to the association. The library, which is recognised as the best of its kind in the Southern Hemisphere, is now in the new headquarters of the association. Members frequently use it as a reference point which is not surprising, as some books go as far back as the 1800s.

'I can quote other examples of Patrick's generosity to the industry, but want to finally say that all of his achievements have not changed the man at all. Throughout his career he has remained a typical Kiwi with all the great attributes that that conveys.'

Hosting charity events and celebrities had long been an integral part of the scene at Cambridge Stud. Visiting royalty, heads-of-state, film stars, sports stars and politicians clamoured for the opportunity to see Sir Tristram, including a memorable 'four Irishmen' occasion.

Irish Prime Minister Albert Reynolds, New Zealand Prime Minister Jim Bolger, Patrick and Sir Tristram lined up for the cameras, and after downing afternoon tea, the 12-car entourage swept down the drive, with the Irish PM clutching a bronze of Sir Tristram.

And it was Sir Tristram who drew Denis Waterman, star of the British television series *Minder*, to the stud after requesting that he wanted to see the famous stallion on his promotional tour of New Zealand in 1982. A keen racing man, Waterman arrived with his female companion to spend a happy hour talking horses.

Olympic equestrian Captain Mark Phillips, the then husband of Princess Anne, was the perfect guest when he stayed with the Hogans in 1984. He was rather nervous and stuttery at first, Justine observed. 'Just relax, you can be at home here,' she told him.

'He invited a couple of his New Zealand friends to dinner and we had a lovely evening,' Justine recalls. 'Later that night he wanted to meet Paddy, but there was this great British police cordon around the house for security and they wouldn't let him out — they were quite rude to us. Eventually they relented and he got to meet Sir Tristram. We weren't to tell anyone that he was staying with us.

'He phoned England that evening and said afterwards, "I'm not very popular. I've forgotten my wife's birthday!" I said Patrick often forgot mine.

'He had put his boots outside his bedroom door to have them cleaned. The next morning I went in to wake him up and said, "By the way, I've left your boots and I'm certainly not cleaning them. My staff would give me hell! Anyway they're such great big whopping feet I'd be there all day. Here's the nugget and cloth, here's the newspaper for you to clean your own, and we'll see you at breakfast." He looked at me quite oddly, I thought, but those boots were clean when he arrived for a general breakfast that we had for everyone. I enjoyed his company — he was very friendly.'

In 1999 Princess Anne had the stud placed on her New Zealand itinerary, following the visit of her mother, Queen Elizabeth, nine years earlier. 'Of all the dignitaries and the diplomats I've had here, the Queen was the most interested and the most knowledgeable,' Patrick commented to *Sunday Times* journalist Peter Sweeney, who was covering the Princess's visit.

This time there was no Sir Tristram. However, the Princess wanted to read the words on his headstone, before being taken to see his paddock, stall, drinking trough and the crash helmets and vests Sir Tristram's handlers wore. Patrick had always admired her for her pluckiness and riding skill, but royalty confers a nervousness on a host which doesn't help the visitor. The visit was correct, but not a raging success.

Joan Collins . . . well, that was Patrick's idea. The Te Rapa Racing Club had the idea of inviting a celebrity to the races as a promotion for its International Day. Patrick was a sponsor for several races, and the previous year's choice of celebrity, rocker Rod Stewart and his New Zealand super-model wife Rachel Hunter, had proved a huge hit with the local racing fraternity. 'Why don't we invite Joan Collins, the Bitch in Dallas?' Patrick suggested at a committee meeting. 'She's pretty glamorous.'

The film star accepted, first coming out to Cambridge Stud for a brief visit to get the feel of things. She clearly didn't enjoy herself and was quite demanding, Patrick observed with dismay.

When she got to Te Rapa, Ms Collins told officials, 'I want only Patrick Hogan to look after me today. No one else!' To his knowledge she didn't invest a cent, but at the end of the meeting she told him she was going to Huka Lodge for the weekend and invited him to join her.

Mistake number one was to invite such a non-horsey person to Waikato, but mistake number two was telling the family he had politely declined her invitation to Huka Lodge. That news cut no ice with the Hogan women, who were livid. 'One sister-in-law wouldn't speak to me for three weeks!' he told Joe Walls.

Premiers, prime ministers, leaders of Arab States, a Saudi Arabian royal, the Amin of the State of Bahrain, representatives from the Royal Racing Stables of the Sultan of Oman, Teruya

Yoshida from Shadai Farm (the biggest stud farm in Japan), the All Blacks, the New Zealand Barbarians, the Japan rugby team, Super 14 teams, rugby league's Parramatta Eels . . . all signed the visitors' book, including 'a visitor from Hawke's Bay' who scribbled in the comments column: 'RICH BUGGERS!'

Justine Hogan, who in a rare magazine interview had explained her low profile by saying 'Patrick does enough talking for both of us', had come up trumps. She had bought her first horse for $20,000 in 1999, which she intended to race with her daughters Nicola and Erin, after receiving a personal invitation from Peter Vela to attend the inaugural fillies' post-race day sale at Te Rapa.

It could be bit of fun to own one, she decided on the day, and inspected several with Marcus Corban and trainer Stephen Autridge. She chose a Danasinga filly.

'I had no part of it. I didn't want her to buy it but, as usual, she didn't listen to me,' Patrick was philosophical. If his wife wanted to race a horse, she should have kept a Danehill filly they sold at Karaka, he said. Justine rejected that option, saying that rather than worry about racing a filly that had fetched $850,000, she was happier to have a share in a cheap horse.

The Hogan ladies called her Singalong, a brilliant choice for a horse who would sing sweetly all the way to the winning post. Singalong, who had barely three weeks' rest between her two-year-old and three-year-old campaigns, and contested the first fillies' race at Wanganui in August 2000, was the toughest filly he had trained, said Autridge. 'She'll go home and eat all her feed, and will do all the work you want. She's really tough.'

In 2001 at Te Rapa came the sweetest moment of all when Patrick presented the trophy for the Cambridge Stud

Sir Tristram Fillies' Classic to his wife and daughters after Singalong's victory. 'It just goes to show,' said Nicola at the presentation. 'The girls can pick the horses as well as Dad can!'

'They're very lucky to have this filly,' her father countered. 'But I do all the payments and they take all the cheques! I suppose next they'll be wanting a free service to Zabeel.'

From Te Rapa came their next trip, a couple of months later; this time to the Wellington BMW awards ceremony, when Singalong was named 2001 New Zealand Bloodstock Filly of the Year.

The success of Singalong took Justine back to the early days when she and her sister-in-law Pat had raced Gay Poss. They had gone to see her at Cummings' stables in Adelaide and, on arrival, Justine had asked to see another Hogan horse, Erin Nicola, the one named for their two daughters. Erin Nicola was no great shakes — she was a weedy type by contrast with Gay Poss who was in great form. However, Justine had always had a soft spot for the underdog, and so she said, 'Pat, you go and see Gay Poss and I'll find Erin Nicola.'

Unlike Gay Poss who resided in the front paddock, no one seemed to know of Erin Nicola when she asked for directions. Erin Nicola had been stuck down at the back of the property and been given the nickname Rabbit by the stablehands.

Justine told Bart: 'Send her home to Cambridge Stud.'

'Who, Gay Poss?'

'No, Erin Nicola. I will love her if no one else does.'

There was a sequel. Some years later, Erin Nicola was in the broodmares' paddock at Cambridge Stud, in foal to the good stallion Sobig, when an Australian buyer offered $30,000 for the mare. She wasn't that good on the racetrack, he knew that, he said — he wanted her for the foal inside.

'What happens to Erin Nicola after that?' Justine asked. That should not worry her, he replied. Well, as a matter of fact, it did worry her, Justine retorted.

They were desperate for money at the time. Patrick took Justine into the kitchen. 'You've got to sell! That $30,000 will finish the fencing of the property.'

But the memory of seeing her mare stuck down in the back paddock was too strong. 'She is not for sale,' Justine told the prospective buyer.

Patrick had been the first to guarantee his horses, but decades later that commitment would take a nasty twist. Not only did he sell horses of his own in the ring, he also sold on behalf of others. In these cases, it was understood by owners that they were to stand by Patrick and all of his decisions over the sale of their horse under the Cambridge Stud banner, including any guarantees he might give. It was a shake-of-the-hand agreement and it had worked well — that is, until the 2002 yearling sales at Karaka.

Patrick had put a filly through the ring on behalf of the vendors and she made $100,000. The purchaser of the filly got her home and shortly after phoned him at Cambridge Stud, saying: 'We're just getting the filly broken in and we've found she's blind in one eye. We've had someone look at her, and it's his opinion that she was probably born blind in that eye, or, if not, she has certainly been blind for quite some time. It hasn't been a recent accident and it hasn't been something that has just developed.'

During her three months at Cambridge Stud while preparing her for the sale, they had never noticed she was blind and therefore disqualified from racing under Australasian rules, Patrick said with surprise. 'We saw nothing to suggest it. I'll get in touch with the vendors.'

He immediately contacted the partnership he represented in the sale ring, and told them what had happened. Their response was, 'That's their tough luck. She's been through the ring — that's their problem.'

'Well, that's not how I operate!' Patrick was furious. 'If the filly was blind before the sale, that means she had something wrong that we weren't aware of. As a presenter, we were ignorant of the fact.'

He returned to the purchaser, whose response was blunt. 'I'll see you in court. We're not paying if the filly is blind.'

There followed a fair amount of to'ing and fro'ing, with Patrick in the middle, hoping that the vendors would do the decent thing. However, the partnership stuck to their guns. 'Sale conditions say *caveat emptor* — buyer beware — so if the vet who vetted it for the buyer didn't see that the horse was blind, that's the buyer's problem, his responsibility,' they argued.

Patrick had always been prepared to take any horse back that had a defect he wasn't aware of at the time, and he also knew that buyer did not get his horses vetted — he picked horses that appealed to him.

There was only one decision he could make, but before he did that he contacted the vendors again and asked them for a final decision one way or the other. One told him, 'We're digging our toes in and we are prepared to go to court.'

Patrick wrote out a cheque for $100,000 to the buyers of the filly and had her brought home to live at Cambridge Stud. The purchaser appreciated the gesture and thanked him profusely. Then Patrick informed the vendors of the filly what he had done. He wrote to the partnership, asking them, again, to honour their commitment, saying he was not prepared to go to court to try and defend the indefensible. He had always stood by his guarantee, he said, and did not believe in what they had done. It was against his principles.

One member of the partnership arrived at Cambridge Stud, pushed a note across his desk, and said, 'You'll find our decision in there. Would you like to discuss it?'

'No!' Patrick said.

What really cut him up was the knowledge that he had been used. He had presented the filly as a favour for the partnership, some of whom were friends stretching back over many years, and his favour had turned to custard.

Today, he talks to one of the partners, who later approached him privately, offering to buy back into the filly. Patrick thanked him, but said he would ride it out on his own. 'It could cause complications for you down the track with your other owners.'

The rest of the syndicate he and Justine have never spoken to again. They pass by one another at the races without a word.

In 2007, that filly is a seven-year-old mare who has produced two foals. Her first sold for next to nothing; her second, a colt, fetched a reasonable price at the 2007 Karaka sales.

'Patrick Hogan: Film Star'. The *Waikato Times*, Saturday 14 June 2003 edition, blasted the news on its billboards and in banner headlines running across the page. 'Sam Neill is wanted to play the part of Sir Patrick Hogan in a Hollywood movie set in part at Cambridge Stud,' wrote Aidan Rodley.

'American novelist Ted Simendinger's book, *12 Miles to Paradise*, has been adapted to screenplay by Hollywood writer Douglas Epoch who wrote *Sweet Home Alabama* starring Reese Witherspoon. Sir Patrick allowed Simendinger to use his name and character for the book after the Denver-based author spent 40 minutes at Cambridge Stud on a trip to New Zealand several years ago. In the book, Sir Patrick becomes a father figure to the female lead character, Cushla, in a romantic comedy also set in Florida and the Bahamas.

'Simendinger told the *Waikato Times* this week that Queenstown-based Neill was both his and Epoch's first choice to portray Sir Patrick. "Sam would be a great Sir Patrick and Sir Patrick deserves to be portrayed by a star like Sam." Anna Paquin and Keisha Castle-Hughes are their leading choices for the role of Cushla.

'Sir Patrick said he had initially taken Simendinger's hopes to have the book adapted to screenplay "with a grain of salt", but accepted now it was closer to happening. "It's mind boggling really," he said. "It would have been great if Sam Neill accepted that role. You never know though — maybe I could have played myself."'

Contacted by another New Zealand media outlet, Simendinger had this to say: 'I believe Sir Patrick is the direct by-product of focus, passion and commitment. He's cocky, confident, decisive — a pure leader.'

It was all too much for Patrick's mates. In November that year, following the running of the Melbourne Cup, they were in a Japanese restaurant in Hamilton, primed for a convivial evening. Some were from New Zealand, including Brent

Gillovic, a Waikato studmaster and old friend of Patrick's, and during the conversation it came up that some people from Hollywood were going to make a movie about him.

Gillovic spoke quietly to an Irish mate seated alongside him: 'Listen, he'll pick my voice, but he won't recognise yours. Let's have him on!'

The Irishman wandered off to another part of the restaurant to phone Patrick on his mobile and, using a phoney American accent, launched into the conversation. 'I got noos of this movie and I'd like to be the director. Can you tell me something about yourself?'

Patrick was all concentration while his friends, who had been tipped off, were almost splitting their sides in trying not to laugh. 'Who do you think you would like to have playing the part of your wife?'

'How about Julia Roberts?' Patrick suggested.

'Julia Roberts?' Brent's mate, the 'movie director', queried. 'Yes, yes! That's the one and we can get her! No problem at all. And what about yourself?'

'Umm . . .' Patrick paused. 'I don't know . . . What's that young joker's name? Brad somebody . . . Brad Pitt! Yeah, yeah, that's him — but I really wouldn't mind playing myself!'

They had to move Nelson Schick away from the table then, because of the noise he was making. He was crying with laughter and had tears rolling down his face. 'Shut up, Nelson, you'll give the game away!' they hissed.

The conversation concluded with a request. 'When can I see you?' the director asked.

'Well, I'm going to South Africa,' Patrick explained. 'I'm away for two or three weeks. Give me your fax and I'll send you my itinerary.'

'Patrick is so great to train for. He always pays his bills straight away, never complains. He's one of the best payers in the industry. He puts a lot of money back into the industry, sponsoring big races, buying horses and encouraging new ventures. He's the most generous bloke and most people don't know the half he does, like sponsoring the Westpac helicopter — the Waikato air ambulance.

'I got a call from Brother Dan recently on behalf of a Catholic charity, so I told him, "Give my mate Patrick a ring," and I gave him his phone number! Brother Dan comes back to me and says, "Thank you very much," in a heartfelt way so I guess that charity got something.

'We've won many races together — he's a great man to have in a syndicate. At the trotting sales at Karaka in February 2007, I was its biggest buyer. I've never bought trotters to this extent, and now we're training them and racing them. Patrick was the first galloping person to contact me. He rang me up at the sales and said, "Put me in." He was straight in for a share in a Christian Cullen colt. That's him.

'I went to Dubai to train for three years and had a sale up there, The Pearls of Dubai. Who do you think comes along? Patrick. He buys a share in four or five horses to help the New Zealand industry and gives them to me to train in the Middle East.

'He's one of my top clients. And I tell you this, he's a very, very good loser. You don't have to make an excuse for Patrick. How would I rate him? Bloody good friend, whatever you want to put. He's got a heart of gold, I'll tell you.

'I train in Sydney, Melbourne and New Zealand and I've probably bought about $30 million worth of yearlings from

Patrick. I've bought a lot of horses off him, but he's good to buy off, though he's very hard. He's a great friend and a great businessman. He says, 'You'll be able to buy this one Rogey, it's about $200,000," and by the time he gets you to the sale it's up to about a million!

'Denise Howell, who's worked for me for more than 30 years, and I have got our first stallion, Duelled, who is in his second season in 2007; his sire is Redoute's Choice. Duelled stands at our Dormello Stud at Tuhikaramea and I was going to stand the horse at $15,000. Patrick gave me all the reasons in the world why I should drop it to $7500 and then he booked a lot of his mares to him!

'He sold me a package of 15 mares and some of them are very good. Two of them went to Savabeel (Zabeel–Savannah Success) who won the 2004 Cox Plate and who now stands at Waikato Stud.

'I always have a table at the Magic Millions sale in Queensland and he always has a draft. Last year we paid $1.5 million for Arlington, Savabeel's half-brother, and I said to him at lunch, "You're in it, 10 per cent." He's always in — never hesitates. I have some blues with him, but when the chips are down, he's the first one there.

'Patrick's very good at picking up the bill. When he sold Don Eduardo, I think that night's restaurant bill came to $26,000. I think he thought it was $2600! I've had some good nights on the drink with him.

'He fancies himself as a singer and he can't sing to save his life. In 2005 we had John Rowles to sing at my partner Debbie's 40th at the Lily Pad in Cambridge. Rowles comes on stage singing 'Danny Boy', and Patrick sprints up and jumps on the stage to join him. When he dies, he's asked John Rowles to sing 'Danny Boy' at his funeral. I couldn't believe it. I thought he was joking, but he's serious!

'What he has done for the industry is just unbelievable. He's so passionate. We need him to keep going for the next 30-odd years. I'd like to see if we could clone him for New Zealand — that would be a great thing! Justine's right there behind him in every thing he does.

Graeme Rogerson, MNZM
International racehorse trainer,
Tuhikaramea, Hamilton, 2007

CHAPTER 16

AT HOME AT CAMBRIDGE STUD

'I have an absolute romance with horses, intertwined with humans.'

— Sir Patrick Hogan

WHAT A RACE. What a thrill! Sir Patrick Hogan, owner, punched the air for joy as his mare Lashed — sporting his colours of Irish green with light-green spots and ridden by Opie Bosson — took out the prestigious Group 1 $100,000 Whakanui Stud International Stakes for 2004 by the closest of margins from Penny Gem.

In front of his home crowd at Te Rapa on the Waikato Racing Club's biggest day and accompanied by two of their grandsons, Liam and James, Patrick and Justine took the most exciting walk in racing as they led the mare back to scale. 'I have been dreaming about and praying to win this race for the last three months,' Patrick confessed on receiving the trophy.

Back in 2002, Patrick had received a phone call from his

old mate Graeme Rogerson in Sydney: 'Patrick, I've bought Lashed off Lloyd Williams and I haven't got an owner for her. You'll have to buy her if you want me to buy any yearlings off you at the sales!'

'I'll take it,' Patrick had replied without hesitation. Lashed, who he had bought for just $85,000 as a two-year-old with sizeable back problems, had now with the Whakanui Stud victory taken her earnings beyond the million mark.

Rogerson had read him the riot act after he had offered race advice to jockey Opie Bosson, when she ran a disappointing fourth in her Wellington outing before the Whakanui. 'Leave the race tactics to me and Opie, Patrick. You're the owner and don't know what you're doing.'

OK, he would butt out, savouring instead the exhilaration and nervousness that is conferred on the owners of well-performed racehorses.

Now, ahead of them lay the Group 1 New Zealand Stakes at Ellerslie a fortnight later on 28 February while, behind them, Patrick was still reliving the triumph of Lashed's stunning win in his sponsored Group 1 Zabeel Classic at Ellerslie on New Year's Day.

Gale-force winds and driving rain had lashed Ellerslie, but it was Lashed the horse who created a storm with an extraordinary late burst to win the New Zealand Stakes. David Bradford, writing in the *Sunday News*, described the finish of the race: 'Coming toward the final 100 metres, Lashed's jockey Opie Bosson thought Deebee Belle had the race won and Hail was still fighting. "I thought we were going to be third," he said. "Then she just dug in — she's something else." Also resigned to third placing until she found her extra gear was Sir Patrick Hogan, who races the mare with his wife Justine.'

Patrick braved the elements when she won, ignoring calls to wait for an umbrella or raincoat before he dashed out in the rain. 'Stuff it, I'm out there. I don't care if I drown.'

And, as he had done when his Rogerson-trained horse Smiling Like won the Wellington Cup on 28 January 2001, he walked down to the horse stall, turned over a bucket and sat on it 'for an age', according to Rogerson, writing out his speech.

'He gets very emotional where his horses are concerned,' Rogie explained to an Ellerslie stablehand, who was gaping in astonishment at seeing a Knight of the Realm crouched on an upturned bucket. Why wasn't he partying up large on the free champagne in the owners' enclosure?

Patrick had dabbled with owning racehorses from the 1980s, when he first sent his Eight Carat filly Diamond Lover to his trainer and friend Colin Jillings. He'd been happy to be part of the magic then, as she won her first race as a three-year-old by a whopping nine lengths in the 1100 metres sprint at Te Awamutu, and later the Group 1 Railway Handicap where she missed the start and recorded an amazing time of 1:7:17, but his business was breeding, not racing. Any spare cash he had was ploughed into Cambridge Stud to produce the yearlings that others wanted to race.

By the late 1990s, that policy was easing. His bank account was healthy in the extreme and he decided he wanted to enjoy the thrill of racing his own horses. That interest-turned-addiction was further triggered by his shared ownership with Sir Michael Fay in a beautifully bred brown gelding called Irish Chance (Sir Tristram–The Dimple). Colin Jillings had bought the horse at a cutdown-price sale in the South Island,

and had contacted Patrick shortly afterwards. 'I think he could be a winner,' Jillings predicted, 'but he'll take a while to strengthen up.'

He had been given a free hand in the preparation of the horse, for which Jillings was grateful. 'Patrick was a true friend to me, rather than an owner,' he later said. However, he was a demanding perfectionist, of which Jillings was well aware. Any horse he raced in partnership or on his own had to be turned out immaculately.

Once though, the perfectionist had the tables turned on him, Jillings laughs. 'We were out having a meal somewhere when the racing commentator Keith Haub, who'd once been a barber, burst out, "Patrick, you know, your hair's parted on the wrong side." We borrowed scissors from a good-natured waiter, put him on a stool, stuck a table napkin around his neck and Haub administered a short-back-and-sides. "Much better!" Haubie purred.'

Irish Chance raced up to April 1998 and, after a six-month break from racing, began a campaign aimed at the 1999 Group 1 Auckland Cup on New Year's Day — the major race on New Zealand's biggest day in the racing calendar.

For Patrick, that race will remain forever etched in his memory. 'Irish Chance was out the back as they came into the straight, so far back that I switched my binoculars to watch the front runners, and then I saw these dark-green and light-green spots come flying through the field. It was fantastic — absolutely fantastic — and the best part was that I didn't have to share the victory walk back to scale with Fay as he was in France! I had it all to myself!'

Between them, the daughter of Eight Carat and the son of Sir Tristram had pulled off New Zealand's most prestigious

347

double for trainer Jillings and the Hogans — Diamond Lover, in winning the best sprint race, the Railway; and Irish Chance, in taking out the best staying race in New Zealand.

Fay may not have been there in body, but he certainly was in spirit. It was the middle of the night at Megeve in France when he roused the family to join him for the running of the race, being relayed via his secretary in New Zealand holding a phone against the radio.

There they sat in their pyjamas on the edge of the bed — Annabel 11, James 13, and Jessie 15, with Sarah and Michael. The kids were getting bored — they couldn't hear much. Their father was playing the commentator, shouting, 'Yes . . . yes . . . he's running at the back of the pack . . . he's coming through . . . he's putting in a huge burst to the finish . . . yes! Yes! HE'S WON!'

But his mate Hogan had got the Cup and was taking it home. 'I'm going to chop it in half, so we can both display it on the wall!' Fay promised his family.

On 7 April 2004, Robert Sangster died of pancreatic cancer at the comparatively young age of 65, leaving his many friends in the racing industry bereft at losing one of their most colourful champions.

For Patrick, Robert's contribution to the Southern Hemisphere's thoroughbred racing industry had been nothing short of huge, introducing shuttle stallions, investing in Australasian breeding, seeing his colours up there . . . He'd been a good friend and a great guy, and although Robert had led a fast life, Patrick would miss him sorely.

Following his death, the South Australian Jockey Club

renamed its Group 1 sprint race for fillies and mares at the Morphettville Racecourse The Robert Sangster Stakes to recognise his contribution to the Australian thoroughbred industry.

Sky City's glittering Mercedes Thoroughbred Racing Awards night in August 2004 might as well have been named the Cambridge Stud and Sir Patrick Hogan benefit function. Lashed was named Champion New Zealand Weight-For-Age Horse of the Year, Cambridge Stud collected the Dewar Trophy for the leading stallion (Zabeel's ninth successive triumph) and Patrick won leading breeder for the fourth time in a photo-finish with Waikato Stud's Garry Chittick. Then came the crowning moment — Patrick stepped up on stage to accept the title as New Zealand's leading owner for the 2003–04 season.

Barely eight months earlier, he had spoken with Barry Lichter of the *Sunday-Star Times*, saying that ownership was his new-found passion and that he would be gunning for the top owner title. 'I've bred Cox Plate winners, Melbourne Cup and Caulfield Cup, Derbies and Oaks winners, but I think I deserve a turn at it myself and seeing my colours up. My greatest dream before I die is to own a Golden Slipper winner and a Melbourne Cup winner.'

He was not racing them to get a return financially, he told Lichter. 'It's my game — my hobby. If we can finish ahead for the year, or just come out square and have a hell of a lot of fun, that's all I'd ask. If I can show a profit, so be it, but I wouldn't allow my racing to cost me a packet.'

Cambridge Stud now had a racing team of 30, divided between 13 New Zealand and six Australian trainers, he added.

'I told four trainers I have these three super fillies, and the one who spends the most buying my horses at the Magic Millions sale will get them!'

It had been a very special night for them all, Patrick said on his return to the stud. 'It meant a lot, not just for Justine and me, but for all of the staff at Cambridge Stud to collect these awards.'

And the accolades didn't end there. His 'new boy' at Cambridge Stud, Stravinsky, was the Champion First Season Sire of New Zealand, while in Hong Kong there was to be international recognition that Cambridge Stud had bred Lucky Owners, who joined Kiwi champion mare Sunline as the only Southern Hemisphere-bred horses to win the Group 1 HK$14 million Hong Kong International Mile and the world's richest 1600-metre turf event.

Lucky Owners had captured that event in spectacular style at Sha Tin racecourse and then went on to beat the highest-rated field ever assembled for the Group 1 HK$14 million Hong Kong Derby in March 2004.

In all, during the 2003–04 season, Cambridge Stud had bred Group 1 winners in five countries — South Africa, Malaysia, Hong Kong, Australia and New Zealand.

The year 2005 got off to a cracking start when Cambridge horse St Reims honoured his father Zabeel by winning the Group 1 Zabeel Classic at Ellerslie on 3 January 2005. The race had been a dogfight throughout, with St Reims, ridden by Leith Innes, edging out Distinctly Secret and Lashed in third place, who was carrying an embryo foal by Zabeel.

Not only was Patrick a part-owner of St Reims (through the February Syndicate) and so had the deeply satisfying experience of owning a horse who had won his sponsored race, but his mare Lashed had come in third, half a length behind the winner.

Could life get better? Yes it could — in mid-2005 he received the highest honour ever awarded to a non-Australian when he was inducted into the Australian Racing Hall of Fame, at Champions in Melbourne.

On being presented with the coveted gold badge and citation, he said it was one of the most moving moments in his life — one which even overshadowed his knighthood because it was something to share with all New Zealand. 'The Aussies have always been generous in recognising our great horses, but taking it another step to honour a New Zealander in this way is quite humbling. And it is nice that my old pal, the late Geoff Murphy, is also being inducted this year.'

The recognition centred on the success of Sir Tristram, who had sired 45 individual Group 1 winners, the second-highest in the world, and was six times Australian champion sire. 'Hogan's skill and judgment as a breeder enabled him to replace one super-sire, Sir Tristram, by another, Zabeel,' the citation read. 'Zabeel's success was phenomenal. In his first crop he sired Octagonal and Jezabeel, in his second Might And Power, Mouawad and Bezeal Bay, in his third Champagne and Zonda, and in his fourth Dignity Dancer and Inaflury.' Zabeel had kept his sire's momentum going with 32 Group 1 wins on the board and was looking poised to eclipse his illustrious sire.

In his acceptance speech, Patrick replied: 'Paddy will always be dear to me — very, very special. In family terms he changed our lives for ever. It is just incredible that Zabeel is doing even more when having to compete against the Northern Hemisphere stallions, something Sir Tristram never had to do.'

Notable Group 1 winners for Zabeel during the 2004–05 season, according to *The New Zealand Thoroughbred Racing Annual*, included the Cox Plate winner Savabeel, Vengeance of Rain (Hong Kong Derby), Dizelle (AJC Oaks), St Reims (Zabeel Classic) and Bazelle (Auckland Cup). For a record tenth time Zabeel was the winner of the Dewar Trophy for the leading sire on the combined Australia/New Zealand progeny earnings list.

The one thing that absolutely got up the nose of everyone in the New Zealand racing industry was the Labour government's failure to deliver on tax promises after pledging to ease the punitive taxes imposed on racing. In June, during the build-up to the 2005 general election, the Minister for Racing, Damien O'Connor, got a roasting when he appeared at Te Rapa for an industry-run political forum.

At the forum he found himself the odd-man-out when New Zealand First, Act and the Greens went along with the promises made by National. 'Governments, not oppositions,' O'Connor pleaded with his stony-faced audience, 'are the only ones who can make good on promises.'

Horses became unusual political billboards with 'Fair Tax' painted on their rumps at the Kelt Capital Group 1 meeting in Hawke's Bay a couple of months later, and New Zealand First leader the Hon Winston Peters arranged yet another meeting with key players in the industry.

The urge for reform had gathered steam from the time Winston Peters had first contacted Patrick and other industry leaders back in 2002 and asked for a meeting to discuss the racing industry. New Zealand First was working on a policy that was something, he believed, that racing desperately needed. 'In fact the base has been there for a long time, since 1993 when we started the party,' Peters said.

Fair Tax had later come up as a separate campaign to their policy, but, coincidentally and happily right in line with what they were arguing, he told them. 'You are in an industry that is being artificially penalised in a climate where we have been absolutely cavalier, as a country, in expanding all forms of gambling and, particularly, forms of gambling which have no employment or cultural enrichment capacity whatsoever — like pokies. That is disastrous. We need to put an industry that employs tens of thousands of New Zealanders on a fair footing.'

In an industry that was staunchly National, Patrick's public support for Winston Peters rankled with many. But he was even-handed. Labour was as upset when he said that Prime Minister Helen Clark was only at the races for a free lunch. New Zealand First was the one party committed to 'walking the talk' on the vexed issue, Patrick claimed.

On election night 2005, National got off to a flyer and, with half the results in, appeared to be bolting home. Then came the votes from the Labour strongholds, in particular South Auckland, and by the end of the evening the result hung on a knife-edge, with neither of the two major parties gaining sufficient votes to form a government.

'Rogey, I think we might be in here!' an elated Patrick was on the phone the following morning to Rogerson. They were thrilled; now it was over to their man, Winston Peters, to negotiate himself into racing's top job.

'It's difficult to get your way and, on election night, we could see the way things would pan out. I knew that neither of the major parties would have the numbers. I knew they would exhaust themselves in negotiations,' Winston Peters later reflected. 'We needed to have our policies set, so that we could say, "We want this policy," and "We want this portfolio," when the time came for negotiating, and that is what made it so easy. There was no demur or argument, given that they had no policy. As the cards played out post-election, I could ask for the job of the Minister for Racing and have the Fair Tax policy put in place.'

The irony was, he said, that most of his colleagues in parliament regarded racing as a Cinderella industry, a Cinderella job. 'I thought to myself, "You guys don't know what you're looking at." I'm pleased and very grateful to have had the chance to turn something around really fast. To have got the backing of Sir Patrick Hogan, someone who is respected worldwide in the racing industry, was enormous. Without the political muscle, you can't do anything, and fortunately that sort of backing gave us the votes we needed.'

Those 2006 Fair Tax policies introduced by Winston Peters — a reduction in racing's tax rates from 20 per cent to 4 per cent in line with casinos and other gaming institutions — and adopted that August provided an immediate boost to the New Zealand racing industry.

On Boxing Day 2005, Patrick was made a Life Member of the Auckland Racing Club, and, as was becoming a nice pattern, his Group 1 Zabeel Classic race was won by a daughter of Zabeel — Bazelle — who had previously won the Auckland Cup in 2004.

In the 4 March 2006 edition of the *New Zealand Herald*,

an article headed 'Inductees put New Zealand on the map — first honours announced for new Hall of Fame at a museum at Ellerslie,' Mike Dillon wrote: 'Fourteen thoroughbred racing icons were last night inducted into the inaugural New Zealand Hall of Fame. They were announced at a dinner in Auckland attended by the Prime Minister, Helen Clark, and the Minister for Racing, Winston Peters.

'Making up the 14 inductees were five horses and nine people. The horses were champions of yesteryear Carbine, Gloaming, Phar Lap and Kindergarten, while representing the modern era was Sunline. Among the nine people were two owner-administrators, two trainers, four jockeys and a breeder.

'The owner-administrators were George Stead and Sir George Clifford. The trainers were Dick Mason and Dave O'Sullivan, the jockeys were Bill Broughton, brothers Bill and Bob Skelton, and Lance O'Sullivan, and the breeder was Sir Patrick Hogan.'

Patrick's citation read: 'With clever planning and intuition he developed a breeding empire to a near art form. Widely regarded as the icon thoroughbred breeding figure in this part of the world, Hogan dominated Group 1 racing on both sides of the Tasman. The blood of Cambridge Stud patriarch Sir Tristram is welded into the pedigrees of many topliners, as is the influence more recently of Zabeel.'

There then followed a list of his many achievements:

- set new standards for marketing stallions and yearlings;
- has sold the most sale-topping yearlings of any vendor in New Zealand history;
- in 2006 was the leading vendor by aggregate at the national yearling sales for unprecedented 25th successive year;
- four times New Zealand breeder of the year;

355

- stood champion sires Sir Tristram and Zabeel (78 Group 1 winners to date between them);
- knighted for services to racing.

Gerald Fell, the Hall of Fame chairman and Manawatu breeder, said the greats of New Zealand racing could now be rightfully honoured. 'It is high time our industry recognised and honoured excellence and achievements that have enriched the New Zealand thoroughbred industry, both equine and human.'

Three months later, America's *Thoroughbred Times* named Cambridge Stud as the world's top stud farm on the basis of the average earnings per stallion and average percentage of stakes winners from starters. It headed off Ireland's leading stud conglomerate, Coolmore, to claim the title.

After more than 20 years the Hogans were leaving their home opposite the stud and moving into a new mansion further along Discombe Road. It had been designed by a local architect, complete with tennis court, swimming pool complex and rose gardens. It would be known as Zabeel Place and would match in style their luxurious beachfront house at Mt Maunganui, built six years earlier, which they named Sir Tristram Place.

Aren't people in their late sixties supposed to downsize and slip off quietly into the night? Not the Hogans. Both houses are lavish, flamboyant, built on a grand scale. Both have drawn disparaging comments from those who prefer a low-key look.

Patrick was unrepentant. They had done the hard yards and been thrifty for years, and now, he said, he and Justine were enjoying the fruits of their labour. 'I guess there's a bit of the entrepreneur in me and a fair bit of Irish,' he says, 'and I've never known an Irishman who didn't want to skite when you've got the opportunity to make a statement. Our statement is that we've worked hard and we've succeeded.'

Melbourne Cup Day had come a month early at Cambridge Stud. Throughout October and early November 2006, the Victorian Racing Club's marketing manager Joe McGrath was taking the famed gold three-handled loving cup on a 35-day tour to 30 destinations — commencing the New Zealand leg in Cambridge. Never one to turn down a party, Patrick decided they would make a grand day of it at the stud, with past winning owners and trainers, jockeys and cups on parade.

The Melbourne Cup haul for Fencourt/Cambridge Stud stood at a New Zealand record of seven: Van der Hum by Hermes, Gurner's Lane by Sir Tristram, Empire Rose by Sir Tristram, Might And Power by Zabeel, Jezabeel by Zabeel, Brew by Sir Tristram, and Ethereal by Rhythm.

The Melbourne Cup was more than just a sporting event, more than just a horse race, Joe McGrath told guests who had arrived from all parts of the country. 'And it was ever so. In 1880 more than 80,000 people turned up to watch the race at a time when the entire state of Victoria had a population of just 300,000 . . . today the $5.1 million Melbourne Cup is a prize that owners and trainers all around the world aspire to take home.

'It is truly The Race That Stops A Nation and it is entirely suitable that today, 11 October, we should start our New Zealand tour in Cambridge, which has given such an out-standing contribution to the Cup.' In all, 11 Melbourne Cup winners were bred in Cambridge, a feat acknowledged later that day in Cambridge township when a Wall of Fame was officially opened by Mayor Alan Livingston, of the Waipa District Council, and local jockey Ron Taylor, who rode Polo Prince to victory in the 1964 Melbourne Cup.

Ethereal, the 2001 cup winner, was unable to parade. Just 30 minutes before the function started she had delivered a colt, sired by Stravinsky, in Pencarrow Stud's foaling paddock. But two great crowd favourites were groomed and ready to meet their fans. Her coat now white and speckled with grey, the champion mare Horlicks was paraded; at 24 and carrying her 13th and last foal, she drew applause both for her deeds on the track and, as the dam of Brew, for producing the winner of the 2000 Melbourne Cup. Zabeel was then brought out to even greater reaction, but as the handsome stallion posed for his admirers and a bevy of cameras, few of those present knew of the tense drama that was being played out behind the scenes.

Zabeel, commanding $100,000 service fees, had commenced serving mares in the first week of September. But by the third week of that month, they knew they were in trouble — the fertility readings were back, and they weren't good. Patrick, Marcus Corban and Jonathan Hope hung on waiting for him to turn around. 'The season never starts well because the weather is cooler,' they rationalised. September was never a great serving period, they knew — as the weather improves, so does a stallion's fertility generally. But still . . .

By 9 October and two days before he hosted the big Melbourne Cup event, Patrick knew he had a responsibility to get in touch with the broodmare owners. He rang them all and admitted, 'We appear to have a problem with Zabeel and we are seeking advice to see if we can fix it. There's no guarantee, but I just want to let you know that your mare is not in foal. It's not her fault, the problem is squarely placed with Zabeel, and I would like to keep the mare right through the season to see if we can fix the problem.'

Some agreed, saying, 'Yes, roll right through . . . he's a great horse and we'd love to get a foal . . . if it's the last foal he ever has . . . we might be one of the lucky ones to fluke it.' Others said they were prepared to give it to the end of the season, while 20 owners in Australia and New Zealand said no, they wanted to put their mares to other stallions.

Some were put on planes, some went to other stallions in New Zealand; the majority said they would like to have their mares put to other stallions at Cambridge Stud. It was a great gesture to stick with him when he was in trouble, Patrick said in thanking them.

Patrick gave Jonathan Hope carte blanche to find a solution, with the proviso that he needed to make it fast. The veterinarian consulted experts around the world, liaising closely with stallion behaviour and fertility researcher Dr Sue McDonnell of the New Bolton centre in Pennsylvania and the Hamilton-based Ambreed semen centre.

Ten days later, Hope came back to Patrick offering a fertility programme that would incorporate cutting-edge technology and some old-fashioned trickery. 'A key to the programme is to make Zabeel believe it is summer,' Hope explained. 'We need to put Zabeel under lights in his box for 16 hours a day and keep him at night in a controlled temperature environment akin to midsummer temperatures.'

The second prong of the programme was to inject Zabeel as closely as possible prior to ejaculation with oxytocin, a natural hormone that would cause his semen storage gland to contract, to increase both the volume of semen and the sperm number produced at service. They would scan every mare after serving to ensure the maximum volume of semen was left in the uterus to improve the prospect of pregnancy, and infuse any remaining semen in the vagina after service into the uterus, Hope said.

By 22 October Zabeel's fertility woes had been turned around and his sperm count would continue to improve. From the 120 mares he served in the 2006–07 season, there were 101 positive 42-day pregnancies.

'The results were far beyond any expectations we might have had,' a delighted Patrick announced, finally going public on the scare. 'We now know what we have on our plate, and in 2007 we will put our management course in two months earlier and have an air-conditioning unit put in his box.'

The magic turnaround had also arrived on race day. On Boxing Day 2006, more than 20,000 people packed into Ellerslie — a crowd reminiscent in both numbers and sartorial style of the heady days of the 1980s — and a Cape Cross sired horse, Mikki Street, won the $200,000 Zabeel Classic, bringing the tally of Cambridge Stud-connected winners in the Group 1 race to four on the trot.

Chris Weaver, chief executive of the Auckland Racing Club, announced that the huge crowds, big profits and good weather had made the Ellerslie Christmas Carnival a winner. After the four-day meeting, the Auckland Racing Club would dedicate a further $140,000 to Auckland Cup week in March 2007, Weaver said. 'As a direct result of the success of the New Zealand Herald Christmas Carnival, the club has been able to make this significant increase.'

On 17 January 2007, a bonus for thoroughbred owners was delivered. They would be the beneficiaries of a net $3 million cash injection through the waiving of nomination and acceptance fees, effective from 1 February when free entry for the majority of New Zealand thoroughbred races would come into force.

Wrote Mike Dillon in the *New Zealand Herald*: 'What has become known as free racing was one of the policy initiatives agreed when the three codes were presented with a $32 million annual rebate, arranged and announced by the Minister for Racing, Winston Peters.' He is the best racing minister New Zealand has ever had, enthused Patrick. 'He's done a wonderful job and I just hope whoever wins the next election will keep him on.'

Winston Peters returned the compliment: 'I'm a great admirer of Sir Patrick, because — I won't beat about the bush — I like the way he dresses and I like the way he talks. He's smart — he's a handsome guy. He's professional to the nth degree. There are not many men who've got that charm and dash and who are straight and direct at the same time.'

During one 10-day period in April 2007, Zabeel emphasised why he had been dubbed 'the prince of heaven' in some avenues of the media. Three of his sons — Vengeance Of Rain, Fiumicino and Gallic — respectively won three top Group 1 events in the Dubai Sheema Classic, the Australian Derby and the Sydney Cup. That win by Vengeance Of Rain in the NZ$7 million Dubai Sheema Classic (2400 metres) was later described by an elated Patrick as the finest hour in the amazing stud career of Zabeel: 'This success at the World Cup meeting by Vengeance of Rain is the biggest result for Zabeel and one of the greatest-ever triumphs for the New Zealand breeding industry. Today, everyone in the New Zealand breeding industry can hold their heads high and share in this awesome moment of racing history.' Vengeance Of Rain's combined earnings in Hong Kong and Dubai were in excess of NZ$11,771,623 — second only to the great Sunline's tally of NZ$12,570,448 — and he was named Hong Kong Horse of the Year later in 2007.

There was a sentimental thrill when Dame Malvina Major dedicated an impromptu solo of 'Danny Boy' to Patrick before a packed house at the Founders' Theatre in Hamilton early in 2007. He and Justine had come to watch Dame Malvina on stage with Sir Howard Morrison in 'A Knight and a Dame' and, in announcing she was departing from the programme, Dame Malvina said: 'I have been told there is a second knight here tonight, and oh, does he like his rugby and his horses!' It was a spellbinding performance. The audience clapped and clapped and Patrick made no attempt to hold back the tears that always flowed whenever he heard that song.

How on earth did he manage to pull that one off? his old friend Graham Wrigley asked after the performance. 'I have no idea,' he answered. 'But, boy, wasn't it something!'

JOE WALLS ON PATRICK HOGAN

'In 2003 we were on a rugby trip in South Africa, following the All Blacks. It was led by Fred Allen who had captained the ABs on the 1949 series there, and we were taking some time off to stay at the Mala Mala Game Reserve at Kruger Park.

'We had a couple of Land Rovers going around spotting various animals. One of the guys radioed over and said, "There's a leopard with a kill up a tree! A leopard has killed a baboon and taken it up a tree." It's pitch black, sometime in the evening, so away we go through the bush, and we're all looking at this thing eating a poor old baboon up a tree. Then Patrick's lot come crashing through in their Land Rover a few minutes later and we all moved off.

'We got back to our lodge and were having a few drinks later that evening when Patrick said, "That was bloody awful. I don't know that I could actually look at that leopard eating that baboon."

'I agreed with him. "Yes, it was awful," then, knowing how soft-hearted Patrick is where any animal is concerned, I thought I'd pull his leg. "But you didn't see the worst of it. When we got the call, the leopard was stalking the baboon, and the baboon had a baby on its back. It bloody bowled this baboon over in front of us and went up the tree with it!"

'Patrick said, "Well, what happened to the baby?"

'I said, "The baby was flung in the air and I wouldn't know what happened to it."

'So he said, "Oh shit. Really?"

'I said, "Oh yes, it was quite a mess. It would have cut you up."

'He went off to bed and I didn't think any more of it. I wised our group up on it, and we went to bed pissing ourselves laughing.

'I got up the next morning and Patrick comes out and says, "Have you got a minute?"

'I said, "Yeah."

'His eyes welling up, he says: "You know that baboon, that baby . . . I wonder if we could find it?"

'I said, "No, Patrick, it would probably be bloody dead now too. It's wild out here. For God's sake, we're in the middle of the bloody African jungle!"

'He said, "Oh shit, it makes me feel sick."

'At that stage one of the game guides came walking past who was in Patrick's truck, and Patrick said to him, "Shit, Joe's just been telling me about that baboon last night. That was shocking!"

'The guide said, "Yeah, it was bloody amazing, while it was up the tree eating the baboon."

'Patrick said, "Yeah, but what about the baby?"

'"What baby?"

'Patrick looked at him. "When the leopard got the baboon, the baby was . . . "

'"Nothing like that happened at all!" the guide said.

'I thought Patrick was going to hit us. "You bastards, you bastards!" he roared. But then he caught the humour of it and cracked up laughing.'

CHAPTER 17

KARAKA — 2007

'I'm as superstitious as buggery. I would never walk under a staircase, even at Karaka — despite the fact that during a typical yearling sale I'd have to make hundreds of repetitive detours simply to avoid it.'

— Sir Patrick Hogan

SCENE 3: NEW ZEALAND, 2007

You sniff the buoyancy in the air as you park in line with a string of continental cars and four-wheel-drives, joining a stream of people heading purposefully towards the scene of the action. It's Premier Yearling Sale time at Karaka for this, the 81st National Yearling Sales Series, and the place looks a treat — a few clouds drifting across the sky, gardens and central fountain in tip-top order, and the splendid complex, topped by cantering horses on the weather-vane, a perfect complement for its surroundings.

A busload of Japanese nationals dismount at the main entrance. Are they here as buyers or as spectators, keen to soak up the excitement and the drama that's about to unfold? Inside, a harassed New Zealand Bloodstock official is replenishing the table where the free sale books are being eagerly snapped up by all who walk through the door. 'They're going out as fast as I can put them down!' she says with a shake of the head.

You face a dilemma — do you head for the sale ring, where the auction is about to begin, or go for a brief wander around the complex to check out the lie of the land, see the location of the big players' marquees, the tents of the smaller ones, where one can get a coffee or a pre-parade glimpse of the prized one-year-old babies? Time dictates it should be the sale ring.

The Prime Minister, Helen Clark, has arrived to officially open the sale and, escorted by Joe Walls, the chairman of New Zealand Bloodstock, she makes her entrance. 'It is a great pride for us to see our horses doing so well internationally . . . we see our horses going to these sales year after year which go on to star in racetracks around the world, greatly benefiting the reputation of New Zealand bloodstock,' Helen Clark says in declaring the 81st yearling sales open.

Now to business. Joe Walls, Steve Davis (of TV's racing show *Trackside* fame) and Michael Kneebone are on the podium, their eyes everywhere, with fellow bid spotters strategically placed around the ring's perimeter as the first yearling, a bay colt sired by Viking Ruler, is paraded. 'Now who is going to start the bidding? Joe asks. 'That's a little bit disappointing, ladies and gentlemen,' he says as Lot 2 is passed in at $110,000.

If Joe is the senior statesman, Steve Davis — when he takes the stand — is pure theatre. 'Give the man a lollipop,' he urges when the bidding stalls at $150,000. 'C'mon, you know you want this horse . . . $120,000? He's worth twice that! I'll give you two-and-a-half . . . going, going . . . thank you sir.'

The prices are good and the sale is ticking along nicely. Not surprising, given that this is the first yearling sale after the government's boost to the racing industry and an announcement that New Zealand Bloodstock is to sponsor a rich new race with eligibility restricted to colts and fillies sold at these sales. All yearlings sold at the Premier, Select, Festival and Carnival sessions of the 2007 national sales at Karaka will be eligible to enter New Zealand's richest two-year-old race, the Karaka Million, to be run at Ellerslie in the summer of 2008.

Peter Vela, founder/owner of New Zealand Bloodstock, is all smiles. 'Winston Peters has been the catalyst to give everybody the confidence the industry needed. We've been waiting a very, very long time — it was truly shocking — but we've turned the corner now. I believe this million-dollar race, which we are sponsoring, is also going to make a very big difference to New Zealand racing.'

Lunch beckons, and outside the sale ring there's an early port of call to catch up with Jo Wilding of Te Mania Stud from Parnassus Station in Canterbury. She is related by marriage to Anthony Wilding, the legendary Wimbledon champion, and says she has been coming to the sales for 'many years now'. She laughs off the oft-repeated tale that her horses are walked across the river from the stud to attend race meetings and sales. Sadly, it's an urban myth. Jo's early Lot No 4, a Pentire–Whey to Go chestnut colt, has fetched $50,000 and now she can relax and enjoy ham-off-the-bone with friends and clients in her hospitality tent.

David Ellis of Te Akau Stud, here to buy and sell on the big scale, is multi-tasking — talking on his mobile, walking towards one group and acknowledging a potential buyer in another.

From Australia, there's John Messara, of Arrowfield, and Nick Columb — partners in many racehorse enterprises, including their current champion Miss Finland — seated at a table under the trees enjoying the scene, a glass or two of wine and a catch-up with New Zealand colleagues in the industry.

A swing past the pre-parade ground and we're at Waikato Stud. Garry Chittick, who took over the stud in the early 1990s when it was in a state of near-collapse, says he is pleased with the prices so far. He has 60 horses in the Premier Sale and more in the Select Sale which is to follow.

An observer has claimed that he, Sir Patrick and Nelson Schick are successful because all have been farmers. Yes, he nods, there's an element of truth in that. 'When I first started in 1975, at about the same time that Patrick went to Cambridge, I said my intention was to be a farm with horses. The three of us have all come from small beginnings and we've coped with the hurly-burly where others haven't. We're not just there to make money. Of course, you've got to make money to survive, but if you've got an element of stockmanship about you, it certainly helps.'

He harks back to the days when the industry was peppered with farmers who had a horse or two for sale, when the patrician old studs of Te Parae and Okawa gave a helping hand to ensure 'young blokes like us got a fair shake of the dice' where stallions were shared to spread the risk. 'The industry has evolved tremendously — I don't think those small operations would survive today; I don't think they could keep pace with the changes in the industry.'

Today they are all committed to huge financial commitments in buying stallions, he says, referring to an overseas trip in 1995 where he travelled with Patrick, Joe Walls and David Benjamin to find a stallion to syndicate. 'We didn't find one, but we did have a very good time!'

Fame and fortune — it's all down to the stallions, he says. 'You wouldn't be writing this book if Sir Tristram hadn't fallen into Patrick's lap. You wouldn't be talking to me if Centaine hadn't fallen into mine.'

And then onto Cambridge Stud. It's a place apart at Karaka, secure in its own large area to the right of the sales complex. There's an expansive parade area, rows of facing stable boxes, grooms dashing around and, in the largest marquee at the place, international guests, sellers and buyers tucking into a magnificent repast washed down by wine, champagne, beer, fruit juice, iced water, tea, coffee . . . your call.

Justine is there with the family — Erin's daughter Katie on her left, Nicola's son Liam on her right — greeting guests and smiling serenely, while her husband darts from one place to another attending to a thousand different issues.

It's time to return to the sale ring for another session in the company of the smart-casual set, a place where heady designer scents vie with the pungency of horse droppings to produce an oddly seductive aroma.

'Coming up we have Lot 119, a magnificent Zabeel–Diamond Lover bay colt. Here you are, ladies and gentlemen . . . here he is, one dam fills the page . . . what am I offered to start the bidding? $100,000?' It's all over in less than a minute: ' . . . $425,000. Nice to see you here, Lee . . . going . . . going for $425,000 . . . ' Bang! Down goes the hammer. 'Sold to Mr Lee Freedman.'

It is fascinating to watch the major buyers in action — a scratch of the nose, a slight inclination of the head . . . The legend, Bart Cummings, sits in the glass-enclosed area, his signal a raise of those bushy eyebrows.

Today has gone swimmingly, but ahead lies day two — the big one. This is the day when Cambridge Stud is offering a Zabeel–Sunline colt, in what is sure to be the biggest-priced ticket of the sales.

As the crowd dissipate on day one, Bart Cummings is in expansive mood, seated in the Cambridge Stud marquee, swivelling a scotch and soda on the rocks in his right hand, while his grandson James, a stud groom at Cambridge Stud, hovers nearby.

What does he look for in a horse? Dumb question perhaps . . .

'Not at all,' he replies courteously. 'Champion horses invariably look similar in conformation. There are certain guidelines which have proven to be successful for centuries — short cannon bone and long arm — if you have a short cannon bone you will have a long arm, because the knee is closer to the ground.

'A fine leg with a hock closer to the ground gives it a longer stride. You've got to have a deep girth and that follows through to a sloping shoulder. Obviously a nice rein — a long rein gives you better balance, a horse turns over a lot of ground and he's got to be well balanced. The centre of gravity of a horse is the wither.

'Some people have got an eye for a horse, but if you're not brought up with them, you will never, ever attain those powers of perception that are necessary to capture the imagination of a horseman. You've always got an eye out for the perfect example of a thoroughbred that will achieve the maximum Group 1 level.'

So how does one get that eye?

'I teach people,' he sighs. 'I show people, but they don't see the obvious. I've always been able to see something unusual, and with horses it's essential to see that, otherwise you are going to miss out. Even the people I bring here or to other sales all the time — they miss things. You explain to them, "When they [the horses] walk, they've got to be balanced, they've got to walk through". A fluent walk is, like they say in the classics, "poetry in motion." A thoroughbred that is, in your mind, a Group 1 winner will always be that type of horse.'

But, of course, it's not just the eye. Cummings is a ferocious student of research with the stud book, and a phenomenal record keeper, writing down every detail of a mare's background and purchase price of other foals she may have had, to call up on cue when wanted. Everything is jotted down in a double-sided hardback Premier Sale book — horses one side, background and comments the other — which he pioneered, and is now copied everywhere. Rather than buying for people, he prefers to buy and sell under his Randwick Leilani Lodge Stables banner. He does not like being restricted to any particular type of horse.

Next question . . . What has made Bart Cummings the King of the Melbourne Cup? No other trainer can claim his record of 11 winners and five first/second quinellas. Well, he says, it all goes back to his great-grandfather, who emigrated from Ireland in the 19th century and was stuck, along with hundreds of other Irish families, in the inhospitable Flinders Ranges where the rainfall was an average six inches a year.

'The good Lord must have looked after them,' Cummings smiles. 'For the first and only time it poured for the next 15 years. They did well and raised large families, but then the weather started to revert back, so my Dad, Jim, who was about 18, accepted an offer from an old bachelor uncle to join him at Ellery Creek Station just out of Alice Springs.'

The year was 1910 and thoroughbred horses that had originally come from South Australia ran wild on the stations. Jim and his uncle's living was made by catching the horses, breaking them in and shoeing them as mounts for use in the Indian army. Then they would walk them down to Port Augusta and ship them out to India.

Jim Cummings rode a horse called Myrtle, which was bred by his uncle, to victory in the Alice Springs Cup later that year. But it was a pretty isolated place for a young chap, says Bart. 'It was about 900 miles to Adelaide, and the train connection from Alice to Adelaide was still years away. After Dad had been there for four or five years he decided to go to Adelaide to seek his fortune.

'He wanted to take a couple of horses with him, he said. His uncle gave him three horses: he had to work six months for the pony and the two horses, as he was only getting board and lodgings. No money, but experience is what he got.'

Jim Cummings picked his trio, including Myrtle, and walked them out. In Peterborough, the horses bolted in terror when they saw a penny-farthing bicycle being ridden up the street by a parson wearing a black hard-hat and carrying a bible under his arm. 'From then on he avoided the towns, going around the back of them until the horses got used to people and traffic,' Bart says.

'When he was walking down to Jamestown, they had thunderstorms off and on all the way down the 800-mile journey from Alice. They grazed on the Mitchell grass that grows wild on the side of the road — that year, because of the thunderstorms, it was three feet six inches high. Mitchell grass is very high in protein — as high as grain — so they looked terrific and were very fit, walking all day every day.'

Along the journey Jim would stop at waterholes, where invariably there was a hotel that might be running two- or three-furlong races. There were bookies, stakes and bets of up to £20, and Cummings, with his fit and healthy horses, cleaned out. 'There was a drought on at the time, so he was racing against horses that looked terrible,' Bart smiles. 'Dad was a terrible rider, so he had to get people to ride for him. He found that the horses who had been broken in and handled by Aboriginals wouldn't go for the white man. Put an Aboriginal rider on it and it would go like the wind.

'He was the first one to figure that out. He put an Aboriginal rider on one of his horses and it couldn't win at all. So he used a white jockey the next time and got twice the odds!'

When he got to Jamestown and the first TAB in the world (the TAB was designed in South Australia, Cummings says) the minimum bet was 2/6d. One of his horses paid £25 for 2/6d and the other £50 for 2/6d.

Jim Cummings made enough money from his horses on their long journey — walking by day, camping with his billycan in scrub or under mulga trees by night, and racing intermittently — to purchase a block of land in Adelaide that would be suitable for the breeding of horses. It would become the first Cummings stable, and later the land that forms the Adelaide airport.

His father would breed a Melbourne Cup winner in Comic Court, who won the 1950 race in dashing style. He discovered whilst transporting his horses from Adelaide to Melbourne that the clean, fresh, sea air was beneficial for his horses' performance. After winning a lot of races in Melbourne, he set up a second stables there and inspired his groom and son, Bart, to make the great staying race his own.

The time allocated for the Cummings interview has long elapsed. There is an urgent appointment in Auckland city. Cummings' entourage is getting agitated, with arms waving wildly behind his head and fingers pointing to watches.

OK, OK — just one more question. Melbourne Cup again — why this race in particular?

'I think staying horses are easier to train than sprinters, easier to develop, more relaxed,' Bart says. 'I'm pretty relaxed myself and the type of training conveys that to the horse. There's an old saying, "The dog's a reflection of his owner." I think the attitude of the trainer — if he is patient — rubs off, and you will find that the horse invariably comes to have a similar attitude if he's got the pedigree to win over a longer distance. 'If they're precocious, that will never happen, because they're differently bred and tuned, and conformation is short-course, grass-speed type.

'The Melbourne Cup is worth a lot of money. If you're going to put all that work in, you may as well go for the best one. After I won the first Melbourne Cup, I thought, "Gee, that was all right."'

He gets to his feet, but then — to the horror of his entourage — sits down again. 'I first came to New Zealand in 1958 because in doing my research I saw that 60 per cent of the Group 1 horses in the eastern states of Australia were bred in New Zealand. "Well," I thought, "if they're going to be bred there, why am I going anywhere else?" The first year I bought a couple, it was more of a learning experience. Then in 1959 I bought three horses and they all won. I never looked back.

'Speaking of New Zealand, I have to say that Patrick's horses do look well and he's been a great success. We always have one or two horses from Patrick. We discuss things regularly and it's proved very fruitful for both sides.'

Bart died on 30 August 2015, aged 87. The man who had lived an extraordinary life and dominated Australian racing – most notably the Melbourne Cup – for so many years was farewelled with a state funeral in Sydney, provoking mass mourning from racing fans across Australasia. In 2012, he had been made an honorary inductee into the New Zealand Racing Hall of Fame.

His grandson James, whose time at Cambridge Stud helped cement a career in the industry, has developed into one of Sydney's leading trainers, having trained in partnership with his grandfather for several years before his death.

The Cummings link with Patrick and Cambridge Stud continued through grand Zabeel stayer Precedence, who contested no less than four Melbourne Cups. Bred by the Dowager Duchess of Bedford in partnership with Patrick and Justine, Precedence raced in the colours of Dato Tan Chin Nam with Patrick and the Duchess of Bedford co-owners. In a remarkable career, Precedence won six stakes races, including the Moonee Valley Cup, but the closest he got to pulling off a Melbourne Cup win was his sixth placing in 2014.

It's day two, and there is a frisson in the air. Like all good dramas, this is going to be a drawn-out one — Lot No 411 and the star of these sales, a Zabeel–Sunline colt, will not be auctioned until towards the end of the afternoon. All the players are here, the television teams, the journos — Mike Dillon from the *New Zealand Herald* with a group of mates; Barry Lichter from the *Sunday Star-Times*; Dave and Sonia Bradford, publishers of the *New Zealand Thoroughbred Racing Annual* — along with hundreds of spectators.

At Cambridge Stud throughout the morning there is a constant stream of visitors to look at Lot No 411, who is paraded up and down by groom Luke Simpson. Bart Cummings and his team request another 'up and down,' and Irishmen Michael Kirwan of Coolmore Australia and Demi O'Byrne — one of the world's biggest buyers of bloodstock — have their heads bent over their sale books and look up only to check out the colt once more.

Sam Kelt, who sponsors the Group 1 Kelt Capital Stakes in Hawke's Bay, is here to inspect the horse and introduce his 11-year-old son Hamish to Patrick. Hamish is already serious about his horses, and will later be the successful bidder for a $350,000 yearling.

Then there's another group, headed by a pleasant-faced Vietnamese man, who have popped up from nowhere. Initially, Patrick mistakes them as being part of the security team, but changes his view when they ask to see the colt. He's got a gut feeling there could be a buyer in this group. They indicate that they are pretty interested in the colt. 'The reserve is going to be very high,' Patrick warns.

'That won't worry us,' they say.

The giveaway is the day of the sale, Patrick tells a friend. 'Invariably, people come for a last look if they are serious.'

Fifteen lots before No 411 and Patrick is pacing in and out of his vantage spot at the edge of the parade ring, always returning to stand alongside his old friend Bob Morris. The place is packed to the gills — every vantage spot has long been taken — as everyone has come to discover how much this glamour son of Zabeel and Sunline will fetch. And, as the incomparable Sunline's first yearling is led into the auction by Luke Simpson, the noise is deafening.

Steve Davis has handed over to Joe Walls for this, the top attraction of the 2007 Premier Sale. Joe signals for quiet, then: 'Ladies and gentlemen, we have been favoured by the owners of Sunline to offer this magnificent colt to you. He's by Zabeel, one of the greatest sires of the modern era, and out of one of the greatest mares of the modern era — who will ever forget those magnificent performances when Sunline carried the nation on her back?

'There he is, ladies and gentlemen. There's the Sunline foal. You've all had time to look at him, now who is going to start the bidding? I've got $500,000 for him as a first bid and I will take bids in $100,000 lots . . . $700,000 . . . $800,000 . . . $900,000 . . . a million.' The first milestone is cleared in just four bids. Joe says he will accept $50,000 bids from now on.

'I've got $1.5 million . . . I've got $1.6 million for this outstanding colt . . . $1.7 million . . . at $1.7 . . . $1.8 . . . at $1.9 million . . . One million nine hundred thousand for this Sunline colt . . . at $1.9 million, the hammer's coming up — and I have been told by the vendors that he is for sale, he will be sold to the highest bidder — at $1.9 million . . . $1.95 million . . . at $2 million, thank you Neil!'

There's a buzz of excitement around the arena. 'At $2 million,' Joe's voice is rising. 'At $2 million . . . is there any further advance? Quickly — he's got to be sold . . . At $2 million . . . ' (There's a loud neigh from the colt and a ripple of

laughter around the saleroom.) 'For the third and last time . . . '
The hammer comes down. 'Thank you very much!'

Applause breaks out from every corner of the arena, the colt
whinnies again and two-thirds of the sale room rise to their
feet to leave. Joe Walls pleads for quiet: 'Please, ladies and
gentlemen, we have other horses to be sold.'

At Cambridge Stud, there's a media scrum around the new
owner of the colt, Don Ha, who admits he only decided to bid
for the horse the night before while taking a shower.

'Did you put a ceiling on how much you would spend on
the horse?' Ha is asked.

'No. He was the only one — there was no other one for
me.'

'Will he go back to Trevor and Stephen McKee's? I know you
have horses with him,' this time from a television reporter.

'We will ask the McKees if they want to train the horse — if
not, we'll have to train it ourselves,' Ha grins.

'You've bought him as a racehorse, Don, but further down
the track do you see him as a stallion?'

'It was for that reason we bought him, and we'll see how he
goes as a racehorse.'

'I think I'm correct in saying you arrived as a refugee from
Vietnam with not a cent in your pocket.'

'Yes, that's true. I arrived in Standard Four and couldn't
speak a word of English. I got into real estate when I was 26
and, with my many bakeries, I have a huge company now. It's
been successful and my people have been successful.'

'Don, have you ever had a more exciting moment in your
life than buying this colt?'

'It has been most exciting, especially as my wife is here to
support me.'

Patrick is fielding his fair share of questions too. 'I thought he would go for between $1.5 and $2.2 million, so that was all right. There were so many people in there. I know Graeme Rogerson opened the bidding and David Ellis was there well past the million, so it was good to see those guys in there. I must say I had a tear in my eye as I left the ring, mostly relief. When Joe slammed the hammer down at $2 million, everything let go inside me. I felt the most enormous relief.

'I've had a huge job to do, to rear this colt out of the greatest race mare we've ever seen. I didn't own a hair on his body . . . if I'd owned the horse it would have been much easier. When you have the responsibility of having that kind of colt on your hands for seven months, you don't want anything to go wrong. You have a sense of responsibility to the horse's owners.

'This last week has been pretty pressured. If I'd fattened him up, I could have had him a lot bigger and with more muscle — but it would have been a shame to do that to him. He's a lovely colt. He's got the quality and is going to be an enormous three-year-old. You can just see the development.

'And, as a bonus, $2 million stays in New Zealand, so that's a great result.'

Another day has ended and we're back in Cambridge Stud's marquee. Marcus Corban's eyes follow his boss and he says he wishes he could slow him down. 'Look at him rushing around everywhere! He's already had a couple of health scares, and I'd like to see him relax and spend more time with Mrs H. She deserves it.'

Duncan Grimley from Australia has a story to tell on the health front: 'We were in Dubai last year, having breakfast at our hotel, when Patrick collapses on the floor. I get him up to his room and shortly afterwards the phone rings. "It's Dr Ali, how is Sir Patrick?"

'"How do you know about this?" I ask. "And who are you?"

'I then discover he is the personal physician to the Sheikh and that word travels fast in Dubai. I assured him that Patrick is OK and he says, "Please keep him quiet and rested for at least a day."

'A few hours later I go up to check on Patrick. There he is, all dressed up, suit and tie and ready to go. "Where do you think you're going?" I say. "You're under orders to rest!"

'But Patrick refuses. "No," he says, "we're off to the races." And that's where we went.'

Michael Kirwan and Demi O'Byrne come over for a chat. The previous morning, they had been taken, courtesy of the Karaka helicopter, on a whistle-stop tour of Cambridge Stud. Patrick introduces them: 'Demi is one of the best judges of horseflesh in the world who buys and inspects for Magnier. Michael Kirwan is general manager of the Coolmore organisation in Australasia and very close to John Magnier,' and he leaves us to it.

'Cambridge Stud is wonderful,' Kirwan enthuses. 'We've had a great relationship with Patrick in the last 20 years plus — from the days when Cambridge Stud was a small farm to now as the premier stud farm in Australasia. We bring shuttle stallions to Cambridge and we buy horses from Cambridge to take back to Ireland. Patrick has really become part of the family at Coolmore in Ireland — there are Irishmen in the thoroughbred industry everywhere. We're horse people.'

What is Patrick? 'A workaholic, that's what he is,' Demi O'Byrne grins. 'He's always diverting the traffic — he's a great innovator, a great mind and a great judge, that's what Patrick is, and Cambridge Stud is a fabulous farm. When we flew down yesterday morning the gardens looked absolutely immaculate, but Patrick couldn't resist snipping away!'

O'Byrne confesses to loving Montjeu-sired horses and at these sales has bought 12 — almost the entire complement on offer — to take back to Ireland to live at Coolmore. He too has a Patrick story. 'Some years ago when I was inspecting Cambridge Stud yearlings here at Karaka, Patrick was hovering close — wouldn't let me be. In the end I got so exasperated I said: "For fock's sake will you fock off and leave me in peace to look at the focking horses!"

'And he says, "As long as they're my horses, I'm not focking off anywhere."'

Every worthwhile record is broken at the Premier and Sale Sessions of New Zealand's 2007 thoroughbred auctions. The series has produced a record turnover of $81,375,700 and for the 26th consecutive year, Cambridge Stud is the largest vendor on aggregate.

PATRICK HOGAN ON IRISH LOGIC

'At the end of a three-day sale at Karaka you always have some yearlings that are passed in or not sold — only a handful — but as Cambridge Stud always has such a large draft, you know you'll have some.

'I really don't want to take my yearlings home. We've got another crop to come along, to be weaned and to be handled, and I think it's a little demoralising going home with four or five yearlings. They go back to the staff — you've got to handle them all again and look after them. To me, it's the end result of the aggregate that counts, not specifically what you get for every individual horse.

'Back in the heady days, when the demand was there, the hype was there and the parties were bigger and hospitality areas were more full-on than today, I did my usual thing on the last night, lit up my area and rolled in with a dinner party for everyone . . . kept the food going, kept the wine and the booze going and, after everyone had been partying for about an hour, I would then bring out my unsold horses.

'Some of them might not have bought a yearling during the sale series, and so once I got the party rolling, I would do my act. I would say, "Now, I've got three or four or five horses that I didn't sell, that I'm going to sell, and I'm going to bring them out one by one and they are available for next to nothing. I have decided it's better to get something for them, move them on and give them an opportunity, than turn around and take them home."

'I would identify the yearlings one by one and target who I thought they should go to. I would say, "Jack and Bob [Ingham], I think this one suits you."

'And they'd say, "How much do you want for it?"

'And I'd say, "Oh, give me $20,000."

'They'd say, "We'll give you $18,000 — is that a deal?"

'I'd reply, "Yes, that's good. It's yours," and they'd be as happy as Larry. But they'd only buy it because they were being entertained and they were having a bit of fun and they were away, and it was a fun thing. They were spending $18,000 — it was a round of drinks for them, so to speak, and we were all mates.

'This particular year, I said to Michael Fay, "Michael, this one's for your mob."

'He said, "Who's my mob?"

'I said, "Well, your mob, your gang — Barney McCahill and you and Hughie Green."

'So he said, "OK, well bring it out, bring it out."

'So I led the colt up and down and they said, "How much do you want for it?"

'I said, "$20,000 — no, no, I mean $25,000."

'Hughie and Michael had a look at it and Hughie said, "Ah, we'll leave it to Barney McCahill. Let Barney deal with Patrick. We'll go and get another drink."

'Barney wasn't with them to begin with, so when he joined them he said to me, "I want to see it." I brought him out and led him up and down, and he said, "How much do you want for him?"

'And I said, "$25,000."

'"Ah, who's in for this horse?" he asked.

'"Well," I said, "I don't know."

'"Well," he said, "I'd better be finding out." So he went back to Michael Fay. "Who's in for this horse — how many of us in this horse?"

'And Michael said, "Well, there's you, and there's me, and there's Hughie, there's Hec McCallum, and Patrick will have to stay in, and we'll bang Colin Reynolds' name in too. There's six of us."

'And Barney said, "Ah, that's six. You want $25,000 for him?"

'I said, "I do."

'So he went back and Hughie says, "Are we buying this horse or not?"

'And Barney says, "Ah, I think he's all right. Yes, I think we'll buy him."

'"Offer him $20,000," says Hughie.

'So Barney says, "We're offering you $20,000 for the horse!"

'And I said, "No, I want $25,000 for the horse."

'So he went back. "No, he says he's digging his toes in."

'Hughie said, "For God's sake, you can't put six into 20 and you can't put six into 25 — it don't fit. For Christ's sake, offer him $30,000 because it goes in $5000 each, and call it a deal. Is it a deal, Patrick?"

'I said, "It's a deal." We did the Irish handshake and everybody had a spit.'

MICHAEL FAY ON PATRICK HOGAN

'Here's a Patrick story. We currently share a horse called Dancing Forever who is being trained by Lance O'Sullivan. I had bought the mare as a yearling — she was known as Forever Dancing then — and raced her. She was trained by Dave O'Sullivan and had a few wins.

'A couple of years ago I did a foal share with Patrick. He provided the stallion, Keeper, and I provided the mare, and we got a filly. Patrick's very smart and knows he can't afford just to be in New Zealand, because he would swamp the local industry which wouldn't be good for other vendors. Anyway, we decided to sell this foal at the Magic Millions yearling sales in Queensland.

'She got over there, but she didn't make the sales: as she was being transported, the floor in the horse float gave way, the horse went through and dragged its back foot along the road. I think that story's a nightmare for anyone who likes horses — the vision of a horse being trapped in a moving truck with its feet dragging on the road. Fortunately a motorist saw what was happening and stopped the truck.

'The horse was seen by a vet. The injuries were horrific, but fortunately he decided he didn't have to put the horse down, he thought he could save her, but of course we couldn't put her in the sales.

'We went ahead with the operations and treatment that she needed. The Irish in us made us feel sorry for the horse. Patrick said, "She deserves a chance. We'll spend a bit of money on her and put her into training if all goes well. She deserves that chance after what she's lived through." Patrick just has this commitment to his horses, this feeling, this softness — every horse is special to him — so we made a purely emotional decision and brought her home to Cambridge Stud, where all the staff loved her, and nursed her back to health.

'We had no idea what we were going to do with a horse that maybe couldn't walk. The staff had the idea of changing the dam name around so she became Dancing Forever. They worked so hard on her bad leg. My goodness, if you'd ever seen that leg, you would be surprised that she could even walk on it.

'When Lance first saw her, he shook his head, but now we're racing her. She's had four races so far for a couple of seconds and a first, and she's racing on Auckland Cup Day. [Dancing Forever retired after 21 starts for four wins and has gone on to a successful career as a broodmare.]

'Maybe if she goes well there, we might have a look at the Oaks. Who knows? We might get her to the Melbourne Cup!

385

Patrick wants to race her lightly this year because he thinks she will go better as a four-year-old.

'The industry is full of these fairy stories, and some fairy tales come true. Wins are not just about the best looks, conformation and so on; it's more about the best heart, the best attitude, the best temperament, the best barrier run, and luck . . . chance on the day.'

Sir Michael Fay
Auckland, New Zealand, 2007

CHAPTER 18

A 31-YEAR STREAK

'It has to be said that Zabeel is as good a stallion as we've seen in the southern hemisphere for a long, long time.'

— Sir Patrick Hogan

WHILE ZABEEL'S ONGOING success remained Cambridge Stud's main headline-grabber, Patrick's savvy selections of associate stallions meant for a steady stream of top-level performers for the farm.

Patrick cut a deal with Darley Stud over Cape Cross, who shuttled to Cambridge Stud for four seasons. As well as siring Group 1 Zabeel Classic winner Mikki Street, Cape Cross left champion Hong Kong miler Able One, and fellow New Zealand Group 1 winners Kindacross and Gaze.

But undoubtedly Cape Cross's best southern hemisphere performer was Seachange, a gangly filly with front legs so wonky that The Oaks Stud general manager Rick Williams couldn't allow breeder Dick Karreman to take her to the sales. That imperative to retain Seachange was repaid in spades as the filly defied her conformation faults to win seven of her first eight starts.

She did enough in her four-year-old season to clinch Horse of the Year honours and repeated the dose the following year. Despite an unsuccessful northern hemisphere campaign in Dubai and England, Seachange was named the world's premier female sprinter on turf for 2008, thanks to her win in the Group 1 Telegraph Handicap at Trentham.

Patrick was particularly enamoured with Cape Cross and was bitterly disappointed when Darley opted not to shuttle him back to Cambridge Stud in 2005. The stallion was retired from stud duties in 2016 with more than 100 individual stakes winners to his credit.

Danehill stallion Keeper was also making his mark with his fillies. The Peter and Philip Vela–bred and raced filly Insouciant claimed the Group 1 1000 Guineas at Riccarton in 2007. Later that month Seachange's younger half-sister Keepa Cruisin claimed the Group 1 Levin Classic at Otaki for Dick Karreman, while Miss Keepsake was victorious in the Group 1 Queensland Oaks and both Keep The Peace and Midnight Oil became Group 1 New Zealand Oaks winners for their sire. Keep The Peace had run second in the Group 1 1000 Guineas earlier that season, denied first place by a horse that held a special place in Patrick's heart. That history-making grey filly was Katie Lee, a spur-of-the-moment purchase for Patrick, who fortuitously had been in the right place at the right time.

'It just happened that by chance I was standing at the ring when this grey filly came in,' Patrick later recalled. 'I hadn't looked through the catalogue to buy fillies because I wasn't a buyer — I was selling a heap of them. But I thought, Whoa, look at this. She just appealed to me. I'd never seen her before so I hadn't got her X-rayed, hadn't got a vet to look at her. I just really liked her, so I looked at my catalogue and saw she was from a family that I didn't have and it was a pretty smart family at that.'

Patrick immediately decided he had to buy the filly. But then an unexpected rival appeared at the sales ring. Noticing Patrick's interest in Katie Lee, the Racing Hall of Fame trainer Graeme Rogerson stepped forward and declared: 'I'm going to buy this filly.' Patrick was taken aback. The pair argued before Rogerson backed off and said, 'Okay, I'll let you have her.'

Recalling the occasion some years later, Patrick described Rogerson's decision to step away from Katie Lee as a masterstroke. 'Knowing me well enough, he had picked up that I was going to have a crack at this filly, so he took the insurance to tell me that he was going to bid on her. He kept telling me he was buying the filly and I kept telling him: "No, you're not."

'The only reason he let me bid on her was that if I succeeded in buying her, there was no way then that I couldn't have him to train her because he backed off and didn't bid against me. It was the greatest trick in the book and I have to give him great credit for it. But if he doesn't think I didn't see right through it, then there's something wrong with him.'

Patrick secured the Pins filly for $340,000 and she joined the Hamilton stable of Rogerson and his now wife Debbie, whose barn she was prepared from. 'She proved right from the word go that she was pretty special, but she was a bit of a bitch and it was to Deb's great credit that she managed her so well,' Patrick says.

In six starts as a two-year-old, Katie Lee won twice, including the Group 3 Eclipse Stakes at Ellerslie, and was second on three occasions. But she had always shaped as a three-year-old Classic type, and the Rogersons set their sights on the Group 1 double of the 2000 Guineas and 1000 Guineas, held a week apart at Riccarton in November — a double that had never been achieved before.

Katie Lee ensured she would be starting among the favourites in the 2009 Riccarton features after flashing home from near last to win the Listed James and Annie Sarten Memorial Stakes at Te Rapa under new rider Opie Bosson; this had followed the Group 3 Gold Trail Stakes at Hastings where she had finished third.

Her first test at Riccarton was expected to be her toughest — competing against the colts and geldings in the 2000 Guineas — and Patrick followed a ritual that bemused many racegoers by sitting on an upturned bucket by the stables so he could keep an eye on his star filly.

'Deb took her out on the lawn under the trees so I just stuck the bucket up against the fence and stayed there all day with her,' he said later.

'It was a good luck omen because when I won the Wellington Cup with Smiling Like, I did the same thing — sat by her stall all day long on the bucket and didn't go anywhere else. It's not that I wasn't interested in all the rest of the racing — I was — but I was there for Katie Lee and that's all there was about it.'

The lone figure of this Knight of the Realm once again sitting on his bucket by the stabling area soon became the toast of Riccarton, as Katie Lee charged home from midfield to win the first leg of the Guineas double, then returned a week later to defeat the fillies. 'It was a great year to win those two races,' Patrick said, recalling the feeling, 'because the 2000 Guineas was that year a million-dollar race. It was huge to win both of those races, especially as it had never been done before.'

One person not so happy with Katie Lee's double was Cambridge trainer Shaune Ritchie, who had to endure the frustration of saddling the runner-up in both races — Military

Move in the 2000 Guineas and Keep The Peace in the 1000 Guineas. However, Ritchie was to get his day in the sun later in the season when Military Move won the New Zealand Derby and Keep The Peace won the Oaks.

Katie Lee went on to win two Cambridge Stud–sponsored Group 2 fillies races over the summer, the Eight Carat Classic at Ellerslie and Sir Tristram Fillies Classic at Te Rapa, but a tilt at the New Zealand Derby proved a bridge too far and she was unplaced. She returned the following season and won the Group 3 Traderacks Stakes at Hastings but she never returned to her three-year-old spring form of Riccarton and was retired to the matron's paddock at Cambridge Stud as one of the finest mares Patrick and Justine ever raced. A future mating for Katie Lee with Fastnet Rock produced a colt that topped the 2014 yearling sales at Karaka, the colt knocked down for $800,000 to Graeme and Debbie Rogerson.

However, there was a tragic chapter to the Katie Lee story. Before her Traderacks Stakes win at Hastings, Katie Lee kicked out as she was being walked through the stabling area and connected with 37-year-old Matamata stablehand Blair Busby, who suffered fatal injuries. There was nothing Patrick could have done but the incident deeply upset him. He attended Busby's funeral and kept a photograph of the handler in his office. He has never forgotten about him. 'He loved his horses and he was at the wrong place at the wrong time,' Patrick says. 'It was something we wished had never happened.'

As ever, Zabeel's star was shining brightly on both sides of the Tasman. Victoria Derby winner Efficient became the first winner of the three-year-old Classic at Flemington since Phar

Lap to return the following spring and win the Melbourne Cup. The grey stayer, bred by Cambridge accountant Scott Williams and Wellington businessman Graeme Hunt, raced in the colours of Lloyd Williams and credited Graeme Rogerson with a coveted Melbourne Cup training triumph, to go with his earlier Golden Slipper and Cox Plate wins.

Efficient became Zabeel's third Melbourne Cup winner after Might And Power and Jezabeel, and Patrick told reporters afterwards that it was rich reward for Williams, estimating the casino magnate had spent more than $20 million on over 100 Zabeel progeny in his quest to find the right stayer to again win the Melbourne Cup.

The following spring Zabeel took his tally of Cox Plate winners to four when Maldivian notched up his third Group 1 win in taking out the Moonee Valley feature. That led to the Moonee Valley Racing Club bestowing a unique honour on the stallion as the most influential sire in the history of the race described as 'Australia's greatest two minutes in sport'.

Patrick was humbled to accept the Kingston Town Greatness Award on behalf of Zabeel. 'It's a great thrill to get it and a huge honour for Zabeel,' Patrick told the *Waikato Times*. 'I'm really chuffed about it, thrilled to bits. The old fella is not getting any younger — he'll be 24 on August 1 — but he's still churning out stakes winners and Group winners the equal of any of his younger rivals. He's had 20 stakes wins this season — four of them Group 1 winners — and not too many stallions of his age can still keep up with the younger brigade and keep on firing out winners like he has.

'I've got to be fair to Zabeel now, too. I said I'd never say it, but he has probably surpassed Sir Tristram now. He's emulated his own sire in every category. But that's not to take away from Sir Tristram. Without him, I wouldn't have had the opportunity to be at the level of involvement I am now in the thoroughbred industry.'

At the 2011–12 Horse of the Year Awards ceremony, Patrick accepted a remarkable 15th Dewar Stallion Trophy for Zabeel, an award for the New Zealand sire with the highest earnings in Australasia for the season. Patrick had four times previously won the Grosvenor Award for New Zealand earnings and once secured the Centaine Award for global earnings. He had also taken out the honours as champion broodmare sire three times, an award he might yet dominate for many seasons to come.

In 2014, Zabeel was inducted into the New Zealand Racing Hall of Fame, joining his own sire Sir Tristram, who was inducted in 2008. 'Sir Tristram made it and now Zabeel has made too — deservedly so. They were both certainties to get there but it was fantastic to see Zabeel join his father in there,' Patrick said.

In 2016, Eight Carat joined them — a fitting honour for his champion matron, Patrick thought. She was just the second broodmare to be inducted after the great Eulogy. 'Till recently, Eight Carat was the only mare in the world to have left five Group 1 winners,' Patrick said after the induction. 'That's an amazing feat and just goes to prove that mares don't need to be great racehorses to be champion broodmares. She raced nine times unsuccessfully and was able to throw five individual Group 1 winners.

'The horses that have got the Eight Carat bloodlines have done an incredible job and her descendants are everywhere now. She has to be the best producing mare that has been to stud in New Zealand up to now.'

In 2016, Cambridge Stud could boast four champions in the Racing Hall of Fame — Patrick, Sir Tristram, Zabeel and Eight Carat — but the studmaster believes the Cambridge farm might still have one or two others worthy of induction, with hopes for Cox Plate winner Surround who was inducted into the Australian Racing Hall of Fame in 2014. And Patrick hopes that one day Justine might also join the list.

'Awards don't always tell the full story,' he says. 'Nobody would have worked harder to make Cambridge Stud a success than Justine. Whether it be mucking out boxes, mowing lawns, leading mares up and down the farm, planting trees and helping out on the studfarm, Justine's influence has been profound.

'It's quite unfair that I have these awards and they are documented as my awards singularly but there's no mention of Justine. That disregards Justine's role as a contributor to making sure we arrived at where we got as a studfarm. The way I look at it, I've received these awards but I've always felt I've accepted them on behalf of Justine and myself.'

Patrick's honours and awards aren't confined to the Racing Hall of Fame either. He was delighted to receive an honorary doctorate from the University of Waikato in 2013, though he jokes it hadn't gone down too well with some younger family members. 'It was pretty special to get. Four grandchildren have all been through university. They're all pretty smart and have worked hard but they have strongly indicated they were more than a little pissed off that I'd done no work whatsoever to get such a high honour at Waikato University. They didn't think that was a bit fair.'

Patrick was presented with his degree at a ceremony officiated by Waikato University chancellor and former prime minister

Jim Bolger. 'It was nice to have the chancellor Jim Bolger do the capping because I've known Jim for a long time and we're good friends,' Sir Patrick told the *Waikato Times*.

'It's nice recognition for the thoroughbred industry, which to my opinion doesn't get recognised enough in the wider community. I'm thrilled to bits I've received that honour.'

The *Waikato Times* reported that Patrick had 'an already impressive list of awards and titles collected over more than 30 years at the forefront of the New Zealand bloodstock industry', and continued: 'The Cambridge horse breeder is a Commander of the Order of the British Empire (CBE) and Knight Companion of the New Zealand Order of Merit (KNZM). He has also been inducted into the New Zealand and Australian racing hall of fame. University of Waikato Vice-Chancellor Professor Roy Crawford said Sir Patrick's contribution to the development and international standing of the New Zealand thoroughbred industry is unparalleled.

'"His hard work and passion for horses have won both him and Cambridge Stud a special place in New Zealand racing history."'

While Patrick's public persona was of a studmaster who never stopped for fresh air, it was becoming clear to those closest to him that he needed to slow down. Patrick suffered a series of health scares that taught him he was no longer a 30-year-old. 'I had 12 months of quite serious issues where I'd pass out and it necessitated that I got a pacemaker,' he later revealed.

'There was a period where I had an enormous number of turns and without the pacemaker, they would have lost me. It's connected to my heart and clicks in when there's a problem.

I've slowed down a lot in recent years. I'm certainly not as fit and healthy as I used to be and stud life is nowadays a little bit tougher than it used to be.'

Patrick wasn't the only one starting to show the signs of ageing. Zabeel was no longer the sprightly stallion he once was — and while his fertility issues were under control, a new, more critical problem emerged. It had become apparent that Zabeel had contracted laminitis, a degenerative hoof disease that can be deadly for horses. It was leaving him in crippling pain.

As always Patrick was straight onto his vets Jonathan Hope and Rob Hitchcock, who wanted to act fast to ensure Zabeel had his best possible chance of beating the disease.

'Rob and Jonathan said: "Listen, he's got this laminitis and he's not going to get over it in a hurry. What we should do is, before the pedal bone rotates any further, we should cut his ligaments." Normally, people don't do it that early, but we agreed to cut them and it was amazing because they healed so well you would never have picked that they had been cut.'

But the ordeal wasn't quite over. Despite the ligaments healing well, Zabeel continued to get worse. 'The flesh around the pedal bone began rotting and it was a hell of a mess,' Patrick says. 'In the end it was so bad, they said if we can't get this gunk out of here, it's the end for this horse.'

Cambridge veterinarians had treated an injury on Victoria Derby winner Lion Tamer by using industrial maggots to eat away dead tissue around the wound. It had been so successful, Jonathan was keen to use the same approach with Zabeel. Farrier Laurie Lynch helped work on the front foot and the vets applied their maggot therapy.

'They put the first lot of maggots in and that was fine. They ate away at the dead flesh but when they put the second lot of maggots in, I went and saw him the next morning and you could see he was in enormous pain,' Patrick says. 'I could see it in his eyes and I could tell how stressed he was. I rang Jonathan in tears. He was doing some work at Trelawney Stud but I said, "You've got to come here straight away. I cannot let this horse put up with this any longer. You need to get here and put him down. He cannot be allowed to suffer after all he's done for us."'

Jonathan arrived with Marcus Corban and after they inspected Zabeel they went to see Patrick. Jonathan said to Patrick, 'I want you to bugger off and don't come near this horse for a few days. He's going to be all right. He's not going to be put down but I don't want you around him.'

Reluctantly, Patrick conceded that he needed to leave Jonathan to his work and put his faith in his care for Zabeel — and slowly but surely the stallion got better. Jonathan and his maggots had ensured the stallion would be around for another couple of seasons yet.

When Patrick finally went public about Zabeel's treatment, he told reporters: 'I didn't want to make too much of it at the time because it could have been blown out of proportion. Every year now is a bonus with him. The last three seasons have been bonus years [for a stallion of his age]. He served 90 mares last season so he's going to have about 70 foals running around from this year's crop. In Australia the perception is that a stallion is past their best once they get to 20 or 21 and the demand drops off. But breeders are still hot on Zabeel.'

With Zabeel's progeny still churning out a regular supply of Group 1 winners across Australasia and reaching the milestone of 1000 individual winners, Cambridge Stud remained a popular vendor at the annual New Zealand Bloodstock National Yearling Sales Series at Karaka.

It continued to make a habit of producing the top-priced yearling, with James Bester going to $2 million to secure a Zabeel colt out of Diamond Like, later named Zephyron, at the 2010 sales. The world-renowned bloodstock agent told media: 'I gave him the highest rating I've ever given a yearling on type.'

Patrick rated the colt the best he had ever presented for sale. 'But in this economic climate if anyone had said you'll sell a $2 million colt you could be taken as a fool. I put an $800,000 reserve on him and I've let everyone know as I always do, and I think that's why we got an opening bid of $900,000. My expectations were that I thought he was a colt who in this climate should make $1 million. When it got to $1.2 million, I thought, Well, that's nice. When it got to $1.6 million, I thought, When is this going to end? When it got to $2 million that was the time for the tear to drop out of my eye.'

Two years later, Cambridge Stud sold a Fastnet Rock colt out of Nureyev's Girl for $1.75 million to David Ellis, the 11th time the farm had sold a million-dollar yearling in New Zealand. But the following year, Patrick found himself in unfamiliar territory.

After an uninterrupted 31-year streak, Cambridge Stud was finally dethroned in 2013 as the national yearling sales's leading vendor. Gordon Cunningham's Curraghmore Stud had sold a Fastnet Rock colt out of Celebria for $1.975 million on the first day of the two-day premier sale, giving Curraghmore Stud an enormous $3 million lead over Cambridge Stud at the halfway stage.

Patrick was immensely proud of his 31-year run and wouldn't give up without a fight. As expected, Cambridge Stud came charging back but at the close of the session was $430,000 behind. Patrick, as always, was humble in defeat, saying it was healthy for the breeding industry to have a new champion. He told the press: 'I'm happy I made a close contest of it anyway and I'm thrilled to bits for Gordon Cunningham. He does a fantastic job and he's an asset to our industry. He always presents himself and his property well and his horses sell exceptionally well in the sale ring. This is an enormous result for him.

'It's been an amazing trip that I've had with Sir Tristram and Zabeel. You've got to have those kind of stallions to go 31 years in a row as leading vendor. I haven't done anything great to achieve that result up till now. I've just had the stallions to make it happen for me.'

For his part, Cunningham said he had nothing but praise and adulation for a man he described as an industry icon and role model. 'I've had the utmost respect for Sir Patrick Hogan and have had since the time I came down from Ireland for the first time in 1984 and saw his professionalism with horses at Trentham. He's led our industry for years and years and, as an industry, each and every one of us owes him so much for his innovation and his marketing.'

Patrick also revealed a measure of relief that his record sequence had ended and the pressure was off, but promised that it would still be business as usual at Cambridge Stud. He told the *Waikato Times*: 'At my age now, I should be doing what my wife keeps telling me and not doing so many horses. She says I should get rid of half of them and I'd enjoy it better — and she's right, but I'm not at the stage to take that advice and listen.'

CHAPTER 19

LIGHTNING STRIKES TWICE

'Zabeel put New Zealand on the world stage. Little did we know that after Sir Tristram, this freak here could get another as good, if not better, with his son. What they've done for the New Zealand and Australian industry is immeasurable.'

— New Zealand Bloodstock Chairman Joe Walls

I T WAS A day that was always going to come but one Patrick had never looked forward to. In the spring of 2013, evergreen stallion Zabeel was still as keen as ever to cover mares but not one returned a positive pregnancy when scanned. After 22 years of siring champion racehorses, the Zabeel era was over.

Now it was up to Patrick to front the media to announce the 27-year-old stallion's retirement from stud duties. He called a press conference and was overwhelmed by the response. The television networks sent their top reporters and photographers, as did the daily and weekly newspapers. Both the general media and racing press were represented, along with Trackside television cameras, radio journalists and racing industry marketing executives. Patrick took time to do individual interviews with them all. He recalled Zabeel's amazing career that had seen him win more than 25 stallion awards and produce champion gallopers the ilk of Octagonal and Might And Power.

'He's had 22 years at stud and done a fantastic job. The staff here at Cambridge Stud have done an amazing job of managing him. To still have him serving at 27 was a huge achievement in itself,' Patrick told the *Waikato Times*. 'It's not a sad day that we're announcing his retirement. At the end of the day, we're doing what's best for him and I'm pretty proud.'

In the *Waikato Times*, Aidan Rodley wrote: 'Zabeel paraded in terrific condition, his coat dappling under the bright Cambridge sun. He walked freely and was playful when his handler Keri Gore stopped him so photographers could have a standing shot. Just as he had done right through his career, Zabeel shone. And Sir Patrick basked in his reflected glory.'

Patrick handled the interviews with good grace and cheer but as Zabeel was paraded for the television cameras and photographers and Patrick stood to pat the stallion's shoulder as requested, the studmaster had to excuse himself. 'I'm about to cry,' he told one reporter, taking himself out of the way of TV cameras to shed a tear and compose himself.

'I'd be biased, of course, but there hasn't been a stallion in the last 60 years do what he's done,' Patrick said, once composed. 'I've got to be fair to both Zabeel and Sir Tristram but he's at least emulated his own sire. I've got to put him on top and Sir Tristram a close second. For anyone to think that we would follow with a stallion such as Zabeel after standing his own sire, Sir Tristram, and getting the achievements and results that we did with him — to think of the result [Zabeel] has achieved internationally, you wouldn't have thought it possible.

'When Zabeel came through the gate, I was certainly rapt in him. I believed he was the right son of Sir Tristram but I did say to myself, "If he's a nice bread-and-butter commercial stallion, I'll be more than happy because I can't get one again like the one I've just had." But as they say — lightning struck twice.'

Not long afterwards, Patrick was approached by sculptor Nichola Lewis, who asked him if she could make a bronze statuette of Zabeel. Nichola's father, Rick, had produced a bronze of Sir Tristram some 30 years earlier and she was keen to follow in his footsteps. They agreed she would create a likeness of Zabeel which would be limited to 300 individual statues to be sold as a collector's item.

Nichola spent hours getting Zabeel just right and took advice from Patrick to ensure the very essence of the stallion was captured in her work. 'We worked together,' Patrick said later, 'getting his head right, broadening his nostrils and lengthening his ears and making sure we got his legs right and his tail flowing. She did a fantastic job.'

Nichola told the *Cambridge Edition* that she was extremely nervous showing Patrick the finished article but was delighted by his response. 'As soon as he saw it, he said, "That is Zabeel." I was blown away by how much he adored Zabeel. He didn't want something arty — he wanted to be able to see the animal in the sculpture.'

While Zabeel was now retired and wouldn't be producing any further foals, he still had two further crops of yearlings to go through the sales and the spotlight fell on them at Karaka in

2015, with buyers keen to get their hands on a commodity that, so to speak, had since gone out of production. Zabeel's final sales draft was just four and it so happened that the final yearling to sell, out of the mare Organdy, was in Cambridge Stud's draft.

Patrick had led the last Sir Tristram yearling in the sales ring and though he was not the young man he was then, he was privately determined to accompany the final Zabeel yearling through the Karaka ring.

Barry Lichter didn't miss the chance to highlight the occasion when he previewed the yearling sales in the *Sunday Star-Times*. 'His knees and hips might be dodgy,' Lichter wrote, 'and he might have a pacemaker to keep him going these days, but if his practice run was anything to go by, Sir Patrick Hogan will be there at the bell to mark the end of one of the most remarkable chapters of the New Zealand thoroughbred industry.

'When the last yearling by champion stallion Zabeel is sold at New Zealand Bloodstock's premier sale at Karaka on Monday, Sir Patrick, 75, is determined to be the one leading him into the ring. He was there at the front end when Zabeel's first progeny went through the ring in 1994 and, even though he hasn't led a yearling for years, the Cambridge Stud boss wants to be there when lot 102 sells soon after 2pm.

'"I had a practice run today walking him up and down the lawn and gathered all the staff around as guards in case it was too much for me," Sir Patrick said. "I'm obviously not as fit and strong as I have been but I reckon I scored an 11 out of 10. I let him know I was in charge but after that I let him do the job for me and it went great."

'The stud grooms were quick to reply they marked the horse 11 out of 10, not the handler, but Sir Patrick was happy just knowing he might still have one more matinee performance ahead of him.

"'It will be an emotional and humbling few minutes because it doesn't just centre around Zabeel. A lot of people have benefited enormously from the horse, not just Justine and I, but all his shareholders. Then there's all the breeders who sold yearlings by him, all the owners who won races with them, the jockeys who got their percentages and the sale agents who got their commissions.'"

The auction itself couldn't have gone much smoother. Patrick was mindful to assert dominance early over the colt and before a packed Karaka auditorium, he morphed back into the young man that led yearlings at Trentham. Again he was the showman, relishing his opportunity to take centre stage.

'The thing I'd always said I missed most was leading yearlings in the ring. It was my stage. I was in Hollywood and I was the lead performer and when I gave it up, it was something I really missed and I still miss it even now,' Patrick revealed later. 'It was difficult to give up but I needed to let others do that job. But I led the last Sir Tristram yearling through the ring at the Sydney sales. Inglis asked me if I would — and I did — so I certainly wanted to lead the last Zabeel through the ring at Karaka.

'I wasn't sure I could do it. I knew I could lead any horse in the early days and no horse would ever beat me because I had it in me that I wouldn't let that happen. But I don't have the same strength in my arms that I did when I was a young fellow and when I saw him in the outer ring, I thought, Gee, can I do this?

'When he came in for the hand-over, I said to myself, "Don't say you can't do this, say you can do it." I got him under the chin and gave him a firm squeeze and a head shake and said,

"Listen, I'm in charge, not you," and as we walked forward he knew he wasn't going to get the better of me and it went great. I loved doing it. I had wanted to do it and nothing would have stopped me.'

After the colt had been knocked down for $160,000, notably to Marcus Corban Bloodstock on behalf of Hong Kong businessman Gene Tsoi, and Patrick had led the youngster out of the ring, he returned to the auditorium to acknowledge the packed audience. They responded with a prolonged standing ovation. 'I felt a fool doing it but I appreciated that people had come to see me lead this yearling and I felt obliged to,' Patrick said of his own encore performance.

With the last of his sales progeny going through the ring, public interest was again piqued in Zabeel. 'He's doing well,' Patrick assured everyone who enquired at the sales.

However, eight months later the mighty stallion took his last breath of Cambridge air. Patrick arrived at Cambridge Stud at 6.30am one Saturday in late September and was informed that Zabeel had died peacefully overnight.

The studmaster let himself through the gate into Zabeel's paddock and slowly walked to where the stallion was lying. He knelt down and shared a final private moment with his champion sire and chum, thanking him for the massive contribution he had made, not only to Cambridge Stud but also to New Zealand breeding and racing.

'He was still on the ball, he didn't suffer. He lay down to have a sleep and his heart stopped. He left in a nice way,' Patrick told reporters, admitting he was taking Zabeel's death pretty hard considering he had been there when he was born at

Cambridge Stud and had formed a close emotional attachment to the stallion over the next 27 years.

Sir Patrick immediately set about burying Zabeel and by midday the stallion was laid to rest on a thick bed of straw, alongside the graves of Sir Tristram and Eight Carat — the three crown jewels of the Cambridge Stud breeding dynasty at rest next to each other. Patrick, Justine and stud staff held an intimate farewell for Zabeel, who like Sir Tristram was buried with his tail to the rising sun and head to the setting sun in keeping with ancient traditions.

Zabeel's death prompted Patrick to think about the journey the sire had taken him on, reflecting on his initial pessimism that he could ever hope to replace Sir Tristram. 'I hit the jackpot with my first stallion and I did seriously contemplate whether I should quit while I was ahead after Sir Tristram,' Patrick said later. 'I even spoke to my brothers about it and they convinced me that this was my calling. They said, "You're crazy. You're meant to be with horses, not anything else."

'I was lucky that I nailed Zabeel and that was probably an even greater ride than Sir Tristram because when he got a Group 1 winner, he got a multiple Group 1 winner.'

With 44 individual Group 1 winners, Zabeel may have had one less than his father, Sir Tristram, but Zabeel's were champion horses like Octagonal and Might And Power who won multiple races.

'Zabeel was a different feeling,' Patrick says. 'With Sir Tristram it was exciting because he took us to the top and with me being much younger, it was the excitement of a young fellow working with a great horse. But with Zabeel and what he achieved, it was more humbling. It was just a privilege to be involved with a son of Sir Tristram who was doing what he did. They were two completely different horses, two different characters. Sir Tristram was an almost unmanageable horse and you had to be very careful handling him, whereas Zabeel was the opposite and just about anyone could have handled him. They were father and son but chalk and cheese.

'I can't explain why but the loss of Zabeel was far more devastating for me. To find him that morning dead in his paddock was extremely upsetting. But with Sir Tristram, he broke his shoulder and we had the chance to say goodbye. We didn't get that opportunity with Zabeel.

'We kept him light in condition because of his laminitis and we always monitored him. When I was home, I would check on him five or six times a day. I needed to know if something was going wrong because there was no way I was going to let him suffer.

'The next day and the day after [his death] were horrible. I was just terribly upset to lose him, but the third day, surprisingly enough, I changed. I knew he was in the right place, he'd done the right thing and didn't suffer — and I suddenly became happy in that knowledge.'

Just as he'd done when sending off Sir Tristram, Patrick asked one final favour from Zabeel — to pass the baton to his emerging new Montjeu stallion, Tavistock. Cambridge Stud's latest acquisition was already making a promising start to his stallion career but surely lightning couldn't strike thrice?

CHAPTER 20

A GOOD TURN OF FOOT

'Cambridge Stud is my kingdom — it's my land, my world.
There's no grass greener on the other side of the fence — there
never has been. Cambridge Stud is me — if I'm not here,
I'm still walking here. It means everything to me because
what you see is me, and I can't get any closer than that.'

— Sir Patrick Hogan

HERE WAS UNDOUBTEDLY a lull in business for Cambridge Stud after Zabeel retired in 2013. The top-class mares were being sent to other stallions, most notably Zabeel's best sire son Savabeel, who was fast making a name for himself as New Zealand's new banner stallion with a steady flow of Group 1 winners across Australasia.

And Waikato Stud, where Savabeel was standing, had claimed its first leading vendor title at the premier sales at Karaka, a massive fillip for new studmaster Mark Chittick, who had only recently taken over from his father, Patrick's great friend and rival Garry Chittick.

After all the hurly-burly of the success of Sir Tristram and Zabeel over the past almost four decades, a quieter life at Cambridge Stud wasn't exactly unwelcome for Patrick.

Though he had recently invested in Tavistock, the rest of his stallions were either shuttle stallions (Cape Blanco and Power) or nearing the twilight of their career (Keeper).

He had given thought to cutting back Cambridge Stud by a third and focusing its activities as more of a broodmare and sales preparation farm. However, the events of the first day of spring of the 2014–15 season had changed everything.

Avisto, a daughter of Tavistock, raced to victory in the Listed Soliloquy Stakes at Ellerslie. It wasn't her first win; she had already credited her sire with his first stakes winner when she claimed the Listed Great Northern Foal Stakes at the same venue late in her two-year-old season. In the very next race in the Group 3 Bonecrusher Stakes, Volkstok'n'barrell announced himself as a galloper of rare talent with a brilliant 4.5–length win, sealing a coveted three-year-old stakes double for Tavistock. Later that day, another son of Tavistock, Diamond Valores, went within a length of beating winner Sweynesse in running second in the Group 3 Gloaming Stakes in Sydney.

Patrick was inspecting stallions in the New South Wales Hunter Valley with good mates and fellow Tavistock shareholders Bob Emery and Gerald Shand when the news of the watershed day for the stallion filtered through. He later recounted: 'Everything just went boom and by the time I got home we were inundated with applications for nominations for services to Tavistock. When I got to the office on the Monday, Margaret was trying to sort through all of these applications and it was doing her head in, there were so many. I remember saying to Bob and Gerald at the time, exact words: "Do I really need this?" Gerald's response was: "You're the first man to say that and have the biggest smile on his face at the same time."'

While Patrick hadn't gone out of his way to look for a replacement sire for Zabeel, he couldn't help but ask whether Tavistock might be available after he had first caught his attention with a phenomenal last-to-first win in the Group 1 Mudgway Partsworld Stakes at Hastings.

'Every studmaster anywhere in the world is always keeping their eyes open and week to week monitoring horses that are running and how they are performing,' he says. 'Even if they are not intending to buy, they are keeping their eye on the ball. When Tavistock won the Group 1 Mudgway Stakes at Hastings, I thought then and there, I must look up that family and see what it's like.'

Tavistock came from an 'overall good-producing' family that included the Japan Cup winner Jupiter Island and Quest For Fame as a damsire. Patrick was impressed. 'That was on top of the Sadler's Wells blood through his sire Montjeu, which I knew would be suited to daughters of Zabeel. I thought, Gee, this horse is worth keeping an eye on.'

Patrick made a special point of inspecting Tavistock first hand before the running of the Group 1 Waikato Sprint at Te Rapa and liked what he saw. 'I kept a close eye on Tavistock in the parade ring before the Waikato Sprint at Te Rapa and in the race. He put in a scintillating sprint to win that race — he showed an amazing turning of foot. I remembered what Colin Hayes told me about a good stallion possessing a good turn of foot when he spoke about Zabeel.

'I didn't know [majority owner] Tommy Heptinstall or [trainer] Andrew Campbell or any of them but I waited till after the presentation was over and approached Tommy and said, "Can I have a word?" I told them I'd like to throw my hat in the ring if the horse ever goes to stud.'

Tavistock's win in the Waikato Sprint earned him a trip to Australia to race. He was out of sorts when finishing fifth in the Group 1 Futurity Stakes at Caulfield in 2010 but on the wider spaces of Flemington next start, Tavistock was back to his best, blitzing his rivals in the Group 2 Blamey Stakes. Campbell and Heptinstall agreed Tavistock had done enough to press on towards Group 1 targets in Sydney but after he was tripped up on an unsuitable slow track in the TJ Smith, they decided to reassess his future.

'I got a phone call from Tommy and he asked if I was still interested in standing the horse at stud. He had met with Andrew and the other owners and they were happy to retire the horse then and there if he could go to stud at Cambridge Stud. If I said no, they were going to race him on,' Patrick says.

Patrick was definitely interested and immediately booked flights to Australia for himself and Marcus to inspect the stallion properly and supervise his vetting. 'There wasn't anything not to like about him so the deal was done. I bought him and syndicated him.'

The price tag was $3 million, with Patrick taking a 50 per cent holding, just as he had done with Sir Tristram and Zabeel. The remaining 50 per cent was syndicated among outside breeders, among them Heptinstall, as well as Tavistock's racing ownership group.

Tavistock covered 127 mares in his first season at a fee of $12,500 and held his own over the next couple of seasons. Patrick strayed from his usual methods and allowed shareholders unlimited services for the first two seasons, so long as they could prove they owned the mare, to ensure his new stallion got the best opportunity possible. 'I'd never done it with the other stallions but I decided that numbers were better than no numbers. I reckon Tim Bodle rounded up all his 20-year-old mares out of the back paddock and sent them!

'It was a new marketing ploy to give Tavistock the best kick-start he could get. The first three years, he got some nice numbers, but then when his progeny started going whoosh on the racetrack, we didn't need to worry about trying to entice breeders to utilise him. And he took it all in his stride. He served 200 mares each of the next two seasons and he is easily the most fertile stallion I've ever had anything to do with. He was able to handle those numbers and that's set him up for the future.'

Tavistock three-year-olds Tavy, Midnitemagicman and Longchamp registered stakes wins or placings for their sire but it was clear Volkstok'n'barrell was the main flagbearer of his crop. He added the Karaka Mile and Group 2 Great Northern Guineas before finishing second to arch-rival Mongolian Khan in the Group 2 Avondale Guineas and in the Group 1 New Zealand Derby after a home straight battle for the ages. Both Mongolian Khan and Volkstok'n'barrell headed to Sydney and squared off again in the Group 1 Rosehill Guineas and this time Volkstok'n'barrell emerged victorious, sparking celebrations among the Tavistock camp. Other successes followed with placings for Werther and Imperial Lass; they added more Classic black-type to Tavistock's resume.

But the best was to come the following season. Tarzino claimed the Group 1 Victoria Derby in the spring and added the Group 1 Rosehill Guineas in the autumn, while Volkstok'n'barrell returned to land the Group 1 double of the Haunui Farm Weight-For-Age Classic at Otaki and the New Zealand Stakes at Ellerslie. Hasselhoof made it six wins in as many starts when he claimed the Group 2 Rich Hill Mile at Ellerslie. Tavago, having won the Group 3 Wellington Stakes in the spring, produced a brilliant performance to win the Group 1 Australian Derby at Randwick. And Werther, who was sold to Hong Kong interests after his three-year-old season, claimed the Hong Kong Derby then destroyed a formidable field of the world's best 2000 metre horses to win the Group 1 Queen Elizabeth Cup.

Before his first crop had even reached the end of their four-year-old seasons, Tavistock had produced four individual Group 1 winners, three of them winning multiple races at that level, while Tavago had already won at Group level as well.

Remarkably, Tavistock's progeny were forming an uncanny nick with the offspring of Zabeel. Tarzino, Werther, Hasselhoof, Diamond Valores and Imperial Lass were all out of Zabeel mares, while Tavago's granddam was a Zabeel mare.

At the end of April 2015, Patrick received a phone call from a breeding analyst in Australia, who asked him: 'Do you know where Tavistock sits in comparison to your previous good stallions Sir Tristram and Zabeel, based on stakes winners and starters to winners at the same age?'

Patrick said he'd 'never cared to check', so the analyst gave him the statistics. 'He told me Tavistock was ahead of them both at the same point of their careers,' Patrick recalls. 'I did say to him, "He'd have to be a very smart dude to stay in front", but at least he's going the right way. There's no question that he's the real deal. Now he's starting to attract a better quality of mare and that could well really set him alight.

'And he's a piece of cake to deal with too, no problem whatsoever. Physically, he's a horse that will never let down into a massive, powerful, muscled-up stallion. He's a horse that's always on the move, though bring him into his box and he's as

413

happy as a sandboy. He'd spend all day in there if we'd let him.'

Writing for UK's *Racing Post*, Martin Stevens interviewed Patrick about Tavistock's remarkable start to his stud career. He filed an article that began: 'It looks as though Sir Patrick Hogan has done it for a third time.'

Stevens's article continued: 'Cambridge Stud's young sire sensation Tavistock has a long way to go to be considered the equal of his illustrious predecessors [Sir Tristram and Zabeel], who must be considered the most important stamina influences on Australasian racing of modern times. But he has made swift progress in the early stages of the journey.'

Patrick explained to Stevens that he was 'very much a breeder who breeds to duplications' and that he was thrilled with Tavistock's form.

'Sir Tristram clicked with the Australasian bloodlines and Zabeel crossed well with the same mares, and now Tavistock is starting to get success through the same families,' Patrick says. 'What's worked well for me is I've always leaned more to the good old English blood. Sir Tristram was all English blood, a real northern hemisphere product. Zabeel, while born in New Zealand, was by Sir Tristram out of a French-bred mare so his bloodline was the same — and now Tavistock is the same. Cape Cross was another. That English blood has just worked for me.'

Before the breakthrough success of Tavistock's 2015–16 season, the stallion had attracted and served his best quality book of mares yet. But for the early part of the serving season, Patrick was absent. 'The All Blacks needed me elsewhere,' he likes to joke. Back in 2007, Patrick had been part of a 14-strong tour group of mainly racing and breeding mates to the Rugby World Cup in France, but the All Blacks' early exit had meant the group had spent more time visiting studfarms and vineyards than they did watching rugby. They had covered most of their travelling expenses by selling their tickets to the final to English fans at premium prices.

The group had decided they would return to the next northern hemisphere Rugby World Cup in England in 2015, and 10 of them eventually did make the return trip. Between matches, they headed to Bordeaux and to the vineyards there, and also to Ireland, where Patrick had teed up a guided tour of Coolmore Stud and its museum. 'Anybody that is fortunate enough to get the opportunity to ever have a look at that museum and especially the history and memorabilia around the O'Brien and Magnier families, the stud and Sadler's Wells definitely should take it,' Patrick says.

They also visited Juddmonte Stud and got to see world champion racehorse and stallion Frankel and one of Patrick's favourite stallions Oasis Dream.

Patrick also took the opportunity to travel to Galway to visit his cousins and family. He visited the family home in Ballindooley where his father Tom was born. 'Before I left home I got in touch with my cousin John and told him I doubted I would be back [again], so I would like to put on a dinner for the family in honour of my father Tom — and Zabeel was going to shout! It ended up a great night. It was a moving experience for me and hopefully meant a lot to them too.'

And of course the trip was a triumph when Richie McCaw's All Blacks won the World Cup final, beating Australia 34–17 at Twickenham.

While Tavistock's unstoppable rise through the stallion ranks continued, Zabeel was to prove he was gone but not forgotten in the winter of 2016, grabbing headlines even from the grave. The reason was his landmark 45th individual Group 1 winner, drawing him level with Sir Tristram.

Cambridge trainer Tony Pike and South Auckland jockey Leith Innes became the toast of New Zealand as Zabeel filly Provocative overcame a wide barrier and taxing trip three-wide in running to prove superior to her rivals in the Queensland Oaks at Eagle Farm. It was a comprehensive victory from a filly tipped as an exciting Cups prospect as an older horse and one that was joyously welcomed at Cambridge Stud.

Sir Patrick told *New Zealand Racing Desk*: 'We've been waiting some considerable time for this victory as it had been a while since Preferment took him to just one win short of Sir Tristram. To think that he could emulate his father is something very special, and when I saw the filly poised to win at the top of the straight I knew that day had finally come. We have a special red rose that is officially known as the Sir Tristram rose and this morning I went and placed one on Zabeel's grave to acknowledge just what he has achieved.'

Sir Patrick was thrilled with the Classic win and the milestone Provocative had provided, but he admitted he was torn about the prospect that Zabeel needed just one further win to surpass Sir Tristram and take the record for himself.

'Now that he has emulated his father I'm a little torn, in that I'm not that sure I want him to go past old Paddy. For them to stay locked together would be good in many ways, not the least in that they have remarkable similarity in their records. I don't have the official figures, but I'm pretty sure that of the

90 individual Group 1 winners between them, it is nearly an even split of both males and females. Often a stallion will have a skew to one sex or the other but for these two it has been quite amazing how even it has been.'

It was another son of Zabeel — Preferment — that anchored Patrick and Justine's fifth breeder of the year title, in 2015–16. Bred in partnership with Mike Moran and Leo and Barbara Anselmi, Preferment added the Group 1 treble of the Turnbull Stakes, Australian Cup and BMW Stakes to the Victoria Derby he had won at three under the guidance of ex-pat Kiwi trainer Chris Waller. Patrick and Justine also had Group 1 breeding success during the season with Victoria Derby and Rosehill Guineas winner Tarzino and Australian Derby winner Tavago, while Titanium won the Singapore Group 2 Stewards Cup and Infantry ran second in the Singapore Group 1 Singapore Guineas. 'It's a good effort to get five breeder of the year awards over four decades. As a breeder, it's the gold medal and to nail that is the most important prize of all. It's a great thrill to get it again,' Patrick said.

At Cambridge Stud in 2016, there is an impressive line-up of the new and the 'great old servants'. On the permanent staff front, and headed by Patrick, is the 30-years-plus club: general manager Marcus Corban, Laurie Lynch, Peter Stanaway, Corrina Holmes, Margaret Fife, Bevan McCallum (who arrived at the age of 15) and Mark Vince.

Add to that the contribution over the same period from bloodstock agent and friend Barry Lee and veterinarian Jonathan Hope, not forgetting the stud's photographer Jenny Kain who goes back to Fencourt days, and you'd conclude that there can't be too much wrong with the way the place operates. Keri Gore, Mark Fox and Gabrielle Potter have contributed immensely to the stud over the years, while Cambridge accountant John Ryan had done the books for Patrick's father and for Cambridge Stud for nearly 60 years up till his death in 2009.

They are the sheet anchors, but the newcomers — the junior stud staff and the kids who arrive on a temporary basis from all corners of the earth every year to work and gain valuable stud experience — are as vital to the stud's wellbeing, says Patrick. 'I'm big on young people. These young stud workers have been tremendous — very rarely have we been disappointed. I see it as a responsibility, because I believe that you have to give young people an opportunity. I don't think any business — and I don't care what it is — should turn its back on young people. I'm sure that the many young boys and girls who have walked through our gates have had their eyes opened and learned a lot.'

Cambridge Stud has been an integral part of many who have gone on to influential careers in breeding and racing. Among them Shane Keating, who spent 14 years at Cambridge Stud before going on to Darley Stud, and Adam Sangster, who arrived in 1984 as a fresh-faced English lad and now runs an arm of the family's empire at Swettenham Stud in Victoria.

Others to have learned the ropes at Cambridge Stud include Trelawney Stud boss Brent Taylor, Westbury Stud's Russell Warwick, Rich Hill Stud's John Thompson, who co-bred 2015 Melbourne Cup winner Prince Of Penzance, Little Avondale Stud's Sam Williams, Widden Stud's Antony Thompson, Brighthill Stud's Nick King, Highview Stud's Brent Gillovic, Seaton Park's Scott Eagleton, JK Farm's Jon Hogan, Ascot Farm's Bruce and Maureen Harvey, Bradbury Park's Michelle and Casey Dando and noted bloodstock agents Gary Mudgway and John White. Mike Fleming is now making his mark at his Victoria studfarm Bhima, while Luke and Mags Anderson, Luke Simpson, Tom Murtagh, Mark Forbes and David Burke have graduated Cambridge Stud and are now forging distinguished careers in the industry.

Patrick says many more ex-Cambridge Stud staffers have gone on to prestigious roles in bloodstock around the world, notably in Ireland and England, among them Coolmore Stud's Colm Santry, Tom Lynch, Paul Gleeson, Bob Davis, Maurice Moloney and Kevin Buckley: 'At its prime, there's no doubt Cambridge Stud was one of the greatest places for learning stud life anywhere in the world.'

In 2016, Cambridge Stud manager Marcus Corban clocked up 34 years of service. He has come to know Patrick as well as anyone. 'He's a self-driven perfectionist. He's a hard boss but you know that from the start. He doesn't often hand out thanks but he's very fair,' Marcus says. 'Because Patrick is such a perfectionist, it is a great place to work. He has good staff and he's always been so positive for the industry. He's given Cambridge Stud such an international profile that it opens doors wherever you go.'

Marcus noted that Tavistock's success had rejuvenated Cambridge Stud and put the spring back into Patrick's step that had been missing since Zabeel's passing. 'Tavistock has really given the boss another burst of life. He's never stopped striving to be the best with his bloodstock or his farming but Tavistock has really given him a boost, given him an outcross for his broodmares and almost a new lease on life,' Marcus says. 'I'd love him to go another 10 years to really enjoy Tavistock because he's put his life into the industry. For him, it's the industry first, then Mrs H, then the family. He's been a great ambassador for the industry.'

On the running of the day-to-day life at Cambridge Stud, veterinarian Jonathan Hope says he would like to make a personal observation. 'Patrick would be the only person I know in a similar position that would be hands-on in the management of the stud. He knows every mare, and we have to report to him on every mare — if there's a problem mare, he wants his input on them. He'll go around every two or three weeks with Marcus, looking at the weanlings right through to the yearlings. He'll examine them, and tell the staff to take this one out of that mob and put it with another mob, so they will end up with a horse that has the best possible presentation. He's unique.'

And, not to be outdone, Laurie Lynch adds: 'Patrick can't help himself with the old feed bucket. Come October/November, he's out there with milk powder and all the high-protein tucker he can stick in there.'

Each year there is a selling ritual to be followed. First up comes the Magic Millions on the Gold Coast, a week later it's the Karaka National Yearling Sales and, finally, the century-old William Inglis & Son Sydney Easter Sales at Newmarket.

There was one particularly memorable year when Cambridge Stud struck the trifecta, topping the sales at Magic Millions, Karaka and Sydney. 'I was determined to try and top the sales in all three,' Patrick grins with satisfaction. 'It hasn't been done before and I doubt very much whether it will be done in the future.'

A convivial man, he likes to attend the great race meetings on both sides of the Tasman and in Hong Kong, at times spreading his net further to South Africa, Dubai or Singapore. He loves to network with friends and clients and observe the progeny of Cambridge Stud wherever they may race.

But his life is not just horses, horses, horses. Today, Patrick has a massive business empire outside his bloodstock interests that extends from commercial properties and supermarkets to his 160-hectare dairy farm in nearby Pickering Road, which backs onto part of the stud and which he bought in 2001. His nephew Sean Hogan is the sharemilker on that property, Erinic Farm, and employs Patrick's grandson Patrick Hunt as farm manager.

These are the products of the man on the big scale. But, beguilingly, there are also the products of a multi-millionaire businessman on the small scale — a studmaster who shooes a rat out of the stables to avoid killing it, or who moves heaven and earth clambering through hedges to rescue a dumped puppy he discovers, through some Irish sixth sense, on a remote part of his dairy farm. Then he phones animal lover and neighbour Gabrielle Potter: 'I've got another one for you to collect and find a home for.' The greyhound-cross puppy finds a new home, as do a miscellany of stray cats and injured ducks and birds who have somehow landed up at Cambridge Stud.

New Zealand studmasters are considered the most hands-on of their profession in the world and Patrick is no different, even as he approaches 80. And while he has the utmost confidence in his loyal, long-serving and capable staff, Patrick is a realist and he understands that the end of the Cambridge Stud era is approaching.

'When Zabeel really slowed down in the stallion barn and he was getting ready for retirement, Cambridge Stud had a two- or three-year lull, a flat period and many people thought that may be it,' he says.

'I'd always thought that when the time came that Cambridge Stud was flattening off a bit stallion-wise, sales-wise and winners-wise, I'd be happy to restructure. The idea was that I would probably put the one-third of the farm that backs onto the dairy farm back into dairy land, and the other two-thirds would continue to run as a studfarm, but I'd ease out of the stallions and cut my broodmares back by 50 per cent. I'd retain shares in outside stallions but cut back and slow down, just enjoying myself breeding a few horses, taking them to the sales and racing a few.

'I'm well conscious of the fact that I've always said I don't want to be involved to this extent when I'm 80 — and I'll be 80 in 2019. It's not an old man's game and that's especially relevant to me because I'm so hands-on and I can't do it any other way. I'm not a bloke who could be offshore and let the stud run in my absence. It's not in my nature — and that's always been in the back of my mind.

'Cambridge Stud and me are intrinsically linked but it can't go on forever. I started it and I'll finish it. That's just the way it is.'

APPENDIX

Cambridge Stud's Group 1 Winners
* bred or co-bred by Sir Patrick and Justine, Lady Hogan

ZABEEL (45 individual Group 1 winners of 90 Group 1 races)
Able Master 2000 Auckland Cup
Bazelle 2005 Auckland Cup, 2005 Zabeel Classic
Bezeal Bay 1998 Emirates Stakes
* Champagne 1998 Mackinnon Stakes, 1998 Ansett Australia Stakes
Cronus 1997 Adelaide Cup
Dignity Dancer 1999 Australian Guineas, 1998 Spring Champion Stakes
Dizelle 2005 Australian Oaks
* Don Eduardo 2002 Australian Derby
Dress Circle 2001 Metropolitan Handicap
Efficient 2007 Melbourne Cup, 2009 Turnbull Stakes, 2006 Victoria
    Derby
* Fiumicino 2007 Australian Derby, 2009 The BMW
Gallic 2007 Sydney Cup
Gondokoro 2013 Queensland Oaks
Grand Echezeaux 2000 Australasian Oaks
Greene Street 2001 Avondale Gold Cup, 2003 International Stakes
Greys Inn 2004 South African Derby, 2004 Durban July Handicap
Hades 1999 New Zealand Derby
Hill Of Grace 2000 Ansett Australia Stakes
Inaflury 1998 One Thousand Guineas
* Jessicabeel 2010 Sydney Cup
Jezabeel 1998 Auckland Cup, 1998 Melbourne Cup
Lad Of The Manor 2005 Mackinnon Stakes
Lights Of Heaven 2011 Schweppes Oaks
* Maldivian 2009 CF Orr Stakes, WS Cox Plate, Yalumba Stakes
Might And Power 1997 Melbourne Cup, 1998 Doomben Cup,
    1997 Caulfield Cup, 1998 Queen Elizabeth Stakes, 1998 Mercedes
    Classic, 1998 Yalumba Stakes, 1998 WS Cox Plate
* Mouawad 1997 Australian Guineas, 1997 Futurity Stakes,
    1997 George Ryder Stakes
* Octagonal 1996 Rosehill Guineas, 1995 WS Cox Plate, 1996 Australian
    Derby, 1997 Chipping Norton Stakes, 1996 Underwood Stakes,

1997 Australian Cup, 1996 Mercedes Classic, 1996 Canterbury
Guineas, 1995 AJC Sires' Produce Stakes, 1997 Mercedes Classic

Our Unicorn 2001 Auckland Cup

* Preferment 2014 Victoria Derby, 2016 The BMW, 2016 Australian
Cup, 2015 Turnbull Stakes

Provocative 2016 Queensland Oaks

Railings 2005 Metropolitan Handicap, 2005 Caulfield Cup

Reset 2004 Australian Guineas, 2004 Futurity Stakes

Savabeel 2004 WS Cox Plate, 2004 Spring Champion Stakes

Shower Of Roses 2003 Arrowfield Stud Stakes

Sky Heights 2000 Yalumba Stakes, 1999 Caulfield Cup, 1999 Australian
Derby, 1999 Rosehill Guineas

* St Reims 2005 Zabeel Classic, 2002 New Zealand Derby

Unearthly 2003 Flight Stakes

Vengeance Of Rain 2005 Hong Kong Derby, 2005 Hong Kong
Cup, 2005 Queen Elizabeth II Cup, 2007 Dubai Sheema Classic,
2007 The Hong Kong Gold Cup

Vouvray 2004 Queensland Oaks

Zabeelionaire 2012 South Australian Derby

Zabrasive 2010 Rosehill Guineas

* Zacheline 1998 South Australian Oaks, 1998 Queensland Oaks

Zagalia 2003 Queensland Oaks

Zavite 2010 Auckland Cup, 2011 Ranvet Stakes

Zonda 1997 New Zealand Derby, 2001 Oaks Stud Classic

SIR TRISTRAM
(45 individual Group 1 winners of 72 Group 1 races)

Admiral Lincoln 1984 Australian Cup

Brew 2000 Melbourne Cup

Cure 1986 New Zealand 1000 Guineas

* Dalmacia 1983 Rawson Stakes, 1982 Epsom Handicap

Dr Grace 1990 Australian Derby, 1990 Chipping Norton Stakes,
1991 Underwood Stakes, 1991 The BMW

* Dupain 1996 Brisbane Cup

Empire Rose 1988 Melbourne Cup, 1988 Mackinnon Stakes

* Fair Sir 1987 The Australasian

Glastonbury 1994 Metropolitan Handicap

* Grosvenor 1982 VRC Sires' Produce Stakes, 1982 Victoria
Derby, 1982 Caulfield Guineas

* Gurner's Lane 1982 Caulfield Cup, 1982 Melbourne Cup

* Irish Chance 1999 Auckland Cup

Isolda 1995 Champagne Stakes

Kaapstad 1987 VRC Sires' Produce Stakes

Limitless 1987 Brisbane Cup

Lurestina 1992 Sky Sport Classic

* Mahaya 1993 Australian Oaks

* Mapperley Heights 1984 South Australian Derby

Marauding 1987 Golden Slipper Stakes

Military Plume 1986 Rothwells, 1987 Australian Guineas

* My Tristram's Belle 1985 Victoria Oaks

* National Gallery 1984 West Australian Derby

* Noble Heights 1981 New Zealand 1000 Guineas

Noble Peer 1985 Australian Cup

Only A Lady 1997 Flight Stakes

* Our Tristalight 1993 Australasian Oaks, 1993 South Australian Oaks

Popsy 1993 New Zealand Derby, 1994 Grosvenor Championship Stakes

Pride Of Rosewood 1983 USA Gamely Stakes

Queen's Road 1982 Brisbane Cup

Riverina Charm 1990 Air New Zealand Stakes, 1988 One Thousand
    Guineas, 1989 Rosehill Guineas, 1989 Canterbury Guineas

* Royal Heights 1986 New Zealand Oaks

Sir Vigilant 1985 New Zealand St. Leger Stakes

* Sovereign Red 1980 Western Mail Classic, 1980 Australian
    Derby, 1981 Rothman's "100,000", 1981 Underwood Stakes,
    1980 Caulfield Guineas, 1980 Victoria Derby

Starline 1987 New Zealand Oaks

Tasman 1980 South Australian Derby

* Trichelle 1985 Marlboro Cup

Trissaring 1989 Television NZ Stakes

Trissaro 1983 Underwood Stakes, 1983 Tancred Stakes,
    1984 Sydney Cup

* Tristalove 1994 Australasian Oaks, 1993 AJC Sires' Produce Stakes

Tristanagh 1989 One Thousand Guineas, 1989 Victoria Oaks

* Tristarc 1985 Caulfield Stakes, 1985 Caulfield Cup, 1985 Underwood
    Stakes, 1986 Queen Elizabeth Stakes, 1985 Australian Derby

Tristina 1985 Queensland Derby

Tristram Rose 1985 Queensland Oaks

Tristram's Edition 1985 Castlemaine Stakes

Zabeel 1990 Australian Guineas

MAROOF (7 individual Group 1 winners of 11 Group 1 races)
Figures 2004 Champions Mile
Hit The Roof 2000 Victoria Derby
Hoeberg 2001 Cape of Good Hope Paddock Stakes, 2000 Kenilworth
    Cape Fillies Guineas, 2001 South Africa Fillies Guineas
Maroofity 2005 Thorndon Mile, 2003 Ellerslie Sires' Produce Stakes,
    2003 Manawatu Sires' Produce Stakes
Natural Blitz 2005 Hong Kong Sprint
* Toccata 1999 Kenilworth Cape Fillies Guineas
Winged Foot 2000 Ellerslie Sires' Produce Stakes

STRAVINSKY (6 individual Group 1 winners of 9 Group 1 races)
Captivate 2007 NZ Bloodstock Breeders' Stakes
Fleur De Lune 2013 Railway Stakes
Keeninsky 2004 Manawatu Sires' Produce Stakes, 2005 Telegraph
    Handicap
Mr Baritone 2008 Stradbroke Handicap
Serenade Rose 2005 Victoria Oaks, 2006 Arrowfield Stud Stakes,
    2006 Australian Oaks
Time Keeper 2010 Easter Handicap

KEEPER (6 individual Group 1 winners of 8 Group 1 races)
Insouciant 2007 New Zealand 1000 Guineas
Keep The Peace 2010 New Zealand Oaks, 2011 Otaki-Maori Stakes,
Keepa Cruisin 2007 Levin Classic
* Linky Dink 2009 TJ Smith Classic
Midnight Oil 2011 New Zealand Oaks
My Keepsake 2010 Queensland Oaks

CAPE CROSS (5 individual Group 1 winners of 13 Group 1 races)
* Able One 2010 Champions Mile, 2011 Hong Kong Mile,
    2007 Champions Mile
Gaze 2007 New Zealand Stakes
* Kindacross 2005 Manawatu Sires' Produce Stakes
Mikki Street 2006 Zabeel Classic
Seachange 2007 Mudgway Stakes, 2008 Telegraph Handicap, 2008
    Waikato Draught Sprint, 2007 Stoney Bridge Stakes, 2006 Mudgway
    Stakes, 2005 New Zealand 1000 Guineas, 2006 Stoney Bridge Stakes

RHYTHM (5 individual Group 1 winners of 8 Group 1 races)
Ethereal 2001 Melbourne Cup, 2001 Caulfield Cup, 2002 The BMW,
    2001 Queensland Oaks
Sir Kinloch 2004 Thorndon Mile
Tapildo 2001 New Zealand Oaks
* Upsetthym 2004 Auckland Cup
* Zabeat 2005 Wellington Cup

GOLD AND IVORY
(4 individual Group 1 winners of 5 Group 1 races)
Magnet Bay 1997 Harrah's Stakes
* Marquise 1996 Captain Cook Stakes
The Message 2000 Kelt Capital Stakes, 1999 Lion Red Stakes
Z'Oro 1994 Thorndon Mile

DANZATORE (2 individual Group 1 winners of 3 Group 1 races)
Key Dancer 1989 West Australian Derby
Wonder Dancer 1988 VRC Sires' Produce Stakes, 1988 West Australian
    Derby

VIKING RULER (2 individual Group 1 winners of 2 Group 1 races)
Court Ruler 2009 Queensland Derby
Red Ruler 2011 International Stakes

MARCEAU (2 individual Group 1 winners of 2 Group 1 races)
Hula Chief 1986 Doncaster Handicap
Hula Drum 1985 George Ryder Stakes

LUCKY UNICORN
(1 individual Group 1 winner of 1 Group 1 race)
Rock Diva 2015 Auckland Cup

TAVISTOCK (4 individual Group 1 winners of 8 Group 1 races,
oldest crop 4 yo to the end of the 2015–16 season)
* Tarzino 2016 Rosehill Guineas, 2015 Victoria Derby
* Tavago 2016 Australian Derby
Volkstok'n'barrell 2016 New Zealand Stakes, 2016 Otaki-Maori
    Weight-For-Age Classic, 2015 Rosehill Guineas
Werther 2016 Queen Elizabeth II Cup, 2016 Hong Kong Derby

Other Group 1 winners
Bred by Sir Patrick and Lady Hogan but not by a Cambridge Stud stallion

Gay Poss* (Le Filou) 1970 Australian Oaks, 1970 Caulfield Stakes

Surround* (Sovereign Edition) 1976 Caulfield Guineas, 1976 Cox Plate, 1976 Victorian Oaks, 1977 Australian Oaks, 1977 Queensland Oaks

Hulastrike (Straight Strike) 1992 New Zealand 2000 Guineas

Millward (Defensive Play) 1997 VRC Sires' Produce Stakes

Foxwood (Centaine) 1997 New Zealand 2000 Guineas, 1998 Captain Cook Stakes

Danske (Danehill) 1998 New Zealand 2000 Guineas

Lucky Owners (Danehill) 2003 Hong Kong Mile, 2004 Hong Kong Derby

*NB Gay Poss and Surround's wins preceded the introduction of the Group and Listed system.

TOTALS

Cambridge Stud: 145 individual Group 1 winners of 246 Group 1 races

Sir Patrick and Justine, Lady Hogan: 43 individual Group 1 winners of 88 Group 1 races

LEADING INTERNATIONAL STUD FARMS, 2005

Rank	Farm	Stallions	Earnings ($)	Average earnings ($)	% SWs from starters	% graded SWs from starters
1	Cambridge Stud, New Zealand	3	12,733,829	47,338	7.43%	4.83%
2	Dalham Hall Stud, England	10	30,876,404	25,021	5.92%	2.76%
3	Coolmore Stud, Ireland	19	84,876,404	23,201	4.04%	2.23%
4	Arrowfield Stud, Australia	9	28,046,541	21,199	4.08%	2.80%
5	Coolmore Stud, Australia	2	16,120,082	29,578	4.04%	2.20%
6	JBBA Shizunai Stallion Station, Japan	14	51,453,635	37,861	2.87%	1.03%
7	Nunnery Stud, England	2	5,024,335	22,232	6.64%	2.65%
8	Gestut Schlenderhan, Germany	3	4,248,837	19,948	5.16%	3.29%
9	Kildangan Stud, Ireland	5	13,027,658	15,810	3.40%	1.70%
10	Lanwades Stud, England	5	8,546,540	17,768	4.57%	1.46%
11	Shadai Stallion Station, Japan	23	217,411,064	67,310	2.35%	0.96%
12	Derristown Stud, Ireland	6	9,829,086	16,859	2.40%	1.72%
13	Haras d'Etreham, France	10	9,422,704	13,538	2.73%	1.72%
14	Haras du Quesay, France	7	17,070,575	15,269	2.50%	0.98%
15	Irish National Stud, Ireland	6	13,925,990	18,062	2.59%	0.91%
16	Haras La Quebrada, Argentina	2	3,655,994	14,566	4.78%	2.79%
17	Cheveley Park Stud, England	7	8,979,954	14,322	2.71%	1.44%
18	Gilltown Stud, Ireland	3	4,140,633	16,302	3.94%	1.57%
19	Arrow Stud, Japan	20	49,200,489	46,902	1.91%	0.76%
20	Haras de Bonneval, France	4	5,100,990	16,780	2.63%	0.99%
21	Whitsbury Manor Stud, England	5	7,604,907	14,767	2.72%	0.97%
22	Haras de Mezeray, France	5	5,401,180	15,656	2.32%	1.16%
23	Highclere Stud, England	2	3,680,448	13,481	3.30%	1.10%
24	East Stud, Japan	10	20,271,165	43,594	1.94%	0.22%
25	Larneuk Stud, Australia	3	2,934,551	13,649	3.26%	1.40%

Standings are based on progeny earnings, average earnings per starter, percentage of Stakes winners (SWs) from starters, and percentage of graded Stakes winners from starters. Each category was assigned equal weight. Statistics are based on progeny earnings of stallions standing at farms in 2005 and of deceased and pensioned stallions for racing between 1 January and 27 November. For a farm to be considered for inclusion, the collective stallions for each farm must have had a combined minimum of 200 starters in that period.

Cambridge Stud achievement awards

SIR PATRICK HOGAN

Honorary Doctorate, University of Waikato 2013

New Zealand Racing Hall of Fame, inducted 2006

Australian Racing Hall of Fame, inducted 2005

Honorary Degree — MSc Sport and Exercise Science, Waikato Institute of Technology 2002

Knight Companion of New Zealand Order of Merit 1999

Companion of the Order of the British Empire 1991

BMW Award for Outstanding Contribution to Racing Excellence 1991

SIR PATRICK and JUSTINE LADY HOGAN

New Zealand Breeder of the Year: 1994–95, 1995–96, 1996–97, 2003–04, 2015–16

New Zealand Owner of the Year: 2003–04

New Zealand Broodmare of the Year: 1981 Taiona, 1983 Taiona, 1995 Eight Carat, 1996 Eight Carat, 1997 Eight Carat

CAMBRIDGE STUD

Leading vendor 31 consecutive years — New Zealand

Octagonal was inducted into the Australian Racing Hall of Fame in 2012 and Surround inducted in 2014.

Eight Carat was inducted into the New Zealand Racing Hall of Fame in 2016.

SIR TRISTRAM

Champion Sire of Australia: 1980–81, 1981–82, 1983–84, 1987–88, 1988–89, 1991–92

Champion Sire of New Zealand: 1986–87

Dewar Trophy (Aus/NZ combined earnings): 1980–81, 1981–82, 1983–84, 1984–85, 1985–86, 1986–87, 1988–89, 1989–90, 1993–94

Champion broodmare sire: 1998–99, 2000–01, 2004–05

Inducted into the New Zealand Racing Hall of Fame in 2008

Sire of 45 individual Group 1 winners (at the time a world record) of 72 Group 1 races and 221 stakes performers

ZABEEL

Champion Sire of Australia: 1997–98, 1998–99

Champion Sire of New Zealand: 1997–98, 1998–99, 1999–2000

Dewar Trophy (Aus/NZ combined earnings): 1995–96, 1996–97, 1997–98, 1998–99, 1999–2000, 2000–01, 2001–02, 2002–03, 2003–04, 2004–05, 2005–06, 2006–07, 2008–09, 2009–10, 2011–12

Champion Broodmare Sire of New Zealand: 2011–12, 2012–13, 2013–14, 2015–16

Champion Broodmare Sire of Australia: 2011–12, 2012–13, 2013–14

Centaine Award (worldwide earnings): 2009–10

Inducted into the New Zealand Racing Hall of Fame in 2014

Kingston Town Greatness Award, awarded by the Moonee Valley Racing Club for siring four Cox Plate winners: Octagonal, Might and Power, Savabeel and Maldivian

Sire of 45 individual Group 1 winners of 90 Group 1 races and 257 Stakes winners

BIBLIOGRAPHY

Newspapers and magazines as quoted in book.

Dillon, Mike (ed.). *New Zealand Racing Annual*, Moa, Auckland, 1988–90.

Dunford, Stephen. *Irish Highwaymen*, Merlin Books, Dublin, 2000.

Hunt, Graeme. *Hustlers, Rogues & Bubble Boys*, Reed, Auckland, 2001.

Ireland Old News, Clare Library, Galway, Ireland, 1909.

New Zealand Thoroughbred Racing Annual, Bradford Publishing, Paeroa, 2005.

Register of Thoroughbred Stallions of New Zealand, Volume XXIX, New Zealand Thoroughbreeders Association, Auckland, 2002.

Simendinger, Ted. *12 Miles to Paradise*, Airplane Reader Publishing, USA, 2003.

Taylor, Mark. *Century of Champions: 100 Great Australian and New Zealand Horses*, HarperCollins, Auckland, 2002.

'The Promise', Sir Tristram documentary video, 1996.

Wishart, Ian. *The Paradise Conspiracy*, Howling at the Moon Productions Ltd, Auckland, 1995.